States of Denial

In memory of Stephanie

States of Denial

Knowing about Atrocities
and Suffering

STANLEY COHEN

Polity

First published in 2001 by Polity Press in association with Blackwell Publishers Ltd

Editorial office:
Polity Press
65 Bridge Street
Cambridge CB2 1UR, UK

Marketing and production:
Blackwell Publishers Ltd
108 Cowley Road
Oxford OX4 1JF, UK

Published in the USA by
Blackwell Publishers Inc.
Commerce Place
350 Main Street
Malden, MA 02148, USA

ISBN 0-7456-1657-7
ISBN 0-7456-2392-1 (pbk)

A catalogue record for this book is available from the British Library and has been applied for from the Library of Congress.

Typeset in 10 on 12 pt Palatino
by Kolam Information Services Pvt. Ltd, Pondicherry
Printed in Great Britain by TJ International, Padstow, Cornwall

This book is printed on acid-free paper.

Each of us is aware in ourselves of the workings of denial, of our need to be innocent of a troubling recognition.

— Christopher Bollas, *Being a Character*

People could find no place in their consciousness for such an unimaginable horror ... and they did not have the courage to face it. It is possible to live in a twilight between knowing and not knowing.

—W. A. Visser't Hooft, Protestant theologian [reflecting in 1973 on the Churches' knowledge of the Holocaust]

All nationalists have the power of not seeing resemblances between similar sets of facts.... The nationalist not only does not disapprove of atrocities committed by his own side, but he has a remarkable capacity for not even hearing about them.... In nationalist thought there are facts which are both true and untrue, known and unknown. A known fact may be so unbearable that it is habitually pushed aside and not allowed to enter into logical processes, or on the other hand it may enter into every calculation and yet never be admitted as a fact, even in one's own mind.... Every nationalist is haunted by the belief that the past can be altered.... Material facts are suppressed, dates altered, quotations removed from their context and doctored so as to change their meaning. Events which, it is felt, ought not to have happened are left unmentioned and ultimately denied.... Indifference to object-ive truth is encouraged by the sealing off of one part of the world from the other, which makes it harder and harder to discover what is actually happening.... If one harbours anywhere in one's mind a nationalistic loyalty or hatred, certain facts although in a sense known to be true, are inadmissible.

— George Orwell, *Notes on Nationalism*

> About suffering they were never wrong,
> The Old Masters: how well they
>   understood
> Its human position; how it takes place
> While someone else is eating or opening a
>   window or just walking dully along.
> —W. H. Auden, *Musée des Beaux Arts*

To know and not to act is not to know.

—Wang Yang-ming

Contents

Preface

My earliest memory that could be called 'political' goes back to a winter night in Johannesburg in the mid-nineteen-fifties. I must have been twelve or thirteen. My father was away from home for a few days on business. Like many South African middle-class families (especially Jewish and anxious ones), we employed for these rare occasions a 'Night Watch Boy': that is, an adult black man – in this case an old Zulu (I vividly remember the wooden discs in his ear lobes) – working for a private security company. Just before going to bed, I looked out of the window and saw him huddled over a charcoal fire, rubbing his hands to keep warm, the collar of his khaki overcoat turned up. As I slipped into my over-warm bed – flannel sheets, hot water bottle, thick eiderdown brought by my grandmother from Poland – I suddenly started thinking about why he was out there and I was in here.

My mother always used to tell me that I was 'over-sensitive'. This must have been my over-sensitivity at work, an inchoate feeling not exactly of guilt – this came later – but that something was wrong. Why did this old man have to sit out in the cold all night? Why had our family (and everyone like us) been allocated black men and women (who were called 'boys' and 'girls' or just 'natives') as domestic servants? Why did they live in tiny rooms in the backyard? Where were their wives, husbands and children? Why did they address me as 'baas', or 'master'?

I don't remember what I did with my bedroom epiphany. Almost certainly, I just dropped off to sleep. But later, even when I began to think sociologically about apartheid, privilege, injustice and racism, I would still return to some version of that early psychological unease. I saw this unease – correctly, I believe – as arising from a sense of knowing that something was deeply wrong, but also knowing that I could not live in a state of permanent awareness of this knowledge. Without my deliberate intention, this awareness would switch itself on or, more often, off. There might be weeks or months of blindness, amnesia and sleepwalking. Political education – later called 'consciousness raising' – made these phases less frequent, just as it should do.

Later, I started asking another question, one that I still discuss with people who grew up with me. Why did others, even those raised in similar families, schools and neighbourhoods, who read the same papers, walked the same streets, apparently not 'see' what we saw? Could they be living in another perceptual universe – where the horrors of apartheid were invisible and the physical presence of black people often slipped from awareness? Or perhaps they saw *exactly* what we saw, but just didn't care or didn't see anything wrong.

My academic life in sociology took me in quite different directions, but my childhood questions continued to float around. I collected and hoarded all sorts of material – newspaper cuttings, Oxfam appeals, Biafra and Vietnam war photos, quotes, book titles, bits of conversations. My fantasy was that one day I would integrate all this into what I pretentiously called a 'sociology of denial'. The subject, if not the pretension, remains the same: what do we do with our knowledge about the suffering of others, and what does this knowledge do to us?

It seemed self-evident that a common – perhaps universal or even 'natural' – reaction is to block out, shut off or repress this information. People react as if they do not know what they know. Or else the information is registered – there is no attempt to deny the facts – but its implications are ignored. People seem apathetic, passive, indifferent and unresponsive – and they find convenient rationalizations to explain themselves. I became stuck with the term 'denial' to cover this whole range of phenomena. I have never been able to find an alternative word – even though its conceptual ambiguities are so gross.

Nor was I entirely satisfied with the term that I adopted as the opposite of denial: 'acknowledgement'. This is what 'should' happen when people are actively aroused – thinking, feeling or acting – by the information. They respond appropriately, in the psychological and moral senses, to what they know. They see a problem that needs their attention; they get upset or angry and express sympathy or compassion; and they do something: intervene, help, become committed.

At first, my original South African questions pulled me only in the political direction: the suffering caused by injustice, racism and repression. Later, I began to think more about personal and family distress. The contrast between denial and acknowledgement seemed to appear everywhere – in the streets, appeals by charities, development or human rights organizations, the mass media. Even my academic subjects – deviance, crime, social control, punishment – became relevant.

By this time, my obsession appeared from an unexpected direction. In 1980, I left England with my family to live in Israel. My vintage sixties radicalism left me utterly unprepared for this move. Nearly twenty years in Britain had done little to change the naïve views I had absorbed while growing up in the Zionist youth movement in South Africa. It soon became obvious that Israel was not like this at all. By the 1982 invasion of Lebanon, I was already disenchanted with the liberal peace movement in which I thought I belonged. I drifted into what in Israeli terms is the 'far left' – the margins of the margins.

I also became involved in human rights issues, particularly torture. In 1990, I started working with Daphna Golan, the Research Director of the Israeli human rights organization, *B'Ttselem*, on a research project about allegations of torture against Palestinian detainees. Our evidence of the routine use of violent and illegal methods of interrogation was to be confirmed by numerous other sources. But we were immediately thrown into the politics of denial. The official and mainstream response was venomous: *outright denial* (it doesn't happen); *discrediting* (the organization was biased, manipulated or gullible); *renaming* (yes, something does happen, but it is not torture); and *justification* (anyway 'it' was morally justified). Liberals were uneasy and concerned. Yet there was no outrage. Soon a tone of acceptance began to be heard. Abuses were intrinsic to the situation; there was nothing to be done till a political solution was found; something like torture might even be necessary sometimes; anyway, we don't want to keep being told about this all the time.

This apparent normalization seemed difficult to explain. The report had an enormous media impact: graphic drawings of standard torture methods were widely reproduced, and a taboo subject was now discussed openly. Yet very soon, the silence returned. Worse than torture not being *in* the news, it was no longer news. Something whose existence could not be admitted, was now seen as predictable.

There was something like an unspoken collusion to ignore (or pretend to ignore?) the whole subject. Thousands of Israelis and tourists walk everyday down the main street of Jerusalem, Jaffa Road, on to which backs the 'Moscobiya', the prison and detention centre in the Russian Compound. This was well known as a place where Palestinians were detained, interrogated and tortured by the *Shabaq*, the General Security Services. On 22 April 1995, a Palestinian suspect, Abed al-Samad Harizat, collapsed there after fifteen hours of interrogation. He died in hospital three days later without regaining consciousness. Harizat had been literally *shaken* to death – yanked up and down by his shirt collar. An Israeli attorney (acting on behalf of the family) petitioned to have this practice designated as illegal. No, the High Court ruled, shaking was perfectly okay.

Pedestrians walk within a few yards of the cells where this happened. In the street and the crowded nearby cafés (in which police and *Shabaq* officers sit) there was no sign of anything out of the ordinary. The day after the High Court ruling, I overheard two fellow bus passengers casually arguing about what the lawyers actually meant by *tilltulim*, the Hebrew word for 'shaking'.

This was time of the *intifada* – the Palestinian civilian uprising that started in 1987, after twenty years of military occupation. The television world viewed the Israeli reactions: beatings, torture, daily humiliations, unprovoked killings, curfews, house demolitions, detention without trial, deportations and collective punishments. Israel got a few bad entries in international atrocity digests, such as the Amnesty annual report. Compared with other censured countries, Israel seems a haven of democracy and the rule of law. Active human rights organizations and good journalists report critically on what happens. And public information can be confirmed by private knowledge. Nearly everyone has some personal experience, directly or indirectly, of army service. Soldiers are not mercenaries or underclass conscripts. Everyone serves or has a husband, son or neighbour on reserve duty. Very few of them keep their activities secret.

Yet even liberals did not react in the way they 'should'. I kept wanting to say, 'Don't you know what's going on?' But of course they knew. I glibly saw this as yet another instance of denial – not the crude lying of cynical apologists, but the complex bad faith of people trying to look innocent by not noticing. Was this time for another report, press release, article or documentary driven by our touching faith in 'if only they knew?' Hardly. The information had been received but not 'registered', or (a better cliché) not 'digested'. It sunk into consciousness without producing shifts in policy or public opinion. Was there some deep flaw in the way we were trying to get our message across? Or was there a point at which the sheer accretion of more and better information would not have any impact?

It was natural to make the claustrophobic assumption that this problem was unique because Israel was uniquely horrible. Luckily our visitors from the international human rights community reminded us that the problem was universal. They were interested in information circulating in the international arena. How did audiences in North America or Western Europe react to knowledge of atrocities in East Timor, Uganda or Guatemala? I started imagining a nice thirty-something couple sitting, with their breakfast coffee and croissants, in

New York, London, Paris or Toronto. They pick up the morning news-paper: 'Another Thousand Tutsis Massacred in Rwanda'. In the mail plop two circular letters, one from Oxfam: 'While you are eating your breakfast, ten more children starve to death in Somalia', and one from Amnesty: 'While you are eating your lunch, eight street-children are killed in Brazil'. What does this 'news' do to them, and what do they do to the news? What goes through their minds? What do they say to each other?

I was back to my original preoccupations: reactions to unwelcome knowledge – especially about the suffering inflicted by human beings on one another. What is meant by saying that 'something should be done' about these atrocities? For governments, this suggests 'interven-tion' in the vague sense used in recent discourse about Bosnia, Iraq, Zaire, Rwanda, Kosovo or Somalia. For the ordinary public – my real interest – it means sympathy, commitment and action: give a donation, boycott a product, join an organization, adopt a prisoner of conscience, sign a petition, go to a demonstration. That is: 'acknowledgement' rather than denial.

I stored away my general 'sociology of denial' files again. In 1992, aided by a grant from the Ford Foundation, I started a project about how information about human rights violations is transmitted. The focus was international organizations, based in either the United States or Britain, and especially Amnesty International, the only one trying to reach the wider public. I also looked at charity, aid and development organizations; market research and advertising companies in the pub-lic interest sector; and mainstream and alternative media organiza-tions. My sources were public reports, press releases, campaign material, advertisements, direct mailings and media coverage; meet-ings and conferences; and interviews with some fifty human rights and aid/development staff and twenty journalists. In 1995, this study was published as a report.[1]

Free at last from the insatiable demands of policy and practice, I returned to the safe world of theory and research. My start was Freud and psychological theories of denial, then topics where the concept was used – whether AIDS, homelessness or global warming. Mean-while the psycho-babble phrase 'in denial' had become part of popular culture. Individuals and whole societies were slipping into denial about everything.

I then submerged myself in Holocaust studies and literature. My theory (almost certainly mistaken) must have been that if you even *tried* to understand this, then you could understand anything. I read more about genocide, massacres and torture, and watched movies about human suffering. My theory (certainly mistaken) was that seeing more *representations* of suffering would teach me how to approach these subjects.

The result was not quite what I had planned. First, although I remain a sociologist, psychological language comes more naturally to me. Someone else will have to write a political economy of denial. Second, though I intended to look only at observers (bystanders) I kept being led to denials by perpetrators and victims. Third, I found myself drawing disproportionately on the Israeli case. This is not because it is especially awful – but because I lived there for eighteen perplexed years.

The 'average reader' whom I address is mostly the ethnocentric, culturally imperialist 'we' – educated and comfortable people living in stable societies. We are the objects of some chapters; but mostly we gaze at distant others in poor, unstable and violent places, which are in the news because of more cruelty and suffering, or in places where juntas, refugees, death squads and famine are never more than a memory away. But they live, construct and resist; they are not just the victims who appear in my pages. And 'we' have our ugly presents and past, our own unacknowledged social problems.

I concentrate on atrocities and human rights agencies, but also consider problems dealt with by aid, relief, health or development agencies and recently subsumed in the concept of 'social suffering'.[2] Unless otherwise stated, I use the general term 'humanitarian' to cover all these organizations. Except in dealing with psychological theory (chapter 2) and research (chapter 3), I have tried to avoid unnecessary academic citations. But now and then, I take pedagogic refuge and switch to writing a textbook for an imaginary course on the sociology of denial.

S. C.

Acknowledgements

As explained in the Preface, this project has passed through various incarnations. I am grateful to many people for helping me so generously along the way. The Acknowledgements in my 1995 report, *The Impact of Information about Human Rights Violations*, lists all the staff members and organizations with whom I worked in the two previous years. I repeat my thanks to all of them. Again, I single out Dan Jones, Karen Sherlock and the staff in the Amnesty International, British Section, office for their unwavering enthusiasm and my friends at the Medical Foundation for the Care of Victims of Torture.

That project was financed by a grant from the Ford Foundation International Affairs Programme. The Foundation's Programme Officer then, Margo Picken, was not only formally responsible, but also supportive, helpful and encouraging in every way. She has remained so till today – always concerned. So has Emma Playfair, a supportive friend and my other early guide (via Ramalleh) into the international human rights community. Margo and Emma have kept me going, walking and thinking. I am also indebted to my new friends in the International Council on Human Rights Policy.

My research assistants – Josie Glausiusz in the year before the original report and Kate Steward in the year before I finished this book – were wonderful. Both gave me the right amount of help and far too much material. Thanks also to Brydie Bethell, Megan Comfort, Rebecca Fasmer, Sharon Shalev, Andy Wilson and my other LSE graduate students for last-minute help, good cover and permanent enthusiasm.

I am grateful for stimulus and comradeship from all my friends in the Israeli and Palestinian human rights and peace communities. Through this work, I met Daphna Golan – who for a decade has been my close friend and colleague, helping on many ideas in this book. I thank her for all this. Through my work in London I was fortunate to meet Bruna Seu. She guided me on the psychology of denial, and also helped me through some difficult times. Her stimulus, advice and enthusiasm have been invaluable.

Many other friends have helped over these years, always mixing the personal with the intellectual. Particular thanks to Judy Blank, Nils Christie, Coline Covington, Maurice Greenberg, Barbara Koltuv, Adam and Jessica Kuper, Kathy Laster, Harvey Molotch, Evely Shlensky, Raja Shahadeh and Penny Johnson, Celia Szusterman, Laurie Taylor, Ruth Towse and Andrew von Hirsch. I am also deeply indebted to Noam Chomsky. At my new academic home, the LSE, special thanks to Tony Giddens, to my old friends David Downes and Paul Rock, and to many new friends, especially Amanda Goodall, Nicola Lacey and Richard Sennet.

My wife Ruth (her patience tried more than ever), my daughters Judith (and husband, Chanan) and Jessica (and husband, Adam) and my brother Robin (and wife, Selina) have always been more than a family. They know my thanks. Lia and Yonatan, my dear grandchildren, reminded me that the world was not the book.

The publishers wish to thank the following for permission to use copyright material:

Faber and Faber Ltd and Random House, Inc. for an extract from W. H. Auden, 'Musée des Beaux Arts' from *Collected Poems* by W. H. Auden. Copyright © 1940, renewed 1968 by W. H. Auden;

A. M. Heath Ltd on behalf of Bill Hamilton as the Literary Executor of the Estate of the Late Sonia Brownell Orwell and Harcourt, Inc. for excerpts from George Orwell, 'Notes on Nationalism' in *Such, Such Were The Joys* by George Orwell. Copyright © 1953 by Sonia Brownell Orwell, renewed 1981 by Mrs George K. Perutz, Mrs Miriam Gross and Dr Michael Dickson, Executors of the Estate of Sonia Brownell Orwell;

The Random House Group Ltd for an extract from Don McCullin, *Unreasonable Behaviour*, Vintage (1992) pp. 123–4;

Routledge and Pantheon Books, a division of Random House, Inc, for extracts from R. D. Laing, *Knots*, Tavistock (1970), copyright © 1970 R. D. Laing.

Every effort has been made to trace the copyright holders but if any have been inadvertently overlooked the publishers will be pleased to make the necessary arrangement at the first opportunity.

1

The Elementary Forms of Denial

One common thread runs through the many different stories of denial: people, organizations, governments or whole societies are presented with information that is too disturbing, threatening or anomalous to be fully absorbed or openly acknowledged. The information is therefore somehow repressed, disavowed, pushed aside or reinterpreted. Or else the information 'registers' well enough, but its implications – cognitive, emotional or moral – are evaded, neutralized or rationalized away.

Consider these common expressions and phrases:

> Turning a blind eye
> Burying your head in the sand
> She saw what she wanted to see
> He only heard what he wanted to hear
> Ignorance is bliss
> Living a lie
> Conspiracy of silence
> Economical with the truth
> It's got nothing to do with me
> Don't make waves
> They were typical passive bystanders
> There's nothing I can do about it
> Being like an ostrich
> I can't believe that this is happening
> I don't want to know/hear/see any more
> The whole society was in deep denial
> It can't happen to people like us
> The plan called for maximum deniability
> Averting your gaze
> Wearing blinkers

He couldn't take in the news
Wilful ignorance
She looked the other way
He didn't admit it, even to himself
Don't wash your dirty linen in public
It didn't happen on my watch
I must have known all along

Now consider the following items:

- The TV screen is full of images of human suffering, faces contorted in agony and desperation. Lost refugees, starving children, corpses in rivers. Sometimes we take a quite conscious decision to avoid such information. Often we are not aware of how much we either take in or block out. Sometimes we absorb all the information, but feel passive, powerless and helpless: 'there's nothing I can do about it.' Or we may feel angry and resentful: this is another demand, another nagging, guilt-inducing reproach – as with this United Nations Association's message: 'There are over 18 million refugees in the world today, fleeing from persecution, rape, torture and war, in Africa and Asia, South America and now here in Europe. You can close your eyes, close your ears, close your minds, close your doors, close your frontiers. Or you can open your heart.'
- Between 1915 and 1917, nearly one and a quarter million Armenians were massacred by the Turkish army or died during forced expulsions. The event was thoroughly documented in official records, survivors' accounts, witness testimonies and historical research. The main details were accepted without dispute soon afterwards by outside observers. But for eighty years, successive Turkish governments have consistently denied responsibility for genocidal massacres or any deliberate killings. Most other countries, particularly the USA and Turkey's other NATO allies, have colluded in this obliteration of the past.
- Villagers who lived around Mauthausen, a concentration camp in Austria from 1942 to 1945, were interviewed forty years later by an American historian, Gordon Horwitz. Many claimed that although they saw the smoke from the furnaces and heard rumours about the purpose of the camp, they did not really know what was going on. They did not ask too many questions at the time, and could not 'put together' what information they did have. Horwitz writes about the villagers' reactions: 'They never sought to inform themselves of what had happened. One encounters not a flat denial of the existence of the camps, only an indifference to their presence so

long ago. In some instances one may not talk of forgetfulness, for one cannot forget what one has never attempted to know.'[1]

- One night in New York in 1964, a woman named Kitty Genovese was savagely assaulted in the street just before reaching home. Her assailant attacked her over a period of forty minutes, during which she struggled, battered and bleeding, to reach her apartment. Her screams and calls for help were heard by at least thirty-eight neighbours who saw her or heard the struggle. But no one offered any assistance, either by directly intervening or by phoning the police. After thirty-five years, the event is still debated.[2] Social psychologists have studied intensely the 'passive bystander effect', publishing 600 pieces of research in academic journals. Every conceivable variable has been manipulated – both in real-life situations and simulated laboratory conditions – to discover how the bystander effect works and may be counteracted.

- A full-page newspaper advertisement from British Amnesty shows a photo of a Muslim woman, screaming with grief. The image is surrounded by a collage of words: *decapitated, massacres, mutilated, burned alive, babies thrown off balconies, pregnant women disembowelled.* The text starts: 'No words – there are no words – to express what this Algerian woman is feeling': her baby dashed to its death, her small daughter disembowelled, her mother's head rolling in the dust. *Words lose power*: 'Shocking headlines no longer touch us. We are not moved, we resent being manipulated. Experience says that you will read this page, turn over and forget it, because this is how you, like the rest of us, have learnt to cope with clamouring ads.'

These are some of the many states covered by my code word 'denial'. This is neither a fixed psychological 'mechanism' nor a universal social process. This chapter simply classifies the ways in which the concept of denial is used. At the risk of repetition, I also preview the themes of the whole book, but in an elementary way – without too many of the endnotes, sidetracks, theories and academic references that appear in later chapters.

Psychological status: conscious or unconscious?

Statements of denial are assertions that something did not happen, does not exist, is not true or is not known about. There are three possibilities about the truth-value of these assertions. The first and simplest is that these assertions are indeed true, justified and correct.

There are obviously many occasions on which individuals, organizations or governments are perfectly justified in claiming that an event
did not happen at all, or not as it was alleged to have happened, or that
it might have happened, but without their knowledge. These denials
are simple statements of fact, made in good faith. Evidence and counter-evidence can be produced, claims checked, lies exposed, reasonable standards of proof presented.

Even without today's post-modernist scepticism about objective
knowledge, these games of truth are highly volatile. It can be genuinely difficult to find out the truth about atrocities within the intricate
circuit of claims and counter-claims made by governments, their
human rights critics and opposition forces. Did the demonstrators
use violence first, or did the police? Is this really torture, or 'intense'
but legitimate interrogation? It is even more difficult to produce legal
evidence, and often virtually impossible to establish causal responsibility. None the less, assertions of denial can be made in perfectly
good faith. This is true for both governments ('there was no massacre')
and individuals ('I didn't see anything').

A second possibility is also logically simple, though more difficult to
identify. This is the deliberate, intentional and conscious statement
which is meant to deceive – that is, lying. The truth is clearly known,
but for many reasons – personal or political, justifiable or unjustifiable
– it is concealed. The denial is deliberate and intentional. At the
individual level, a few common words (lying, concealment, deception)
will do. At the organized level (perhaps indicating the pervasiveness
of lying in public life) more terms are in currency: propaganda, disinformation, whitewash, manipulation, spin, misinformation, fraud,
cover-up. These are standard responses to allegations about atrocities,
corruption or public wrongdoing. In the absence of evidence that the
government must be telling the truth while everyone else is biased,
unreliable and lying, most of us assume that most such official denials
are indeed lies. A different form of conscious denial is the deliberate
choice not to expose ourselves to certain unpalatable information. We
cannot live in a state of continuous awareness of the fact that thousands of children are starving to death each day or dying of easily
preventable diseases. So we make a conscious decision to switch off
the sources of such information. This is like taking a different route to
avoid seeing homeless beggars on the street.

Sometimes, though, we are not entirely aware of switching off or
blocking out. This is the third and most intriguing set of possibilities.
Denial may be neither a matter of telling the truth nor intentionally
telling a lie. The statement is not wholly deliberate, and the status of
'knowledge' about the truth is not wholly clear. There seem to be states

of mind, or even whole cultures, in which we know and don't know at the same time. Perhaps this was the case with those villagers living around the concentration camp? Or with the mother who doesn't know what her husband is doing to their daughter?

The complex psychology of denial is the subject of my next chapter. The best-known psychological theory – well known enough to have entered into everyday language, though in a sense the most extreme – derives from psychoanalysis. Denial is understood as an unconscious defence mechanism for coping with guilt, anxiety and other disturbing emotions aroused by reality. The psyche blocks off information that is literally unthinkable or unbearable. The unconscious sets up a barrier which prevents the thought from reaching conscious knowledge. Information and memories slip into an inaccessible region of the mind.

Can this really happen without any conscious awareness – in the uncharted territory between deliberate choice and unconscious defence? Is this the normal suppression of background noise – allowing attention to be paid to more important matters – or a defence against a personally threatening perception? And is denial malignant (as with high HIV-risk groups denying their vulnerability) or benign (like the false hopes that allow terminally ill patients to continue living)?

The psychology of 'turning a blind eye' or 'looking the other way' is a tricky matter. These phrases imply that we have access to reality, but choose to ignore it because it is convenient to do so. This might be a simple fraud: the information is available and registered, but leads to a conclusion which is knowingly evaded. 'Knowing', though, can be far more ambiguous. We are vaguely aware of choosing not to look at the facts, but not quite conscious of just what it is we are evading. We know, but at the same time we don't know.

The political echoes of these states of mind may be found in the mass denial so characteristic of repressive, racist and colonial states. Dominant groups seem uncannily able to shut out or ignore the injustice and suffering around them. In more democratic societies, people shut out the results not because of coercion but out of cultural habit – turning a blind eye to the visible reminders of homelessness, deprivation, poverty and urban decay. Knowledge about atrocities in distant places is more easily rendered invisible: 'I just switch off the TV news when they show those corpses in Rwanda.'

Denial is also studied in terms of cognitive psychology and decision making. This approach emphasizes the normality of the process, and plays down its emotional component. Denial is a high-speed cognitive mechanism for processing information, like the computer command to 'delete' rather than 'save'. But this assumes the *denial paradox*. In order to use the term 'denial' to describe a person's statement 'I didn't know', one has to assume that she knew or knows about what it is that she claims not to know – otherwise the term 'denial' is inappropriate. Strictly speaking, this is the *only* legitimate use of the term 'denial'.

Cognitive psychologists use the language of information processing, monitoring, selective perception, filtering and attention span to understand how we notice and simultaneously don't notice. Some even offer the neurological phenomenon of 'blindsight' as a model: one part of the mind can know just what it is doing, while the part that supposedly knows, remains oblivious of this. More obviously, information is selected to fit existing perceptual frames and information which is too threatening is shut out altogether. The mind somehow grasps what is going on – but rushes a protective filter into place. Information slips into a kind of 'black hole of the mind' – a blind zone of blocked attention and self-deception. Attention is thus diverted from facts or their meaning – hence the 'vital lies' sustained by family members about violence, incest, sexual abuse, adultery and unhappiness. Lies remain unrevealed, covered up by family silence, alibis and conspiracies.[3]

Not only families. Government bureaucracies, political parties, professional associations, religions, armies and police all have their own forms of cover-up and lying. Such collective denial results from professional ethics, traditions of loyalty and secrecy, mutual reciprocity or codes of silence. Myths are maintained that prevent outsiders knowing about discreditable information; there are unspoken arrangements for concerted or strategic ignorance. It may be convenient not to know exactly what your superiors or subordinates are doing.

This sounds close to the philosophical interest in self-knowledge and self-deception, especially the famous notion of 'bad faith'. For Sartre, contrary to psychoanalytical theory, denial is indeed conscious. Self-deception refers to keeping secret from ourselves the truth we cannot face. Sartre ridicules the theory that this happens through an unconscious mechanism that maintains the duality between deceiver and deceived. His alternative, 'bad faith', is a form of denial that the mind *knowingly* directs towards itself. But how do you lie to yourself? How do you know and not know the same thing at the same time?

These are the concerns of chapter 2. Political denial – the normal disinformation, lying and cover-up by public authorities – seldom calls for these subtle psychological questions. Denial is cynical, calculated and transparent. The grey areas between consciousness and unconsciousness are far more significant in explaining ordinary public responses to knowledge about atrocities and suffering, This is the zone of open secrets, turning a blind eye, burying one's head in the sand and not wanting to know.

Content: literal, interpretive or implicatory?

There are three possibilities as regards *what* exactly is being 'denied': literal, interpretive and implicatory.

Literal denial

This is the type of denial that fits the dictionary definition: the assertion that something did not happen or is not true. In *literal, factual* or *blatant* denial, the fact or knowledge of the fact is denied. In the private realm of family suffering: my husband could not have done that to our daughter, she is making it up, the social worker doesn't understand. In the public realm of atrocities: nothing happened here, there was no massacre, they are all lying, we don't believe you, we didn't notice anything, they didn't tell us anything, it couldn't have happened without us knowing (or it could have happened without us knowing). These assertions refuse to acknowledge the facts – for whatever reason, in good or bad faith, and whether these claims are true (genuine ignorance), blatantly untrue (deliberate lies) or unconscious defence mechanisms.

Interpretive denial

At other times, the raw facts (something happened) are not being denied. Rather, they are given a different meaning from what seems apparent to others.

In the personal realm: I am a social drinker, not an alcoholic; what happened was not really 'rape'. President Clinton smoked marijuana while he was a student, but never inhaled; so this was not really using drugs. As for later allegations about his sexual relations with Monica Lewinsky, he followed his literal denial (nothing like this happened at all) by some original interpretive denial: oral sex was 'inappropriate behaviour' but not really a 'sex act' or 'sexual relations', and therefore there was no adultery or marital infidelity or screwing around. Indeed, there was no sex. So the president was not lying when he said that his relationship with Ms Lewinsky was not sexual.

In the public realm: this was population exchange, not ethnic cleansing; the arms deal was not illegal and was not really an arms deal. Officials do not claim that 'nothing happened', but what happened is not what you think it is, not what it looks like, not what you call it. This

was 'collateral damage', not killing of civilians; 'transfer of populations', not forced expulsion; 'moderate physical pressure', not torture.
By changing words, by euphemism, by technical jargon, the observer
disputes the cognitive meaning given to an event and re-allocates it to
another class of event.

Implicatory denial

At yet other times, there is no attempt to deny either the facts or their
conventional interpretation. What are denied or minimized are the
psychological, political or moral implications that conventionally
follow. The facts of children starving to death in Somalia, mass rape
of women in Bosnia, a massacre in East Timor, homeless people in our
streets are recognized, but are not seen as psychologically disturbing
or as carrying a moral imperative to act. As a witness to a mugging in
the underground, you see exactly what is happening, but you deny
any responsibility as a citizen to intervene. Such denials are often
called 'rationalizations': 'It's got nothing to do with me', 'Why should
I take a risk of being victimized myself?', 'What can an ordinary
person do?', 'It's worse elsewhere', 'Someone else will deal with it.'
    As with literal denial, such assertions may be perfectly justified,
both morally and factually. There is nothing you can do about death
squads in Colombia; it might be quite stupid to try to stop a mugging.
Rationalization is another matter when you do know what can and
should be done, you have the means to do this, and there is no risk.
This is not a refusal to acknowledge reality, but a denial of its significance or implications. My clumsy neologism 'implicatory denial'
covers the multitude of vocabularies – justifications, rationalizations,
evasions – that we use to deal with our awareness of so many images
of unmitigated suffering.
    At one extreme this vocabulary is wholly bland and unapologetic.
We are either unable or unwilling to decode these messages. The folk
idioms of detachment, unconcern and self-centredness are casually
invoked: 'I don't care a shit', 'It doesn't bother me', 'Not my problem',
'I've got better things to think about', 'What's the big fuss about?',
'So what?' When these denials seem grotesquely inappropriate, we
reach out for explanations: 'He obviously doesn't grasp what's going
on' (he needs more information); 'she can't really mean that' (she is
being disingenuous ... deep down she really cares). Or, depending on
the favoured discourse: he must be a psychopath, a moral idiot, a
product of late capitalist Thatcherite individualism or an ironic post-
modernist.

At the other extreme is the rich, convoluted and ever-increasing vocabulary for bridging the moral and psychic gap between what you know and what you do, between the sense of who you are and how your action (or inaction) looks. These techniques of evasion, avoidance, deflection and rationalization should draw on good – that is, believable – stories. These stories are difficult to decipher. Passivity and silence may *look* the same as obliviousness, apathy and indifference, but may not be the same at all. We can feel and care intensely, yet remain silent. The term 'implicatory denial' stretches words to cover all such states. Unlike literal or interpretive denial, knowledge itself is not at issue, but doing the 'right' thing with this knowledge. These are matters of mobilization, commitment and involvement. There is a strong sense, though, in which inaction is associated with denial – whether it comes from not-knowing or knowing but not caring. Hence the apocryphal reply by a British civil servant to a question about whether his government's policy in the Middle East derived from ignorance or indifference: 'I don't know and I don't care.'

Each mode of denial has its own psychological status. *Literal denial* may be a genuine and non-culpable ignorance; a deliberate aversion of your gaze from a truth too unbearable to acknowledge; a twilight state of self-deception where some of the truth is hidden from yourself; a cultural not-noticing because the reality is part of your taken-for-granted view of the world; or one of a variety of calculated forms of lying, deception or disinformation. *Interpretive denial* ranges from a genuine inability to grasp what the facts mean to others, to deeply cynical renamings to avoid moral censure or legal accountability. *Implicatory denials* come from some rather banal folk techniques for avoiding moral or psychological demands, but are invoked with mystifying degrees of sincerity.

Denial, then, includes *cognition* (not acknowledging the facts); *emotion* (not feeling, not being disturbed); *morality* (not recognizing wrongness or responsibility) and *action* (not taking active steps in response to knowledge). In the public arena of knowing about the suffering of others – mass media, politics, charity appeals – action is the issue. Oxfam and Amnesty want their information not to allow you to bracket off, ignore, forget and just go on with your life.

Organization: personal, cultural or official?

Denial can be individual, personal, psychological and private – or shared, social, collective and organized.

Personal denial

At times, denial appears to be wholly individual, or at least comprehensible in psychological terms: patients who forget being given a diagnosis of terminal cancer; spouses who put aside suspicions about their partner's infidelities ('I just don't want to know whether he is having an affair'); refusal to believe that our family and friends – our 'own people' – could act so cruelly. There is no public access to how these processes take place in a person's mind. In the Freudian model, they even remain unconscious and inaccessible to the self unless exposed with professional help.

Official denial

At the other extreme are forms of denial which are public, collective and highly organized. In particular, there are denials that are initiated, structured and sustained by the massive resources of the modern state: the cover-up of famines and political massacres, or deceptive violations of international arms boycotts. The entire rhetoric of government responses to allegations about atrocities consists of denials.

  In totalitarian societies, especially of the classic Stalinist variety, official denial goes beyond particular incidents (the massacre that didn't happen) to an entire rewriting of history and a blocking-out of the present. The state makes it impossible or dangerous to acknowledge the existence of past and present realities. In more democratic societies, official denial is more subtle – putting a gloss on the truth, setting the public agenda, spin-doctoring, tendentious leaks to the media, selective concern about suitable victims, interpretive denials regarding foreign policy. Denial is thus not a personal matter, but is built into the ideological façade of the state. The social conditions that give rise to atrocities merge into the official techniques for denying these realities – not just to observers, but even to the perpetrators themselves.

Cultural denial

Cultural denials are neither wholly private nor officially organized by the state. Whole societies may slip into collective modes of denial not dependent on a fully-fledged Stalinist or Orwellian form of thought control. Without being told what to think about (or what not to think about) and without being punished for 'knowing' the wrong things, societies arrive at unwritten agreements about what can be publicly remembered and acknowledged. People pretend to believe information that they know is false or fake their allegiance to meaningless slogans and kitsch ceremonies. This happens even in more democratic societies. Besides collective denials of the past (such as brutalities against indigenous peoples), people may be encouraged to act as if they don't know about the present. Whole societies are based on forms of cruelty, discrimination, repression or exclusion which are 'known' about but never openly acknowledged. These denials may be initiated by the state, but then acquire lives of their own. They may refer to other, distant societies: 'places like that'. Some are public and organized, but not 'official' in the sense of being sponsored by the state. A notorious example is the Holocaust denial movement.

The mutual dependency between official and cultural denial is most visible in the mass media coverage of atrocities and social suffering. The media image of the Gulf War was a masterpiece of collusive denial between the producers and reproducers of reality. Nor did the public really want to know more. The combination of official lying and cultural evasion is also clear in the language of the nuclear arms race: the use of war games analogies and other linguistic tricks to neutralize catastrophe. An entire language of denial has been constructed in order to evade thinking about the unthinkable.[4]

The point of 'consciousness raising' (feminist, political, human rights) is to combat the numbing effects of this type of denial. Assertions such as 'I didn't really know what happened to the Kurds in Iraq' call for radical changes in the media and political culture rather than tinkering with private, psychological mechanisms. We must make it difficult for people to say that they 'don't know'. Amnesty once prefaced a report with these words by Arthur Miller: 'Amnesty, with its stream of documented reports from all over the world, is a daily, weekly, monthly assault on denial.'[5]

There are also micro-cultures of denial within particular institutions. The 'vital lies' sustained by families and the cover-ups within government bureaucracies, the police or the army are again neither personal nor the result of official instruction. The group censors itself, learns to keep silent about matters whose open discussion would threaten its self-image. States maintain elaborate myths (such as the Israeli army's 'purity of arms', which asserts that force is used only when morally justified for self-defence); organizations depend on forms of concerted ignorance, different levels of the system keeping themselves uninformed about what is happening elsewhere. Telling the truth is taboo: it is snitching, whistle blowing, giving comfort to the enemy.

Time: historical or contemporary?

Are we talking about something that happened a long time ago and is now a matter of memory and history – or is it happening now? 'A long time ago' is a vague notion, but is a common-sense point between historical and contemporary denial.

Historical denial

At the personal, biographical level, historical denial is a matter of memory, forgetting and repression. It is commonplace to talk about remembering only what we want to remember. A more controversial claim is that memories of traumatic life experiences, notably childhood sexual abuse, can be totally blocked for decades but then be 'recovered'. Here we will be more interested in the denial of public and historically recognized suffering. Memories are lost or regained about what has happened to you (as victim), what you have done (as perpetrator) or know about (as observer). The Nazi period contributed two folk clichés to the lexicon of bystander denial: the 'good Germans' and 'we didn't know'. Such denials belong to the wider cultural pool of collective forgetting ('social amnesia'), such as the grossly selective memories of victimization and aggression invoked to justify today's ethnic nationalist hatreds. Sometimes, this amnesia is officially organized by the state, covering up a record of genocide or other past atrocities.

The Armenian and Holocaust cases combine both literal and interpretive denial (it didn't happen; it happened too long ago to prove; the facts are open to different interpretations; what happened was not genocide). More often, historical denial is less the result of a planned campaign than a gradual seepage of knowledge down some collective black hole. There is no need to invoke conspiracy or manipulation to understand how whole societies collude in covering up discreditable historical truths, as in the French myth of resistance that masked the record of collaboration with the Nazi occupation. Historical memories about suffering in distant places are even more prone to speedy and thorough deletion through the 'politics of ethnic amnesia'. Atrocities were denied at the time by the perpetrator government; the information flow is limited; there are either no geopolitical interests, or they are too strong to be sacrificed; victims are unimportant, isolated peoples in remote parts of the world. Some people make more suitable and memorable victims than others.

'Coming to terms with the past' becomes an urgent, fateful question when regimes change after periods of state terror and repression. How does the new government confront past atrocities? Democratic transitions in South Africa, Latin America and post-Communist societies have raised complex questions about whether and how the past is to be uncovered, recovered and represented: Are some wounds too fresh to open? Does 'living in the past' interfere with social reconstruction and national reconciliation? Should previously covered-up and denied information always be brought to light?

In the Soviet bloc, history was officially rewritten to help people forget what the state preferred them not to know. But most people knew the past all too well. Their private memories were intact, and no one believed the official lies. Private knowledge, though, has to be officially confirmed and enter into the public discourse, if it is to be acknowledged. Truth Commissions provide an arena for the symbolic recognition of what is already known but was officially denied. I will return frequently to the distinction between *knowledge* and *acknowledgement*.

Contemporary denial

At any moment, we can justifiably claim (that is, we are not lying) that we cannot and do not notice everything that is happening around us. Cognitive psychology confirms that people are bombarded with far too many stimuli for the mind to process. The media present us with so much information ('information overload') that we have to be highly selective. A perceptual filter is placed over reality, and some knowledge is shut out: 'literal denial of the present'. Nor can we feel emotionally moved or compelled to act in response to all that we do absorb. Even if there is no literal denial of the daily bulletin of social suffering, there is no choice but to deny most of its implications. Each item cannot carry the same overwhelming demand. According to the 'compassion fatigue' thesis, the potential for response is gradually blunted ('I just can't take any more photos of starving children'), and filtering becomes even more selective. In our message-dense environment there is no need to wait for historical denial; the information slips away the instant it is presented. The problem is not to explain how anyone 'denies', but how anyone's attention is ever held.

There are some intriguing links between historical and contemporary denial. The rhetoric of historical denial is prefigured in the accounts used by perpetrators at the time to hide from themselves and others the implications of their actions. Deceptive planning and implementation – by deliberate use of euphemism, commands that have an encoded double meaning, destruction of incriminating orders – live on long after the event.

Agent: victim, perpetrator or observer?

There is an atrocity triangle: in the one corner, *victims*, to whom things are done; in the second, *perpetrators*, who do these things; in the third, *observers*, those who see and know what is happening. These roles are not fixed: observers may become either perpetrators or victims; and perpetrators and observers may belong to the same culture of denial.

Victims

Victims suffer from something terrible that 'happens' to them or is deliberately done to them. Victims from all causes – whether hurricanes, wrongful arrest or sexual abuse – say to themselves, 'This can't be happening to me.' Sometimes this is just a superficial and automatic cliché. Sometimes it expresses a more profound sense of denial: an almost bodily dissociation, a sense that what in fact is happening to oneself is happening to somebody else. It is commonly said by women who are raped, people told that they are HIV-positive, parents informed that their child has been hurt in a road accident, political activists who are tortured. Chapters 2 and 3 explore the psychic manoeuvres that we use to keep troublesome knowledge from ourselves.

This also happens at the cultural level. Whole groups of potential or even designated victims may deny their approaching fate. Even when the warning signs were clear, Jewish communities in Germany and the rest of Europe refused to believe what was about to happen to them – or was already happening to their fellow Jews. Explicit warnings were ignored; each incremental increase in persecution was seen as the last one; initial reports were disbelieved; the unbearable knowledge was suppressed that you and your loved ones were going to be killed and that nothing could save you; the belief was sustained against all odds that innocent people will not suffer. Observer governments refused to believe clear reports about the annihilation programme. There was moral indifference, but perhaps also a zone of denial shared with the victims: the refusal to acknowledge a truth which seemed too impossible to be true.

While such refusal is patently maladaptive for victims, who then fail to protect themselves against impending danger, in many other situations denial is healthy and adaptive. The inhabitants of Beirut, Bogotá or Belfast cannot live in a permanent state of heightened awareness that a car bomb may go off any minute. Some switching off is necessary to get through the round of everyday life.

Perpetrators

A recurrent question about perpetrators of political atrocities and serious crimes is this: how can ordinary people do terrible things, yet, during or after the event, find ways to deny the meaning of what they are doing? These denials play a causal role in allowing atrocities to be committed initially and allowing offenders to continue with the rest of their lives as if nothing unusual was happening. The same denials – whether contrived lies or sincere beliefs – appear in official discourse and government appeals to persuade their citizens to do terrible things or keep quiet about knowing them. And they reappear in the rhetoric later used to deflect any criticism. These continuities are reviewed in chapter 4.

Bystanders

This is my main interest: the responses of onlookers, audiences, witnesses, observers, spectators and bystanders: those who come to know, see or hear, either at the time or later. There are three types of audience: (i) *immediate, literal, physical* or *internal* (those who are actual witnesses to atrocities and suffering or hear about them at the time from first-hand sources); (ii) *external* or *metaphorical* (those who receive information from secondary sources, primarily the mass media or humanitarian organizations); and (iii) *bystander states* (other governments or international organizations).

Immediate bystanders

Much human suffering takes place in private, invisible to any outside observer. We never know the secret agonies of those closest to us. Domestic violence may remain hidden indefinitely, belonging only to victim and perpetrator. But even some secret atrocities may become known to others. Torture goes beyond detainee and interrogator: police or soldiers escort prisoners to be interrogated; doctors check them before, during or after; judges and lawyers hear their testimony.

Mass refugee displacements, ethnic cleansing and famines cannot be hidden. Observers are present at the scene or hear first-hand evidence: the villagers living next to a concentration camp, the passers-by watching someone being mugged, people seeing their neighbours being abducted and 'disappeared'.

The iconography of the classic 'passive bystander effect' – the indifference of urban strangers to visible public suffering, their reluctance to help a victim – derives from one of my opening vignettes, the Kitty Genovese case. Research (chapters 3 and 6) suggests that intervention is less likely when *responsibility is diffused* ('So many others are watching', 'Why should I be the one to intervene?', 'Besides, it's none of my business'); when people are *unable to identify with the victim* (even if I see someone as a victim, I won't act if I can't empathize with their suffering; we help our family, friends, community, 'people like us', not those excluded from our moral universe, who may even be blamed for their predicament – a common experience of women victims of sexual violence); and when they are *unable to conceive of effective intervention* – even if you do not erect barriers of denial, even if you feel genuine moral or psychological unease ('I just can't get those pictures from Somalia out of my mind'), this will not necessarily result in intervention. Observers will not act if they do not know what to do, feel powerless and helpless themselves, don't see any reward, or fear punishment if they help.

These explanations of bystander passivity have been applied to routine urban sights like street crime, homelessness and accidents. Social psychologists have used experiments and simulations to discover how passivity is caused and may be counteracted. How do we encourage altruistic responses – whether to banal troubles or mass suffering? Bystanders may be too similar to perpetrators: belonging to the same ethnic group, exposed to the same ideology and stereotypes, prone to beliefs such as 'just world thinking' and victim blaming (wanting to believe that they themselves won't become victims of random circumstance, they see victims as deserving their fate). Bystanders, like perpetrators, are gradually drawn into accepting as normal actions which are initially repugnant. They deny the significance of what they see by avoiding or minimizing information about victims' suffering.

Research on bystanders to the Holocaust finds a 'history of inaction, indifference and insensitivity'.[6] Observers stand by even when their neighbours are abused, walk past victims as if they were not there, and take the jobs and possessions that victims leave behind. Chapter 10 searches for the reverse: observers who acknowledge and help, even at great personal risk.

External bystanders

We are all external or metaphorical bystanders, sitting in our living rooms facing texts and images of suffering. Switching newspapers, cruising to another channel, even going on holiday – these tactics buy only a little time. The children especially won't leave us alone – killed in the streets of Rio, suffering from AIDS in Romanian orphanages, sold as slave labour in Bangladesh, the twelve-year-old 'clean' girls in Thai brothels, the Sierra Leone child soldiers with their limbs sliced off. Then, as if to reinforce the unease induced by the media, the organizations keep up their pitch: donate money, sponsor a child, sign a petition, attend a demonstration, become a member, *do something*.

There are few theories and even less data about how we respond to such appeals. Some of us do something; most of us scan our rationalization list or just feel helpless or (metaphorically and actually) switch off. Televised images of distant misery don't seem to belong to the same world as our familiar daily round. But the distant and the immediate bystander raise common questions: Is this really my problem? Can I identify with these victims? What can I do about it anyway?

Bystander states

Whole governments and 'the international community' are also external bystanders. The term 'bystander nations' was originally used to describe the lack of response by Allied governments to early knowledge about the unfolding destruction of European Jews: the reluctance to believe allegations of genocide and the refusal to adopt policies such as bombing concentration camps. The repeated mantras calling on Western governments to 'do something' about Rwanda, Kosovo and Chechnya are part of a long history of selective refusal to intervene in certain national and international conflicts.

There is now an intensified debate about peace-keeping and international humanitarian intervention: conceptions of national self-interest; disputes about whether nation states are moral agents with moral obligations; doctrines of non-interference and national sovereignty; beliefs in moral relativism. Without stretching concepts such as 'denial' and 'bystander' too far, they at least suggest some analogies. Literal denial occurs when observer governments have to react to the depredations of their client states or arms-dealing partners. Cynically, and with full intention to deceive, they deny knowledge about what their partners are doing. The State Department's Annual Human

Rights Review reinterprets its own embassy's *evidence* as 'allegations'. Information is assigned a different cognitive frame ('ethnic conflict', 'restoring order', 'security needs', 'furthering the peace process'), or its political implications are denied. These reactions are virtually institutionalized in international bodies such as the United Nations. Kuper remarks on 'the technology of denial developed by member states of the United Nations as they shield offending governments'.[7]

Bosnia was the most explicit case in which the Holocaust experience was invoked. Early reports – about atrocities, mass rapes, detention camps, ethnic cleansing – were initially disbelieved by official sources. Eventually, no bystander nation denied these realities, but rationalized non-intervention: using the familiar mixture of high-sounding principles, pragmatic doubts, political expediency and self-interest. The Rwanda case, though far more similar to the Holocaust, was deemed too unimportant and distant for principled arguments.

Space and place: your own or elsewhere?

The difference between knowing about the sufferings of our family and loved ones, compared with strangers and distant others, is too primeval to need to be spelt out. These ties of love, care and obligation cannot be reproduced or simulated anywhere else. But the boundaries of the moral universe vary from person to person; they also stretch and contract historically – from family and intimate friends to neighbourhood, community, ethnic group, religion, country, right up to 'the children of the world'. These are not just psychological questions, but draw on a wider discourse about responsiveness to 'the needs of strangers'.[8]

In your own society, you know about social suffering (past or present) from personal observation and experience. But information about other countries, often strange and remote places, comes primarily from the mass media or international humanitarian organizations. Leaving aside extreme cases of insulation because of near-total state control over information, local people normally have more and better-quality information than outsiders – from first-hand experience, memory, personal contacts, national media, rumour, linguistic nuances and shared public culture. This information is rich, personal, multi-dimensional and historically layered. You can smell the tear gas; you know of somebody who has been tortured; you have a cousin in the army; you have participated in recent political history; you have a deep sense (prejudiced or not) regarding the evils of the enemy (the 'victim'?) and a fear of what might happen if you make any concessions. This dense picture is quite unlike the flat, one-dimensional information (headlines, sound-bites, and fifty-second TV clips) we receive about foreign places.

Past atrocities may be genuinely unknown: the clandestine torture cells and unmarked mass graves. But within these societies, people usually know most such things – and the government knows that they know. The culture of state terror is neither secret nor openly acknowledged. Information circulates – neighbours witness disappearances or kidnappings, torture victims return to their families, newspaper readers know exactly what was censored – but is simultaneously denied. Fear inside depends on knowledge *and* uncertainty: who will be picked up next? State legitimacy outside depends on permanent official denial.

If the perpetrator is your own government, this must touch your own identity and political role. You are not responsible for the atrocities – you may be an opponent of the government or even a potential victim. But this is your country. As a citizen, however distant or critical, you are bound by collective ties of culture, history and loyalty. These are not horrors in some remote place about which you have no feelings. There are few similar competing pulls of guilt, shame and loyalty when it comes to other countries.

Interests and risks are at stake in your own country: material interests and personal safety. Any outcome of the conflict will directly affect your life. Israeli citizens' interest in what is happening in their country is not the same 'interest' as that of Canadian citizens reading about Israel. And doing something about your own country asks more of you, that you pay especially the price of standing up against the consensus: ostracism, isolation and stigmatization as a 'traitor'. You may even risk becoming a victim yourself.

International observers, by contrast, do not have to understand much in order to take a stand. And they are asked to do very little – write a cheque, sign a petition, send a postcard to a prisoner, join an organization – and with almost no risk to themselves. A Swedish citizen signing an Amnesty petition against the death penalty in Singapore is not doing very much. The distant bystander should be far more easily mobilized to take a simple stand: 'Sure, I'm against the occupation of East Timor'; 'Sure, I support Kurdish rights'. In your own country, even the most undemanding action may put you outside the consensus. Moral indignation about a remote place is safe, cheap and uncomplicated.

Other reasons, though, make active involvement less likely in the international arena. I know why I should be interested in (and not 'deny') crime, unemployment, child abuse, homelessness, racism or environmental pollution in my own country. But why should I take any interest, let alone 'do something', about the fact that a hundred people were massacred in Algeria or a poet was gaoled in Malawi? The powerful moral meta-rule is to look after your own people first: 'Charity begins at home.' Pressing domestic social problems should take priority over the perennial demands of far-off places. This meta-rule was graphically expressed by the former British Defence Minister, Alan Clark, in a 1994 television documentary about East Timor.[9] Asked whether he knew that British arms exported to Indonesia were being used to carry out massacres in Timor, Clark replied: 'I don't really fill my mind much with what one set of foreigners is doing to another.'

International organizations have to ask their audiences to make an effort even to think about what is happening in a foreign place, let alone acknowledge the implications of this information. It is not natural to step out of the rhythms of private life in your own society to engage with these distant issues. And the channels through which this information is conveyed – whether the mass media, a direct mailing or a public appeal – are so structured that they can easily be segmented from the rest of life. We turn off the television, throw away the begging letter, and go back to daily life.

But a deeper form of denial is more universal: the inability or refusal to be continually 'facing' or 'living with' unpleasant truths. Domestic and foreign problems, for example, may be avoided by the same sentiment that 'worse things are happening elsewhere'. In your own society, this allows you the evasive reassurance that what is happening is not so bad. And for a remote society, this locates information on a relativistic atlas of other terrible places: why should you concern yourself about this one place if even worse things are happening elsewhere?

As Auden's Old Masters knew, suffering is always happening elsewhere.

2

Knowing and Not-Knowing

The Psychology of Denial

After looking at the everyday uses of the term 'denial', I review the concept's origins in psychoanalysis, then its appearance in theories of self-deception and cognition.

Everyday denial

Imagine typical denial responses to these statements: 'The Turkish police routinely torture political detainees'; 'Smoking tobacco increases the chances of getting lung cancer'; 'Your wife is having an affair with your neighbour'. There are five ways to deny such information.

Reality ... knowledge   The truth-claim of the statement itself may be denied: 'There is no torture in Turkey'; 'Smoking has nothing to do with lung cancer'; 'No way is my wife having an affair'. Or the existence of the reality is not contested ('Yes, this is probably true'), but you deny that you *knew* or *know* about it ('I had no idea that this was happening'). Denying the facts and denying your awareness of the facts are very different matters. Thus, the Turkish government's official response is that torture is not used and indeed is prohibited in that country. The response of British tourists being persuaded not to holiday in Turkey is that they have never heard allegations like this.

Asserting that a statement about factual reality is untrue is *literal (total, complete, factual* or *flat)* denial. The same adjectives, rather confusingly, are also applied to the quite different response of denying past or present *knowledge* about this reality: I knew nothing about it, I never thought that my wife could have done that, I could not have known.

Existence ... interpretation ... implication   Interpretive denial concedes that something is happening. But this 'something' must be seen in a different light from what is alleged, or does not really belong to this designated class of events. The police may treat detainees a little roughly, but this is not torture; the statistical correlation between smoking and lung cancer doesn't prove causation; my wife and our neighbour have an intimate relationship, but they aren't having an affair.

Implicatory denial concedes the facts of the matter and even their conventional interpretations. But their expected implications – emotional or moral – are not recognized. The *significance* of the reality is denied. These are 'denials' in the loosest sense. They evade the demand to respond by playing down the act's seriousness or by remaining indifferent ('It doesn't concern me. . . . Why should I care?').

Truth ... deception   At one extreme, statements that deny either that something exists or is known about may be true and made in good faith. You are genuinely ignorant ('know' only in the unconscious and therefore in an inaccessible sense). At the other extreme, there is deliberate deception, blatant lies offered cynically and in bad faith: such as the denials made by the Turkish government or by tobacco industry executives. Charny notes a continuum between the 'innocent' and 'malevolent' denial of known genocides: on the innocent side, deniers (like Holocaust 'revisionists') may really believe in their world-view, so their denials are sincere; on the malevolent side, people know all the facts, but blatantly lie and conceal the truth.[1] This is what politicians and public figures do much of the time. A husband's denial of his wife's infidelity allows for more subtle variations: he may genuinely not know; he may suspect, but not seek to prove his suspicions; he may know but deliberately pretend to others not to know.

Denial is always partial; some information is always registered. This paradox or doubleness – knowing and not-knowing – is the heart of the concept. It creates what Wurmser nicely calls 'pseudo-stupidity'.[2]

Conscious ... unconscious   In the discourse of public responses – to a human rights report about torture, research proving the carcinogenic effects of tobacco, newspaper exposés of sleaze and corruption – professed denials of fact or knowledge are hardly 'unconscious'. Any such explanation is redundant. Public figures knowingly lie about what they obviously know. In the personal, private realm, however – infidelity, illness, family violence, grief, addictions, sexuality – the opposite is true. Even those not committed to the Freudian meta-narrative routinely (unconsciously?) describe and explain virtually any form of denial as being an unconscious defence mechanism. Uncomfortable truths are too threatening to 'know', so they are unconsciously banished to some inaccessible zone of the mind. Such theories fill most of this chapter.

Experience . . . action Three of the standard four components of human action fit naturally: *cognition (knowing)*: you deny the facts or your knowledge of them; *emotion (feeling)*: you deny your feelings ('I didn't feel a thing when they told me'); *morality (judging)*: you approve of what was done or profess not to have any judgement ('I can't see what was so wrong').

The fourth component, *action (behaviour)*, applies to denial in a less obvious way. You are given conclusive information about the smoking/cancer connection. But you ignore this and continue smoking ('Its my problem'). Other ways of doing nothing – indifference, apathy, passive bystanding – agree that 'It's not my problem'. These are better explained by political beliefs, cowardice, laziness, selfishness and sheer amorality than by intricate states of psychic denial. Unless, that is, we agree with the Chinese sage that 'To know and not to act is not to know'.

Thankfully, the subterfuges of everyday consciousness undermine any attempt to convert these five dimensions into a neat scheme. Literal denial alone, in the 'not-knowing' sense, could mean: 'I didn't even think of that', 'I hid the truth from myself', 'I suspected', 'I partly knew', 'I knew some of the time', 'I thought that I didn't know, but I must have known'. Clinical psychologists, alas, try to measure these variations. At the low end of one denial scale are minor lapses of awareness, efforts at minimizing discomfort and looking for the good in difficult situations. At the high end, external reality is grossly denied: 'I am not in hospital; this is a Holiday Inn.' In the mid-range, the painful or frightening implications of events or perceptions are denied, although the evidence itself is acknowledged.[3] Besides a reactive blocking-out of known facts, denial may be an advance decision to avoid situations in which such facts might reveal themselves.

These fine distinctions remain salient when we move from the psychic to the political realm. As an ordinary citizen, you know that your government is doing terrible things to an ethnic minority, the situation is getting worse, and there is talk of 'transfer'. In what sense can you 'deny' all this?

- You deliberately avert your eyes from reality, because you don't want to hear more disturbing information, or you don't want to be forced to take a stand. So you stop watching TV or reading newspapers or talking to your politically involved friends.

- You don't notice this reality or comprehend its nature, because it is just part of your taken-for-granted view of the world. You literally don't perceive that anything special or unusual is happening.

- You see what is happening, but you refuse to believe it, or you can't 'take it in'. If these apparent facts and their manifest interpretations were true, this would seriously threaten your sense of personal and cultural identity.

- You are well aware of the emerging reality, but you vocally deny this because you support the policy, or are not bothered by what is going on. You are oblivious to what is happening; you simply don't care. Or you are following either the state's formal injunction or the tacit cultural understanding that you should not speak out about certain matters and should trust those who know better.

- You are bothered, disturbed, even outraged about what is happening, but for many reasons (fear of standing out, powerlessness, self-protection, the absence of a visible solution) you remain silent. You don't make a personal protest (write a letter, blow the whistle, resign your government job); you don't participate in any collective protests.

Political states that look similar from the outside – apathetic and submissive – may harbour different psychological states. Their common thread may be called 'denial', but would not necessarily fit a formal definition:

A statement about the world or the self (or about your knowledge of the world or your self) which is neither literally true nor a lie intended to deceive others but allows for the strange possibility of simultaneously knowing and not-knowing. The existence of what is denied must be 'somehow' known, and statements expressing this denial must be 'somehow' believed in.

Many other uses of the concept don't fit these criteria, and may utterly miss the paradox of denial. Only psychoanalysis comes near to the elusive quality of the concept. The analyst deals with the subject's unconscious need not to know about troubling matters: the distressing ideas and emotions that mobilized the denial in the first place must be uncovered; the patient resists, but eventually becomes conscious of the denied content. Bollas comments: 'Each of us is aware in ourselves of the workings of denial, of our need to be innocent of a troubling recognition.'[4] I take this simple formula – the 'need to be innocent of a troubling recognition' – as my guiding definition.

The entire chapter now deals with the perplexing state of knowing and not knowing at the same time.

The psychoanalysis of denial

Origins: Freud on denial and disavowal

The standard Freudian lexicon presents the first puzzle. Rather than a separate entry on 'denial', we find 'Disavowal (Denial)'.[5] Following earlier scholars, the editors prefer 'disavowal' as the translation of Freud's German term *Verleugnung*. They suggest that although 'denial' is the more common translation, it carries different and stronger connotations than Freud intended, as in 'I deny the validity of your statements'. It also has the quite different and irrelevant meaning of denying (that is, withholding) goods, services or rights.

The next puzzle comes from the obscure – not to say bizarre – initial application of the concept. Freud first used *Verleugnung*, 'disavowal', in the specific sense of 'a mode of defence which consists in the subject's refusing to recognize the reality of a traumatic perception – most especially the perception of the absence of the woman's penis. Freud invoked this mechanism particularly when accounting for fetishism and the psychosis.'[6] (The reference to psychosis is misleading, because Freud soon distinguished disavowal from the more radical, psychotic denial of reality.)

As early as 1894, Freud noted that 'The ego rejects the unbearable idea together with its associated affect and behaves as if the idea had never occurred to the person at all'.[7] The term *Verleugnung*, however, first appears in his 1923 paper on infantile genital organization. Freud suggests that the little boy notices, perhaps by accident – seeing his mother or little sister naked – that not everyone has a penis. Ho hum, there's something different there. 'We know how children [that is, boys] react to their first impressions of the absence of a penis. They disavow the fact and believe that they do see a penis all the same.'[8] It is as if they refuse to accept what they are seeing. They may find ways to gloss over the contradiction between observation and preconception – for example, 'it might grow later'. Only gradually do they come to face the awful truth: the penis is absent – and permanently so – because of castration. Unable to face the possibility that little girls have been castrated and that this could happen to them, boys would rather believe that they actually *have* seen a penis. Really?

Two years later, Freud tried to show how an equivalent disavowal operates for girls.[9] The girl's destiny is to convert her momentous discovery – that she does not have this large, visible and obviously superior organ – into envy. In contrast to the little boy who instantly disavows, or 'sees nothing', the girl awards psychic importance to her discovery only much later. But even at the time, she behaves differently. In a flash, she makes a judgement: 'She has seen it and knows that she is without it and wants to have it.'[10] This hope of obtaining a penis and the desire, in spite of everything, to become a man may persist, Freud tells us, till an incredibly late age, and may become the motive for strange and otherwise unaccountable actions. 'Or again a process may set in which I should like to call a "disavowal", a process which in the mental life of children seems neither uncommon or very dangerous but which in an adult would mean the beginning of a psychosis.'[11] 'Thus', he continues, 'a girl may refuse to face the fact of being castrated, may harden herself in the conviction that she *does* possess a penis and may subsequently be compelled to behave as though she were a man.'[12] Deep denial, indeed.

A year earlier, Freud had distinguished between neurotic and psychotic denial of reality – but created some confusion by seeing them both as forms of *repression*.[13] In neurosis, the ego, depending on reality, suppresses a 'piece of the id', that is, of instinctual life. In psychosis, however, the ego, in the service of the id, withdraws from reality. Neurosis is repression that has failed. Thus the repression of instinctual demands (such as the love of a forbidden object) is neurotic: you 'forget' (always in inverted commas) through repression. Freud's illustrative case is prototypical: a patient is in love with her brother-in-law; at her sister's deathbed, she is horrified to have the thought 'Now he is free and can marry me'. Instantly, the forbidden desire is repressed. The psychotic's reaction, by contrast, would be a disavowal of the actual event – that is, the fact of the sister's death.

This is all a little confusing. Freud's paper shows both the similarities and the differences between neurotic and psychotic reactions. Both express rebellion by the id against the external world's unwillingness to adapt itself; but 'neurosis does not disavow reality, it only ignores it; psychosis disavows it and tries to replace it'.[14] Eventually he finds a definition close to the mundane (and not particularly neurotic) experience of denial: 'A neurosis usually contents itself with avoiding the piece of reality in question and protecting itself against coming into contact with it.'[15]

In 1927, Freud published his paper on fetishism – usually and incorrectly cited as the origin of his concept of disavowal or denial.[16] The fetishist, he claims, perpetuates an infantile attitude by holding two incompatible positions at the same time: he simultaneously disavows and acknowledges the fact of female castration. The object choice of the foot fetishist is not a substitute for *any* penis, but for the childhood penis later 'lost'. Freud desperately tries to clarify this weird thesis:

> The fetish is a substitute for the woman's (the mother's) penis that the little boy once believed in and – for reasons familiar to us – does not want to give up. What happened therefore, was that the boy refused to take cognisance of the fact of his having perceived that a woman does not possess a penis. No, that could not be true: for if a woman had been castrated, his own possession of a penis was in danger.[17]

And so on. The explanations only become more obscure. Suddenly, Freud switches to the *workings* of denial, rather than its supposed contents. Now we see the paradox of knowing and not-knowing. Should we say, he asks, that the boy 'scomatizes' his perception – that is, wipes it out in a psychotic, even physiological sense? No: psychoanalysis already has a perfectly good term for this – 'repression'. But the vicissitude of the idea is distinct from the affect (emotion). *Verleugnung*, 'disavowal', refers to the idea; *Verdangung*, meaning 'repression', should be reserved for the affect. 'Scomatization' is an unsuitable explanation, because it implies that the perception is entirely wiped out, like a visual impression falling on the blind spot of the retina.[18] True denial is quite different: the original perception persists, and energetic action must be taken to maintain the disavowal. The child has not at all preserved unaltered his belief that women have a phallus. 'He has retained his belief, but he has also given it up.'[19]

Only if this contradictory state exists or is suspected, does the concept of denial have any significance. Freud describes two young men who might look as if they had 'scomatized' their father's death. But this is more a split in consciousness. Their lack of recognition of their father's death was 'only one current in their mental life...there was another current which took full account of that fact. The attitude which fitted in with the wish and the attitude which fitted in with reality existed side by side.'[20]

Freud was fascinated by the idea that awkward facts of life could be handled by simultaneous acceptance and disavowal. They are too threatening to confront, but impossible to ignore. The compromise solution is to deny and acknowledge them at the same time. Freud hardly admired this solution: it was a 'false resolution': a protection against reality rather than learning to confront it. Instead of using insight to try to integrate these split perceptions, the subject uses 'perverse arguments' to misrepresent the facts – a way of dealing with reality which, in Freud's words, 'almost deserves to be described as artful'.[21]

Many denials are certainly 'artful'. Indeed, the term hints at some conscious intent in a process supposed to be unconscious. In any event – gnostic speculations about penis envy, castration and fetishism aside – Freudian meta-psychology still frames the contemporary debates.

Reality and meaning

Freud insisted that what is denied is the 'unwelcome idea' associated with the perceived reality, rather than the objective existence of the phenomenon itself. Unless there is a wholly psychotic interference, the subject is perfectly able (in theory, at least) to describe things accurately. 'Disavowal or denial as originally described by Freud involves, not an absence or distortion of actual perception, but rather a failure to appreciate fully the significance or implications of what is perceived.'[22]

This distinction is far, far trickier than it looks. First, despite Freud's insistence that the object of denial is the significance of reality (interpretation and implication) and not its literal existence, many expositions, including his own, are inconsistent. They often do claim that reality (events, facts, things) is being denied. Second, this strict distinction between perception and meaning is hardly straightforward. Third, how can we be sure that the person indeed does know or knew – or, even more difficult, would or should have known – what is denied? The therapist knows, because she sees the symptoms, the dreams, the slips of the tongue and the acting out. But as a journalist talking to witnesses to a long-past massacre, how do I know that they 'must' have seen what they claim not to have seen?

Split perceptions

Freud's fetishism paper introduced the notion that the psyche contains incompatible, or split, perceptions. The child's disavowal of the anatomical distinction between the sexes indicates, for Freud, a split in the subject's ego. Some years later, he returned to the splitting of the ego as an explanation of disavowal.[23] The fetishist has two attitudes: *disavowal* of the perception of a woman's lack of penis and *recognition* of this absence and the anxiety it arouses. Disavowal, Freud insisted, is

always supplemented by acknowledgement; these incompatible positions are always there. You take account of reality and detach the ego
from reality. These psychic states 'persist side by side throughout their
lives without influencing each other. Here is what may rightly be
called a splitting of the ego.'[24]

The ecological trope of a 'split' in consciousness appears in virtually
all theories of denial and, moreover, in popular discourse. It is astonishing that such a disturbing idea is so readily accepted. Freud supposedly referred to disavowal as 'blindness of the seeing eye in which
one knows and does not know a thing at the same time.'[25] This
conveys the image perfectly. But how can it be? How can we deny
the existence of a fact, yet simultaneously, apparently in another 'part'
of the mind, acknowledge that this fact does indeed exist?

Repression versus denial

Freud tried, with increasing inconsistency, to distinguish between
repression and disavowal. In one version, repression refers to an
emotion, disavowal to an idea; in another, repression is a defence
against internal instinctual demands, whereas disavowal/denial is a
defence against the claims of external reality. Later theorists went on to
blur all such distinctions. Common tales of denial – the mother denying hostile wishes about her infant, the son denying Oedipal fantasies,
the male denying homosexual desires – hardly even attempt to distinguish between acknowledging external reality and wishes about that
reality.

Repression, as Freud intended, soon became the driving force
behind the entire psychoanalytical narrative. It became used especially
to describe the forgetting of actual, imagined or desired childhood
sexual experiences. 'Denial of the past' became synonymous with
'repression of the past', while denial itself became indistinguishable
from other defence mechanisms such as repression and dissociation.

Conscious versus unconscious

The psychoanalytic model is taken to assume – as it mostly does – that
the whole process of denial is unconscious. It does allow, however, a
partial awareness – albeit less than outside critics demand – of disturbing perceptions being banished to the zone of unawareness. After
this initial awareness (which may be denied), the 'loss' of information
over time is unconscious. This sequence sounds more plausible than
invoking a mysterious inner barrier, its workings impenetrable to
conscious thought, that so effectively censors the information as to

render it inaccessible – but then emits a warning light every now and then to tell you that something strange is going on. Sometimes, rather cruelly, we don't accept this sad tale: 'You really knew all along what she was up to,' we say.

In Freudian theory, though, the defence mechanism *must* be unconscious. Denial in the 'vernacular sense' of declaring something not to be true is not necessarily denial in the 'scientific sense' of an unconscious process.[26] Nor is this the arcane matter it seems. Many witnesses to an unfolding atrocity draw on popular versions of the topographical metaphor of splitting: 'I didn't know,' but (usually later), 'Another part (portion) of my mind knew (or must have known).' Thus, 'part of the ego can, speaking anthropomorphically, be regarded as "declaring" not to be true something which another part of the ego "recognizes" as true'.[27] But if the denying 'portion' of your self is entirely *unconscious* and split off from reality testing, how can you be held responsible for anything?

Later developments

Later theories remained close to the original. Anna Freud's first elaboration pointed to the frequency of denial in childhood play and fantasy.[28] Young children cannot draw on more sophisticated defence mechanisms; they often use denial as a coping mechanism to block out perceptions that disturb or frighten them. She claims that positive assertions (that is, fantasies) place a screen over the negative denials: 'The denial of reality is completed and confirmed when in his fantasies, words or behaviour, the child reverses the real facts.'[29] As most Freudians do, she then keeps switching from external reality to internal emotion, and from denial to repression.

She also points out that denial in adulthood is more rigid than in childhood. Children may deny some aspect of reality one moment, then acknowledge it the next. Adults, especially those who build a large part of their lives on denial, remain entrenched in their position, and are more threatened when confronted with reality. In mob-rousing politicians and bigots, she later argued, 'the denial goes over into lying and falsification.'[30] This is an appealing but confusing claim: how does an unconscious defence mechanism 'go over' into the deliberate lies and manipulations of political bigotry?

The notion of denial as normal (positive, healthy, necessary, even benign and valuable) is homeostatic: denial protects us from painful emotions – just as a literal turning of the head or blinking of the eye shields the retina from intense light. Our pre-conscious appraisal of a situation as dangerous brings about painful emotions that direct our focal concern to something else.[31] But when are defensive manoeuvres adaptive? If the patient gets better, we say that denial has been healthy; if worse, that denial was pathological.

Little distinction is made between repression, denial and disavowal: all arise from a 'basic drive' to ward off unconscious danger and 'plug the leaks' of what was to stay repressed.[32] Wangh asserts that we are never 'spontaneously aware' of our denials; only an outside observer notices. But at the same time, we mobilize *conscious* mechanisms against the 'leakages' of repression. These are further 'plugged' by means of such constructs as religious beliefs or plain lies. You convince your listeners by lying, and this reinforces your own denial of the real facts. This is a crucial theoretical compromise, especially in the polit- ical realm. Here Wangh finds a better metaphor than 'plugging leaks': 'Negating the existence of an object – meaning by this, of course, its psychic representation – or disavowing a feeling, are akin to having a "negative hallucination". Where there should be something, there is nothing. Such a perceptual vacuum is, however, not easily tolerated under the growing pressure of a sense of reality and the hunger for percepts.'[33] You can't live too long with the emptiness of 'nothing happened'. So 'positive hallucinations' (fantasies, myths, rationaliza- tions, fairy stories, ideologies) come to the aid of the failing denial, fulfilling the hunger for some image. These 'images' are obviously not idiosyncratic and private, but derive from the culture.

Getting to this point hardly requires such a circuitous route. And even if most denial is not a psychotic negation of manifest facts, but an evasion of their significance, there are many non-psychotic forms of literal denial. Some persistent denials – 'My father didn't really die' – are indeed psychotic; others – 'Elvis Presley didn't really die' – harmless cultural *meshugas*; yet others – 'Our Holy Man didn't really die' – the bases of religious belief. The need for an alternative story is especially acute when the manifest interpretation of the acknowledged 'something' is unthinkable. This is the response to the most extreme forms of mass human suffering. Wangh gives a painfully relevant example: the beliefs adopted by Jews in the Warsaw Ghetto to deny that they were in danger of liquidation: it can't happen here in Europe, only Communists will be killed. Why, though, is it a 'paradox' that denial relieves us from immediate anxiety, but that we must 'renounce its comforts' to remain alert to long-term dangers?

These considerations apply more to denial by victims than to denial of the suffering of others. Denying unwelcome and potentially dan- gerous news about ourselves obviously needs explanation. But there is no compelling reason to even notice the suffering of others. Denying the significance of a massacre in East Timor is not irrational; nor does it carry any dangers for us. A price has to be paid, some analysts claim, for rendering psychologically non-existent something that is 'really real' to us. 'Such crass handling of reality', Ehrlich sternly warns, 'cannot go unnoticed or uncompensated. Sooner or later with a greater or lesser degree of psychiatric righteousness, the culprit ego will have to face the music.'[34] This may be true for the hapless 'culprit' who denies hating his father – but in the world of atrocities, neither the best-informed observers nor even the culprits may ever face any music. In the public if not the private realm, denial carries no necessary psychic price.

In both realms, denial may be *active* (repudiation, rejection, negation, disavowal) rather than *passive* (the mere withdrawal of attention, deflecting the gaze).[35] People living in the midst of political horrors may do some active denying, but mostly they can just ignore and forget, going on with their daily lives. Even more so with news of distant suffering: we don't *actively* deny that thousands of children are starving to death every day; we merely put this knowledge aside, bracket if off, learn to live with it. We don't *dwell* on it, as we say. But 'bracketing' is another spatial metaphor – like splitting, compartmentalization and isolation. Such metaphors hardly explain how vital information is both registered and denied. Still less can they deal with the elusive distinction between perceiving and interpreting. If Little Red Riding Hood had perceived the bed as empty, this would have been psychotic denial. But does her 'ordinary' denial really *begin* with the instant and gross misperception that this is her dear granny on the bed (her face a little odd, that snout, such a big scarf, hair on her cleavage)? Surely Little Red Riding Hood knows instantly and certainly that the wolf cannot possibly be her grandmother. But she does not appreciate the *significance* of what she recognizes. This is why she needs therapy, education and consciousness raising – as we all do – to address the implications, demands, messages or risks presented by reality: 'Listen, Ms Hood, this is what the Dirty Old Wolf will do to you if you get much closer.'

Instead of dwelling on the difference between fact and interpretation, the issues in our personal and political lives should be: 'What inhibits us from searching further for the truth?' and 'What do we do to the truth when we discover that it is the truth?' Let us ask these questions of the greatest denier of all time, Oedipus. Steiner's reinterpretation of the Oedipus drama starts with a case-study of a patient who, despite appearances, was neither ignorant of the reality he was evading nor the victim of splitting or repression: 'I think he turned a blind eye and then tried to maintain a cover up as he became superior and morally righteous.'[36] Sophocles saw his hero, Oedipus, as the quintessential tragic figure, struggling with reality and self-knowledge, both knowing and not-knowing the truth of what he had done or was doing. The story of Oedipus as a victim of fate who bravely pursues the truth becomes an allegory for the patient in analysis to whom the secrets of the unconscious are gradually revealed. With the therapist's long and patient help, denial eventually leads to insight.

But Steiner reminds us that, alongside the epic of Oedipus as an innocent man caught up in relentless fate, Sophocles also conveys another message. Far from being ignorant and hence innocent of what he did, Oedipus must have realized that he had killed King Laius, his father, and married the widow, Jocasta, his own mother. Oedipus did not, of course, fully know all these facts; rather, 'he half knew them and decided to turn a blind eye on this half knowledge'.[37] All the main characters in the drama must also have been aware of the identity of Oedipus and realized what he had done. There is, to be sure, considerable ambiguity about just how much each knew. Certainly all the participants – Tiresias, Creon, Jocasta, the court officials, the elders – had good reasons to evade their knowledge or suspicions. If any of them had made some enquiries, or followed up some leads, the truth would easily have come out. Instead, consciously or semi-consciously, they join Oedipus in staging a collusive cover-up. He, in turn, erects a plausible facade to hide even the half-knowing that he is reluctant to acknowledge – and persuades himself and others to accept this.

Far from being about a relentless pursuit of truth, then, the legend is about the systematic denial of truth. This is a cover-up story like Watergate or Iran-Contra. The questions in those cases are those of the Oedipus story: How much, and when, did Nixon or Bush or Reagan really know? How did the collusion get under way? In whose interests was the cover-up sustained? The legend is also relevant to 'the good German' question: 'How much did they know?' And to Truth Commissions: did this official know that his underlings were running death squads?

Denial as 'the need to be innocent of a troubling recognition' exactly fits this reading of the tragedy: 'we seem to have access to reality, but choose to ignore it because it proves convenient to do so.'[38] The phrase 'turning a blind eye' also conveys 'the right degree of ambiguity as to how conscious or unconscious the knowledge is'.[39] These are not simple lies or frauds where facts are accessible – but they would lead to a conclusion you knowingly evade: 'we are vaguely aware that we choose not to look at the facts without being conscious of what it is we are evading.'[40] We turn away from our insights and hide their implications. We half-know, but don't want to discover the other half.

This revisionist interpretation does not replace the traditional version. Both may be true: knowing and not-knowing. Indeed, much of the drama's tension comes from the conflict between the wish to know and the fear of knowing. Each of these states may dominate – as they do for all of us – at different times. What gives Oedipus a heroic stature is that eventually 'he is able to persevere in his search for the truth, overcoming his reluctance to know which had so dominated him in the past'.[41] As *Oedipus the King* reaches it climax, his ambivalence disappears. Now shattered by the open revelation of the truth, he acknowledges the facts and his guilt; he offers no excuses. But the act of blinding himself shows that the truth fully revealed is too terrible to endure. The next part of the drama, *Oedipus at Colonus*, shows a further retreat from reality, leading to wild denial, self-justification, self-righteous innocence and, in extreme states, a psychotic-like sense of omnipotence.

These are two modes of evading the realities of personal and mass suffering. First, *turning a blind eye* – keeping facts conveniently out of sight, allowing something to be both known and not known. Such methods can be highly pathological but nevertheless 'reflect a respect and fear of the truth and it is this fear which leads to the collusion and cover-up'.[42] Turning a blind eye is a social motion. We have access to enough facts about human suffering, but avoid drawing their disquieting implications. We cannot face them all the time.

The second mode, *retreat from truth to omnipotence*, is more insidious and more resistant to therapy or insight. This is the preferred move of perpetrators, rather than mere bystanders. When Oedipus, now actually blind, can no longer turn a blind eye, he shows a contempt for the truth. He shifts to implicatory denial. This takes a particularly dangerous form of a self-righteousness that exonerates all atrocities and obsessively blames others. 'He does not deny the facts themselves, it is too late to pretend that he did not kill his father and marry his mother, but he denies responsibility and guilt, and claims that these wrongs were wrongs inflicted *on* him rather than by him.'[43] He is haughty and arrogant; he has no respect for reality, no shame, and makes no attempt to conceal his crimes. This is surely the true voice in the 'new barbarism' of ethnic nationalist conflict, with its delusionary circuits of self-righteous omnipotence and self-vindication by blaming others.

This is an analogy, not a causal link between psychic and political denial. A recent thesis that looks back to *The Authoritarian Personality*, shows the perils of extrapolating from personal to political levels.[44]

The claim is that states of denial result from parents using rigid, harsh child-rearing methods, especially physical punishment, while denying their own malevolence ('We're doing this for your own good'). Children of such parents learn early to deny the reality of their pain, repress their feelings of anger and humiliation, and to construct imaginary worlds. As adults, they deny aspects of reality that remind them of the emotional pains suffered in childhood – fear, anger, helplessness. As parents, they transmit to their own children the pain denied as a result of their experience. Denial is transferred across generations and echoed in the wider political culture: 'If we deny reality, if we don't feel the pain of what is happening in Bosnia or in the house next door, we don't act . . . to change these realities.'[45] These empirical links are highly tenuous, and the causal chain is stretched to cover too much: the rise of the religious Right, violence against gays, punitiveness in schools, the death penalty, child abuse and just about any rage associated with American white males.

The increasing popularity of dumbed-down notions of 'in denial' derives more from therapeutic psycho-babble. It is reassuring to invoke a 'professional' term to explain the strange existence of people who know yet do not know, who are neither simply lying nor unable to perceive reality.

The authoritative DSM thus instructs clinicians to follow a seven-level 'Defensive Functioning Scale', ranked in order of adaptiveness.[46] At the second level, dissociation and repression are doing good work in keeping potentially threatening stuff out of awareness. This also happens at level four, *Disavowal*, where denial keeps 'unpleasant or unacceptable stressors, impulses, ideas, affects or responsibility out of awareness'. By level seven, the most maladaptive, *Defensive Dysregulation* has led to 'a pronounced break with objective reality'. Other 'scientists', needless to say, rate denial differently. In one league table ranking defences according to their 'maturity', denial is relegated to the lowest category, *narcissistic defences*, 'the most primitive and . . . used by children and psychotically disturbed persons'.[47]

In these texts the intelligent ambiguity of psychoanalytical theory is converted into spuriously exact 'scientific' classification and a fetishized 'medical' diagnosis. The DSM, though, notes a criterion usually taken for granted: that the 'painful aspect of reality' which the person refuses to acknowledge [*is*] *apparent to others*. But unless we are certain that this reality actually *is* (or *was*) apparent to others, we can only speculate about what these others saw but the subject 'refuses to acknowledge'.

If clinical sources are hardly sophisticated, the New Age psychology that popularized the notion of being 'in denial' sounds more

promising: self-reflection and subjectivity, rather than scales and syn-
dromes. I intended to devote much space to the self-help, growth, New
Age, alternative, complementary and spiritual movements. But after
paging through some thirty such books, I found the discourse too
repetitive and simplistic to be worth much comment. It conveys two
messages about denial.

First, there's a lot of it around. Every reader is assumed to be 'in
denial' about whatever happens to be the subject of the self-help
book,[48] which in turn happens to be 'really' your problem. You are
denying your dependence (on drugs, alcohol, junk food, destructive
relationships, men from Mars, or too many vitamin supplements);
your low quota of self-esteem or emotional intelligence; your high
quota of self-destructiveness or narcissism; your lack of contact with
your inner being, true self or child within.

Second, denial is always something that can and should be overcome, undermined, broken through or down. This leads to insight,
acceptance and acknowledgement; the hidden truth emerges; and, the
healing process then begins. You tick off the boxes in the diagnostic
table, keep a daily denial diary, and do the suggested exercises. You
can now check how much better you are (that is, how much *worse*,
because you are no longer in denial). I once attended a series of
lectures in Santa Cruz, California, on 'Self-Actualization'. I was
pleased to see R. D. Laing's work on the reading list – until I realized
that Laing's patently (even heavy-handed) ironical accounts of therapy
were being read *literally* as bad cases of denial:

> *He does not think there is anything the matter with him because*
> *   One of the things that is*
> *the matter with him*
> *is that he does not think that there is anything the matter with him*
> *therefore*
> *   we have to help him realize that,*
> *   the fact that he does not think there is anything*
> *   the matter with him*
> *   is one of the things that is*
> *   the matter with him.*[49]

The original Freudian discourse was aware of its internal tensions.
Take the assumption that there is, or could be, a unified self. Attempts
to explain and overcome denial use tropes of slippage, isolation and
splitting that only make sense if this integrated self exists. By contrast,
the late-modern and post-modern self has in essence no essence. To
this fragmented, fluid and compartmentalized self, denial, far from
being an aberration, is only to be expected. This, however, is not

just a change in world-views. Freud himself was quite clear that the unitary self of even the healthiest, 'integrated' person was permanently under siege. The self could never be fully socialized; denial and self-deception are part of being human.

The insistence that in normal (non-psychotic) denial, the perceptual evidence remains intact, only its significance disavowed, leaves other unresolved tensions. But it does allow talk about meanings, interpretations, symbols and subjectivity. There is no room for this language in the mechanistic theory of defence 'mechanisms'. Think of the means, conscious and unconscious, used by residents of Jerusalem, Belfast, Beirut, Bogotá and Algiers to keep violence out of daily awareness. You cannot allow your knowledge of the risk to govern your routine; nor can you act without this knowledge. The language of 'mechanisms' cannot do justice to these nuances, anymore than talk about cognitive 'loss', or 'holes' in perception.

Then there is the recurrent issue of the normality of denial. Denial supposedly protects us from dysfunctional anxiety by keeping us from thinking about or expressing whatever threatens us. But it is also taken as evidence of a failure, distortion or 'cognitive arrest' that has to be remedied. If the defence functions so well, why should anyone try to erode it? My final chapter struggles with a grander version of this question: is there an absolute value in facing and telling the truth?

Lies and self-deception

Plain lying, we have assumed, is a far simpler matter than denial. 'The government of Ruritania strongly denies that its armed forces were responsible for any killings.' If this assertion is untrue, is known by the government to be untrue, so is knowingly intended to deceive, then this is not 'denial' in any puzzling sense. 'Strongly denies' is merely the conventional phrase for lying. Such deliberately deceptive statements do not call for any taxing thoughts about 'denial' in the psychoanalytic sense.

In some states of mind and political states, however, the difference between obvious lying and paradoxical denial becomes blurred. This is the terrain of *self-deception* and bad faith. What can it mean to 'lie to yourself' – the conventional (and bizarre) meaning of self-deception? A lie is 'a statement intended to deceive a dupe about the state of the world, including the intentions and attitudes of the liar'.[50] The liar, that is, intends to cause the dupe to adopt an understanding about the world and/or the mind of the liar that the liar believes to be false. The distinction between truth and deceit, Barnes reminds us, refers to the intentions of the liar, not the nature of the world. Robinson nicely identifies the 'prototypical, fully fledged lie as a proposition (P) asserted by S (sender) to an addressee (A) such that (1) P is false, (2) S believes P to be false, and (3) in uttering P, S intends that A shall come to believe P'.[51] Despite its ungainly appearance, this is a helpful tool to weed out those denial statements (surely the majority) that are 'merely' fully-fledged lies.

But what about self-deception? If this means *lying to yourself* rather than to others, it looks similar to prototypical denial. A literal application of the P-S-A definition, however, is quite implausible. It is semantically difficult to imagine this sequence of lying to yourself – you as S (one distinct part of the self) trying to dupe you as A (another part). The notion of self-deception, though, must suppose inner dialogues or many-sided conversations just like these: the roles of liar and dupe are indeed played or thought out by the same person (the 'I' and the 'me').[52] These are more like ongoing internal reality negotiations, which – like external negotiations between real, different people – can include denial, lying, delusion, illusion and deceit. In this looser sense, self-deception is imaginable. So is self-delusion: the liar begins to believe that her lie is not a lie, but true. In order to live with yourself, you allow yourself to be 'taken in' by your own deceptive style. So internal denial is similar to self-deceit or self-delusion.

But how much do people 'really' believe the lies they tell to themselves and others? In chapter 4, we will see perpetrators of dreadful atrocities who not only deny culpability, but insist (and convince others) that they were morally right: 'they started shooting...we are the real victims...they deserved what they got...this was the will of God.' This self-righteousness may be only a tactical ploy, a rhetorical gesture, a pretence. Such people know that they are lying, and don't for a minute believe their own clichés. Alternatively, however, they (and their audiences) may be convinced that this is the truth: the self is the text. It takes long practice, cultural learning, indoctrination, routinization or conversion to enable people to believe their own lies and not see themselves as deluded. You become sincere when, in Riesman's classic definition, you start believing your own propaganda. Remember that the truth or falsity of such narratives does not tell us whether they are fully-fledged lies, empty rhetorical chat or utterly sincere beliefs. More likely, from the lips of a Serb soldier talking to the CNN, they are a mixture of the three.

But assume that he does mean what he says – either after assuring himself that he does or because he has never questioned his beliefs. Is this self-deception or sincerity? And is it better (less dangerous) that soldiers, press officers and politicians believe their own rhetoric than know that it is only rhetoric? Do they start believing, then become cynical, or begin to believe what they were cynical about?

In any talk about deceiving ourselves by hiding the truth 'from' ourselves, terms like 'deceive' or 'hide' surely negate the idea that denial is an *unconscious* process. Freudian theory does not require us to be, at every stage, totally unconscious of what we are doing. Thus we knowingly choose not to make enquiries that might confirm some hidden cognition: 'I just don't want to know what he gets up to at those conferences.' Nor are we unconscious when we profess not to recognize what we are doing or protest against the (quite correct) name that someone else gives to this: 'It's not that I'm actually *leaving* you.' But the master force must be unconscious to allow us to go on thinking that we are doing something quite different from what we acknowledge, to others as well as ourselves. Protected thus by denial – we are not responsible for this evasion of the superego's judgement – we not only avoid anxiety, but enjoy the forbidden.

This looks pretty close to self-deception. According to a standard account, people in states of self-deception defensively avoid 'spelling out' what they are doing: 'The self-deceiver is one who is in some way engaged in the world but who disavows the engagement, who will not acknowledge it even to himself as his.'[53] Fingarette notes that this is like Freud's 'splitting of the ego'. Even if they have a clear personal self-identity, people act in ways they know to be morally unacceptable, but do so in pursuit of isolated projects disengaged from the rest of the self. This type of disavowal – the act has no connection with who I really am – may be sincere, and hence self-deceiving. As we will see, it is critical in the perpetuation of atrocities. I might engage in an even more radical form of denial: the person who did (or observed) all those horrible things in Vietnam *was not me*.

Self-deception is a way to keep secret from ourselves the truth we cannot face. As Bok notes, 'To see the self as deceiving itself has seemed the only way to explain what might otherwise seem incomprehensible: a person's failure to acknowledge what is too obvious to miss.'[54] But this explanation is troubling: 'Exactly how can one be both insider and outsider thus, keeping secrets from oneself, even lying to oneself? How can one simultaneously know and ignore the same thing, hide it and remain in the dark about it?'[55] Without this simultaneity – knowing *and* not-knowing the same thing at the same time, being in the light *and* in the dark, keeping a secret *and* ignoring it – both self-deception and denial lose their paradoxical character. Yet there is no way to 'show' any of this. If I am told that I am deceiving myself or in denial, I have no convincing way to deny this. All my denials are further proof of the depths of my denial, the force of my resistance, or the falsity of my consciousness.

The Freudian solution is appealing because the topology of splitting – 'portions' of the mind – keeps these dualities in place. This is just what Sartre famously ridiculed: 'the hypothesis of a censor, conceived as a line of demarcation with customs, passport division, currency control etc. to re-establish the duality of the deceiver and the deceived.'[56] His alternative, *bad faith*, is a form of denial that consciousness directs towards itself – but it is not 'lying' to oneself. The person practising bad faith is, to be sure, hiding a displeasing truth. But this is not a falsehood – simply because you are hiding the truth from yourself. There is no duality of deceiver–deceived; everything happens within a unified single consciousness: 'It follows . . . that the one to whom the lie is told and the one who lies are one and the same person, which means that I must know in my capacity as deceiver, the truth which is hidden from me in my capacity as the one deceived. Better yet, I must know the truth very exactly *in order* to conceal it more carefully.'[57]

This makes sense. But Sartre now becomes his most opaque. Bad faith, he insists, is not something one is infected with; it is precisely not a 'state'. Consciousness 'affects itself' with bad faith: 'There must be an original intention and project of bad faith.'[58] But just what sort of project can this be in the world of social suffering? Sartre insists that knowing the truth 'very exactly' and concealing it 'more carefully' do not happen at different moments, but 'in the unitary structure of a single project'. If the project is neither unconscious nor a deliberate and cynical attempt (obviously doomed) to lie to oneself, then just what is it?

One result is the refusal to spell out one's engagement in the world. Elster interprets this as the deliberate refusal to collect threatening information.[59] Thus, the dictator tells his underlings that he doesn't want to know any details; he knows that something unsavoury is going on, but his self-imposed lack of detailed knowledge allows him later to tell himself and others that he had no knowledge of what was happening. Hence the ability of millions of Germans to overlook the extermination programme: they must have known that something terrible was happening, but as long as they remained ignorant of the details, they could say later, 'We didn't know'. This is not a hard or paradoxical form of self-deception to explain, 'because we do not have to impute to the self-deceiver a knowledge of the facts that he does not want to know, only a knowledge that there are such facts'.[60] We have all, I believe, dabbled in this particular project of bad faith.

The essence of self-deception, though, remains elusive. Philosophers do not agree about what self-deception is, or how it relates to rationalization, wishful thinking or other self-manipulative psychic strategies. Indeed, a recent review concludes that 'there is no agreement on whether there *are* bona fide cases of self-deception'.[61] Rorty's view brings self-conception closer to denial.[62] She puts aside, first, the notion of lying to yourself in the sense of deliberately believing what you know to be false, and second, being simultaneously aware and not aware of your beliefs. Her post-modern alternative is the fragmented self, composed of relatively autonomous micro-systems. This allows 'compartmentalization, self-manipulated focusing, selective insensitivity, blind persistence, canny unresponsiveness'.[63]

Comparing the tragic view that we are all doomed to perpetual self-deception (we cannot help being false to ourselves) with the thesis that self-deception is impossible (because this would entail the same person both knowing and not-knowing the same thing in the same respect), Elster can only conclude: 'Between the two stands common sense, which tells us that men sometimes but not always deceive themselves.'[64] Common sense also tells us that 'sometimes but not always' we slip into modes of defensive denial without our conscious awareness that this is happening.

The psychic world is complex enough to accommodate both denial as unconscious defence and self-deception as bad faith. Let us imagine that both the Freudian and Sartrean homunculi are present, each getting to work on different material at different times. In one part of your mind, without an invitation and without you even being aware of her presence, sits a rather benign Freudian aunt. She may be smiling, but she is working hard all the time – and without much conscious help from you – to protect you from the psychic costs of living with threatening and unwelcome knowledge. She doesn't want you ever to feel too anxious. She helps you by means of all sorts of weird folk techniques (projection, dissociation, reaction formation), but her favourite trick is to nudge you into denial. She works so quickly that you don't realize what you had noticed. Literally without you knowing it, any 'troubling recognition' – feeling, fantasy, fact, the realization of what you have done or seen – disappears. Later, every now and then, you get a quick, anxious flash, an intimation of the denied knowledge. This, of course, your aunt immediately helps you to deny yet again. 'It's all in your mind,' she chuckles, and goes back to her knitting.

In another part of your mind, stands a rather stern and malignant Sartrean uncle. You are aware of his presence almost all the time. He too works hard at his job – which is to save you from the moral costs of acknowledging and taking responsibility for your own (stupid) decisions, amoral fantasies, selfish impulses and nasty actions. With your collusion, he has drawn you into the project of bad faith. You are contemplating doing something (or have already started) which is morally dubious or contrary to your self- and/or public image. You are too terrified, however, to face the abyss of your own freedom, the knowledge that you can choose. So you give each other a knowing wink – and out you pour the sad tales about 'no choice', 'compulsion', 'unconscious motivation', 'just obeying orders' and 'didn't know what was happening'. He half-listens while smoking his pipe. You eventually turn into your uncle – and never do anything authentic for the rest of your life.

Cognitive errors

The cognitive revolution of the last thirty years has removed all traces of Freudian and other motivational theories. If you distort the external world, this means that your faculties of information processing and rational decision making are faulty.[65] No cognitive psychology textbook today even lists terms like 'denial' or 'repression' in its index. The topics are attention, perception, awareness and memory, backed by advances in cognitive science, neuro-psychology, artificial intelligence and brain functioning.

Denial-like phenomena might appear in five contexts.[66]

Perception without awareness

If perception depends on full conscious awareness, the subject must be able to introspect and report on what is perceived. Cognitive and neuro-psychologists, however, have long pondered the evidence for modes of perception without awareness, sometimes referred to generically as 'subliminal perception'.[67] Three forms are relevant:

Negative hallucinations   The metaphor of denial as a 'negative hallucination' suggests that instead of imagining that you see something, you imagine you see nothing. Negative hallucinations can, in fact, be experimentally induced, and look like prototypes of perception without awareness. Hypnotized subjects, who were told that they would not see a chair, none the less avoided bumping into the chair when they were instructed to walk around the room. Apparently they had formed a visual registration of the object without representing it as a 'chair'.

Blindsight   Some brain-damaged patients have lesions in their visual cortex. They are blind in part of their visual field in the sense of having no conscious awareness of objects that appear there. Despite this, they can make some accurate judgements and discriminations about visual stimuli presented in the blind area. They seem to 'register' the occurrence without being subjectively aware of it. This strange combination is known as blindsight – most thoroughly investigated by Weiskrantz in his patient 'DB', who was left partially blind after a brain operation.[68] But is this really perception without awareness? DB claimed to have a sense that 'something was there', although he also claimed not to 'see' anything. Such patients, Weiskrantz suggests, may be in an intermediate state of awareness in which they have a 'gut feeling' that there is something there.

Whether or not this should be termed 'blindsight', clearly something remarkable is going on. 'Blindsight suggests a startling possibility about the mind: that one part may know just what it is doing, while the part that supposedly knows – that is awareness – remains oblivious.'[69] In this sense, blindsight – also found in 'normal' people[70] – is analogous to everyday denial. The mind can know without being aware of what is known.

Subliminal perception   Studies of subliminal perception were popularized in the early sixties by findings that consumer choices of cinema audiences could be influenced by flashing subliminal advertising messages. The chances of buying a particular brand of soft drink or cigarette were increased even if there was no awareness or memory of seeing the brand-name image on the screen. These early findings are controversial. But there are indeed mental and physical reactions – changes in galvanic skin response, EEG, emotions, even decision making – to stimuli not consciously perceived. The *objective threshold* of perception (where the mind detects and registers a stimulus) is lower than the *subjective threshold* (conscious awareness of this). This is, perhaps the nearest 'scientific' evidence for denial as seeing, yet not knowing *what* or even *that* you have seen.

Perceptual defence and selective attention

But why are some stimuli filtered out rather than others? The standard explanation was the perceptual defence model of the late nineteen forties. Stimuli – photos, flashing lights, subliminal messages – were controlled to show how people either ignore or pay attention to particular inputs. Focal attention, rather than a more diffuse and peripheral sort of sensing, is redeployed and inhibited. Emotionally charged stimuli are perceived less readily than more neutral stimuli. This protects you from awareness of objects that have unpleasant emotional connotations. Without you knowing, the mind 'activates' your internal filter or censor. If you were aware of what you had seen, but denied this, this would be mere dissembling or lying. But stimuli can arouse autonomic reactions of anxiety or pleasure *prior* to any conscious awareness.[71]

This explanation is psychoanalytical in all but name. Some stimuli are avoided, blocked or distorted because they are disturbing or stressful. The subject either assigns to them a less disturbing meaning or resists any perception. To avoid the threat, you divert attention to something less painful, more neutral or more pleasurable. This 'motivated denial' calls for a non-commonsensical view of perception: awareness of the meaning of an event before it enters awareness. You somehow know reality in order to avoid knowing it. Is this what the villagers living near that concentration camp were doing? This is the denial paradox again: 'if the perceptual defence is really perceptual, how can the perceiver defend himself against a particular stimulus unless he *first perceives* the stimulus against which he should defend himself?'[72] Howie's early criticism applies to all 'explanations' of denial: 'To speak of perceptual defence is to use a mode of discourse which must make any precise or indeed any really intelligible meaning of perceptual process impossible, for it is to speak of perceptual process as somehow being both a process of knowing and a process of avoiding knowing.'[73]

The Freudian censor gave way to a model of perception as not a 'frozen' event, but a multiple, simultaneous set of mental processes: instead of emotionally motivated defence, just errors of cognition and rationality.[74] Popular social psychology still tries to combine these somewhat incompatible ideas. When we deny our awareness of threats or edit our thoughts, 'a looming anxiety is appeased by a twist of attention'.[75] This creates a blind spot, a solace from pain – whether arising from deep memories of childhood, current emotional wounds, unbearable images of others' suffering, or fear of illness. Pain is numbed by dimming attention, a universal process grounded in such neurochemical systems as the damping of endorphins.

Selective attention short-circuits the arousal of stress and anxiety. 'Denial is the psychological analogue of the endorphin attentional tune out.'[76] It also works like an analgesic. In response to a devastating event such as the death of a loved one, we oscillate between intrusion (invasion) and varieties of denial (avoidance, disavowal of obvious meaning, numbness, etc.). These are the two sides of attention; neither is healthy, and both result in bias. Denial is only a palliative: anxiety is reduced, but the threat remains. There is always a trade-off, Goleman argues. The dimming of awareness protects the mind and gives a sense of security – but the resulting blind spots of blocked attention and self-deception may ultimately be self-defeating. These palliatives, especially when used habitually, distort our ability to pay full attention, to see things as they are. In the cognitive model, the emotional part of the filter is not salient; more important is its *intelligence*.[77] Our 'smart filter' automatically scans our internal and external messages, letting through only the 'pertinent' stuff.

These attentional tricks may be shared between people. Indeed, distortions and self-delusions are most often synchronized – within families, intimate relations or organizations. Whole societies have unmentioned and unmentionable rules about what should not be openly talked about. You are subject to a rule about obeying these rules, but bound also by a meta-rule which dictates that you deny your knowledge of the original rule:

> *They are playing a game. They are playing at not*
> *playing a game. If I show them I see they are, I*
> *shall break the rules and they will punish me.*
> *I must play their game, of not seeing that I see the game.*[78]

Cognitive errors and inferential failures

The mental resources that we can mobilize at any instant are limited. Only a tiny portion of available information is processed, and this happens without conscious monitoring.[79] Motivation plays no overriding selective or defensive role in explaining attention or consciousness. Subliminal perception is merely 'pre-conscious processing' or 'priming': particular stimuli activate mental pathways that enhance the ability to process later related stimuli. Priming also occurs when the background is too 'noisy'.

The distinction is between *automatic processes* (those concealed from consciousness, unintentional, consuming few attentional resources, running parallel rather than in sequence) and *controlled processes*. In implementing the automatic processes – habits and routines of daily life – we are literally 'absent-minded'; the mind goes walkies. To explain errors in attention and data processing, there is no need invoke a mysterious motivational state like denial. An error is simply an error. A 'Freudian slip' is merely one of the predictable mistakes that occur in any complex data-processing system.

The process nearest to denial is *thought suppression*. We try to keep a particular thought from entering consciousness; when we stop this conscious effort, our automatic scanner continues to 'search out' the unwanted thought and it eventually enters consciousness. Cognitive scanning is made easier by *habituation*: as we become accustomed to a stimulus – a homeless man sleeping in a doorway, news headlines about another Balkan massacre – we gradually notice it less and less. Motives and emotions are irrelevant. This is just another cognitive phenomenon like vigilance (waiting for a signal to occur), signal detection, search (scanning the environment) or divided attention (performing multiple tasks).

There are two theories about how this happens.[80] In *filter and bottleneck* theories, multiple incoming sensations pass through a bottleneck which sorts out what should receive attention. In *attentional resource* theories, people have a fixed amount of attention, which they can choose to allocate according to the task. Attention is coming to see, sense, know and hear; perception is recognizing and making sense of these sensations: not what we notice, but how we decipher its meaning or significance.

Expressions used to explain everyday failures of perception could be metaphors for bystander denial: you 'can't see something that's right under your nose', and you 'can't see the forest for the trees'.[81] People with the neurological condition of visual agnosia have normal sensations of what is in front of them, but cannot recognize what they see. Denials used by ordinary people sometimes look as extreme as this. But brain lesions aside, why can't observers see something that is right under their noses? To cognitive science, they are not deliberately lying, nor ensnarled in Freudian defences, nor bamboozled by self-deception, nor acting in bad faith. They are simply lousy data processors; they are making errors of inference.

How do these errors occur? Models of information processing and decision making have identified our many dismal ('non-optimal') strategies for decision making.[82] These biases, mental short cuts and 'heuristics' lighten the cognitive load when making decisions, but also lead to perceptual errors and irrational decisions. The way we gather information and reach inferences is pathetic: 'Instead of a naive scientist entering the environment in search of the truth, we find the rather unflattering picture of a charlatan trying to make the data come out in a manner most advantageous to his or her already-held theories.'[83]

The creatures of cognitive theory are not subservient to infantile and unconscious wishes, but are capable of astounding perceptual judgements, decisions and rationality. Even their biases, illusions and rationalizations result from *rational* errors in problem solving, rather than buried needs, desires or traumas. Their life as intuitive scientists is unfortunately compromised by 'inferential shortcomings'. No point in agonizing about denial; that's all there is to it.

The mystery of consciousness

If 'interpretive denial' is just another inferential error, then literal denial is something like attention without consciousness: a high-speed psychological mechanism programmed like a computer to 'DELETE' rather than 'SAVE' the information. But unlike a computer, the brain does not process information step by step. It can engage in multiple operations on myriads of data all at once ('parallel distributed processing', as they say in the business).

Denial is just a 'knowledge-avoidance pattern of information processing'. Interruptions and distortions occur somewhere between the stages of pre-attentive registration, focal attention, comprehension and then full cognitive elaboration. Unlike in the common-sense view of consciousness, there is no inner spectator, no 'I' in a Cartesian theatre. To an outsider, this mechanistic view – which tries to dispense with a conscious mind not reducible to brain functioning – is wholly counter-intuitive.[84] Certainly nothing very interesting about denial can be said without assuming a conscious self who is doing the denying.

Oddly though, Dennett's very mechanistic theory suggests a vivid image of some forms of denial.[85] In a 'multiple drafts' model of the mind, you cannot settle on one moment of brain processing as *the* moment of consciousness. There are no functional differences, Dennett argues, between 'prior' stages or revisions that are pre-conscious and 'subsequent' stages, revealed by recollection to be memory-contaminated. You cannot even distinguish between what the subject is conscious of and what the subject is oblivious to at any given instant. You don't first separate out the entities and then make a pattern. There are, rather, instant multiple drafts, in which the observer's point of view is 'smeared' over the brain at a single time.

Dennett compares a 'Stalinesque' with an 'Orwellian' account of what the brain does. In the conventional, Stalinesque model, the censor holds up transmission until a more acceptable, properly edited version is available for release. The Stalinesque editor splices extra frames *into* the film before it is sent out to the theatre – whose sole spectator is the conscious subject. Denial takes place by the editor splicing *out* unwelcome information before it reaches full subjective awareness and reporting. The Orwellian editor, on the other hand, notices that the unvarnished history does not make enough sense. So he interprets the raw events (in the typical experiment, a red dot followed by a green dot on a blank screen) by making up a causal narrative about the intervening passages, and then installs this history into memory for future reference. You say and believe that you saw the illusory motion and colour change – but this is really a memory hallucination, not an accurate reflection of your original consciousness.

Dennett prefers the Orwellian version – the extra processing is done after you become conscious – to the Stalinesque version, in which this precedes consciousness. But you cannot choose between them: there is no subject, no ghost in the machine to 'whom' images are relayed. Instead of a knowing theatre of the mind, there is just a software package of simultaneous multiple drafts. A lovely metaphor – which explains nothing much about denial.

Cognitive schema: frames, adaptations, illusions

In one cognitive model, information about the world derives directly from accessible external stimuli. This is known as *bottom-up*, or *data-driven*, processing. The alternative model gives causal priority to internally stored, past knowledge. This is called *top-down*, or *conceptually driven*, processing. Neither model can be taken literally. If everything is bottom-up, there can never be any inaccurate perception; if everything is top-down, there can never be accurate perception. These processes work together. Internal residues of knowledge direct perception (top-down) towards sampling particular stimuli; this in turn leads to modification (bottom-up) of the scheme.

Theories about top-down cognitive framing – variously termed 'maps', 'assumptive worlds', 'schemata' – explain how some information gets shut out. These 'new' theories are old news to any sociologist. The notion of 'assumptive worlds' simply means that people live with unchallenged assumptions about themselves and the external world. These assumptions are organized into strategic packages – which help make sense of major unwelcome and traumatic events.[86] Cognitive schemata are our own private and unarticulated ways of guiding the flow of information – scanning, screening, simplifying, organizing. These are filters working simultaneously: encoding, interpreting and retrieving information consistent with our prior theories and beliefs. We are all 'cognitive misers', trying to save energy by picking out only the stimuli we 'need'. We persevere in our cognitive conservatism (the need to maintain the schema's stability) even when we know that the selected information is false.

What are our 'prior beliefs'? According to cognitive psychologists (but nobody else I have ever met), we all assume that (i) the world and people are benevolent; (ii) life is meaningful (outcomes are distributed according to goodness and justice, people can directly do something to control things); and (iii) the self is worthy. You have a decent moral character, you do what is necessary to control outcomes, and fortune will protect you.

A traumatic life event – illness, disaster, victimization – confronts you with anomalous data that are too painful and too vivid to ignore, but do not fit these assumptions. Instantly, without intellectual cogitation, this information is assimilated into existing schema. What looks like denial is an accommodation to cognitive threat. The attack on your life assumptions is blunted, and threatening information is cut down to tolerable doses. This leads to the provocative idea that mental health depends largely on our ability to sustain what are really *illusions*.[87] These are 'positive illusions', buffers against events that threaten our sense of meaning, control and self-esteem. These illusions do not necessarily negate known facts (literal denial), but they manifestly slant these facts (interpretive denial) to enhance self-esteem and confirm our map of the world. Paradoxically, these positive misinterpretations (poor information processing) are adaptive, especially under adversity. Far from indicating mental illness, these modes of 'being out of touch with reality' are necessary for healthy functioning.

There is a darker side to this happy story: these adaptive principles are analogous to totalitarian strategies of information control depicted in *1984* and other dystopias.[88] Three states of mind are shared. The first is *egocentricity* – organizing memory around a self which is the axis of cause and effect; the second is called by Greenwald *beneffectance* – taking credit for success (good effects) while denying responsibility for failure (ill effects); the third is *conservatism* – the cognitive disposition to preserve what is already established. New evidence or contrary arguments are ignored or made to fit the schema. My epigraph from Orwell on nationalism shows the homology between personal and ideological denial.

Denial is a presence that evaporates, the nearer you get to defining it. Unconscious defence mechanisms, splitting of the ego, cognitive paradoxes, self-deception, bad faith, inferential schemata: these constructs spin away into their own spaces. As it moves further from the rich Freudian and Sartrean originals, the academic discourse becomes shallower than the thoughts of even the most minimally self-conscious adult – let alone the sense of knowing and not-knowing to be found in literature.

These psychological concepts cannot simply be transposed to the political level. They are not grounded in roles and relationships; nor do they take into account differences between victim, perpetrator and bystander. There is also little sense of social setting: a court room, an everyday conversation, a confrontation with a jealous lover, a psychotherapy session, a parent–child soap opera, being witness to a mass atrocity, caught up in wars, the cancer ward of a hospital, watching the news on television, or passing a beggar on the street. Moreover, the considerations used in attributing denial – the value of telling the truth, the credibility of appeals to the unconscious, the ideal of self-integration – are not universal brain mechanisms, but highly contextualized linguistic devices and cultural practices that vary across time and social space.

Above all, the scientific discourse misses the fact that the ability to deny is an amazing human phenomenon, largely unexplained and often inexplicable, a product of the sheer complexity of our emotional, linguistic, moral and intellectual lives. This is the ability well appreciated by Saul Bellow's wonderful character Mr Sammler. Sammler finds himself in one of those situations that makes us all into psychological theorists, expert thinkers about knowing and not-knowing, deception and self-deception. His nephew, Elya Gruner – only a few years younger and himself a doctor – is lying in hospital after an operation for a blood clot. Sammler reflects: 'Elya would die of a haemorrhage. Did he know this? Of course he did. He was a physician, so he must know. But he was human, so he could arrange many things for himself. Both knowing and not knowing – one of the most frequent human arrangements.'[89]

A frequent human arrangement indeed. But not always benign. Mr Sammler, of all people, must have learnt that the state of 'both knowing and not-knowing' serves not only those who suffer. It is indispensable for those who deliberately inflict terrible suffering on their fellow human beings – and for others who come to know about this.

3

Denial at Work

Mechanisms and Rhetorical Devices

In the first two chapters I showed the versatility of the concept of denial and reviewed some traditions of inquiry into its psychology. Here I look further at the concept's status and different uses. In this bridging chapter, before entering the worlds of mass suffering and public atrocities, I look at denial of the sufferings in everyday life.

Normalization

The most familiar usage of the term 'denial' refers to the maintenance of social worlds in which an undesirable situation (event, condition, phenomenon) is unrecognized, ignored or made to seem normal. Consciousness raising, politicization, economic change, professional interests, pressure groups or victim demands then construct this 'thing' into a category of deviance, crime, sin, social problem or pathology. The worlds of personal suffering now enter the public discourses. This process conforms to Wright Mills's famous injunction about turning private problems into public issues. Take the cases of domestic violence against women.

The gaps between acts of physical violence and the 'appropriate' reaction are forms of micro-denial: 'It didn't happen' (victim, friends, neighbours); 'He's perfectly okay without drink' (victim); 'You can't call that real violence' (offender); 'She really enjoys it' (offender, some observers and therapists). Variants of this normalization will be our constant themes: accommodation, routinization, tolerance, putting up with it, collusion and cover-up.

Macro-denial takes place at the societal level. Domestic violence went through a familiar sequence from denial to acknowledgement. In the denial phase, the phenomenon was hidden from public gaze; normalized, contained and covered up. The wall of public silence was built from the designation of women as property, the exercise of domination as a male right, the protection of the family as a private space, etc. The acknowledgement phase began with exposure by victims, feminist-inspired movements and professionals. Eventually a separate discourse emerged – supportive, empowering and political – and a set of institutions: legal sanctions, powers of intervention for welfare and law enforcement agencies, shelters for battered women, self-help agencies, etc.

As with mass suffering, these narratives draw us to the interface between historical (macro-) and personal (micro-) denial. As the problem becomes politically fixed, so it becomes easier for the individual victim to overcome residual denial, self-blame, stigma or passivity and seek appropriate intervention. It becomes correspondingly harder for the offender to offer denials ('She asked for it') that have much chance of being accepted. There are contemporary societies in which this public construction has hardly taken place or is unevenly spread according to social class. Here we find not literal denial but cultural interpretations and neutralizations which encourage a dulled, passive acceptance of violence: this is what men are like, this is the fate of women, there's no point in telling anyone, these things should be kept in the family.

'Dulled, passive acceptance' is only one of the nuanced possible reactions. Terms like 'tolerance', 'normalization' and 'accommodation' all convey other variants of denial. They are often invoked to answer the stereotypical (and stupid) question about why women stay in abusive relationships rather than leaving or seeking outside intervention. One study of a traditional Palestinian society shows that women's apparent 'tolerance' of abuse – not making public claims or seeking outside intervention – does not mean 'acceptance'.[1] The women do not ignore or condone abuse; nor are they in some psychic state of victim denial. They are trapped in a culture where tolerance is a form of social control, discouraging or even forbidding any acknowledgement of the problem. (They cite the proverb: 'A hidden defeat is better than being disgraced in public.') Not only is the wife blamed for her husband's violence, but her tolerance is a mirage, hiding the fact that passivity ('Why doesn't she tell?', 'Why doesn't she leave?') results not from free choice but lack of choice.

Defence mechanisms and cognitive errors

Denial and normalization reflect personal and cultural states in which suffering is not acknowledged. The models of 'motivated defence mechanism' and 'cognitive error' purport to explain why observable denial occurs at all. I take my illustrations from the area of illness, especially serious physical illness, HIV/AIDS, and depression.

Denial is a predictable reaction to information about the 'stressful, serious or catastrophic life events' contained in the expanding syndrome of PTSD (Post-Traumatic Stress Disorder). It includes serious illness, crimes, accidents, psychic trauma, torture, war, natural disasters, the sudden death of a loved one, etc. You may deny the information itself; its threat, personal relevance and urgency; your emotional vulnerability and moral responsibility.[2] A standard sequence of responses is outcry, denial, intrusiveness, working through and completion.[3]

A similar sequence applies to dying and death: your own risk and the eventual approach of death, your reaction to fatal illness and the death of loved ones. When terminally ill patients deny their impending death, do they really not know the truth? Do we hide the truth from ourselves if we claim not to realize the seriousness of the patient's condition? There are many variations: unconscious spirals of self-deception between the patient and others; unstated complicity not to openly acknowledge the truth; a calculated deception orchestrated (usually with the best of intentions) by various combinations of patient, doctor or family, then at the later stage of grief and bereavement, refusal to believe what has happened, incomplete mourning, and preserving intact the loved one's room.

There is a rich stock of folk knowledge and personal and family experience about how people first react to being diagnosed as having a fatal or serious illness and then cope with their condition. For some, the initial information is shocking and hard to believe; for others, it confirms what they already somehow 'knew'. Most people eventually settle down and accept the diagnosis and comply with the treatment offered, while vacillating between acceptance of the new condition and a reluctance to come to terms with it: 'This can't be happening to me', or 'Why me?' Some people sink into despair; others energetically resist, exhausting every possible avenue of treatment; others are stoical, optimistic and hopeful, even to the point of behaving as if the illness did not exist.

But is there a right way to cope with information about traumatic, catastrophic or disabling losses? Even the cautious assessment that a patient is 'not so distressed as might reasonably be expected' allows for quite different possibilities. People may not realize the emotional implications of their loss or may not be too stressed by the loss. There cannot be any objective measure of the amount of distress that can 'reasonably be expected'. Nor is there any evidence for the dogma that (at the 'right' stage) people must 'work through' rather than deny their feelings of grief. Exactly when and how can denial be observed? An early study looked at 345 male heart patients about to be discharged from hospital three weeks after treatment for a first myocardial infarction.[4] Denial was operationally defined as replying either 'no' or 'don't know' to a question about whether the patient thought that he had suffered a heart attack. Some 80 per cent responded 'yes', 12 per cent 'no', and 8 per cent 'don't know'. These 20 per cent were defined as 'deniers',[5] and were said to show attributes such as a 'denial-style of personality', a disavowal of their unfavourable personality traits. They minimized their symptoms and the effects of the heart attack on their lives, and tended not to comply with medical advice.

I cite this study only to show the problems of detecting denial. The researchers admit that the non-deniers may have included people who were unconsciously denying, but for some reason replied 'yes', and those who were denying to themselves, but felt a social obligation in the interview to give a reality-based response. But yes/know/don't know is surely a very literal index, even of literal denial. Measurement nowadays is more refined. The Levine Denial of Illness Scale (LDIS), for example, contains two dimensions: *cognitive disavowal* (displacement of symptoms, minimization of diagnosis and prognosis, avoiding information and signs of health problems) and *affective disavowal* (absence of anxiety, denial of depression, disavowal of anger, detachment/indifference).[6]

But the contrast between deniers and non-deniers assumes that denial is a property of personality rather than situation. There is indeed evidence that some people use denial as habitual coping strategy. But denial is not a stable psychological condition that can be assessed like this. Unless psychotically cut off from reality, no one is a total denier or non-denier, still less either 'in denial' or 'out of denial' permanently. People give different accounts to themselves and others; elements of partial denial and partial acknowledgement are always present; we oscillate rapidly between states. Families and treatment staff are often exasperated at seeing newly disabled patients fluctuate between awareness and radical denial of their condition. 'The fluctuations over time suggest that a patient must "know", but may at different moments have more or less ability to tolerate what is known and to integrate the knowledge into a meaningful reality.'[7] For people newly diagnosed with a serious disease, denial and acceptance flicker on and off like the filaments of a dying light bulb. Just when you think that you have finally 'come to terms' with the illness, you realize that this acceptance was truly self-deceptive – a mere internal public relations exercise – and that layers of reality remain unconfronted.

What about the intriguing possibility that denial might increase chances of recovery? Is there an optimal denial level? Too much is maladaptive, but *some* denial – either by protecting patients from stress or by eroding self-fulfilling fatalism – improves the treatment rates of some illnesses. This has been shown in a series of recent studies of groups of London women diagnosed with early stage breast cancer.[8] Three months after the initial diagnosis, the women were divided into three groups according to psychological response. Group 1 faced their situation with a fighting spirit, an optimistic belief in their ability to survive. Group 2 adopted a stoic, passive acceptance of their disease or felt completely overwhelmed, hopeless and defeated. Group 3 effectively denied that they had cancer, refused to discuss the subject, and showed no emotional distress. At a five-year follow-up, the women in groups 1 and 3 were significantly more likely to be alive and without a recurrence. The two (rather different) states of fighting spirit and total denial were found to be better than stoic ('realistic') acceptance and helplessness. In a follow-up fifteen years later, the first and third groups continued to fare better: 45 per cent of them were still alive and free of cancer, as against 17 per cent of the second group.

So how does this work? In the perceptual defence model, disabled people cope by denying their differences from normality, a cognitive shield protecting them from awareness. For most people, though, knowledge of having a serious illness creates more, rather than less, awareness of relevant information. You begin to notice previously ignored bodily functions; changes are seen as 'symptoms'; friends send press cuttings about latest cures; you take special note if a famous person has the same disease. This is the opposite of a perceptual shut-out.

Cognitive theories are more sophisticated. People actively negotiate their realities, and successful treatment does not depend on accurate perceptions. Even patients with severe injuries try to maintain positive self-conceptions under the most threatening circumstances.[9] They don't make excuses; they try to bolster their self-esteem and sense of agency; they work on techniques to decrease their impairment. Their 'denial' might be better described as a search for some hope in the wreckage of their lives.[10] Like the breast cancer deniers, they do not literally disavow the fact of their condition. Rather, they play down its threatening implications and emotional impact, in order to better adapt and function.

Analogous forms of 'constructive denial' include searching for meaning in the experience, believing that they can control the disease by taking active treatment decisions, and efforts to bolster self-esteem by making 'downward' comparisons to ensure that they come out looking good.[11] Faced by threat, perceptions are changed in self-enhancing and ultimately beneficial ways. Mental health, it turns out, depends not on being in touch with reality, but on illusion, self-deception and denial.

The 'optimistic bias' thesis is that in perceiving health risks, there is a tendency for people to claim that they are less at risk than their peers.[12] Failure to take precautions – seat belts, no smoking, low-fat diet, safe sex – reflects the bias that 'It won't happen to me'. The thesis assumes – utterly implausibly – that the optimistic bias is universal, and corresponds to neither the perceived seriousness of the risk or the actual risk (high- and low-risk people similarly get it wrong). This is a cognitive version of 'splitting': people keep their thoughts about their behaviour and about their vulnerability in separate mental compartments.

These models all use an intra-psychic language, that gives no hint of a life with others. Even at the most intimate moments of illness and dying, others are there. This opens up a possible theatre of collusion, complicity and lying. Many patients, at early or later stages of a life-threatening disease, participate in densely layered games with their doctors and family. Any one or any combination of these players may know the diagnosis and prognosis – but not let on that they know or that they know that any others know. The collusive edifice of denial is kept intact.

The theme of denial is integral to the story of AIDS. The public narrative began with cultural silence and evasion. Some societies have not quite passed this stage: the cultural equivalent of 'It can't happen to me' is 'It can't happen here' ('AIDS is an African disease'). Cultural denial may arise from good faith: genuine ignorance, lack of resources, or a policy not to create unnecessary panic. More often, there is a refusal to allocate resources to stigmatized groups. Full acknowledgement is difficult – the syndrome's menacing and mysterious emergence, the finality of the diagnosis, the association with stigmatized groups and sexual practices, the potent metaphor of depravity.[13]

There are many opportunities for micro-denial: continuing with unsafe sex, delay in being tested or getting the results of tests, difficulty of believing or 'taking in' an HIV-positive diagnosis, withholding of the truth from others, finding adaptive strategies for living with the disease – ranging from organizing your life around the most pessimistic outcome to stoically carrying on as if nothing has changed. The split between factual knowledge and behavioural change remains. This is the difference between what is 'epidemiologically accepted as risk behaviour' (the scientific information in educational campaigns) and what men themselves regard as risky.[14] Even if well informed, they created their personal – far more risky – category of 'acceptable risk'. This 'folk construction' transforms group data into personal data. The binary distinction between 'safe' and 'unsafe' becomes a spectrum, with few absolutes.

Poor, black and other disadvantaged women use a different language of denial.[15] 'AIDS facts' are taught and known, but in a disembodied way. Factual information is dismissed, reinterpreted or neutralized by cultural cynicism: 'experts' are fallible; the health care system is racist; AIDS is unavoidable; the idea of safe sex is nonsense. The belief that 'AIDS can't happen to me' is found whatever the objective risk – if only because admitting risk is too shameful.

My final example is the relationship between depression and denial. However elusive the concept of mental health, all definitions refer to the accurate perception of reality. An official 1958 review defines perception as mentally healthy when 'what the individual sees corresponds with what is really there' and 'is able to take in matters one wishes were different without distorting them to fit these wishes'.[16] By contrast, mentally ill people are 'out of it', 'not in touch with reality', 'living in a world of their own'. Some cognitive theorists tell a different story.[17] Moderately depressed people may seem more pessimistic, but their clinical profile shows *less* cognitive distortion than in normal people. Far from distorting reality, they see it only too clearly. They also have a more balanced view of themselves, the world and their future. Unable to sustain 'positive illusions', they are doomed to a state of depressive realism. They lack the biases that normally shelter people from the harsher side of reality.

Normal people know how to deny things; they are not immobilized by intrusive thoughts about how terrible everything is. They sustain themselves precisely by the denials and self-deceptions they so easily condemn in others. Their 'positive illusions' show a fair amount of self-deception and escape from reality.[18] But they are not delusions, false beliefs that persist despite the facts. As illusions, they reluctantly accommodate to facts. They promote mental and physical health by decreasing stress and creating the optimistic mind-set that helps treatment to work – as in the placebo effect.

Attractive as the thesis might sound – with its ironical nod at the idea that only depressives accept reality (or that accepting reality will make you depressed) – it hardly deserves stretching too far. This is a simplistic view of mental health; there is little evidence for the widespread existence of these illusions, and their differences from delusion or denial are hardly convincing. Moreover, Taylor's ideal people are not activists who keep their own and others' morale high with a measured self-deception. This would be fine; all inspiring leaders radiate a sense of greater hope than the situation warrants. They know the slogan 'Pessimism of the head, optimism of the heart'. But Taylor's creative self-deceivers are not like this. All they do is to minimize the 'harsher side of reality' and to deny feeling guilty about much. Why, then, should they have the motivation to make the world any better? The prospect of entrusting the cause of social justice to these pseudo-stupid optimists, with their positive illusions and creative self-deceptions, is not reassuring. I would rather take my chances with a few depressed realists or realistic depressives. People highly endowed with positive illusions – notably about their own omnipotence – commit the most appalling atrocities. The admired qualities of high self-esteem, a sense of mastery, faith in their capacity to bring about desired events and unrealistic optimism were possessed in abundance by Mussolini, Pol Pot, Ceauşescu, Idi Amin and Mobuto.

Accounts and rhetorical devices

Perpetrators of gross atrocities and offenders against ordinary criminal codes invite the same set of questions: 'Why did they do something like that?' Further, 'How could they do it, but still believe in the rules they break?' Yet further, 'How could they do such atrocious things, yet think of themselves as good and decent people?'

Denial theory claims to understand not the structural causes of the behaviour (*the* reasons), but the accounts typically given by deviants themselves (*their* reasons). It is concerned less with literal denial than with interpretations or implications – especially attempted evasions of judgement ('It's not as bad as you say').

Offender and bystander denials belong to a wider category of speech acts known as *'accounts'*, 'motivational accounts' or 'vocabulary of motives'. Motives, Wright Mills argued, are not mysterious internal states, but typical vocabularies with clear functions in particular social situations.[19] They serve to realign people to groups whose norms and expectations they have confounded. There is no point in looking for deeper, 'real' motives behind these verbal accounts. Unlike the Freudian 'rationalization' – an *ex post facto* mechanism invoked after an action to hide the secret, unconscious, unacceptable, unknown but 'real' motive – verbal statements of motives are *initial* guides to behaviour. An account is not just another defence mechanism to deal with guilt, shame or other psychic conflict after an offence has been committed; it must, in some sense, be present *before* the act. That is, to make the process sound far more rational and calculating than it usually is, I must say to myself, 'If I do this, what will I then be able to say to myself and others?' Contemplated acts may be abandoned if, despite a strong urge, need or desire, no acceptable reason can be found.

Such internal soliloquies are not private matters. On the contrary: accounts are learnt by ordinary cultural transmission, and are drawn from a well-established, collectively available pool. An account is adopted because of its public acceptability. Socialization teaches us which motives are acceptable for which actions. Denial of intent ('I didn't mean to break the glass...it was just an accident') is probably the earliest evasive account learned by small children. When rules are broken – whether minor infractions of daily norms, ordinary crimes or political atrocities – offenders have to 'give an account' of themselves. This phrase carries the crucial dual meaning: not just telling a story ('This is what I did last night') but also being morally accountable ('This is why I stole that book').

Such moral accounting may remain private, secret and inward looking ('how can I live with myself if I do this?'). The denials we see are those offered in the expectation that they will be accepted: by victims, friends, family, journalists, political comrades, police, defence lawyers, judges, public inquiries, human rights reporters, organizations and therapists. As Wright Mills originally noted, the fact that each audience may be offered a different account, far from undermining the theory, confirms the radically sociological character of motivation.

Accounts may be justifications or excuses.[20] Justifications are 'accounts in which one accepts responsibility for the act in question, but denies the pejorative quality associated with it', whereas excuses are 'accounts in which one admits that the act in question is bad, wrong or inappropriate, but denies full responsibility'.[21] A soldier kills, but denies that this is immoral: those he killed were enemies who deserved their fate. He is *justifying* his action. Another soldier admits the immorality of his killings, but denies full volition for his action: this was a case of involuntary obedience to orders. He is *excusing* his action.

Excuses look like techniques described by psychoanalysis as denial, defence mechanisms, rationalization and disavowal, or by sociology as remedial actions, apologies, normalizations and neutralizations. Such accounts are passive, apologetic and defensive – what Goffman called 'sad tales'. By contrast, ideological justifications are active, unapologetic and offensive; they deny pejorative meanings, ignore accusations or appeal to different values and loyalties. This distinction does not always work. 'I was just following orders' may be offered as an excuse ('denial of responsibility') or as an affirmation of higher allegiance to values such as patriotism and obedience to legitimate authority.

I will often use Sykes's and Matza's classification of the accounts invoked by ordinary delinquents to neutralize, permanently or temporarily, the moral bind of the law.[22] This vocabulary, they suggest, functions *after* the act to protect the individual from both self-blame and blame by others, and *before* the act to weaken social control – and hence make delinquency possible. Between contemplating the act and doing it, the anticipated social disapproval by significant audiences must be neutralized or deflected. This is necessary because delinquency, they claim, does not arise from an inversion of conventional values and commitment to alternatives. Confronted (made accountable) by parents, police, teachers, courts and social workers, delinquents do not justify their offences by appealing to values opposed to those of the wider society. There is an allegiance, however weak, conditional and compromised, to conventional morality and legality. This is precisely why these values have to be neutralized, rather than completely ignored or rejected by a fully-fledged ideological alternative. The delinquent cannot entirely escape condemnation. Denials and neutralizations are indeed rhetorical devices, but cannot be dismissed as mere manipulative gestures to appease authority. Three of these five techniques use the word 'denial'.

Denial of responsibility   Appeal to accident – 'I didn't mean to do it' – is the childish, simplest way to deny intent and responsibility. Even the most cognitively challenged offender can go well beyond this: their action resulted from forces beyond their control; they had no will and could make no choices; the self is determined, more acted upon than acting. Popular psychological accounts include: 'I just blew my top', 'Something came over me', 'I didn't know what I was doing', 'I must have blacked out'. More sociological versions appeal to broken homes, slum neighbourhoods, deprivation, discrimination and bad friends.

The more extreme the offence and the greater the suffering inflicted, the more radical are the denials of responsibility needed. Thus sex offenders typically offer (and judges prefer) fully non-responsible accounts: cortical breakdown ('Can't remember a thing'), inner impulse (a sudden urge, the animal theory of sexuality) and under-socialization (misreading the cues).[23] Except for the occasional postmodern de Sade, courts seldom hear aesthetic or ideological accounts that accept full responsibility.

Denial of injury   This technique – a form of 'act adjustment' or redesignation (rather than 'actor adjustment') – tries to neutralize the wrongfulness of the act by minimizing any resultant hurt or injury.

Vandalism is only 'mischief' – and, after all, the owners of the property can afford it; auto theft is 'borrowing'; gang fighting is a private quarrel, of no interest to the wider society. The delinquent is not criticizing the existence of these formal legal prohibitions, but – 'in a hazy fashion', as Sykes and Matza put it – feels that his behaviour does not cause great harm despite its illegality.

Denial of the victim Even if some responsibility and harm are acknowledged, delinquents may still protest that the injury is not wrong in the circumstances. In fact, the victim was the original wrong-doer ('He hit me first'), what I did – vandalizing the property of an unfair teacher or a crooked shop owner – was only rightful retaliation or punishment. Other targets or circumstances are inappropriate (this shows your residual allegiance to the general norm), but this 'victim' only got what was coming to him.

Condemnation of the condemners Delinquents try to deflect attention from their own offence to the motives and character of their critics, who are presented as hypocrites or disguised deviants. Thus the police are corrupt and brutal, teachers unfair and discriminatory. By attacking others, the wrongfulness of your own behaviour can be more easily repressed or lost to view. (This defence is close to the psychoanalytic mechanism of projection.)

Appeal to higher loyalties Social controls are neutralized by playing down the wider society's demands in favour of demands from intimate groups (friends, gang) who are owed more immediate loyalties. If caught in these conflicting demands, delinquents respond to the more pressing ties of subcultural loyalty – thereby, unfortunately, breaking the law.

These accounts prepare the ground for the offence to take place. Afterwards, they also perform the defensive task assigned to denial: 'I didn't really hurt anybody'; 'They had it coming to them'; 'Everybody's picking on me'. Such rhetorical devices are normally invoked for non-political offences. Indeed, the point of neutralization theory is that, unlike political actions, these violations do not reflect commitment to an oppositional ideology. In my next chapter, however, I show that these same accounts appear, suitably modified, in the vocabulary of political perpetrators. Denial of responsibility is the master account. Mundane and trivial delinquency, like the worst political atrocities, relies on 'socially approved vocabularies for mitigating or relieving responsibility when conduct is questioned'.[24]

Accounts must have currency: that is, they should be honoured by victims (if necessary), bystanders and those who have the power and authority to make people accountable. The point is not to persuade audiences to agree with the account – that is, to support the action – but to make it sound credible and reasonable. The journalist or judge who 'accepts' an account like 'I was just following orders' is saying, 'Yes, I accept that this person could have done this for these reasons'.

Each kind of everyday deviance – whether pilfering at work, cheating at exams or extra-marital affairs – has its own portfolio of denials, either act adjustment ('It's not what it looks like') or actor adjustment ('I am not the sort of person who does things like this').[25] Good accounts evoke, as they are meant to, an intuitive sense of recognition – 'this is just what I tell myself' – even if the action in question is not something we have done or even contemplated doing. We are all 'rationalizing animals'. Denial is hard work, because our actions nearly always conflict with our self-image. Our rationalizations keep escalating.

Act adjustments (interpretive denial) are popular accounts of everyday misdemeanours such as the prohibited use of the university e-mail system for personal and family messages. Denial of both injury and victim easily glide from 'Everybody does it' into self-righteous moral entitlement: 'It's nothing'; 'It's not really a crime'; 'They won't miss it'; 'We all do it'; 'They all do it'; 'They invite it'; 'Look how they treat us'; 'Look what they pay us'. These act adjustments are clearly preferable to pathetic actor adjustments such as: 'It started by chance; then it became compulsive; now I can't help doing it.'

A radical actor adjustment – invoked for the most ordinary acts of deviance through to mass atrocities – is to deny responsibility by attributing the action to another part of the self that has been disengaged from the 'real' me. This is a lay version of Freud's 'splitting of the ego'. Pilferers create a special part-time self, the 'work self', who is doing all these bad things condemned by the real self. This real self becomes an observer – sometimes perplexed, sometimes oblivious, sometimes judgemental – to what the work self is doing.

Men convicted of sexual offences against children use 'deviance disavowal' for acts that are difficult to justify, without a legal excuse and too odious to normalize.[26] Being drunk is the most common disavowal: 'If I were sober, it never would have happened.' The offender admits his behaviour, but retains his self-concept as normal by substituting a lesser, more acceptable, temporary form of deviance. This works better than denying the offence completely. Incarcerated rapists may be *admitters*, who acknowledge forcing sexual acts on their victims and define this as rape, or *deniers*, who admit sexual acts, but deny that they constitute rape.[27] The deniers' accounts claim to involve much less violence. They explicitly implicate the victims, and claim that more were picked up in a bar or hitchhiking.

Is offering such denials purely Machiavellian, a cynical manipulation to tell the audience what it wants to hear, a mere tactical manoeuvre to appease authority and to get off the moral hook – or is this what the offender 'really' thinks? A moderate reply is empirical: it may sometimes be one, sometimes the other, or a mixture of both. Accounts range from the true, consistent and totally believed, to *ad hoc* and *ad lib* improvisations or carefully calculated deception. Offenders unaware of their motives offer accounts suggested to them by psychiatrists, defence lawyers and criminologists. A more radical reply is that this question is beside the point: in Goffman's aphorism, 'There are no true stories or false stories, only good stories and bad stories.' The study of denial is the study of giving and receiving accounts: how accounts enter the culturally available pool, how they differ over history and social context, when they are accepted or rejected.

What if offenders' behaviour is blatantly out of line with their accounts? Virtually no acts of rape, for example, fit the animal image of sexuality. The offender doesn't casually walk down a street, suddenly see a woman and be overcome by an irresistible impulse to rape her. Rather, he chooses his target in advance, plans the sequence, selects a situation that minimizes his risk of being caught. Virtually no crimes are as compulsive as 'kleptomania' sounds. But such accounts can be learnt at the time, or suggested afterwards by others, such as sympathetic probation officers. They easily become rhetorical devices which, if routinely honoured by others, allow people to actually see themselves in terms of them.[28]

Denial talk is so integral to alcoholism that 'overcoming denial' is central to all treatment strategies – whether conventional therapy, New Age healing or Alcoholics Anonymous. One manual is entirely organized in terms of denial: *denial of facts* ('I have not been drinking'); *denial of implications* ('Sure I like to drink, but that doesn't mean I'm an alcoholic'); *denial of feeling* ('It doesn't bother me'), and *denial of the need to change* ('So, I'm alcoholic – so what?').[29] Items on a 'Denial Scale' deny your inability to control your drinking ('I can drink when I want and stop when I want') and deny that you need treatment. The 'Rationalization Scale' contains justifications and excuses for drinking.[30]

Vocabularies of political justification should not require the sad tales of sex offenders, alcoholics or 'compulsive' shop-lifters. Far from entailing a defective capacity to heed constraints, ideological crime denies the very legitimacy of these constraints. But even when people do appalling things for noble reasons, they may still search for a culturally recognizable language to evade conventional judgement. The result is a potent combination: in part ideological, in part defensive neutralization. This may escalate into a hermetic self-righteousness. People facing total moral condemnation for carrying out atrocities manage to maintain a self-image of being good (idealistic, sacrificing, noble, brave) or else just 'ordinary people'.

Vocabularies of denial derive from the fact that social rules are negotiable, flexible, conditional and relative. The more tolerant, pluralistic and 'multi-cultural' the society, the richer and more varied will be its motivational accounting system. This may sound benign enough. But accounts that are embedded in coherent world-views – drawing their legitimacy from appeals to God, the state, the revolution or the *Volk* – become malignant in exactly the ways that Orwell warned about. By 'nationalism', he meant not just nationalism in the narrow sense, but all ideologies that maintain themselves by denial of other realities.

Collusion and cover-up

Denials draw on shared cultural vocabularies to be credible. They may also be shared in another powerful sense: the commitment between people – whether partners (*folie à deux*) or an entire organization – to back up and collude in each other's denials. Without conscious negotiation, family members know what trouble spots to avoid, which facts are better not noticed. These collusions – mutually reinforcing denials that allow no meta-comment – work best when we are unaware of them. The resulting 'vital lie' in the family may become a literal blind spot. But the facts are too brutal to ignore. They have to be reinterpreted, using techniques like minimization, euphemism and joking: 'If the force of facts is too brutal to ignore, then their meaning can be altered. The vital lie continues unrevealed, sheltered by the family's silence, alibis, stark denial. The collusion is maintained by directing attention away from the fearsome fact, or by repackaging its meaning in an acceptable format.'[31]

Family members have an astonishing capacity to ignore or pretend to ignore what happens in front of their eyes, whether sexual abuse, incest, violence, alcoholism, craziness or plain unhappiness. There is a subterranean level at which everyone knows what is happening, but the surface is a permanent 'as if' discourse. The family's distinctive self-image determines which aspects of shared experience can be openly acknowledged and which must remain closed and denied.

These rules are governed by the meta-rule that no one must either admit or deny that they exist. This is a consistent pattern in the families of alcoholics. Denial is an early stage in the family's adjustment to the disruption caused by an alcoholic member.[32] The drinking is min- imized or seen as a private matter; there is cultural support for 'social drinking', especially by men; husband and wife try to avoid the sub- ject; increasingly desperate attempts are made to shield the children from the problem and cover it up from the outside world. The primary behaviour is drinking; the primary pathology is 'alcoholic thinking' – denying that you are drinking too much, while doing precisely this. Core beliefs – having no problem with drinking, drinking because of other problems, being in control of your drinking – are sustained by altering, ignoring or denying any anomalous incoming data. Informa- tion must fit this collusive version of reality. The alcoholic is the 'elephant in the living room'. The presence of this permanent visitor must be denied, ignored, evaded or explained as something else – or you risk betraying the family. As the alcoholism progresses, engulfs more of the family's life, and threatens exposure of the secret, so the pressures to maintain denial increase.

A more sinister form of collusive denial is that termed by Bollas: 'violent innocence'.[33] His text is *The Crucible*, Arthur Miller's drama about the Salem witchcraft trials, his extended metaphor of McCarthy- ism. Reverend Hale is brought into the village to investigate stories about the devil's presence. Abigail denies Reverend Parris's accusa- tion that he saw her dancing naked in the woods. The more he asserts what he saw, the more intense becomes her insistence on her inno- cence. But she is lying, and demands silence from the other girls involved. She is manipulative and devious, because she fears being publicly whipped for her erotic dancing. But she is also the victim of another denial: John Proctor disavows any knowledge of their earlier sexual intercourse. Mary, one of her girl-friends, later confronts Abi- gail and reveals her culpability. Abigail, infuriated, now assumes the pose of innocent witness to the implied presence of evil. She sets up Mary to embody this evil.

Bollas takes Abigail's reactions to illustrate his definition of denial as 'the need to be innocent of a troubling recognition'. She initially denied knowledge of her naked dancing, because its recognition disturbed her. This denial is quite conscious, and Parris is in trouble because Abigail refuses to validate what they both saw. This is damaging enough for him: 'But Abby changes the scenario when she becomes a radical innocent, disavowing responsibility for her action, accusing the village elders of acting on behalf of Satan.'[34] She has become a 'violent innocent', passing her deviance off on an other, who now stands accused. Denial is not confined to the self's (or organization's or nation's) sense of its own realities. In the transitional moment from simple denial to violent innocence, a relationship is created: the other takes on an unwanted perception. Violent innocence is a form of denial 'in which we observe not the nature of the subject's denial of external perception, but the subject's denial of the other's perception'.[35]

Denial is no longer a personal matter: other people – family, friends, lovers – are drawn into its field. The violent innocent creates confusion in another person – and then disavows any knowledge of this. 'I just can't understand how you can think that I don't trust you.' The newly created victim is utterly confused. The subject refuses to acknowledge the self-evident perception, offers an 'innocent gaze', and withholds help. 'Is anything wrong?', 'You don't seem content', the subject innocently enquires, taking on the posture of 'false wonder' – patently to disturb the other.[36]

Whole organizations and political cultures take on collective false selves. An elite university department may be ridden with strife, but maintain a glossy, false public self. Privately, its members may admit the strife to their spouses or close colleagues. But in the public domain they talk about how 'inspiring' or 'stimulating' it is to work there. Thus 'each appears innocent of the more disturbing truths that are part of the place. And those who are exceptionally gifted at false self technique will contribute to the structure of innocence that climatizes the institution.'[37] People who 'know the score' can more easily adjust to the split between false and true self. Others suffer, not quite grasping what's going on.

Some may become exasperated enough to speak out. This is whistle blowing – now a familiar tactic to uncover organizational denial such as political corruption, corporate malpractice, violations of professional codes, and the rest. Codes of silence – whether in the Mafia, large corporations, government, army, church, police or professional groups – range from strict, formal and enforced to barely conscious collusive denials. Webs of complicity may draw innocent observers into protecting the worst of perpetrators, denying the gravity of their actions or keeping silent about matters that threaten the group's conception of itself.

Organizations work by what Janov termed 'groupthink': a collective mind-set that protects illusions from uncomfortable truths and disconfirming information.[38] The group sees itself as invulnerable and unanimous; personal doubts are suppressed; incoming information is screened; accounts are circulated to bolster the members' sense that whatever they do must be justified; unspoken arrangements allow for concerted ignorance, thus insulating individuals from culpability or even knowledge about what the rest of the organization is doing; and strategic myths are crafted about the organization's high morality. Members gradually come to disavow what they know that they once knew – all along denying the influence of any group pressure.

This is more than the crude cover-up that even small children can manage. The strategy of 'maximum possible deniability' is used for administrative massacres as well as petty organizational sleaze: deniability is built into each stage *in advance*. Planners and managers keep the full truth from key players ('nobody told me') or arm them with denial techniques. Those 'in the loop' or 'in the know' have to anticipate that one of their own people or someone just on the edge of the loop will eventually talk.

The Watergate and Iran-Contra cases in the USA and the Scott 'Arms to Iraq' Inquiry in Britain offer rich narratives of denial.[39] Denial of knowledge is a precarious tactic in the face of outside scrutiny. The 1996 Scott Inquiry quickly established that while the British government officially denied that it was licensing the export of lethal weaponry to Iraq, everyone in government knew that blind eyes would be turned and the export would go through unimpeded. (This artifice was exposed after the collapse of the trial of the businessmen prosecuted for selling arms-related equipment to Iraq, a transaction in which the government itself had connived.) Civil servants worked frantically to come up with a plausible denial – or some formula to protect their ministers from the charge of deliberately deceiving Parliament.[40] Helped by officials and politicians trying to save their own skins, the inquiry easily cracked the denial code. The policy changes in the export guide-lines that actually authorized arms sales were disguised as being merely 'flexible' and 'liberal'. This was cleverly done: the message of flexibility managed to suggest *at the same time* that the policy had and had not been changed. Alan Clark, the minister who changed the guide-lines (and openly supported the 'tilt' towards Iraq), was contemptuous of these 'slightly Alice in Wonderland suggestions'. He recalled the Foreign Office minister saying that 'because something was not announced, it could not have happened'.

Lord Justice Scott was astonished not that the ministers and civil servants had tried to deceive Parliament and the public, but that they seemed actually to *believe* what they were saying. They had succeeded, that is, in deceiving themselves with their own deceptions. Sartre would have relished this senior official's testimony: 'I think there was an element of mutual reinforcement of belief or misunderstanding. . . . I quite simply misled myself on what I thought the situation was.' As the head of the Ministry of Defence arms sales correctly noted, 'Truth is a very difficult concept.'

There are two symbiotic accounts at work: collective blindness (cover-ups, half-truths and being 'economical with the truth') and denial of responsibility. In organizations exposed for causing mass suffering, low-rank perpetrators and bystanders deny their cognitions ('We didn't understand the big picture') and their culpability ('Each act was harmless in itself'). But in the 'Arms to Iraq' story, offenders and collusive observers denied their own role by pointing not upwards, but downwards. The Cabinet Secretary told the Scott Inquiry: 'It was all happening below my eyesight level.'

Careful management is needed to sustain the convenient fiction that those in charge knew nothing of what was going on. The key to successful conspiracy, as I. F. Stone noted, is that the higher-ups do not ask what's going on, and the lower-downs do not tell them.[41] The powerful need reassurance that they are kept *fully uninformed*. Middle-level conspirators manufacture 'genuine' deniability by hiding the truth from top people whose later denials are better if they are true. These key people are protected in advance by being designated (how-ever implausibly) as having no need to know. They do not need to turn a blind eye: there is nothing to not-know.

When Watergate was first being investigated, one official asked Nixon's campaign finance chairman what Gordon Liddy intended to do with huge amounts of cash. The answer was: 'I don't want to know and you don't want to know.' This cliché expresses the denial paradox (how can you decide not to know something if you don't know what that something is?), but is also a simple (too simple?) way to ensure later deniability. Mitchell told the Ervin Committee that he kept quiet in front of Nixon not to spare the president from having to decide, but to let him make a decision as to whether he wanted to be informed for the record – and then face the consequences of a denial that was obviously untrue.

It would have been better for Oedipus had he really been able not to know what he said he did not know.

Everyday bystanders

More than thirty years after it happened, the 1964 Kitty Genovese incident (summarized in chapter 1) still shapes both the popular and the social-scientific iconography of the 'passive bystander'. The image of this named but unknown woman, her desperate screams for help ignored by her indifferent neighbours, became a metaphor for urban malaise, a moral panic about 'what has happened to us'.

Social scientists became preoccupied with the policy question: how can the passive bystander effect be reversed?[42] Can we identify and create conditions under which people could be induced to help others?

The Kitty Genovese case was soon joined by other equally distressing and poignant tales. In Britain there were: neighbours who didn't report hearing children next door being beaten by their parents; a young woman dragged screaming from a Birmingham shopping centre in daylight and raped in partial view of dozens of shoppers; a woman in a suburban railway carriage threatened and abused by three youths, while fifteen passengers sit quietly, ignoring everything. And then, most resonantly, the blurred closed-circuit television images of Jamie Bulger, wandering from his mother's side in a Liverpool shopping centre, being dragged away by two ten-year-old boys, then (witnessed by some thirty people) being shoved, kicked and thrown in the air, before eventually being led out of sight and killed on a nearby railway line.

Such images have generated a slightly hysterical discourse about the passive bystander. The contrast is too sharp and melodramatic: on the one side, indifference, emotional numbing, desensitization, coldness, alienation, apathy, the anomie and loneliness of urban life; on the other, responsibility, moral sensitivity, compassion, good citizenship, bravery, altruism, community, the Good Samaritan. For humanistic psychology, bystanding became a concept that covers everything from keeping quiet when you hear a sexist joke or hear someone being given wrong street directions, to observing a Nazi commando shooting Jews in a village square, to 'doing nothing' about mass killings in Rwanda viewed on television. Drawing, she says, on her political consciousness as a South African and her experience as a clinical psychologist, Clarkson claims that her book, *The Bystander*, deals with 'our responsibility for ourselves *and* for others; our ineradicable existential connectedness with others and the devastating effect of bystanding'.[43]

'Bystander' is a tricky term – its usage already implies the judgement of *passive* or *unresponsive* witness. Terms like 'observer', 'spectator', 'audience' and 'passer-by' by contrast, should be strictly neutral descriptions. In practice, this distinction is difficult to maintain, and the term 'bystander' is used with both connotations: 'A bystander is the descriptive name given to a person who does not become actively involved in a situation where someone else requires help.'[44] Furthermore, 'requiring help' is extended to 'knowing that something is wrong'. This usage puts a heavy burden on the term.

The strongest claims about bystanding are ethically resonant, but empirically unproved: that the passivity of those who watch, know and close their eyes becomes a form of complicity or approval that allows, or even encourages, further atrocities and suffering. This applies both to the ordinary troubles of everyday life and the mass tragedies of history. There is a consistent repertoire of what Clarkson calls bystander 'patterns' or 'slogans'. These accounts are similar (as the theory would predict) to those used by offenders. They also function in the same way: as preparation for withdrawing from a demanding situation and afterwards as retrospective justifications for past inaction. The same words, though, mean different things for offender and bystander. 'Responsibility' (as in 'denial of responsibility') implies culpability for the offender, but *obligation* for the bystander. We will come across many variations of the 'slogans' on Clarkson's list:

> It's none of my business.
> I want to remain neutral; I don't want to take sides.
> The truth lies somewhere in the middle.
> I don't want to rock the boat; I don't want to raise a difficult issue.
> It's more complex than it seems; who knows anyway what's
>   happening?
> I don't want to get burned again.
> My contribution won't make much difference. (Who? Me?)
> I'm only following orders.
> I'm just keeping my own counsel.
> They brought it on themselves really (victim blaming).

Social-psychological experiments simulate a condition that calls for intervention – either within the laboratory (smoke pumped through a door, a cry for help) or in staged real-life settings (an associate collapses in a subway train or fakes a heart attack on a jogging track). 'Variables' are then manipulated: the number of people present, whether the observer is rewarded, or the ambiguity of the distress. As with all such experimental work, many findings are banal, contradictory or of limited application to more complex social settings. The following is simply a list of situational influences on bystanders, each of which needs placing in the political cultures of the next chapter.

Numbers   When too many others are present and in a position to help, any one onlooker is less likely to do so. Individual responsibility is diffused, and thus reduced. Subjects in such experiments were not apathetic or indifferent to (faked) suffering, but upset and puzzled. They held back because of a diffusion of responsibility ('Whose job is it?'), fear of social blunders or an unreflecting selfishness and alienation. People are inhibited less by indifference than by the presence of passive others. Lone bystanders are more likely to help – but so too are those who are encouraged by the presence of active others.

Ambiguity and interpretation   Distress and calls for help that are totally unambiguous lead to more intervention than situations with potential ambiguity. The individual relies on the reactions of others to resolve ambiguity. The cognitive thesis goes further: bystanders may simply be making cognitive errors. They may have *misinterpreted* the Kitty Genovese incident as a lovers' quarrel and therefore unsuited and too complicated for outside help. This is a preposterous explanation. But ambiguity does influence reactions. Most of the passers-by watching Jamie Bulger and his two young companions, may, in good faith, have misinterpreted a situation that looks unambiguous only with hindsight.

Anticipated reaction of others   The inhibiting presence of large numbers applies less in a group where people know each other well. If people are concerned about what others will think of them, they are quicker to offer help. Uncertainty leads to apprehension about being ridiculed for doing something wrong, intrusive or unnecessary.

Expected rewards, utility and risk   In the rational choice model, people weigh up their desire to help against the possible costs involved. They actively avoid situations in which they anticipate being asked to help; the stronger the request, the greater the avoidance. The greater the good you think you can do, the more likely you are to help. Helping itself is rewarding: it will be repeated if previously rewarded, if there is evidence that it really does help, and if future rewards are expected. The 'bystander calculus' leads to altruism when prospective rewards are high (self-benefit and expected success) and costs are low. Possible risks of helping range from mere loss of time, monetary cost or embarrassment to the dangers of becoming a victim yourself, arrested, physically injured or even killed.

Social justice and equity   Helping may result from a strong commitment to social justice. But some victims are seen as more deserving than others, especially when appeals are morally based. Combining equity with social justice means that deserving victims should be helped more than undeserving victims. (The staged 'victim' collapsing on the subway was more likely to be helped if he appeared to be an invalid rather than drunk.) The 'just world hypothesis'[45] complicates matters. Its assumption of a stable, controllable, beneficent world is undermined if victimization seems due to random forces. This raises the threatening possibility that the same could happen to you. The hypothesis now becomes slightly bizarre. People who don't see the world as being just will be more ready to help. People who do believe that the world is just will less readily help if they believe that victims have done something to deserve their suffering ('If she hadn't walked in the park on her own, she wouldn't have been raped'). Only undeserved suffering threatens your faith in a just world. You must therefore do something to restore this faith. But only if your actions will be effective: just world thinkers want to re-establish justice, but to avoid futile actions. The suffering should be brief and finite, rather than lasting a long time and beyond immediate remedies. So all three models – just world, utility and social justice – assume that intervention depends on perceived effectiveness: the promise that helping will indeed help.

Guilt and responsibility   It might seem that people who feel guilty are more likely to help than people who do not feel guilty. In most research, however, the helping situation has no necessary connection with the original (experimentally induced) guilt-arousing situation. Real organizations often try to induce in audiences a vague sense of responsibility and even guilt about suffering which they had no direct responsibility for causing.

Sympathy and empathy   It seems obvious that a helpful response to suffering must be motivated by emotions like compassion, sympathy and empathy. The evidence, though, is vague at best.[46] Sympathy is insufficient in itself to arouse active helping responses. Empathy – awareness of the consciousness of others – can be aroused by giving people an 'observational set': on how to view others and picture yourself in their position. But too much empathy causes the observer distress – an even greater risk if the help is seen as too demanding or the need not deserving enough.

Identification   Being able to identify with the other is usually associated with sympathy and empathy. It places a very special type of cognitive demand on bystanders: to imagine being in exactly the same predicament as the victim. This is what public appeals try to induce: 'This could happen to people like us' or 'I could imagine myself in their situation'.

Witnesses to real-life emergencies or demands for help do not quietly sit down, make a list, and leisurely assess these eight conditions, needless to say. The perceptual flash is instant: Just what is happening? What should be done? Why aren't these other people doing anything? You are part of an audience, but fellow members are the audience for your actions: they inhibit you from doing foolish things. If bystanders see each other as momentarily frozen, each may be misled into thinking that nothing too serious has happened and that the best thing is to do nothing.[47] But lack of engagement is not a matter of lost cognitive opportunities. The problem lies in the vocabularies of denial that allow initial recognition (and even distress) to go no further.

When knowledge is mediated, rather than immediate, situational bystanding – the observer in a finite, temporary setting facing an instant demand or call for help – becomes less urgent anyway. Television audiences may be 'metaphorical bystanders' to the suffering presented by the global media, but even this suggests something too immediate. The mediated voice-over images from Mozambique do not make the same demands as those on Kitty Genovese's neighbours.

There are other, everyday settings for bystanding: notably the beggars, runaways, homeless people, bag ladies, the slightly deranged, druggies and alcoholics who inhabit the streets, pavements and doorways of most of our cities. They have become a familiar feature of the urban landscape, normalized and expected as something that has just 'happened'. Those of us afflicted with guilt are sensitive to each of these encounters. There is an unreflective, if not unconscious, repertoire of reactions: passive accommodation (walking past, averting your gaze, trying hard to look as if you have not noticed), avoidance and evasion (stepping over the person, crossing over to the other side of the street, even taking a different route to work).

We know very little about people's thoughts and emotions as they make these routine adjustments. Carlen talks of accommodation and 'psychic closing off', borrowing from Lifton the notion of 'doubling at the centre' (the creation of a separate functional self, which acts contrary to your usual conscience) and 'numbing at the periphery' (a blocking of normal sensitivity).[48] There may be 'splitting' – but this is not literal denial. You notice, but your perceptions are instantly framed, as if by an automatic camera lens. What is astonishing is the utter shallowness of the accounts that even sophisticated people exchange with themselves. These include a weary sense of familiarity, even irritation ('That guy again with the *Big Issue*?'); an equally weary sense of powerlessness ('I have no idea what can be done about this'); self-righteousness and balance ('Why should I have to give every time?'); being clever (giving money or showing sympathy 'only perpetuates the problem'); a run-through of causal theories that Carlen calls 'myths of creation' ('It's their fault, there's enough alternative care available for them, but they don't want to settle down'; 'It's all because of alcohol/drugs/mental illness') and, in post-Thatcherite Britain, a vocabulary of selfishness and unapologetic indifference: 'So what? I can live with it; I don't care a shit.'

Seeing child abuse in streets, shopping malls, supermarkets and other public settings is different. Homelessness has become normalized, but cultures of denial about child abuse have been severely eroded, thus lowering the tolerance threshold. Even if they don't actively intervene, observers are less likely just to accept the sight of a parent hitting or humiliating a child in public. In a study of 567 college students, half recalled witnessing a child being abused in public; of these, only 26 per cent reported that they intervened: 70 per cent directly with victim or perpetrator, 30 per cent indirectly by telephoning authorities, encouraging others to intervene or reporting the abuse to the victim's relatives.[49] Of the *eighty* separate variables ploddingly correlated with 'intervention', one cluster stands out: racial similarity between interveners, other witnesses and the victim. Afro-American children were less likely to be helped by the mostly white sample. All these correlations, however, are vitiated by the absence of any concrete definition of 'child abuse'. The only interesting conclusion, consistent with other research, is that the passive witness was *not* an indifferent bystander. 'On the contrary, most non-interveners reported experiencing as much concern with the child as the interveners.'[50]

This is a critical – if sometimes implausible – point. Blocking out knowledge, moral obliviousness and 'concern' without action are three very different states of mind. These distinctions may be irrelevant to the hapless victim, but they do make a difference to educational or political attempts to overcome bystander passivity.

Bullying at school is, I believe, the archetypal everyday setting for witnessing the bystander effect. Most of us have vivid memories of such childhood scenes, with ourselves playing or being close to roles of perpetrator, victim or bystander. It is this personal experience that makes the image of crowds watching a political atrocity so painfully resonant. The violence literally gets inside you – even though you are the observer, watching an image relayed by another observer (the photographer) of other observers watching a victim being humiliated or beaten. There has been almost no theoretically informed work on the subject. Only psychoanalysis has dealt with the shifting dynamics in the bully–victim–bystander relationship. Bystanders may become like victims – not necessarily identifying with them, but becoming passive, helpless, frightened and frozen.[51] Or they may become like bullies – taking vicarious and voyeuristic pleasure, egging them on or even aiding them by screening off playground incidents from the teachers' view or creating diversions.

The family, site of so much noisy angst, is also a place for silent witnessing. Psychologists dealing with violence and sexual abuse against children note the particular sense of betrayal and abandonment felt by the child towards family members, neighbours and friends who know or suspect, but do nothing. A more tragic role is assigned to the mother who comes to know about father–daughter incest, but remains in a perpetual state of not-knowing or just retreats into helplessness. Every clinician mentions this, but there is no evidence regarding its extent. Russell cites mothers who either refused to believe their daughters or were not helpful. But she takes issue with the 'collusive mother' image, along with the 'seductive child' image, as forms of scapegoating and victim blaming. The mother who does not actively intervene, she argues, is powerless rather than collusive.[52]

If there is any literal denial in situations like these, it must happen in an instant. This saves us from having to react immediately – but fails because the image does not fade away. This is exactly why we say, 'I must have known all along.' A wider circle of bystanders – relatives, neighbours, friends, doctors, social workers and teachers – do even less about their suspicions. But, as the discourse about sexual abuse shifts the cumulative – and intended – effect is to allow less cultural space to the old vocabularies of denial. In certain circles, 'I didn't mean it that way' or 'It was just a joke' are accounts that are no longer honoured. They are more likely to be seen as forms of violent innocence.

The story of changing reactions to the sexual abuse of women might be seen as a hopeful parable for changing people's reactions to public suffering and atrocities, the subject of the rest of the book. There are indeed psychological obstacles at the public level – normalization, defence strategies, evasive accounts, collusion – and these concepts can be given a political spin. But these cannot explain the political conditions under which people are kept silent, nor the cultures of denial sustained by the state, nor the construction of indifference to the suffering of selected others. Contrary to both situational and societal explanations, though, it may be that passive bystanding is a small enduring part of the moral character of all people and a major part of some. All of us don't care sometimes or about some things; some of us don't seem to care about anything most of the time. The next chapter places these reactions in political settings.

4

Accounting for Atrocities

Perpetrators and Officials

This chapter looks at public and political atrocities: the denials used by individual perpetrators of some well-known atrocities and the official reactions by governments today to allegations about human rights violations. These two sets of accounts will look very similar. It cannot be otherwise. The cultural stock of denials accessible during the 'real time' of an atrocity is used by perpetrators who are later brought to account and by governments that make these accounts acceptable. The language used by the state to persuade people to do terrible things or to keep quiet then reappears in responses to outside criticism. Note also that armed oppositional groups (national liberation movements, political factions, ethnic separatists, terrorists or guerrillas) use very similar vocabularies of exoneration.

More surprisingly, accounts normally associated with non-ideological offences also reappear. This does not mean that genocide, political massacres, disappearances or torture can be explained in the same way as ordinary crime.[1] The drift of the question, though, is similar: how can people act in appalling ways, yet continue to disengage themselves from their actions and deny their meaning as evil, immoral or criminal? Such disavowals are not private states of mind. They are embedded in popular culture, banal language codes and state-encouraged legitimations – hence the dual meaning of 'states of mind'. These culturally shared mind-sets that allow people to be perpetrators or collusive bystanders do not constitute an explanation of the origins and aims of atrocities. I take as given the Big Theories about how nationalist, racial, ethnic or religious conflicts are transformed into institutionalized violence. These social-scientific theories form the background against which vernacular accounts – not knowing the big picture, just following orders – are offered.

Perpetrators: accounts as denials

According to neutralization theory, ordinary delinquents do not typically justify their offences: either by claiming full responsibility or
opposing conventional values or appealing to alternative moral
codes. Instead, they dispute the conventional meanings attached to
their offences or try to evade moral blame and legal culpability. The
ubiquity of such accounts shows that conventional values remain
salient, even when violated. By definition, such delinquent accounts
should not be lumped together with political atrocities.

Yet political accounts most often follow the same internal logic and
assume the same social function as ordinary deviant accounts. The
narrative acknowledges that something happened, but refuses to
accept the category of acts to which it is assigned. The equivalent of
'you can't call this stealing' is 'you can't call this torture'. My inventory
of denials consists mostly of ideological versions of the core five
techniques of neutralization. But two especially important accounts
must be added to this list: at the start, *denial of knowledge* – perpetrators
profess not to know what they or others around them did – and at the
end, *moral indifference*: the absence of even token appeals to conventional morality – no neutralization because there is nothing to neutralize.

Political accounts are as jumbled and inconsistent as any other.
There is no contrast between pure, prior ideological commitment and
situational pressures such as obedience. In the current acrimonious
use of such a contrast, Goldhagen argues that perpetrators of the
Holocaust were not just ordinary people – passive, non-ideological
and unwilling – who were pressured into social conformity or forced
to obey orders, becoming robotic carriers of the banality of evil.[2] They
were ordinary *Germans*, true believers motivated by a historically
rooted, widespread, and virulent anti-Semitism that logically encouraged an 'exterminationist' ideology that existed well before the opportunity to act on it. In this sense they were 'willing executioners'. They
could have refused, but they didn't; they not only acquiesced, but
acted with zeal and gratuitous cruelty. They did not need excuses to
allow them to do what they already wanted to do. Later accounts ('just
a cog in the machine') are wholly tactical and manipulative.

Compare this with Bauman's sociological extension of the obedience
to authority thesis.[3] The Holocaust is not the repudiation but the
product of modernity. The bureaucratic mind-set allowed this to
happen: bureaucratic organization and rationality, separation of

functions, ethical indifference and specialization. The 'obedience to authority' model explains how ordinary people do terrible things if ordered and authorized to do so. They are not 'naturally' willing, nor are they morally degenerate. As products of the civilizing process, they have innate moral inhibitions. At the very least, they have to overcome the animal pity aroused by the prospect of killing. Their denials of ideological motivations such as extreme anti-Semitism and their refusal to accept full responsibility for their actions are genuine.

Does Goldhagen place 'eliminationist anti-Semitism' far too early historically, completely overstate its coherence, intensity and influence, and misunderstand the obedience thesis? Does Bauman overestimate the influence of ideal-type modern bureaucracy, ignore the historical specificity of Germany, underestimate the role of ideology, and have no idea about other genocides? Our subject is only the verbal shadows that these contrasts cast.

Denial of knowledge

Ordinary offenders claim mistaken identity ('It wasn't me') and use endless legalistic strategies to achieve a not-guilty verdict. Smoking gun in hand, they struggle with astonishing persistence and ingenuity against admitting to have done *anything* that they knew to be criminal. We should not expect to hear this from ideological perpetrators: they knew exactly what was happening and what they did, it was justified at the time, and in retrospect still is.

But many alleged perpetrators, especially at the lower levels, do not talk remotely like this. Their accounts make them sound like ordinary delinquents: 'I wasn't even there at the time'; 'Why pick on me (when everyone else was doing it)?' Many of them are so pseudo-stupid that they claim not even to have figured out what was going on – despite the fact that many fellow participants (or even bystanders) at the same vantage-point could understand pretty well. Among a group of defendants in the same court – Nuremberg was a notable example – accounts vary from innocent ignorance to arrogant self-justification.[4]

'We didn't know' may be true for many people. Public knowledge of atrocities and social suffering varies according to political setting, length of conflict, control over mass media, visibility, geographical spread, proportion of the population involved, and much else. Peripheral bystanders or even perpetrators may have no idea of the big picture. The majority of citizens of a country seized by a military junta for a year would know little about secret disappearances or torture. In virtually all mass atrocities of the post-war period, though, cynicism is justified: the phrase should remain in inverted commas. But do we need the opaque concepts of denial, psychic defence, self-deception and bad faith? Are there states – in the psychic and political senses – in which something is known and not-known at the same time? I originally asked this about bystanders. But what about perpetrators, even those who gave orders, who were undeniably at the heart of the machine, who had access to information – yet still insist that they knew neither the essence nor the details?

Despite the differences between this and other atrocities, there is something more general in Gutman's enigmatic claim that the Holocaust was already being denied as it happened: 'The denial, the blurring of reality and the eradication of traces and vestiges of the stark truth were part and parcel of the act of murder itself.'[5] Denial is an integral stage in the unfolding of genocide beyond its 'practical purposes'; denials are 'in continuation of the complex motivations that inspire genocides to begin with'.[6]

This applies not merely to retrospective accounts, but to initial warnings, planning and implementation. Advance planning for 'maximum deniability' may merely be more explicit. The case of Nazi Germany has been the most scrutinized, yet there are still disputes about who and how many knew what and when. Certainly the creation of a genocidal state required more mass involvement than earlier historians recognized. Most of the general public knew or figured out the nature of the extermination programme if not its precise details. This was a prototypical 'open secret'. The extreme denial story is literally incredible: that a small group of fanatic perpetrators planned and carried out the killings while most of the public were a passive, distant, anonymous mass who knew nothing. 'Open secret' does not mean collective responsibility, or that the secretary filing papers about confiscated Jewish property and the Nazi doctor at Auschwitz are psychologically identical. But it does imply gradations of collective knowing: not just *how much*, but how much is acknowledged. Here, the distinction between bystander and perpetrator is less relevant. The tiny cog inside the machine may indeed know less than the informed outside observer.

Some knowledge was clear even in the years before the war. When the social exclusion of Jews, gypsies, the mentally disabled and homosexuals became routinized, the expulsion and then extermination stages were in sight, even apparently unconnected arms of government and business became involved.[7] The Interior Ministry supplied birth records of Jews; the Post Office delivered notification of expropriation and deportation; the Finance Ministry confiscated wealth; businesses fired Jewish workers. And later, pharmaceutical companies tested drugs on camp inmates; some companies bid for the contract to supply gas ovens, others to receive the shaved hair from women's heads (to process into felt) and melted down gold (10–12 kilograms a week by 1944) from jewelry and dental fillings (each transaction meticulously recorded by clerks). Doctors, lawyers and other professionals all played supporting roles.

Imagine, though, that assertions of ignorance were not intentional lies, but belonged to the 'twilight between knowing and not-knowing': alleged perpetrators and collusive bystanders caught in the web of denial that is 'part and parcel of the act'. Later cover-ups and excuses are more plausible when deception is built into the initial warning, planning and execution – by euphemism, ambiguity, secrecy, double-track or coded orders, blurring the chain of command.

Himmler's 1943 Posen speech is remarkably 'frank' in stating and justifying the extermination policy – and warning that this cannot be publicly admitted:

> I also want to talk to you quite frankly on a very grave matter. Among ourselves it should be mentioned quite frankly and yet we will never speak of it publicly. I mean the evacuation of the Jews, the extermination of the Jewish race.... Most of you must know what it means when one hundred corpses are lying side by side or five hundred or one thousand. To have stuck it out and at the same time – apart from exceptions caused by human weakness – to have remained decent fellows, that is what has made us hard. This is a page of glory in our history, which has never been written and is never to be written.

But this is not a 'pure' (that is, ambiguous) denial text. It could hardly have left its audience in a twilight state of knowing and not-knowing. This is merely an instruction on what to lie about. Other public Nazi texts, were encoded, two-track communications. The extermination message was hidden, but barely. It was a pretend concealment – like 'hiding' objects from children in a game. Concrete terms like 'murder' and 'killing' were seldom used. The actions of the *Einsatzgruppen* were referred to as 'deportations', 'special actions', 'special treatment', 'executive measures', 'cleansing', 'resettlement', 'finishing off', 'liquidation' and 'appropriate treatment'. The text allows the author to disavow its meaning and the audience to claim that they did not understand it.

Hannah Arendt refers to 'language rules': on one track, the language was brutally clear; on the other, there were instructions on how to disguise reality by lies, cover-up and euphemism.[8] Even after the nature of the Final Solution became obvious, those directly informed were formally converted from being 'bearers of orders' to 'bearers of secrets'. Correspondence was subject to rigid language rules: never 'liquidation' or 'killing', but prescribed code names. Only among themselves could the 'bearers of secrets' talk in uncoded language. 'Moreover the very term language rule... was itself a code name; it meant what in ordinary language would be called a lie.'[9]

In itself, this is an obvious point. Intelligence agents, corporate lawyers and Mafia bosses also use coded language in this way. But Arendt claims far more: that the same 'mendacity' and self-deception ingrained in Eichmann's character were integral to the *whole* of German society. This is what shielded Germans from 'reality and factuality'. But can mendacity really be a national character? Intentional, planned lying is not the same as self-deception. Arendt suggests an alternative which in this context is more 'radical' and frightening than a simple fully-fledged lie: 'The net effect of this language system was not to keep people ignorant of what they were doing, but to prevent them from equating it with their old, "normal" knowledge of murder and lies.'[10]

This is a perfect definition of interpretive denial – although 'people' can hardly mean 'all people'. Recall those images – so wonderfully conveyed by Claude Landzmann in *Shoah* – of the railways, the link between people's lives and their deaths. Was the organization of 'transports' a deliberate deception or a grotesque, but unreflecting continuation of German bureaucracy doing business as usual?[11] *Reichsbahn* employees knew the routes and destinations of these hundreds of thousands of 'passengers' and exactly how they were being deceived. These employees (1.4 million, of whom 500,000 were civil servants who ran the system) continued to allocate personnel, obtain freight cars, co-ordinate timetables, drive and clean cars. The officials who devised, gave and recorded orders might have deliberately used a coded language, but ordinary workers had no need to construct and deconstruct texts. Right in the middle of these bizarre, horrible scenes, 'all' they had to do was keep up an appearance of normality.

> The SS used travel agents to book one-way passage to the camp at the rate of four *Pfennig* ... per kilometre of track they would travel. Children under ten rode for half fare; those under four travelled free. A group rate of half the usual third-class charge was introduced for deportations of more than four hundred people.... *Reichsbahn* employees used the same forms and procedures to book tourists going on vacation as they did to send Jews to Auschwitz.[12]

It cannot be that these railway workers had no idea what was happening. But what *sort* of idea: an ideological conviction? knowing but not caring? twilight knowledge? All normalization – that is to say, all living – calls for some pretence, living 'as if' what is happening is not happening. People can live a long time with horrors, yet continue as if everything were normal. These booking clerks and train drivers must have recognized that something abnormal, if not morally wrong, was going on. They must have eventually slipped into a state of dulled routinization – as if this was more or less business as usual. 'You can get used to anything.' This slippage may have come from an unconscious emotional defence, but just as easily from a conscious, knowing pretence, a decision to proceed as if everything were normal. There is no need to defend or neutralize without the internal conviction that something wrong is happening or without anyone present to challenge you. Or else – a devastating possibility – the 'language system' indeed prevented the equation with 'their old, "normal" knowledge of murder and lies'. These clerks used routine booking procedures for transporting hundreds of thousands of people to be slaughtered. What looks to us more terrifying sixty years later: that they were too insulated to be aware of anything very odd, or that, with full awareness, they continued doing their jobs?

There are atrocities where the political authority is too insulated to require either elaborate deception or linguistic codes. The Khymer Rouge in Cambodia made little attempt to disguise their crimes at the time. In the interrogation manual found at the Tuol Sleng execution centre, there is a section entitled 'The Question of Doing Torture'. It includes detailed instructions on how to inflict pain and warns against any hesitancy or half-heartedness in 'doing torture'.

No country today combines such total internal repression and external isolation. This is why the *simultaneity* of literal denial and ideological justification is essential – for perpetrators at the time, for later official rhetoric, and for bystanders. The Argentinian junta created the most intricate version ever of the double discourse. This was an intensely verbal regime, obsessed with thoughts of its opponents. It invented a special language, a clandestine discourse of terror, to describe a private world whose official presence was publicly both denied and justified.[13] At the official level, the junta's discourse was not merely ideological, but messianic: ultimately, the 'Dirty War' was a defence of Western and Christian civilization. Argentina had become the place for the final battle of the forces of life against the forces of death. The public discourse was highly coded, full of sanctimonious – even metaphysical – references to purity, good and bad, and the sacred responsibility to eliminate opponents. At the private level, though, a new lexicon of daily life was improvised to make atrocities look normal. In the secret world of torture – where the infliction of pain is so personal – pre-junta meanings of words change and neutral words are retranslated. *Assado* (a barbecue) is now a bonfire to burn dead bodies; *la parrilla*, the grill for cooking meat, becomes the metal table on which victims are laid out for torture; *Comida de Pescado* (fish food) describes the prisoners thrown from planes into the sea, either drugged or dead, with their stomachs slit open. *Submarino* was not a submarine, or a sandwich, or a traditional children's treat of a choc-olate bar melting in milk, but repeatedly holding the victim's head under foul water (often containing urine and faeces), stopping each time short of suffocation.

Every torture regime uses the same linguistic technique: something awful that is *being done*, a verb, is transposed into some mundane *thing*, a noun. Israeli torturers gave Palestinians the *banana* (being tied in a painful floor position), the *sack* (prolonged hooding in a dirty muslin sack) and the *fridge* (being locked up in a coffin-sized cupboard, cold air blown in).

Torturers cannot literally 'deny' at the time what they are doing. The theatrical perversion of language is more a torment for the victim, a sadistic pleasure for some torturers, and an 'enabling device' for others in the chain of command.[14] But torturers construct a social reality that distorts facts and events, relocating the infliction of pain in a different cognitive world.[15] Torture may be referred to as 'work' ('What hours are you working tomorrow?'), and interrogators may be given banal *noms de plume* ('Uncle'). In some Argentinian detention centres, tor-turers, guards and victims lived together in the same building. Daily life was often like a hallucination. Prisoners played card-games with their tormentors. Everyone (prisoners in handcuffs and shackled) watched the 1978 World Soccer Championship, chanting support together for the national team. In the Buenos Aires camp, Olympus, pregnant women prisoners – still undergoing torture – went on out-ings with guards to a nearby park and café. They sat together, talking, partly in code, about daily life in the torture centres.

The humour of Paraguayan torturers in the seventies was cruder. They mocked President Carter's human rights rhetoric by naming their different sticks according to size: 'Constitution', 'Democracy', 'Human Rights'. As they beat people, they would shout, 'Here is your Human Rights.' In Brazil, torturers (referring to the UN Declara-tion on Human Rights) would say, 'Time to apply the Declaration again', while tying a prisoner on the parrot's perch and fastening the wires to his body.[16]

Common-sense explanations of the discrepancy between official and private discourses would talk of hypocrisy and cynicism. The public discourse, however, is not just self-righteous rhetoric for justifying atrocities, but rather 'a kind of re-arranged truth, a mythological

reality in which the Junta's words and deeds were integrated components of a single coherent agenda'.[17] The regime denies responsibility
for atrocities – which are anyway not happening – and maintains the
hermetic mythology about the dangers posed by 'subversives'. External criticism make the denials stronger and the ideology more
sacrosanct. Even in the 1985 trials, the junta accepted only an occult
sense of responsibility and continued denying all concrete allegations.
The prosecuting counsel became an expert on denial: 'General Videla's
empty references affirming that he takes full responsibility but that
nothing happened expose a primary thought process which, giving
magical power to words, tries through them to make reality disappear
because one wishes to deny it.'[18]

Magical realism indeed. The double discourse appeared throughout
Latin America as a way of 'talking terror'.[19] A leading Colombian
general referred to the dirty war as 'said to be going on'. It is and it
isn't. Taussig uses Garcia Marquez's novel, *Chronicle of a Death Fore-
told*, as a paradigm of state terror in Colombia. In the story, the
residents watch two armed men follow another man through the
town's street; they search from place to place; they are going to kill
him. The spectators sense this, but can't quite believe that he will be
killed – or rather, 'they believe and disbelieve at the same time'.[20]
Marquez conveys that strange sense of unreal reality experienced in
many cultures of terror: there is a 'war of silencing', nothing is official,
no disappearances, no torture. Factual knowledge is driven into a
private realm of fear and uncertainty. Talk of terror is silenced; you
say nothing in public that could be construed as criticizing the Armed
Forces.[21]

The 'double discourse' can almost be visualized. For a more pictorial
image of the known and said-to-be-unknown, look at the administrative office of the Nazi 'euthanasia' programme. The clerks are faking
death certificates, writing standardized letters of condolence, and
tying up loose financial ends. A map on the wall ensures that the
asylum was not reporting a suspiciously high number of deaths to
small places. With coloured pins representing a given month, staff
could stagger the bad news.[22]

I will end this section with Albert Speer, the most intensely studied
case of 'I didn't know' since Oedipus. From Nuremberg and Spandau
until his death in 1981, Speer continued to deny full knowledge about
the Final Solution. Most historians see these denials either as cunning
lies or as the products of wilful, culpable blindness. Speer knew
enough, anyway, to make any residual ignorance irrelevant. Sereny's
biography – 750 pages devoted to the subtitle *His Battle with Truth*[23] –
makes the story more complicated: too complicated for those who

think that she was charmed by Speer into accepting a bogus account of his life as a long moral agony about how much he knew, suspected or should have known. They are rightly sceptical about Speer's 'double claim to unique knowledge of Hitler's regime and to contemporaneous ignorance of the extent if not the very existence of the genocide that was its driving force'.[24] Sereny reminds us, however, of the historical period in which such accounts were originally offered. As knowledge increased of the horrors, so Speer's whole generation were driven to maintain their declarations of innocence and present themselves in a less damaging light to others and themselves. Sereny exaggerates the extent of de-Nazification and the intensity of any resulting stigma. But she shows how knowledge itself became as bad as action. 'Knowledge was like a tower built of dominoes – the smallest admission and the tower collapsed.'[25]

The other Nuremberg defendants told blanket lies about their knowledge, and refused to accept any responsibility. Speer's lies were more careful, specific and plausible. He accepted blanket responsibility for what happened: he didn't know any details at the time, but his position in government meant that he should have known more. He would never go beyond this: 'a droplet of apparent admission at times escaped him. But it was invariably followed by a veritable torrent of denials, and quite often convincing rationales for them.'[26] His mantra was constant: 'he should have known, he could have known, but he hadn't known.'[27]

The 'should' and 'could' are beyond all doubt. 'Hadn't' is more complicated. Sereny cautiously accepts his denials about some events, dismisses others as 'entirely untenable', and concludes that even in 1942, Speer was not yet 'consciously aware' of the genocide. The symptoms of his supposed 'unconscious awareness' could be the Table of Contents of a textbook on the psychology of denial.

Virtual blindness   Speer claims to have seen nothing ominous during the build up from 1934 to 1939. Something comes to your attention, but you take so little notice that you might as well be blind. Speer's account of this period shows 'the virtual blindness he displays to real events'.[28] In his own words 'People will never believe me or understand when I say this, but my mind was on other things. When it was actually happening, of course, one could hardly avoid being "aware" as you put it. . . . But I certainly didn't see it as it was considered historically and politically later.'[29] Ominous things 'eluded him', or 'bypassed his awareness'.[30] In a memoir, he did not even refer to Kristallnacht. He 'seemed exceptionally unaware of what was going on'.[31]

Not needing to know   Speer and his circle 'could have known but didn't need to, unless there was a practical need or a psychological or intellectual determination to confront rather than ignore the issue'.[32] Speer's loyal secretary, Annemarie Kempf, is profoundly clear: 'Now of course, I think we should have sensed something wrong and we should have asked ourselves the same questions you are asking. But we didn't and it was normal enough not even to think about it.'[33] This is a devastating claim: what was happening for a decade was 'normal enough not even to think about it'. Even when they came to know later about the camps, the latter weren't seen as important enough to warrant discussion. The fate of the Jews was simply not interesting enough.

Not wanting to know, refusing to know   The principles of the 'euthanasia' programme were known to Speer's wife and her elite circle of women friends, but never discussed. Annemarie and Speer had seen a propaganda film on the subject, but she claimed that none of them knew that this was actually happening. Perhaps, she speculates now, they might have had a 'buried suspicion' that if they had known or had tried to find out, this would have made things too difficult. She explains: 'If one had known, one would have had to question it, one would have had to face the reality of it and – much more than talking about it theoretically, as the subject of a film – one would have had to question one's own attitude toward it.'[34] Even in 1943, when things were very clear, they continued their 'determined ignorance', their deliberate refusal to acknowledge what was going on. Sereny often notes Speer's tendency to refuse to know about things he couldn't accept. Again, Annemarie Kempf gives the best explanation: 'In a way, I think that he felt that what he didn't know didn't exist.'[35]

Compartmentalization   At the end of 1943, Speer visited a slave labour camp; he also knew what Himmler said at Posen. He could no longer profess ignorance. Now he saw the reality of the atrocities which up to then he had only suspected or 'sensed'. He could not live with this knowledge – and thus started the compartmentalization that would continue till his death. This is different from Lifton's blocking mechanism: 'much harder than "blocking" the truth, which in its most extreme form can mean no longer being consciously aware of lying, Speer was living a lie, saw no way of ending it and – I think his one great merit – suffered atrociously under it.'[36] He suffered, Sereny claims, because he was morally ambivalent. Others are less sympathetic: Speer's 'ability to compartmentalize (to put it no more strongly) stayed with him for life, enabling him later to plead unawareness of major events in his immediate vicinity with a straight face'.[37]

Moral ambivalence, moral indifference or moral blindspot? The same straight face accompanied Speer's expressed guilt about not doing anything about the 'little' he knew. His litany never changed: how much he knew was unimportant compared with the 'horrors I ought to have known about and what conclusions would have been the natural ones to draw from the little I did know'.[38] Speer and his circle did not know everything, but they knew more than a 'little'. What conclusions did they draw *at the time*? And what were the 'natural ones' for that time? These people were not deluded, hypnotized or persuaded that wrong was right. They were persuaded to 'accept the legitimacy of forbidden knowledge'.[39] Some things are better not known about. If knowledge can't be faced, there must at least be moral ambivalence about this knowledge. Sereny thinks that Speer's ambivalence between the moral necessity to confront the long-repressed guilt of his terrible knowledge and his desperate need to deny it was the great dilemma of his life. Responding to a request to rebut a Holocaust denial claim, he restated his 'overall responsibility', conceding that his main guilt was his 'tacit acceptance [*Billigung*] of the persecution and murder of millions of Jews'. Sereny translated *Billigung* as 'tacit consent', and Speer added a footnote explaining the term as 'looking away, not by knowledge of an order or its execution'. 'The first', he added, 'is as grave as the second.' The contrary and simpler explanation is that Speer's supposed moral sensitivity or ambivalence was just indifference – certainly at the time – about the knowledge. These were things not worth thinking about. As one of Sereny's interviewees said about Speer's circle and other Germans of his generation: 'There was and perhaps lingered a moral blind spot about the Jews.' This was not, and could not have been, a *literal* cognitive blind spot: whether *Billigung* means acceptance, tolerance, connivance or consent, it must be about *something* of which one is aware. It is semantically impossible to be 'ambivalent' towards something you have no knowledge about.

Speak memory Only after his release from Spandau, Speer recalled things that *at the time* looked different but were hardly noticed. He remembered, some forty years later, a sense of 'momentary unease' when seeing at Berlin railway station crowds of German Jews being evacuated. This sort of afterthought was 'only an inept attempt to claim that he had not been morally blind, only blinded'.[40] Why, Sereny asked him, if he had any unease – there were, after all, many population movements going on – Speer was irritated. He replied: 'I was blind by choice . . . but I was not ignorant.' Of course he knew that Jews were a 'special problem'. But he didn't answer the crucial question about 'unease'. If he had this state of mind ('foreboding' or 'suspicion') it could only mean that he knew *at the time* what he constantly denied afterwards: that he had some idea of the extermination programme. Sereny pursued the matter. She recalled that Speer wrote: 'I can say that I sensed that dreadful things were happening with the Jews.'[41] She kept pressing him: 'If you sensed, then you knew. You cannot sense or suspect in a void. You knew.'[42] He knew, that is, what he so successfully denied at Nuremberg, thus saving himself from the death penalty. Sereny pushed home: 'You say you sensed something. . . . But you cannot sense in a void; "sensing" is an inner realization of knowledge. Basically, if you "sensed", then you knew.'[43]

Speer's only reply was to thank God that Sereny was not a Nuremberg prosecutor. He immediately understood that the moral implications of the denial paradox apply to sensing as well as knowing. Some things he never knew or even sensed: in a hierarchical organization obsessed with secrecy, top-level people are sheltered from reality. For *passive not-knowing*, I cannot be blamed: 'disingenuous', we might say. For *active not-knowing* (not trying to find out), *passive not-doing* (indifference) and *active not-doing* (silence), I am sorry: 'sanctimonious', we might say.

Denial of responsibility

The most accessible and popular accounts for ordinary offenders are various *denials of responsibility* (or of *agency, intent, autonomy* and *choice*). These range from total excuses and full incapacity ('I didn't know what I was doing', 'I must have blacked out') to the more moderate vocabularies of social determinism (bad homes, bad friends, bad neighbourhood, bad luck). These tales sound nothing like ideologically inspired accounts, which, by definition, must *accept* full moral responsibility.

Instead, the ideological realm contains an even richer repertoire of denials of responsibility. Indeed, as Bauman comments, evasion of responsibility, far from being a convenient after-the-fact excuse, is the 'unanchored responsibility' which is the condition for ordinary people to participate in atrocities: 'Free-floating responsibility means in practise that moral authority as such has been incapacitated without having been openly challenged or denied.'[44] The best-known in this repertoire is *obedience to authority*, but I will also consider three other accounts: *conformity, necessity* and *splitting*.

Obedience

The most facile and comprehensible way to evade personal responsibility is to appeal to authority and obedience. You deny agency,
intent, disposition and choice: 'I was just following orders...I had
no choice...I couldn't have refused...I had nothing against those
people, but they told us we had to kill them.' Such admissions come
from underlings who implement rather than make policy, receive
rather than give orders. The iconic image of such obedience is Eichmann (who, of course *did* make policy and gave many orders): a cog in
the machine, obeying only the orders that covered him; performing
duties as a good citizen, conforming to the new 'laws of the land'.

Just as 'good Germans' are icons of not-knowing, so Milgram's
laboratory volunteers have become icons of obedience. The scene of
the experiment is unforgettable: people sitting in front of fake meters,
ordered by a fake 'instructor' to give fake electric shocks to fake
victims faking heart attacks. This is a powerful reminder of the un-
edifying ways in which most people comply with authority.[45] The
concept of 'crime of obedience' has been refined and applied to the
case of the 1968 My Lai massacre committed by American soldiers in
Vietnam.[46] Crimes of obedience are immoral or criminal actions that
occur in hierarchical organizations (army, police, security forces, guerrilla cells) and are linked to orders from a superior in the chain of
command. The generic notion of obedience applies in different ways.
The lower you are in the hierarchy, the easier it is to deny personal
responsibility. You are the most passive recipient possible, at the end
of a long chain of command, unable to exercise any initiative. But the
higher you are in the authority structure (short of initiating the orders),
the further you are from the end results. You are subject to weaker
social controls and restraints, because you don't directly carry out or
even see the atrocity. This allows a denial of responsibility especially
potent in high-tech or multi-staged killing operations – all that you do
is transmit a stand-by code number to an underling at the next stage.

Kelman and Hamilton have identified three conditions for crimes of
obedience by low-ranking personnel. The first is the *authorization* of
violence via orders from a legitimate authority. You are not required to
deny moral values, but only their application to this particular situation: you are allowed to harm *these* others here (surely a better explanation than 'splitting of the ego'). There is no general ideological
justification. Indeed, your own morality is irrelevant; a superior
authority makes the moral decisions. Your 'appeal to higher loyalties'
is to the code of obedience itself. The second is *dehumanization* –

enemies or victims are placed outside your moral universe. You have no normal human obligations to them. Third is *routinization*: once you overcome the initial moral restraints – the soldier kills his first civilian, the torturer first uses electric shock – then each subsequent step becomes easier. An account for stopping is harder to find, because this would question the earlier steps. Each step becomes a mechanical action, solely means-directed. In Calley's chilling words, each My Lai killing was 'no big deal'.

These conditions usually exist already in the perpetrator's organization or political culture. If not, they have to be taught. The training of Greek torturers during the 1967–74 Junta started by desensitizing them to their own pain, suffering and humiliation. Trainees were forced to watch films which became progressively more gruesome. They learned to deny the big picture by being made to concentrate on small details like the motif on a knife handle. 'A steady diet of this desensitizes the soldier so that he can dissociate his feelings from the act of killing and inflicting pain.'[47] Recruits feel progressively less, while their 'object' is stripped of any identity except terrorist or enemy. Training encourages a 'task-oriented frame of mind': conscience is narrowed, and consciousness is focused on the single obsessive task of getting information. What is being done to *someone* just becomes 'what is being done'. These Greek recruits needed re-educating to be persuaded that people, who had previously seemed just like them, were actually hidden subversives.

Most atrocities are carried out from within organizations like armies. This makes them inconceivable without some degree of obedience. But conforming to authority is itself an ideological value, just as the rhetoric of even the most dedicated perpetrators may dignify little more than obedience, ignorance, bad faith, pretence and self-deception. These states of mind combine or vacillate among themselves. The most dangerous is bad faith. In the moral void of state terror, perpetrators may adopt *as their own belief* that they are acting against their will. During the four-year mass killings in Castle Hartman in Austria (K4 'mercy deaths' for the incurably ill, then gas chambers for children, sick and weakened inmates from Mauthausen and other nearby camps), the administrative employees diligently did their jobs and followed their orders, all the while reassuring themselves with the 'conviction that their co-operation had been forced contrary to their personal will'.[48] In the void was a sense of helplessness: the consolation that nothing else was possible, that there was no point in trying to resist. Just accept (in one secretary's words) that 'there was nothing to be done'. The result: 'Resignation led to a belief in helplessness, the ultimate inner justification of submission.'[49]

If obedience is a causal requirement for atrocities, so participating in atrocities creates obedience.

The psychological profile of perpetrators as either willing or obedient is not the issue. What matters is only whether the cultural climate and the authority of the state accept people's motivational account that they kill, maim, torture and rape because they were ordered to do so.

Conformity

The simple word 'conformity' does not have the resonance of 'obedience to authority', but deserves equal attention. In both its delinquent and ideological versions, the appeal to conformity – 'I was just doing what everyone else was doing (so why pick on me?)' – is widely used, highly plausible and makes obvious empirical sense. The delinquent versions – bad friends, neighbourhood or school – appear in folk sayings such as 'he was a nice boy until he got in with that crowd'.

At first glance, the ideological version is not attractive. A soldier will hardly tell journalists that he raped and killed a mother in front of her children because 'everyone else was doing it'. In more elaborate accounts, though, the pressures, demands and expectations of the situation – 'You don't know what it was like to be in the village then' – may convey a vivid sense of a temporary loss of choice. Other denials stretch conformity beyond the immediate situation into longer-lasting alibis: 'I just went along unthinkingly with what everybody else around me was doing at the time.' This sad tale may mutate into the most ideologically radical version of the conformity defence: 'If you were there, you would have behaved in just the same way. Therefore you have no right to judge me.' This claim is frighteningly plausible.

Necessity and self-defence

Denial of responsibility by appealing to necessity is a well-established account in criminal law. The sub-text may also appeal to self-defence: 'he was about to stab me', 'we had to save ourselves'. As with obedience, this refers to the immediate situation. You are faced with obvious dangers and threats: the terrorist is about to throw a grenade, so you start shooting. This may be panic, a reflex action, or the result of weighing up the odds. But any reasonable person would do much the same. More controversially, the threat can be less immediate or more hypothetical: torturing the terrorist to reveal the location of the 'ticking bomb'.

'Necessity' has a somewhat different meaning in the 'dirty work' theory. Every society has dirty work that just has to be done. The political equivalent of disposing of the garbage, this is unpopular and often done secretly, behind the scenes. We should not associate this work with bad people. On the contrary, these selfless tasks need good people – whose secret contribution to collective necessity we take for granted.[50] An Israeli psychiatrist asked a mid-level *Shabaq* (internal security services) officer about criticisms of using torture against Palestinians. How did he feel about his job? He replied that he never took such criticism personally. He knew that he wasn't a sadist, nor was he doing anything morally wrong. Ordinary Israelis – including these same human rights critics – can get on with their comfortable lives and know that their children are safe only because they can depend on the hidden, dirty work done by people like him. It was time we understood: 'Every palace has its sewers.'

Splitting

A radical denial of responsibility is to attribute your action to another, autonomous part of the self: as in Freudian models of dissociation, compartmentalization and ego splitting. Traditional deviant accounts ('I couldn't have done anything like that', 'That must have been another part of me') have been augmented by the discovery of 'dissociative states' and 'multiple personalities'.

The model's best-known ideological application is Lifton's study of Nazi doctors.[51] The real self separates, in three ways, from the person carrying out the evil. First, a *dissociative field* is set up, a 'place' where a portion of the self separates from the rest of the self. This is the detached state in which repressed memories and multiple personalities are formed. Second, there is *psychic numbing*: a diminished capacity or inclination to feel any emotion or the radical separation of knowledge from feeling. Finally, there is *doubling*: the formation of a part self that becomes functionally a whole self. The person doing these horrible things belongs to the 'Auschwitz self', a self comfortably attuned to that environment – giving lethal injections, performing fatal experiments, supervising the killing process. The doctor returns home for weekend leave; there he calls forth his prior, relatively more humane self, and functions as a nice, caring husband and father. Back at work, the healer is transformed into a killer, who 'awaits' within the sincere persona, but without having the killer's awareness. When the killer emerges, he denies this, and continues to think of himself and his behaviour as good.

Despite Lifton's vivid imagery of 'doubling at the centre' (the perpetrators) matched by 'numbing at the periphery' (bystanders, the public), the splitting thesis is not a convincing explanation of the Nazi doctors or similar perpetrators. It is impossible that a doctor on weekend leave with his family could either be unaware of his actions during the week or assign these actions to another part of the self. And if the doctor while giving lethal phenol injections to 'patients' thinks of himself as a noble healer, this is not because he has 'dissociated', but because in this setting, his own ideological autism is in harmony with the social reality of others.

The subtleties of splitting are hardly needed to explain how these doctors deluded themselves into thinking that they were doing noble medical and scientific work. Doctrines of socio-biological purity were in place well before Auschwitz, and so was the amoral professional mentality of doctors and lawyers.[52] Some doctors had already participated in earlier coercive sterilization programmes. Lifton concedes these ideological influences, but rightly notes that not all these doctors were true believers; they embraced fragments rather than the whole ideology. True, but these doctors seemed to know what they were doing – even though at the time (possibly) and afterwards (probably) they preferred not to see their behaviour as indicative of their 'real' selves. Ordinary people do not become unreflective serial killers for years because of splitting and doubling. Referring to a particularly ambitious and callous doctor in the 'euthanasia' project, Burleigh comments: 'I rather doubt whether men such as Gorgass spent the day as two different people in the manner posited by some psychiatrists who write about these matters.'[53]

Psychopathological mechanisms such as 'splitting' are too dramatic to convey the everyday forms of role distancing, compartmentalization and segmentation by which people separate themselves from what they are doing. We all do this normally, and we are normally aware of what we are doing. Far from being so private and secret that they deceive even the self, these states result from publicly available, even clichéd cultural denials, such as 'My job is not me'. Our societies encourage and reward the successful practice of splitting; dissociation and numbing are integral parts of late-modern cultures of denial. Here are four types:

- *Limited or situational morality* This allows you to isolate your offence within a specific situation or place without seeing yourself as immoral in general. In Israel during the *intifada*, reserve soldiers would return for weekend leave after a month of brutalities in Gaza, change out of uniform, pin a dove of peace button on their shirts, and then appear at a *Peace Now* demonstration. Civil liberties lawyers wrote articles and lectured to visiting delegations, denouncing the military justice system for Palestinians, but carried on doing their army reserve service as lawyers in the same military courts. These forms of institutionalized hypocrisy and bad faith were widely *praised* as signs of the society's 'tolerance'.

- *Means–end dissociation*   According to the ubiquitous 'cog in the machine' metaphor, people are not entirely responsible for the outcome of an enterprise in which they play only a limited part. In organizations with a clear division of labour, many fragmentary tasks seem harmless in themselves. Morality is easier to suspend if these routine, fractional contributions are isolated from the eventual function or end-product. You concentrate less on the effect of what you are doing than on doing a good job. Any suffering caused is remote and invisible. In many cases, however, even bureaucrats who have highly limited tasks (say, drawing up train timetables) have some sense of where these lead. It is simply impossible that clerical staff in an administrative office of the 'euthanasia programme' did not know exactly what they were doing. Burleigh describes how Irmgard Huber, a senior nurse directly involved in killing inmates maintained the psychological fiction that she was removed from the actual murders. 'She used various strategies of denial and evasion to distance herself from what she was doing.'[54] She attended the doctors' morning conferences, but passed instructions to kill patients on to her subordinates. Maintaining the fiction of the self as merely a passive vessel relaying orders was highly conscious.

- *Moral balance*   Perpetrators who are quite aware of the harm or immorality of what they are doing nevertheless consign these actions to a small self-contained compartment of themselves. This is not a Hollywood split-off personality, Mr Evil, doing these terrible things, unknown to, and beyond the control of, the nice Ms Good. The claim is not that the bad compartment is self-contained, unconscious or secret, but that it is *small*. In a moral atlas of our whole lives, this space is not significant; don't judge us just by this. In the moral ledger, the overall balance is in our favour. Lithuanian villagers who readily handed over their Jewish neighbours to the Nazis, then moved into their neighbours' houses, today remind visitors (many of them 'memory tourists') that previously they admired Jews and treated them with great kindness. They still have nothing against them.

- *Bad faith and role distance*   Many societies, especially democratic ones, encourage a radical disjunction between belief and deed. People who are reluctant to do bad things, and find them awkward to justify, are given space to believe that what they say to themselves is not the same as what they do. A Palestinian public figure detained for questioning was told by his Israeli interrogator that he felt uncomfortable with the situation. He himself was in favour of reconciliation, had for some time supported the aim of a Palestinian state, and looked forward to meeting Dr A there one day. There is even a special expression in Hebrew – used with increasing irony – to describe the dissociation between action and emotion. *Yorim V'Bochim* means literally 'shooting and crying': after doing all these unpleasant things – out of self-defence, necessity or duty – you express loud public regrets, even sympathy for the victims.

Perpetrator and bystander denials invariably contain some elements of splitting, dissociation and distancing. These may be states of mind, but they are also indicators of wider cultural patterns. The longest-lasting 'anti-denial' movements – the Black Sash in South Africa, Mothers of the Plaza de Mayo in Argentina, Women in Black in Israel – were started and sustained by women. Does this mean that men find it easier than women to compartmentalize their cognitive, emotional and moral reactions to suffering?

Denial of injury

Delinquents can draw on many variants of 'No one really got hurt'. These include something close to literal denial ('What's all the fuss about?'), playing down the injury ('They won't even miss a small sum like that'), and legalistic reinterpretation ('This was ordinary business practice').

Gross political atrocities do not easily allow these types of denials of injury. Perpetrators of massacres or disappearances can hardly claim that the victims did not really get hurt. Reframing – 'this does not fit the legal definition of torture' – figures more in the official discourse than in the vocabulary of individual perpetrators. When victims belong to a devalued ethnic group, though, it is common to claim that they don't feel pain as other people do: their culture is used to violence, it's the only language they understand, look what they do to each other.

We don't know whether and which perpetrators always, sometimes or never deny injury *at the time*. Some survivors and outside observers claim that prior contempt creates a shut-down mechanism, blinding perpetrators to the suffering they are inflicting. In the literal sense, however, most perpetrators are surely aware of the victim's suffering; this is what they want. Or an awareness intrudes, however dim, peripheral and momentary. If the suffering is then denied or neutralized, this is more a moral than a cognitive blindspot. Sometimes, though, the eye was blind from the start – a cumulative result of total control of whole populations for extended periods (for example, years of military occupation). Dramatic atrocities are felt less acutely than the daily indignities, petty harassment and minor humiliations of road blocks, restrictions on movement, stop-and-search procedures and curfews. Just as sensitively as these minor injuries are felt – an old man being searched and verbally abused in front of his granddaughter – so are they utterly invisible to the powerful.

Denial of the victim

'They started it' is the primeval account for private violence. The offender's claim to be the 'real' victim refers to immediate, short-term defence and provocation. In political atrocities, denial of the victim is more ideologically rooted in historically interminable narratives of blaming the other. Recent spirals of virulent political violence all draw on the refrain of 'Look what they did / are doing to us'.

The discourse is melodramatic: legendary heroes and persecuted victims, conquest and defeat, blood and revenge. Narratives from quite different histories and cultures have the same ending: 'history' proves that the people whom you call victims are not really victims; we, whom you condemn, have been the 'real' victims; they are, in the 'ultimate' sense, the true aggressors; therefore they deserve to be punished; justice is on our side.

This text may also draw on 'just world thinking'.[55] In a just world, suffering is not random; innocent people do not get punished arbitrarily. They must have done something. They deserve to suffer because of what they did, must have done, support doing, or will do one day (if we don't act now). Even when there is no objective symmetry, each side may feel its very existence threatened. The self-righteous claim to victimhood was most famously stated by Golda Meir, queen of Israeli kitsch, in her reproach of *Arabs* (Palestinians, she had said, did not exist) for 'making' nice Israeli boys do all those terrible things to them.

Full-fledged historical appeals are more likely to come from leaders, ideologists and official apologists than from ordinary perpetrators. In many conflicts, though – like the Israel–Palestinian, the Bosnian–Serb or Northern Ireland – individual participants on each side have an acute political consciousness and a detailed historical sense of their victimhood. In these societies, the victim-reversal myths of ethnic nationalism flow easily between leaders, media and ordinary people. Participants, even if their lives are totally grounded in a hedonistic and apolitical subculture of cruelty and male violence, glibly appeal to 'history' for vindication. A Serb soldier in 1999 talks about the Battle of Kosovo as if it happened the week before. This nationalism, Ignatieff points out, is supremely sentimental: kitsch is the natural aesthetic of an ethnic cleanser.[56] This is like a Verdi opera – killers on both sides pause between firing to recite nostalgic and epic texts. Their violence has been authorized by the state (or something like a state); they have the comforts of belonging and being possessed by a love greater than reason: 'Such a love assists the belief that it is fate, however tragic, which obliges you to kill.'[57] This is your destiny. You must get rid of your enemies – the aggressors who started everything – and live in peace and security with your own people. A collective memory that denies full humanity to the out-group allows for various shades of 'getting rid of' – from forcible segregation to ethnic cleansing or mass deportation ('transfer') to even genocide.

This is not situational cruelty. To be co-operative perpetrators or complicit bystanders for years requires a sense of the world in which the others' presence is hardly recognized. They get what they deserve, not because of what they do, but because of who they are. All ideologues exclude others from their moral community, placing them outside the boundary within which values and rules of fairness apply.[58] Ignatieff applies Freud's observations about the 'narcissism of minor difference' to the nationalist representation of the enemy. Nationalism abroad, like identity politics at home, seems not merely narcissistic but autistic: 'the pathology of groups so enclosed in their own circle of self-righteous victimhood, or so locked in their own myths or rituals of violence, that they can't listen, can't hear, can't learn from anybody outside themselves.'[59]

Not all perpetrators know, let alone articulate, the ideological history constructed by elites, leaders and officials. The reverse is also true. Populist racism (stereotypes, jokes) may be routine among low-level soldiers in private conversations with each other, threatening victims or confiding to their own families. The vocabulary is censored and sanitized in the official discourse meant for the outside world. Political leaders keep the official and populist cultures of denial separate from each other. Victim status is denied not by referring to 'the Arab mind' or 'the Jewish mentality' but by brushing up on the accepted international vocabulary of disputes, boundaries, agreements, the Geneva Convention, historical records and violations of UN resolutions.

Condemnation of the condemners

In its delinquent form, 'condemnation of the condemners' is already a slightly anomalous account because it expresses some kind of ideology. Attention is deflected from your own behaviour ('everyone is doing this – why pick on me?') to questioning the critics' right to criticize. The police are corrupt and biased; teachers and social workers are hypocrites. The wrongfulness of *others* is the issue. Perpetrator language is more explicitly political. External critics are attacked for being partial or are said to have no right to interfere. These accounts – no right to judge, double standards, it's worse elsewhere – are elaborated in the discourse of official denial.

Appeal to higher loyalties

Delinquents appeal to their loyalties to friends, peer groups or gangs. In the political world, these higher loyalties become transcendent, and the language of justification is total and self-righteous. Documenting the origins and contents of these loyalties is far easier than knowing what the ideology means to those who act in its name. There is a vast range between the Hamas suicide bomber and the GDR border guard shooting from the Berlin Wall.

The Serbian version of ethnic nationalism is closer to the 'nationalism' that Orwell warned about: 'The warlords are nationalists, but their convictions are uninteresting. They are technicians of violence rather than ideologues.'[60] The rhetoric of nationalism works as a 'moral vocabulary of self-exoneration', as if drawn from a handbook of motivational accounts.

Moral indifference

By definition, neutralization theory has nothing to say about truly radical and consistent repudiations of conventional moral codes. *Radical* means not a psychotic denial of the existence of such codes ('I didn't know that rape was wrong') but an ideological denial of their moral legitimacy. Fundamentalist religion is even more radical, by excluding the very possibility of secular law or morality. *Consistent* means that the justification is not picked up in an opportunistic way, but is inherent in (before and after) the act. Pure ideological crimes do not require any neutralization, because there is no morally legitimate universe outside the ideology. There is no need to be innocent of a 'troubling recognition' – because the recognition is not troubling.

Pure ideological narratives become increasingly strident and impervious to outside reality checks – the lesson from Festinger's famous study of a doomsday cult. If people hold two contradictory cognitions

– the world will end today *and* it has not ended as we predicted – then, as rationalizing creatures, they try to resolve the dissonance by denying or distorting reality. The cult followers not only found an account to resolve the dissonance (God saved the world because of our faith), but also spread the message with a new zeal. They had to convince themselves and others that their prior commitment and sacrifices were neither absurd nor in vain. They changed from mere believers into bigots, which is just how 'ordinary' perpetrators (and audiences) become more ideological. Every step taken escalates into justifications for further action; the action is followed by another round of rationalization. If forced to look backwards – testify in trials or Truth Commissions – these offenders, by definition, stick to their narrative of ideological indifference: 'I still think that what I did was right.' Others, sincerely or not, adopt a vocabulary of 'repentance': 'I thought I was right at the time, but only now do I see that it was wrong.'

There are many variants of moral indifference, even within a single historical case. Klee's anthology of writings by German perpetrators – diaries, letters home, reports, later testimonies – cautions against a simple reading of this type of denial. He quotes gas-van driver Walter Burmeister, whose job it was to load people into the van, switch on the engine to send gas fumes from the exhaust pipe into a hole in the floor, then drive to the wood to dump the bodies. Was he just obeying orders? Did the ideology influence him? His reply (in his 1961 trial): 'I can no longer say today what I thought at the time or whether I thought of anything at all.'[61]

These personal texts describe the mass killings (hundreds of Jews in a village lined up and shot or clubbed to death) in banal, factual tones. The events are barely recorded – as if only to give enough background information to appreciate the writer's concerns, such as:

- Correct military decorum: 'dignified arrangements', 'decent soldierly attitude', avoiding shameful practices such as looting for personal gain or 'degenerative sadism'.
- Pride: 'I can say with pride that my men, however unpleasant their duties might be, are correct and upstanding in their conduct and can look anybody squarely in the eye and back home they can be good fathers to their children.'[62]
- Decency: SS-Mann Ernst Gobel watches a soldier lift children (between two and six years old) by the hair, shoot them in the back of the head, and throw them in a grave. 'After a while I just could not watch this any more and I told him to stop. What I meant was that he should not lift the children up by the hair, he should kill them in a more decent way.'[63]

- Morale and stress: they are doing a thankless job, no one appreci- ates just how difficult their work is. Officers must watch out for this: 'I cannot say whether I had misgivings about the use of gas- vans. What was uppermost in my mind at the time is that the shootings were a great strain on the men involved and that this strain would be removed by the use of gas-vans.'[64]

Another state of absence, similar to dissociation, takes perpetrators (and many bystanders) even further beyond moral reach. The self denies its very presence by becoming a spectator. People in a car accident often recall feeling that this was happening to someone else – 'it was like watching a movie'. 'There's been an accident,' not 'I've been in an accident.' There are some perpetrators who care so little, whose sense of personal responsibility has so atrophied, that they act like bystanders who just happen to come across something. This is marvellously conveyed in McCarthy's account of the trial of Calley's company commander, Captain Ernest Medina, for his involvement in the My Lai massacre.[65] His own and other testimonies portray him as a chance spectator, a casual passer-by. In the village, he tried to keep as faraway as possible from the carnage: 'When unavoidably he had to pass a body or a pile of bodies, he walked rapidly on, looking to neither the right nor the left, the way one skirts garbage in a big city street. On the stand, except for the technical know how, he seemed no more "involved" in My Lai than a newspaper reader perusing a famine story from Biafra or Bangladesh.'[66]

This is not a state of mindless social conformity. During the event, these perpetrators seem not to have reflected on its meaning; years later they may still profess not to understand why the event was so condemned. This may be either an obvious lie (they know exactly what happened) or a form of self-deception, classic twilight area denial. The more frightening possibility is that they really saw nothing wrong at the time and behaved, like everyone else, without reflection. This, I believe, is the meaning of Arendt's much misunderstood concept of 'the banality of evil'. Far from minimizing the evil, she warns that unimaginable evil can result from a constellation of ordinary human qualities: not fully realizing the immorality of what you are doing; being as normal as all your peers doing the same things; having motives that are dull, unimaginative and commonplace (going along with others, professional ambition, job security), and retaining long afterwards the façade of pseudo-stupidity, not grasping what the fuss was about.

Thus Lt Calley's 'no big deal'. His soldiers did not confess, because they were literally unaware of their actions; they were not in a state of psychotic disavowal, nor were they like Oliver Sacks's neurological patients who mistook their loved ones for items of furniture. It is only in the moral sense that Arendt wrote of Eichmann: 'He *merely*, to put the matter colloquially, *never realized what he was doing.'*[67] This becomes a powerful account: 'As Eichmann told it, the most potent factor in the soothing of his own conscience was the simple fact that he could see no one, no one at all, who was actually against the Final Solution.'[68] This is the pure test: create a moral void without people knowing that this has happened.

A terrifying image: the absence of anyone to test your old moral reflexes. But no totalitarian state has been total. Even in extremities, some people's moral instincts remain intact. Between those who actively refuse to see anything wrong and those who see everything as wrong, the vast majority in between can be nudged into acknowledging that something was wrong – yet *at the same time* sustain their denials. Cultures of denial encourage turning a collective blind eye, leaving horrors unexamined or normalized as being part of the rhythms of everyday life.

Arendt made a strange claim about Eichmann: 'Except for an extraordinary diligence in looking out for his personal advancement, *he had no motives at all.'*[69] This makes perfect sense. The more self-evident the culture's amorality, the easier it is for motives to be picked up and tried out in a wholly opportunistic way. It is interesting, but irrelevant, to contrast the unprincipled, obedient automaton, looking after number one, adopting any convenient motivational camouflage, with the fully informed, ideologically motivated monster, evil but acting out of principle. Both occupy the same moral void.

The discourse of official denial

For obvious reasons – benign, neutral and malignant – our cumulative knowledge of recent and current atrocities is incomplete, uneven and unobjective.[70] Some countries are closed to outside scrutiny, shielded by patron states, obscure and politically uninteresting; others are highly scrutinized, especially those with the rare combination of visible violations and relatively open access. There is no exact correspondence between the severity, duration and extent of violations and the amount of attention any particular country receives from the media or human rights reports. So government responses to international criticism ('Why pick on us again?') may be justified, even when disingenuous or distracting.

Despite this selectivity, most countries and issues have been covered, rather than covered up: suppression of political dissidents in China, police violence in Brazil, war crimes in Bosnia, child labour in Pakistan, land-mines in Angola, prison conditions in Poland, female genital mutilation in the Sudan, genocidal massacres in Rwanda, deprivation of women's rights in Afghanistan, the destruction of civil society in Haiti, political massacres by Indonesia in East Timor, disappearances in Peru, atrocities in Iraq, Aboriginal deaths in custody in Australia, torture in Turkey, persecution of Roma in Hungary, extra-judicial killings in Somalia, death squads in Colombia, amputations and public floggings in Saudi Arabia, the death penalty in the USA . . . And despite occasional legendary mistakes, this reporting is generally fair and reliable.

Governments respond in the global media, diplomatic channels, press conferences, refutations of Amnesty reports, UN special committees or the General Assembly. Their denials are sometimes justified: allegations may be exaggerated, reports unbalanced, details inaccurate, violations may happen without official knowledge. But words take on their own, unanchored lives as they flit through the textual loop of report (claims) followed by government reaction (counter-claims), followed by further rounds of exchanges. The discourse grows, becoming increasingly self-referential, slipping on to the agendas of Washington subcommittees and into documents floating around UN offices in Geneva and New York.

In these arenas 'denial' is just another public relations term. 'The government of Freedonia strongly denies that . . .' may refer to domestic or foreign policy, corruption, personal scandals, public health risks, etc. Today's benign image of not telling the truth is to 'put a spin' on information. The same public relations agencies – based in Washington, New York or European capitals, and hired by corporations, movie stars, football players and political parties – handle the accounts of governments trying to clean up their human rights image. These are difficult clients ('New Zaire?', 'Democratic Syria?', 'North Korea Welcomes You?'). But the task is seen as technical, rather than as 'thought control' or 'manufacture of consent'; deriving from what Chomsky calls 'the sacred right to lie in the service of the state'.[71]

There are three forms of government response: the classic discourse of official denial, the conversion of a defensive position into an attack on the critic, and the partial acknowledgement of criticism. These are all active reactions. Many countries – including, and especially, those with the worst records – pay no attention to outside criticism. They close their shell and withdraw from any engagement. Because of pressures from outside (stigmatization, sanctions, boycotts, isolation) and their own internal ideology (everyone is against us, no one understands us), they do not react at all. They see no political necessity for dialogue with the rest of the world; nor do they have to contend with internal criticism. Their silence is the most radical form of denial possible.

Fewer countries of this type remain in the new world order. Most have to appease the Super Powers, the United Nations, the International Monetary Fund or 'international public opinion'. But even countries that normally respond actively complain of unfair attention and bias. Israel, for example, sends more detailed responses to Amnesty International than any other country, each offering exquisite legalistic denials of all allegations.

Classic official denial

Each variant of denial appears in the official discourse: *literal* (nothing happened); *interpretive* (what happened is really something else) and *implicatory* (what happened is justified). Sometimes, these appear in a visible sequence: if one strategy does not work, the next is tried. If literal denial is countered by irrefutable evidence that something indeed happened – video footage of passive demonstrators being shot, corpses in mass graves, autopsy reports showing torture marks – the strategy may switch to legalistic reinterpretations or political justifications. But these forms seldom run in sequence: more often they appear simultaneously, even within the same one-page press release.

How can one say that a massacre *did not take place*, but also that 'they got what they deserved?' Trying to 'expose' this contradiction misses the point. As the apocryphal US army spokesman said in Vietnam: 'There was no massacre and the bastards got what they deserved.' The contradictory elements form a deep structure: their relationship to each other is ideological, rather than logical. With respect to torture, the infliction of pain is immediately accompanied both by a literal denial that any torture took place and reinterpretations and justifications for the act.[72] Torture victims who hear their interrogators' dreadful words 'Scream as loud as you like, no one will believe you,' face a double problem when they are released. They are indeed not believed, but are also confronted with the response that they 'must have done something'. The ideology of state terror justifies action whose existence is never officially admitted: 'On the one hand ... the repression is justified, and on the other, those who have suffered at its hands are accused of being liars.'[73]

The Argentinian junta patented a uniquely self-righteous version of the double message. When talking to foreign governments and reporters, General Jorge Videla's note was outright and outraged denial: Argentina was 'born free', political prisoners don't exist, no one is persecuted for his ideas. Yet on US television in 1977, Videla patiently explained: 'We must accept as reality that there are missing persons in Argentina. The problem is not in ratifying or denying this reality, but in knowing the reasons why these persons disappeared.'[74] There had been, he conceded, some 'excesses'. But many people thought to be missing had secretly disappeared to devote themselves to subversion; they turned up on television in Europe, 'speaking ill of Argentina'.

'Nothing is happening': literal denial

With most authoritarian and repressive regimes, there is only literal denial, the laconic disavowal that 'nothing happened'. Without domestic accountability and insulated from external scrutiny, no elaborate response is needed. Internal counter-claims are impossible, because of government controls on information and the mass media.

For different reasons, more democratic societies may also practise literal denial. Indeed, governments paying strong formal allegiance to human rights values prefer to contest allegations at the literal, factual level. 'We would never allow something like that to happen, so it could not have happened.' This response is needed in the international diplomatic arena, where financial aid or strategic alliances depend on an image of conforming to human rights standards. Danner's account of the US government's active collusion in the cover-up of the 1981 El Mozote massacre in El Salvador is a model case-study.[75] At the same time as claiming that El Salvador was making every effort to improve its human rights record (and therefore was eligible for aid to be certified by Congress), US Embassy officials in El Salvador and the State Department were involved in baroque manoeuvres to deny what they knew about the massacre.

There are no limits to the methods that are used to deny, cover up, explain away, or lie about the most apparently obvious realities. This is clear in the well-known episodes of historical denial. As soon as events become assigned to 'history', further denials become available: it happened too long ago, memory is unreliable, the records have been lost, and no one will ever know what took place. Increased human rights monitoring, the spread of international reporting and advances in information technology (instant global TV footage, electronic mail that can bypass censors) have made the literal denial of *current* events more desperate. For example, the Serb government response to the February 1993 market massacres in Sarajevo: either there was no massacre (the Bosnians had faked it by substituting dummies or corpses from previous incidents) or the Bosnians had cynically shelled their own citizens to obtain political advantage by blaming the Serbs.

Literal denial is usually implied by attacking the reliability, objectivity and credibility of the observer. Victims are lying and cannot be believed, because they have a political interest in discrediting the government. Witnesses are untrustworthy or drawn from the political opposition. Journalists and human rights observers are selective, biased, working from a hidden political agenda, or else naïve, gullible and easily manipulated. Or denial magic is evoked: the violation is prohibited by the government, so it could not have occurred.

The phenomenon of 'disappearances' takes its very definition from the government's ability to deny that it happened. The victim has no legal *corpus* or physical body; there is no evidence to prosecute, not even a sign of a crime. In the Argentinian junta's discourse, the physical acts of abduction, torture and execution were complemented by the speech act of denial; otherwise terms such as 'arrest' or 'detention' could have been used.[76] For a disappearance to be a disappearance, it has to be denied. Someone 'vanished without a trace' because denial obscured the traces. *Desaparecidos*, 'the disappeared', were people who would be, in army commander General Roberto Viola's words, 'absent forever'; some were living in exile, working with false identities in a subversive organization; some had been eliminated as traitors by their comrades. Officially they were neither living nor dead. Their 'destiny' was to 'vanish'.[77] The authorities could tell no more to parents searching for their children; as for kidnappings in cars, secret detention centres and torture, these simply did not exist.

Literal denial is more credible to foreign audiences: the sources of information are unknown; patron states are willing to look the other way; things are too complicated to understand. Within the domestic setting, however, these denials are not easy. Too many people know what is happening. State terror must be known by everyone, but they must be induced into knowing collusion in the silence.

'What is happening is really something else': interpretive denial

Greater international visibility and transparency have made the more literal forms of literal denial difficult to sustain. Even repressive governments – dependent on global economic controls and exposed by the collapse of cold war alliances – are less likely to ignore criticism or issue crude denials. The standard alternative is to admit the raw facts – yes, something did happen: people were killed, injured or detained without trial – but deny the interpretive framework placed on these events. No, what happened was not really torture, genocide or extra-judicial killing, but something else. The harm is cognitively reframed and then reallocated to a different, less pejorative class of event.

This is a complex and subtle strategy, because the naming of all social events requires interpretation. The human rights ethos, however must assume that such definitions can be made in good faith and with some consensus. There must be sharable definitions of minimum prison standards, a fair trial, torture or rape. The definition will have some ambiguities, but should be able to exclude official interpretations that are evasions made in bad faith. This is the point of concepts like 'standards'. These evasions are most evident when the label is universally stigmatic: even the most self-righteous governments will contest the public labels of 'torture' and 'genocide'.

There is room for legitimate controversy, claims and counter-claims, not because of the sociological truism that all actions are interpreted, but because the dominant language of interpretation is legal. The common-sense meanings of terms such as 'genocide', 'political killings' and 'torture' have all been superseded by the legal definitions on which international standards and prohibitions are based. Concepts such as 'genocide', 'crimes against humanity', and 'war crimes' are notoriously difficult to define, even in good faith – a condition hardly evident in official denial. Such international prohibitions are always subject to the politics of definition. What degree of 'intent to destroy' is needed to fit the Genocide Convention's definition of genocide? How severe is the 'severe pain' prohibited by the Convention on torture. The interest of governments to apply the most restrictive formal definition is self-evident.

These definitional battles occur because law is a 'plastic medium of discourse', capable of varied, though certainly not infinite, interpretations. In this sense, a dispute between Amnesty International and a government about whether a particular method of interrogation is 'acceptable' rather than 'ill-treatment', or 'ill-treatment' rather than 'torture', is no different from disputes in an ordinary trial about manslaughter rather than first-degree murder. Without these legalistic games of truth, the institutions of international human rights enforcement would collapse and return to the older moralistic language that they replaced. The term 'ethnic cleansing' is admirable and exceptional in remaining both moralistic and pictorial.

Reinterpretation is a compromise. The elephant on the dining-room table is there, but the state and its allies collude in defining it as something else, something not very significant. Harm may be acknowledged, but its legal or common-sense meanings are denied, contested or minimized, by four common methods.

Euphemism   The function of euphemistic labels and jargon is to mask, sanitize and confer respectability. Palliative terms deny or misrepresent cruelty or harm, giving them neutral or respectable status. The classic source remains Orwell's original account of the anaesthetic function of political language – how words insulate their users and listeners from experiencing fully the meaning of what they are doing.[78] His examples have become only too banal: 'pacification', 'transfer of population', 'elimination of undesirable elements'. In each instance, 'such phraseology is needed if one wants to name things without calling up mental pictures of them'.[79] Half a century later, the dictionary of euphemisms has been vastly enlarged. But Orwell would recognize the new entries – even those derived from the specialized jargon, convoluted verbiage and techno-babble of modern warfare:[80] 'strategic hamlets', 'interdict', 'relocate', 'take out', 'safe havens', 'smart bombs' and 'collateral damage'.

The vocabulary of torture is rich in euphemisms. Under the Argentinian junta, softening the violation was complemented by hardening the nature of the enemy. In a 380-page secret manual issued in 1976, the army chief, Roberto Viola, set out two columns of linguistic regulations: *Terms not to be Used* and *Terms to be Used* ('Guerrillas' became 'Armed bands of subversive criminals', 'Wearing uniform' is 'Usurping the use of insignia, emblems, uniforms').[81] The best-known torture euphemisms were the 'intensive interrogations' used by the British in Northern Ireland; the 'special procedures', the 'long-established police procedures', 'services' and 'excesses' used by the French in Algeria;[82] the methods of 'moderate physical pressure' used by Israelis against Palestinian detainees.[83]

Whole organizations devoted to committing atrocities may be euphemistically named. There was the CHARITABLE FOUNDATION FOR INSTITUTIONAL CARE (the re-named Nazi 'euthanasia' programme for killing the mentally handicapped and other unworthy people) and the STATE RESEARCH BUREAU (Idi Amin's Ugandan death squads).

Legalism   Powerful forms of interpretive denial come from the language of legality itself. Countries with democratic credentials sensitive to their international image now offer legalistic defences, drawn from the accredited human rights discourse. This results in the intricate textual commentaries that circulate between governments and their critics or within legal-diplomatic loops and UN committees. Does the second clause of article 16(b), para. 6, apply to all the state parties? Do the minimum standards of prison conditions apply to detention during interrogation? Interesting questions indeed.

The legal discourse depicts a wholly non-pictorial world. This is a board game with a limited repertoire of fixed moves. One side claims that event X does not fit the appropriate category (right, law, article or convention). Yes, this demonstrator was arrested and detained, but this was not a violation of freedom of expression. Yes it was, comes the counter-move. Event Y may have been a violation of the Fourth Geneva Convention, but the Convention does not apply. Yes, it does. Some legalistic games are unplayable (or infinitely playable) because of the original definition. The Convention Against Genocide has not registered a single case for fifty years, partly because the original politicized drafting resulted in so many restrictions – hence Kuper's thesis, 'that the sovereign territorial state claims, as an integral part of its sovereignty, the right to commit genocide, or engage in genocidal massacres against people under its rule, and that the United Nations, for all practical purposes, defends this right'.[84] He notes of the 1954 Draft Code of Offences, 'It reads, sadly, like a manual for contemporary international practice'.[85]

Magical legalism is a method to 'prove' that an allegation could not possibly be correct because the action is illegal. The government lists domestic laws and precedents, ratifications of international conventions, appeals mechanisms and provisions for disciplining violators. Then comes the magical syllogism: torture is strictly forbidden in our country; we have ratified the Convention Against Torture; therefore what we are doing cannot be torture.

Many such legalistic moves are wonderfully plausible as long as common sense is suspended. A nice example comes from Israel: in 1991, a deputy attorney-general wrote an official letter of guidance regarding a compensation claim from a Palestinian from Gaza whose sixty-three-year-old wife was beaten and shot by soldiers after going into the street to see what was happening during a clash. The letter (withdrawn in the wake of public criticism) read: 'Aside from the usual arguments [*sic*] we should claim that the plaintiff only profited from the death of the deceased because he had to support her while she lived and now he no longer had to; thus his damages are zero, at the most.'

The type of legalism that appears to recognize the legitimacy of human rights concerns is more difficult to counter than crude literal denials. The organization has to show that behind the intricate legal façade lies another reality (Orwell's 'mental pictures'). Interpretive denials are not fully-fledged lies; they create an opaque moat between rhetoric and reality.

Denial of responsibility   Techniques for evading responsibility – so rich and versatile for individual perpetrators – are more limited in official discourse. More is needed than the agentless passive form ('Four rioters were killed yesterday'): the linguistic device creating the impression that atrocities just happen, rather than being caused by human action.

Another move is to attribute responsibility to forces – named or unknown – that supposedly have nothing to do with the government and are beyond its control. Yes, something bad happened, but don't blame us. Responsibility lies with shadowy armed groups, vigilantes, rogue psychopaths, proxy armies, vague 'third forces', paramilitaries, mercenaries, private death squads or 'unknown elements'. Or the violence is 'endemic' – communal violence, civil war, war-lords, bar-ons, tribal rivalry, ethnic tensions, traditional justice or drug wars – and for ever beyond the reach of the state. Or no responsibility can be found *anywhere*: political authority has collapsed, the massacre could have been ordered by any number of forces.

Instead of the subordinate claiming obedience to orders, the super-ordinate denies giving the orders. The ministry certainly did not author-ize anything like death squads and had no idea that this was happening. Or else they gave orders, but these were misunderstood. This defence is more often offered – in Truth Commissions, trials, and inquiries – than believed. General Coetzee, former head of the security police, was asked by the South African TRC what the State Security Council meant when it gave an instruction to *eliminaar* (Afrikaans for 'eliminate') its opponents. He produced two Afrikaans dictionaries to prove that *eliminaar* does not *per se* mean to kill or assassinate. Why, then, did so many of his forces go out killing and claim that this was authorized? No one at the 'grass-roots level', Coetzee replied, had ever asked him what the word meant – or other words like *neutraliser* ('neutralize'), *uitwit* ('obliterate or wipe out') or *permanent uit die saamelwing verwyder* ('remove permanently from society'). If they had, he assured the commission, he would have told them that murder was forbidden.

Isolation The government concedes what happened and accepts responsibility – but denies the systematic, routine or repeated quality attributed to the act. It was an 'isolated incident'; you cannot even put us in the same category as governments which systematically do this.

What's happening is justified: implicatory denial

A list of justifications for the infliction of human suffering would be endless. Government accounts in the international arena make up a tiny subcategory. Some of these explain why the violations occurred; some are retrospective inventions. Some are sincere and offered in good

faith; some are blatant, knowing lies. Some are closer to pure justifications; others look more like excuses; yet others are intermediate
neutralizations. Some need decoding; others are openly stated. Some
are confined to perpetrator governments; others are offered on their
behalf by patrons, allies and clients. Some are transparent in the state's
internal ideology, but are never used in the international setting.

Despite the demise of the cold war, the End of History and the death
of meta-narratives, there is no shortage of ideological accounts.

Righteousness Appeals to higher loyalties claim that the values
enshrined in international human rights standards are not universal
at all, and therefore that any society can act according to its own
morality. A weaker variant asserts that alternative sets of values can,
under certain circumstances (or in regard to certain people), override
universals. The strongest justifications invoke a transcendent ideology,
righteous cause or sacred mission. Your nation is exalted, extraordinary and possessed of a higher wisdom and morality that permits –
even demands – any means towards the higher good. The Argentinian
junta member Admiral Emilio Massera noted that 'God has decided
that we should have the responsibility for designing the future'. A
more common version appeals to less transcendent but equally binding ideologies – the revolutionary struggle, ethnic purity, Western
civilization.

Necessity A less strident justification is utilitarian and expedient: 'we
had to do it', 'there was no alternative'. The theme of security now
dominates the responses of virtually all governments. There is no
principled denial of human rights values in favour of other values.
The government, reluctantly, acted out of necessity: self-defence,
national survival, prevention of greater harm, anticipation of danger,
or for the protection of its citizens. Necessity may not refer to actual or
imminent threat, but the calculated prevention of a long-term foresee-
able danger – which requires preventive detention, states of emergency and restrictions on freedom of movement.

A potent version of the necessity defence is the image of a Darwinian struggle for survival: the conflict has gone on for centuries; only
one side can win; no compromises are possible; it's either them or us.

Denial of the victim The primeval sentiments of 'they started it', or
'they got what they deserved' – displacing blame on to those who are
harmed – provide official justifications as well as personal exoneration.
Again, the defence is situational (reacting to immediate provocation)
or historical (the narrative of current victim as primal perpetrator). The

atrocities of the last few decades show that there is no end to the historical spirals of conflicting claims about which group is the original, 'real' or ultimate victim.

Contextualization and uniqueness   In a sense, all justifications such as necessity and blaming the victim are forms of contextualization. Governments always accuse their critics of not knowing, understanding or mentioning the context in which the violations took place. They say, in effect: 'If only you really understood our history, politics, the nature of the conflict, then [the weak version] your judgement would not be so harsh or [the strong version] you would support what we are doing.' Many government responses consist of a detailed, didactic (and, by definition, tendentious) historical review of the conflict.

A stronger contextualization asserts that normal standards of judgement cannot apply because the country's circumstances – terrorism, isolation, nuclear threats – are unique. This is not to reject universal standards: we only wish we could observe them; but, alas, history does not allow us to be like everyone else.

Advantageous comparisons   A more oblique justification is the self-righteous comparison of your own moral standing with that of your critics:[86]

- By contrasting your own harmful acts with the more reprehensible inhumanities committed by your adversary, your record looks good. The major part of a government response may be a comprehensive (and often credible) catalogue of the atrocities perpetrated by armed oppositional groups. So: whatever we do is nothing compared with what they do. Indeed, under the circumstances, we behave with great restraint and according to the rule of law.
- 'Condemning the condemners' means making comparisons with your outside critics, accusing them especially of hypocrisy ('Their hands are not clean') or selectivity ('Why do they keep picking on us?'). They are themselves too morally compromised to have any right to judge us. The Israeli version of this tactic is especially resonant: when Jews were being slaughtered during the Holocaust, the very countries now condemning us either colluded or stood by in silence; the international community has thereby abdicated its right to criticize us now.[87] Former colonies make equivalent historical appeals: their former colonists can hardly condemn brutalities. More generally, all democracies were born out of violence, slavery, occupation and the extermination of indigenous peoples; they have no right to judge us now.

- Besides our adversaries or critics, compare us with other governments facing similar provocations and dangers. They would have
  acted, and do act, worse – without any of our self-imposed
  restraints.

These comparisons may be combined in a unified discourse of righteous indignation: our adversaries behave terribly (and you don't condemn them); your own moral record is flawed (so you have no right to
judge); other countries with lesser problems behave worse than us
(and you say nothing about them). No such comparisons can be
made without a universal measuring rod – just the pre-condition that
many governments reject as impossible and undesirable. I will return
(in chapter 11) to the intellectual fandangos around the theme of
universality.

Counter-offensive

In today's political culture, accounts are negotiated through spectacle,
simulation and stage management. Governments have to contend with
victims, social movements and pressure groups that have been
empowered and humanitarian organizations that are visible and tele-
genic. Moreover, these sources of denunciation have access to powerful communication methods – electronic mail, internet, fax, video – not
easily subjected to state power. In this market-place of accounts, governments defend themselves by pre-emptive attack and 'shooting the
messenger'.

The simplest strategy rejects all allegations as lies, propaganda,
ideology, disinformation or prejudice. Techniques include citing errors
in previous reports (this detainee was interrogated in March not May,
this prisoner later withdrew his allegations); impugning the sources of
an organization's financing or the political affiliations of its inform-
ants, field-workers or board members; and attacking the timing of its
report as 'politically motivated'. If any allegations look undeniable,
evade them by discrediting the source. Human rights organizations
are mouthpieces or fronts ('pro-Sendero', 'pro-Tamil', 'PLO sympathizers').

Internal critics may be defined as treacherous, unpatriotic or irresponsible. Or their *bona fide* human rights status is conceded – they
have good intentions, they are not merely taking political sides – but
they are 'useful idiots', whose reports will be ruthlessly exploited.
Critics who publish their allegations abroad or talk to the international
media are especially vulnerable. Israeli human rights activists are

denounced as *malshinim* – literally 'informers'; they are playing into the hands of anti-Zionist or even anti-Semitic forces. Internal critics of Arab regimes are accused of washing their dirty linen in public and reinforcing anti-Arab or anti-Islamic forces.[88]

Accusations of treachery and lack of patriotism cannot be applied to international critics, but the rest of the strategy is similar. Particular organizations may be singled out ('Amnesty International is known for its anti-India record') and denounced for ignoring the victims of terrorism. These organizations are not genuinely concerned with the rights of all people; they are, in the words of President Fujimori of Peru, 'the legal arm of subversion'.

Partial acknowledgement

Just as there are varieties of denial, so there are gradations of acknow-ledgement. In certain circumstances, governments may acknowledge at least some claims and appear to take the allegations seriously. This is often the response of observer governments. Either because of chan-ged political alliances or because the evidence is too embarrassing to explain away, they will threaten to abandon their ally or client and demand that it acknowledge criticism and act as requested. Admit that this was an extra-judicial killing; it cannot be justified; it must be stopped; no more aid for you unless something is seen to be done.

Such acknowledgement is rare from perpetrator governments left to themselves. But most countries with a democratic image to maintain have to go some way in this direction. They cannot indefinitely sustain strategies of ignoring allegations completely, crude denial, ideological justification or aggressive counter-attack. One response goes like this: 'We welcome constructive criticism; in fact, we are the only democracy in the region, and we allow human rights organizations to do their job without restrictions. We met with your delegation and will meet with them again. The human rights situation is not perfect, but we are showing restraint and doing what we can to improve things. The situation is difficult; things can't be changed overnight; you must be patient.'

Such expressions hardly add up to full acknowledgement – in par-ticular, because they avoid the specific details of the alleged violations. If these details are conceded, they are qualified by three devices:

- *Spatial isolation* Yes, the alleged event happened, but is 'only an isolated incident'. This is not systemic or normal; the circumstances were special; the victim was atypical; any violations arose from 'individual excesses' within the ranks of the security forces and are not condoned by the government.

- *Temporal containment*   Yes, this is what *used* to take place, in the past – before the new government took office, before we signed this treaty. But it cannot happen anymore.
- *Self-correction*   Yes, we are aware of the problem, and we are doing our best to deal with it. We have ratified the relevant human rights instruments, passed new domestic laws, met with human rights observers, set up judicial commissions of enquiry, appointed a human rights commissioner, and disciplined, punished or removed offenders from office.

This response is often genuine enough. In partial transitions to democracy, a government may be unable to go further, given limited resources, in-built corruption and inefficiency, the fragility of democratic structures, risk of sabotage by the armed forces. Even a genuine response may be interpreted by mid- and low-level officials as being merely the usual nod and wink (the two-track message) to go on doing what they always did.

The official discourse is inevitably a mixture of blatant lies, half-truths, evasions, legalistic sophistries, ideological appeals and credible factual objections. The success of the human rights movement is reflected in the fact that it seldom encounters a public dismissal of its agenda. But this success heralds dangers. The translation of the moral and pictorial image of atrocities into the legalistic, diplomatic, UN-speak and decidedly non-pictorial language of 'human rights violations' passes ownership of the problem into the professional and bureaucratic cartel.

However fascinating their commentaries on these texts of denial may be, they have little political impact. Even the most devastating exposures followed by even the most patently bogus denials do not disturb the order of things. Powerful governments, most notably that of the United States, still shield their allies and clients and deny their own involvement. As long as it suits them, they will stick to the denial narrative. They know that they can rely on a reciprocal – and unreflective – turning of many blind eyes. Everyone recognizes the lie, but no one cares.

Human rights advocates have a limited stock of responses to official counter-claims. They can reaffirm the human rights litany of absolute principles, universal standards and total ('non-derogable') prohibitions. This moral absolutism is easily ignored or dismissed with condescension. 'Get real,' says the government, explaining the circumstances that allow principles to be compromised by obvious necessity. Critics anticipate the exact details of these standard neutralization techniques and counter them in advance. Human rights reports thus *begin* by explaining: 'No, we have not singled you out for special criticism. We regularly produce equally critical reports about other countries.... Yes, we unequivocally condemn the acts of terror by armed oppositional groups in your country; we consistently take this position elsewhere.... No, we do not take sides in the conflict, nor do we favour any particular political solution.... Yes, we understand the long history of your conflict; we know about the atrocities against your citizens; we take seriously the threats to your security.'

Needless to say, there is no guarantee that these pro-active responses will prevent another round of government denial.[89] Nor will they evoke an active public response. The reason is that official accounts are not mere fictions or rhetorical flourishes. They are deeply rooted in national and international political cultures. Even well-informed and well-meaning people think, 'Yes, these allegations sound true – but what else do you expect the Freedonia government to do?' The exposure and denial of atrocities have become familiar rituals in media and public culture. This is what governments usually do; this is what Amnesty usually says.

Internally, the state naturally prefers a reliable public indifference to enforced compliance. No matter how strongly international prohibitions insist that no putative threat to public security can justify torture, virtually all citizens accept that any method to extract information is permissible to prevent an act of terrorism. No matter how strong the moral critique of accounts such as 'obedience to orders', there will be sympathy for soldiers who claim that they 'just followed orders'. These accounts have been offered and accepted long enough to be part of the moral fabric. A culture of denial is in place – with the equivalent coded messages, areas of evasion and meta-rules that are found in 'disordered' systems of family communication. This is what Havel calls 'living within the lie'.

Official denial means denial only in the vernacular sense; these are simply lies and deception, with no devious currents below the level of consciousness. But what about self-delusion? At least some people in the denial business, from political commissars to press officers, are sincere. They may begin as opportunists and careerists, then start believing in their own untruths. They become converted – in ways they seldom succeed in converting others. But the sequence may be reversed. Officials may start out with sincerity (or self-deception), but then become knowingly cynical and deceptive. These deceptions become desperate, almost a parody of official denial; the government knows this and knows that the public know.

The enigmas of denial and bad faith are encoded within the language we use to converse with ourselves about atrocities and suffering. The public texts of perpetrators and their apologists hardly need much decoding: listen to a spokesperson, political leader or bureaucrat come out with the usual patent lies, desperate evasions, subtle half-truths, pathetic reassurances, convenient fictions, absurd analogies. Where are these people in that cognitive space between knowing and not-knowing that they are lying? Perhaps they have already entered a post-modern version of the Oedipal state: knowing and not-knowing at the same time, but also not caring.

5

Blocking out the Past

Personal Memories, Public Histories

Before turning from perpetrators to bystanders, this chapter moves the time frame backwards: seeing these events as subjects of memory and history. In every part of the world, societies that seem relatively tranquil now are still dealing with terrible histories of atrocities and social suffering. The modern iconography of denial and acknowledgement still draws on the pasts of Hitler, Stalin and Mao. These have now been supplemented by the cluster of cases rather blandly termed 'democratization' or 'transitional justice': the collapse and dismantlement of the former Soviet Union and state Communist regimes in Eastern Europe; the transitions in Latin America (Brazil, Argentina, Chile, Uruguay, El Salvador, Paraguay) from dictatorships and military juntas to formal democracies; and the collapse of apartheid and the emergence of multiracial democratic society in South Africa.

There is no exact line between denying the *past* and denying the *present*. At what point does public knowledge of atrocities and suffering become a matter of forgetting, memory, history and commemoration? If we talk about the bloodshed of the Congo, Bangladesh or Biafra as having being 'consigned to memory' or 'belonging to the past', when will these phrases start applying to Chechnya, Angola and Kosovo? The media draw the clearest line: the events disappear from 'current news'. Wars end with an official peace; famines are declared to be over. The distinction may be banal, but denial talk about not noticing the present is different from talk about not remembering the past.

The distinction between *personal* and *public* will remain blurred. There is a realm of personal, private or autobiographical memories – about our private lives (childhood, family, school, being in love) or about our response to public events (how we felt during the Cuban missile crisis). The public realm is a shared, collective, sometimes 'official' past; what happened is slotted (in museums, textbooks, ceremonies) into recorded history. Individual memory is the subjective experience of this public past as recalled in the present.

The line between *denial* and *acknowledgement* is the hardest to sustain. It looks simple: the opposite of denying that something once happened is acknowledging that it did happen. An example: experiments on Afro-American prisoners deliberately not treated for syphilis were immediately covered up; the facts were suppressed for decades of rumour and allegation; the truth was eventually uncovered and finally acknowledged. In recounting such narratives, though, we cannot always isolate our knowledge of the denied past from the modes of acknowledgement (trials, Truth Commissions, confessions) by which this past became known. In the case of repressed memory therapy, this is an impossible separation. But for public atrocities and suffering, I leave issues of acknowledgement to chapter 9, followed by a chapter on acknowledging the present.

The fragility of all these distinctions is a major theme in Havel's writings about private memories and public histories in Czechoslovakia and the rest of Communist Eastern Europe. In the early seventies, he saw what was to come. People were aware that the price for daily pretence, denial and outward conformity was permanent humiliation and loss of dignity. Solemnly performing ritual acts which you privately find ridiculous, you deny yourself in public. But none of this is forgotten; the dissimulation remains buried in consciousness, caged up in emotional memory like a toxic substance. So, 'when the crust cracks and the lava of life rolls out', the search for public acknowledgement is formed by a private bitterness, a vengeful wrath.[1]

After introducing the concept of repression, I will look at personal denial of the private (autobiographical) past, using the case of the 'repressed memory syndrome'. My main subject, though, is the personal denial of publicly known past atrocities.

Prelude: repression

I follow convention by using 'denial' to refer to the present and 'repression' to the past. Freud's original contrast, though, was quite different: repression refers to *inner states* like emotions, while denial refers to *outer realities*. Repression is a far more significant concept in Freudian theory than denial, and its meaning even more elusive. Often repression is seen as entirely unconscious; at other times, it mutates into 'suppression' – a conscious decision to forget. Freud eventually used repression as a generic term for all defence mechanisms, and saw

it as the foundation of his whole theoretical edifice. One of his definitions of repression is a fine statement about denial: 'the effortless and
regular avoidance of anything that has once been distressing. . . . It is a
familiar fact that much of this avoidance of what is distressing – this
ostrich policy – is still to be seen in the normal mental life of adults.'[2]

Repression became the archetypal defence mechanism: keeping out
of awareness information that evokes the psychic pains of trauma,
guilt and shame. This generic use ignores the distinction between
troubling external events and troubled feelings about these events.
We may remember what happened, but repress the emotional tone –
or else remember feeling bad, while forgetting what we felt bad about.
These tactics are anyway doomed to fail. The repressed pain 'is not
really forgotten': it remains somewhere 'in there' – causing distortions,
pathological inner states and generally rotten 'symbolic behaviour'.
Therapists try to uncover these hidden layers; patients are generally
uncooperative: they resist, protest, whine and deny ('What, me?'). The
deeper the probe – today's unacceptable sexual desires, childhood
traumas, the infant's ur-memories – the greater the pain. But, in the
metaphor that Truth Commissions came to favour, the more profound
the wound, the more rigorously it has to be exposed.

Freud takes us a little further: 'The most peripheral strata contain the
memories which are easiest remembered and have always been clearly
conscious. The deeper we go the more difficult it becomes for the
emerging memories to be recognized, till near the nucleus we come
upon memories which the patient disavows even in reproducing
them.'[3] We enter a state of double unawareness – both of the original
repression and of our efforts to hide its emergence now. This is really a
triple forgetting: we forget, we forget that we have forgotten, then we
forget what we start to remember.

There are terrible penalties for all this fun and games. The first is
repetition. We keep doing the same stupid, destructive things.[4] But we
don't realize that we are repeating ourselves. This is the problem: the
diversionary cognitive schemata we habitually use keep the fact of
repetition from awareness. We forget that we did this before and don't
recognize – even deny – that we are doing it again. This is classic and
heavy self-deception: keeping even from ourselves the secret that this
'new' place, face or problem is not new at all. The second penalty is
leakage. Desperately as we press and repress, there is no way to keep
the hatches down. In the end, 'the truth will out'. Sooner or later, the
repressed will pay you an unwelcome visit. This is what Archbishop
Tutu means about the past coming back to haunt you – a metaphor
used even by secular advocates of truth, justice and reconciliation. The
clinical and the political become a metaphor for each other.

Personal memories, personal past

Probably the most bitter psychotherapeutic controversy ever to have reached the wider public is the story of the Repressed Memory Syndrome (RMS), False Memory Syndrome (FMS) and Recovered Memory Therapy (RMT). This troubling episode raises many issues about psychoanalytic theory, the concept of repression, the psychology of forgetting, and the vagaries of truth telling in personal life.[5] At the risk of tunnel vision, I use the story only to raise a rather simple matter: not everything that is denied must be true.

The RMS thesis is that very many women are sexually abused as children (usually by their father). Especially if this happens very early in life, the event is immediately repressed from consciousness; this is a major cause of much unexplained depression and other continuing psychic distress often labelled as hysterical or neurotic symptoms. The repression is total: there is literally no knowledge or memory of the experience. But the hidden trauma remains intact. Recorded as by a videotape, it is perfectly preserved while locked away for decades in a timeless zone of the mind, all the time silently working its damage. Current symptoms are mnemic symbols (often expressed somatically) referring back to unconscious memories of the original trauma. Forgetting – the inability to access a particular event – can only be caused by repression. But just as the event is 'lost' by repression, so it can be 'recovered' or 'retrieved'. RMT, Recovered Memory Therapy, is a combination of techniques – classic psychoanalysis, hypnotherapy and all imaginable New Age talk therapies or body work – to assist patients to recall their long-repressed memories of childhood sexual abuse.

The theory assigns extraordinary powers to the workings of repression. The version variously known as 'strong', 'massive' or 'robust' repression claims that 'Many children are able to forget about the abuse, *even as it is happening to them'*.[6] Conscious access to traumatic memories is then completely blocked off. These patients will believe that for years, even decades, they 'lived with' memories of two separate childhoods. The story they knew of normal (even 'happy') memories turns out to be a fantasy, a front protecting them from the awful truth. The other, the one they knew nothing about – the subconscious record of their abuse and suffering – is real. Strong repression is not the same as conventional motivated forgetting (we forget what we don't want to remember), which does not happen unconsciously or immediately; and does not consign memory to a solid-state pristine form. The avoided memory is accessible until it fades away through the normal process of forgetting.[7]

Two related notions strengthen the repression model for its proponents, but weaken it further for its critics. The first (close to the original Freudian idea of the 'split ego') is *dissociation*: one part of the self can so split away and distance itself from external or internal realities that it looks as if 'it' did not see (let alone do) what happened. The trauma of the sexually abused child is so unbearable that she dissociates by no longer experiencing the suffering as part of her sensed self. The mind thus deals with 'memories of traumatic childhood abuse which cannot be forgotten in the usual way, because they never succeeded in being fully known in the first place'.[8]

The second is the notion of *multiple identities* and the specific diagnosis of Multiple Personality Disorder (MPD). This extends the dissociation thesis further, with even more radical implications for the recovered memory debate.[9] The unconscious of the MPD sufferer registers secrets so dreadful that 'mere' repression – massive and motivated forgetting – cannot contain them. Memories do not even reach the stage of being repressed; the abuse is so awful that the mind cannot survive any awareness. Pieces of the self are created that function like self-contained personalities, each autonomous enough to cordon off forbidden or traumatic memories from the self as a whole. Each unintegrated piece of split self – over time, more fragments may join the original primal fragment – is termed an 'alter' (from the Latin word for 'other'). These alters are not aware of the core personality (what is left of it) or of one another; the core seems to have no idea of their presence. By the mid-eighties, these people ('multiples' as they are known in the business) were reporting sensational repressed memories: not just incest, but rape during satanic cult rituals, human sacrifice, baby breeding and abduction by aliens.[10]

The repressed and recovered memory thesis soon moved from its therapeutic setting to become a mixture of social movement, urban folklore and cult. This is when it began to attract increasingly lethal criticisms (labelled as evidence of further denial):

- Many acts of abuse indeed go unreported, but most of these are unreported not because they are forgotten, repressed or denied: the regime of denial enforced by patriarchal power is sufficient reason for silence.
- The thesis of robust repression, the notion that human beings can completely forget being repeatedly abused over a prolonged period of time, runs counter to everything known about memory. Its workings are inherently uneven and improvisatory – and so is

the gradual avoidance, then atrophy, of painful recollections. Single events are forgotten this way, but continuing abuse over years leaves behind a spider's web of intrusive and unwanted memories. It is similarly implausible that the hitherto repressed experience can be 'recovered' from the brain's storage-room and then re-presented in vivid cinematic detail.

- The RMS literature presents open-ended check-lists of human behaviour and feelings which are taken to indicate *symptoms* of repressed childhood sexual abuse and/or (with total inconsistency) *coping mechanisms* for dealing with these symptoms. These lists of items – feeling lonely, being afraid to succeed, low self-esteem, feeling different from other people, dreaming about spaces or objects, avoidance of mirrors, being overweight (or underweight), being sexually promiscuous (or having no sexual experience at all), having ambivalent relationships – are useless, but not harmless, for the millions of self-help consumers checking up on their victim status. Even more useless is the therapist's expert diagnosis: that your denial of abuse is definitive proof that it did happen to you.[11]

- Most people, especially those in mental turmoil, are highly suggestible. The methods used to recover memories – hypnosis, thiopental sodium (the 'truth drug'), body re-mapping, re-autobiography, primal screaming, age regression and guided imagery – leave patients open to therapeutic suggestion. These are vulnerable people, looking desperately for a causal narrative that makes sense of their misery. They are willing to fill in vague memories with details that are easily accessible in the mass culture – through self-help literature, talk shows and the media. This creative memory work is induced and rewarded (if only by an encouraging nod) by zealous memory recoverers. The results are often fantasies and fictitious memories. The suggestible patient joins the therapist (more well-intentioned than fraudulent) in a self-fulfilling spiral. Having been carefully created, the abuse narrative is believed and tenaciously defended.

- If the accused perpetrator, his family or other therapists allege that some element of imagination, suggestibility or fantasy is at work, this is indignantly rejected by patient and therapist. The victim, at painful psychic cost, goes through a 'gradual awakening'.[12] The accused is stigmatized, refused the legal presumption of innocence, and never believed. From beginning to end – the original events, the years of lying, and now the dramatic confrontation – he has obviously been *in denial*.

- Repressed childhood sexual abuse was soon assigned to the category of Post Traumatic Stress Disorder (PTSD), shared with victims such as Holocaust survivors and Vietnam veterans. But these comparisons weaken the robust repression thesis further. Clinical repression does not strike those who survive repeated and prolonged horrors. Langer suggests that for survivors and witnesses of the Holocaust and similar atrocities, time is durational as well as sequential.[13] Durational time is experienced continuously, not in a sequence of memories from which you can be liberated. Memories are not 'symptoms' to be uncovered and narrated to bring psychic peace and social integration. Indeed, 'Painful memories are not always disabling, and narratives about them ... rarely "liberate" witnesses from a past they cannot and do not wish to escape.'[14]

So, only the victim's original repression is authentic. Alleged perpetrators cannot possibly be believed. At the same time, the psychiatric establishment is blamed for refusing to acknowledge that childhood sexual abuse memories are *always* real. This refusal can be traced back to the Great Betrayal by Freud himself. According to this narrative, Freud in his early work (from 1893) believed that his patients' accounts of having been sexually seduced as children were true. Moreover, girls so abused were very likely to develop hysterical symptoms as grown women. By 1897, he rescinded this theory – bullied according to some by criticism, even faking patients' case histories – claiming now that memories of childhood seduction were false. These reported events did not actually happen, but were based on fantasy. The triumphant end of the narrative – after half a century of denial – is the success of feminists, psychologists and the Recovered Memory Movement to vindicate Freud's original position.

Three aspects of this debate go well beyond the subject of childhood sexual abuse. First is the muddle about the possibility of objective truth. The therapist's gradual recovery of her patient's memory is taken to replicate the triumphalist narrative of cultural acknowledgement. At both the personal and the social level, this is an essentialist model. There was and is only one truth: the facts of abuse and repression are there, just waiting to be uncovered. Faced, however, with requests for proof and evidence, the movement proclaims not merely scepticism and total epistemological relativism, but unapologetically states that whether the allegations are true or false *doesn't matter*: The patient and therapist must trust their 'inner voices'. The point of therapy is to validate the patient's subjective experience – her wellbeing is the therapist's concern, not whether the event happened or not: 'You can become too caught up in seeking external proof rather than internal relief.' The point is to 'avoid the truth trap'.[15]

The second confusion – knowingly spread by therapists – is between denial of child abuse at a societal level with denial on a personal level. The hard-won cultural acknowledgement of childhood sexual abuse as a social problem does not axiomatically mean that abuse has occurred in each particular alleged case. As Ofshe and Waters note, telling patients to accept their memories because society has denied them for so long is the ultimate confusion of the slogan 'The personal is political'.[16]

The third assumption is that mental health requires the excavation, explanation and even *reliving* of painful experiences; the deeper we dig, the harsher are the truths to confront, but the better off we will be. This project has a deep mythical appeal – the heroic journey back-wards in time, reliving the pains of the past, finally arriving at the truth that heals. There is, alas, no evidence that to get well, you must remember, or that you must reconstruct the past *honestly* to be happy in the future. Discovering and confronting painful truths may be valuable in itself, but cannot be taken for granted as a way to 'free yourself' from the past. The promise of liberation and wholeness is even harder to sustain, as we shall see, when referring to the collective 'working through' of the uncovered truths of whole societies.

Personal denials, public histories

For sexual abuse, incest, child abuse and rape in ordinary life, the confrontations between denial and acknowledgement take place in the private realm: the family, the therapist's consulting room, only rarely in a criminal trial or media story. Personal accounts are very different when played out against histories of known atrocities. The moment the account appears, if only to deny knowledge of the past, it is compared with public narratives, either shared ('our shameful col-lusion with the Occupation') or contested. Without these comparisons and discrepancies between the personal and the public, collective memory would become what it can never be: the arithmetical sum of the identical memories shared by all survivors, perpetrators and bystanders.

The perpetrator who did nothing and the onlooker who saw nothing symbolize the best known of these discrepancies. Let me mention, though, a far more unusual story of denial: Bar-On's study of people who were children of major Nazi activists.[17] Virtually all children of perpetrators were protected by their families from knowing the truth, about either their fathers' personal role or the extermination process as a whole. Moreover, the children didn't ask any questions – not of their fathers at the time, nor of their mothers and other family members afterwards. Bar-On describes the mutual interest of parent and child in denying or avoiding knowledge of what the perpetrators did, as a 'double wall of denial'. But the wider culture set up a third wall. These patterns of family collusion were not private and insulated: the fifties, when these children were growing up, was the period when German society as a whole did not talk about, let alone 'acknowledge' the past.

The democratic transitions of the nineteen-eighties reached their moments of truth much sooner. Each was different – what happened in Chile is not what happened in Czechoslovakia – but there was one fateful common question: what to do about the atrocities and suffering of the past? The search for *truth* or *knowledge* became a powerful form of accountability – meaning, as chapter 9 shows, not just uncovering factual evidence, but 'coming to terms' with the past. The rhetoric appeals to the same objectives as Recovered Memory: denials overcome, repression undermined, dreadful secrets disclosed, reality confronted, truth faced.

But 'doing something' about the past means more than getting the accounts right. The dominant meaning of accountability is *justice*. How should one deal with perpetrators from the old regime – death squads, torturers, informers, collaborators and their political superiors? Should their deeds be investigated and they themselves (like the perpetrators in family dramas of sexual abuse) hunted down, exposed, brought to trial and punished, suffer pain and humiliation, or make restitution? Or should not much be done at all: to let old wounds heal, to achieve national reconciliation, to preserve a fragile democracy, so that we may 'draw a line under the past' and 'close the book'? This could mean a collusive silence, a preparation for further cultural denial – but could also mean 'doing something' very different: forgiving the offenders, seeking reconciliation between them and their victims, integrating them into a reformed social order.[18]

Here we consider how the pasts of perpetrators (and some concurrent bystanders and victims) are denied and blocked off. I start at the personal level: with the ways people forget or 'forget' unpleasant memories. The public historical record is acknowledged, but one's own role is excised. There are two major symptoms of what may be called the 'Kurt Waldheim Syndrome': first, 'At the time, I didn't know what was happening', and second, 'I might have known at the time, but afterwards I forgot it all'.[19] The syndrome was evident in the 1994 Versailles trial of the French wartime collaborator Paul Touvier, a Milici official accused of killing seven Jewish prisoners near Lyon in

1944. Asked whether he was aware of the Vichy government's anti-Jewish decrees, he replied, 'No, I missed that.' Did he know of the mass deportations to Germany? 'We didn't have television then. I didn't know about it'; or 'I don't remember. It was all too complicated for me'.[20]

I am interested mainly in perpetrators. But the prototypical denial, 'we didn't know' ('we didn't have television then'), is shared with bystanders. There are three variants: *literal innocence, not-knowing* and *forgetting*. The simplest opposite is *admission*.

Literal innocence

In the public arena today, literal denials of the past are becoming more difficult to sustain. This is not to say that all mass atrocities and suffering are known about. But once exposed, they are more difficult to deny. The new political spaces and technological methods for scrutiny and recording cannot easily be patrolled by the powerful: global media reports, electronic communication, instant histories, victim testimonies, international monitors, opening of secret files.

Any one alleged perpetrator, though – at the Rwanda or Bosnia War Crimes Tribunals, for example – can still claim literal innocence. The defence will never offer an ideological justification, so the trial becomes not a political event, but – as was intended – a legal game. The plea is mistaken identity: 'you've got the wrong person'. Issues of identity and culpability appear in genocide or war crimes trials as much as they do in regular criminal courts. No international system can guarantee that literal denial cannot be sustained all the way: the chaotic conditions at the time, the breakdown of internal legal systems, deliberate revenge accusations, the fading away of media interest.

Not-knowing

The state of mind of 'not-knowing', for all its psychic complexity, is more open to some objective comparisons. Except in the most obscure cases, we can reconstruct enough to determine who could not have known, could have known, must have known, or should have known what. Most societies today have 'informed publics'; neither they nor those in the lowest loops of state power can easily be left in total ignorance by deception or segmentalized structures of responsibility. The sixties slogan, *Don't Say You Didn't Know*, was intended to combat the bad faith of radicals; it now applies more widely. Not-knowing does not sound a good account to offer a Truth Commission today.

As we move from core perpetrators (those 'in the know') to peripheral bystanders, memories are more difficult to organize. A decade after the events, Argentinian citizens would say, 'I was there; I saw it,' but also, 'I couldn't have known a thing'.[21] In fact, most of the disappeared were kidnapped from their homes; neighbours and observers knew exactly what they were witnessing. But some 'saw and didn't see, understood and didn't know,' and seemed to remain in this state even after the Sabato Commission and the trials of the generals. This was more than regular denial: some of the mental space of Argentinian citizens had been captured: 'The Terror needed a setting that was largely undisturbed. For if the setting radically changed, how could one assimilate what was happening there? If the missing were eerily present by virtue of their absence, in what sense were those present really there? Space was manipulated to make one thing clear: It was strictly forbidden to get one's bearings.'[22]

There will always be circumstances in which some people, even those in official positions, only knew some fragmented bits of the whole picture. But, as Arendt argued, moral, rather than factual, knowledge is at issue: 'Eichmann needed only to recall the past in order to feel assured that he was not lying and that he was not deceiving himself, for he and the world he lived in had once been in perfect harmony. And that German society of eighty million people had been shielded against reality and factuality by exactly the same means, the same self-deception, lies and stupidity that had now become ingrained in Eichmann's mentality.'[23]

Forty years later, South Africa's Truth and Reconciliation Commission heard some similar stories. In October 1997, the commission and almost the entire public, even those seemingly inured to decades of public lying, were amazed at the consistent denials by the notorious former Minister of the Police, Adrian Vlok. There was not the slightest doubt about his participation in the State Security Council, his overall responsibility for the police, and his specific control over police-organized death squads. Yet he stuck with two denial techniques. The first, was *denial of responsibility*: not only could he not be blamed for any human rights abuses, but, as minister, he had tried his best to instruct the police to treat blacks and whites equally. Any abuses that may have occurred were not explicitly ordered. 'We at the top took certain decisions and used certain terminology without thinking about it. It worked its way to the ground, where people misrepresented it.'[24] Other witnesses also claimed that their intentions had been 'misrepresented' in precisely the same way: instructions to 'eliminate' a particular ANC activist meant to remove him from the area, not to kill him. The second appeal was *denial of knowledge*. Vlok claimed to have been kept in the dark by the lies of his own police commanders. He never knew about torture and death squads. His language now became concrete and absurdly literal: 'There was never any report on my desk [saying] "we tortured someone or we killed someone and buried his body". I never approved it, it was never brought to my attention.'

Vlok's most senior police commander, General Johan Coetzee, used the same language to disavow all knowledge of these murders: 'it never came to my knowledge', 'it was not reported to me', 'it would have been completely out of the correct procedure'. Asked by a lawyer whether this meant that he was incompetent, turned a blind eye, or was complicit in the killings, Coetzee did not hesitate: he chose incompetence.

Someone slightly lower in the hierarchy than Vlok gave the Commission a different narrative of 'knowing' about the same reality. Leon Wessels, former Deputy Minister for Law and Order, presented a fine analysis of this type of denial:

> I do not believe the political defence of 'I did not know' is available to me, because in many respects I believe I did not want to know.... In my own way, I had suspicions of things that had caused discomfort in official circles, but because I did not have the facts to substantiate my suspicions, or I lacked the courage to shout from the rooftops, I have to confess that I only whispered in the corridors.... It may be blunt, but I have to say it...the Nationalist Party did not have an inquiring mind about these matters.

Not having an inquiring mind – just like Oedipus. But Wessels is a better source than the Greek classics: this is a clearer, more comprehensible and more accurate description than any tale of blind eyes, averted gazes, heads in the sand and ostriches. Many institutions – armies, police forces, government departments, cabinets, the arms industry, care institutions where children are abused, work-places where women are harassed – are full of people who do not have inquiring minds. These people and their states of mind appear in every Truth Commission and war crimes trial. They are also present in investigations of illegal arms dealing, political corruption, discrimination and abuse of authority. This is not a flat denial of any knowledge at the time, but a claim either not to have grasped the significance of the event or not to have known the big picture. Information was transmitted on a 'need to know' basis; tasks were compartmentalized; everyone deceived us; work was focused on means rather than ends; *no one* figured out the whole story.

Let us make the unlikely assumption that this was indeed the case – a deception of Le Carré–like complexity and impermeability. But let us also assume that isolated role players sensed (with their third eyes?)

that something bad was happening. At this point, Deputy Minister Wessel's admission of bad faith – whether this came from remorse or further posturing – makes all the difference. His muted understatement – even irony, if this is possible – conveys the essence of not-knowing: 'the Nationalist Party did not have an inquiring mind about these matters'.

The same questions apply to all historical bystanders, perpetrators and victims: how much did they *know*, *could* have known, or *should* have known. In the Nazi years, denial of knowledge by millions of Germans no doubt derived from not caring enough to have inquiring minds. But millions more – besides those directly implementing the extermination policy – in government and public offices (and their employees, from train-drivers to postmen) knew something about the mass murders: not the big picture or all its components, but certainly where specific tasks and segments were leading. Hilberg concludes: 'The indispensability of every function in the destruction process and the interconnection of all the actions performed by the perpetrators were not obscure, opaque phenomena. The nature of the process could be recognized and understood by its lowest ranking practitioners.'[25]

This is not the context in which to use terms like 'function', 'process', 'phenomena' and 'action'. Memories of atrocities and suffering are more concrete. Imagine the scene in an ordinary-looking suburban villa in Berlin in 1940, the operational centre for 'Aktion T-4', a code name for the 'euthanasia' programme. The men and women sitting there are busy at their jobs of organizing and covering up the murder of thousands of people. Burleigh comments:

> It is no use describing them as 'desk-bound murderers', somehow remote from murder, since even the secretaries shared their offices with jars of foul-smelling gold-filled teeth, listening to dictation which enumerated 'bridge with three teeth', 'a single tooth' and so on. To bring this account down to the moral level at which these people operated, one should mention that all T-4 employees could avail themselves of cut-price dental work, which utilized gold recycled from the mouths of their victims.[26]

Could these employees totally repress all memory of where those gold teeth came from?

Forgetting

Yes, this is just what some people claim: 'It was so many years ago'; 'I'm an old man now'; 'That whole period is buried in time'. They have forgotten whether and how much they participated in such events.

Perhaps they were not even there, and only heard about these things from others. Or a more opaque 'interpretive forgetting': they remember something happening but not knowing just what was happening. There are, to simplify beyond simplification, two extreme possibilities. One is 'genuine', very robust repression, memory loss or amnesia. That is: Someone who was a functioning adult at the time simply *forgets* being in the Aktion T-4 office or in Rwanda watching twenty people hacked to death with a machete. This claim is literally incredible – whether an account of instant repression through dissociation (a bizarre notion) or the long-term drip of normal memory loss. At the opposite extreme, forgetting is simply a 'prototypical fully-fledged lie'. You remember what you did or what happened – whether perfectly, partially or vaguely – but for obvious reasons, you deny this.

There are infinite possibilities in between. Without them (like the nuances of denial) twentieth-century literature would not exist: the weaknesses and failures, the blank and blind spots of memory, but also its powers, conscious and unconscious, to create, invent, imagine and rearrange the past. The experience of having our memory 'jogged' is enough to prove that the 'recovery' of things past is not always in our control. Memory is less a filing cabinet that we open to examine a pre-selected file (*my childhood, the war*) than a book we are writing and editing. The more ambiguous the event, the more room there is for this 'memory work'. Garton Ash has nicely shown that the network of informers, agents and collaborators revealed by opening his own (or anyone else's) Stasi files does not yield a clear memory of 'what really happened'.[27]

The political guile of state officials has combined with information technology to allow new modes of forgetting. The Iran-Contra hearings in the USA and the Arms to Iraq (Scott) Inquiry in Britain revealed more than the crude destruction of incriminating evidence.[28] Documents need not be burnt or shredded in mass, nor computer data simply wiped out. They can be electronically rearranged to create an entirely false chronology of events (and cast list) to present to later inquiries, trials or historical scrutiny. These post-modern histories, moreover, are constructed not just after the event (or change of regime), but while things happen. Ideally, deniability should be so planned at the time that when participants testify later, they don't have to lie. As Oliver North told the Select Committee, 'My memory has been shredded.' In this strange world (parodied by the Clinton–Lewinsky saga) memory is not what you can remember, but what other people are allowed to tell you that you knew. Ministers told the Scott Inquiry that they often had to ask their civil servants which documents they had seen in the past and therefore what they could be considered later to have known. Memories of the present are falsified in advance, to ensure that future claims about forgetting and not-knowing are true.

But whether in modern or post-modern times, there are some atrocities, some images of suffering, that simply do not belong in these halls of mirrors. Perpetrators and observers only pretend to forget. This hardly ever happens to victims. They may have phases of forgetting or denial, but most of them, most of the time – contrary to the repressed trauma model – are quite unable to shut out their memories. In the recent revelations about children sexually abused in Catholic orphanages, some thirty years elapsed before private memories became public. But during all this time, these private memories were never repressed. For the most powerless of victims, like families in South Africa silenced for decades, the pain of telling replicates the original suffering: 'This inside me . . . fights my tongue. It destroys . . . words. Before he was blown up, they cut off his hands so he could not be fingerprinted . . . So how do I say this? – this trouble . . . I want his hands back.'[29]

After the first waves of revelations, the testimony literature of Holocaust survivors became more about the collective acknowledgement of memory. The problem is not remembering the story – most listeners know the public narrative – but you have to locate and make sense of memories which you yourself cannot fully believe. The impossibility lies not in seeing the past reality, but in perceiving it *as* reality: 'to recapture through memory what, because of the impossibility of its content, has already . . . fallen outside memory.'[30] Some survivors recall trying to convince others to believe what they themselves cannot quite believe.

Such testimony demands more than normal powers of recall. Survivors have to strain against disruptive memory to find any continuity between their recollections and the rest of their life. The horrors were experienced in a 'counter-time'. Ordinary, 'common memory' tries to locate these experiences in some familiar narrative, to 'mediate' or even normalize the atrocity. But beneath the surface is a 'deep memory' that corrodes these comforts and suspends belief.[31] The chasm between ordinary and deep memory arises because of the reality that could not be known – in the sense of assimilated – at the time. The attempts to record, transmit and preserve evidence during the actual occurrence of events (smuggled notes, buried diaries, secret photos) were not enough to 'bear witness', because it was beyond human ability and willingness to grasp what was happening.[32] It was 'the very circumstance of *being inside the event* that made unthinkable the very notion that a witness could exist'.[33]

Admission

Perpetrators, of course, may also be visited by a sense of unthinkability: 'How could I have done something like that?' But this is already an admission, if not yet a testimony. In a war crimes tribunal, few defendants can be expected to 'come clean' and say something like, 'Yes, I did everything listed in the indictment. Do with me what you will.' Like ordinary criminal defendants, they (and their trained advocates) are defending their right to deny. Some pasts have been so atrocious, and the lies so blatant, that even if admission is accompanied by acceptance of responsibility and expression of remorse, this may be (and is often interpreted as) a tactical ploy to get a lighter sentence. This is more likely in settings like the South African Truth and Reconciliation Commission, where public truth telling ('full disclosure') and the expression of remorse help to gain indemnity from prosecution.

Many feel that this type of acknowledgement comes too easily. The sight of previously unrepentant racists suddenly turning into tolerant multi-cultural liberals is not pleasant. Have they 'really' changed, or only been swept up by the tides of history into public revisions of their politically incorrect autobiographies? It turns out that everybody really was more innocent, even far better, than they seemed at the time. No, it wasn't that they 'did not know', but they were always secretly *unhappy* with the old system. This is what Arendt originally described as 'inner opposition' or 'inner immigration'.[34] After the war, many people – even those who had been in the Reich leadership – told themselves and the world that they had always been 'inwardly opposed to the regime'. The slogan of 'inner immigration' has now become a bad joke in many parts of the world. South Africans are particularly cynical about the apparent ease with which some of the worst perpetrators have adopted the rhetoric of the 'new South Africa', as if the past never existed. It now appears that nobody, not even civil servants and politicians, ever believed in apartheid.

Collective denials, public histories

Cultural versions of psychological concepts – collective memory, cultural repression, collective denial, shared forgetting, social amnesia – assume that an entire society can forget, repress or dissociate itself from its discreditable past record. This may happen either through official state policy – the deliberate cover-up, the rewriting of history –

or through cultural slippage in which information just disappears. Personal denials of historical events draw on these shared narratives. It is easier for you to 'know nothing' if your society claims that 'things like that could not have happened here'. Organized denial works best when people prefer 'not to have an inquiring mind'. Slow cultural forgetting works best when powerful forces have an interest in keeping people quiet.

The classic cover-up

Here are two prototypes of the atrocity cover-up. One: the 1941 Babi Yar massacres. The Germans shot 33,000 Jews in two days; the bodies were buried in mass graves, then dug up again to eradicate all evidence, bulldozers working for a month, bodies doused with gas and burnt; the concentration camp workers used for this project were then themselves killed. Two: the elaborate hoax staged in 1943 in Theresienstadt for a visiting Red Cross delegation. Gardens were planted, a building refitted as a synagogue, and a monument erected to honour dead Jews; a band played Strauss waltzes, a film showed how well the inmates were living, and a children's opera was performed. (Afterwards, most of the cast, including nearly all the children, were sent to Auschwitz.)

Variations on Babi Yar (numbers, circumstances, methods) can be found in any human rights report on political killings. And all politicians, journalists and political pilgrims have been taken to less extreme versions of Theresienstadt – happy prisoners, smiling peasants, cheerful workers. (Times have changed – political figures and international humanitarian workers are now likely to be shown even *more* suffering than there is.)

State-organized denial

Those two variations of the instant cover-up merge into the standard discourse of official denial reviewed in the previous chapter. Charny has even proposed a set of 'templates for the denial of a known genocide'.[35] These include:

- Do not acknowledge that the genocide took place.
- Direct denials should not be attributed to the government or high leaders, only to functionaries and anonymous spokesmen.
- Deny the facts of the genocide by transforming them into other kinds of events.

- Represent the perpetrators as victims and the victims as perpetrators (or as lesser victims than others were).
- Not only deny the facts of the genocide outright, but advance counter-claims that the victims were treated well.
- Insist as long as possible that all the data are not available, that allegations are forgeries and hoaxes, and that further research is needed and/or that new research disproves the claims of genocide.
- Question the statistics, so that the number of dead victims is smaller than usually stated.
- Move from the facts of the genocide to some kind of relativist comparison that mitigates the horror of these events.
- Distance the event in time – it all happened so long ago, there is a new generation of the (perpetrator) people today, why not let the wounds heal?

The most consistent, strident and elaborate state-organized attempt to conceal a record of past atrocities fits most of these templates: the eighty years of denial by successive Turkish governments of the 1915–17 genocidal massacres of the Armenians. At least a million Armenians were killed directly or through starvation or forced deportation. These events are documented in Ottoman sources as well as in diplomatic reports at the time, survivor testimonies and later historical research.[36] This is not the usual story of initial unconfirmed rumours giving way to certain truths (as in the recent saga of the former Yugoslavia). Rather, the opposite: truths that were certain at the time and the object of international attention were transformed into speculation, rumours and uncertainties. The initial denials entered collective culture in Turkey and slowly became more prevalent outside: the events did not take place; Turkey bears no responsibility for any loss of life; Armenian deaths were an unintentional by-product of bad conditions; the term 'genocide' is not applicable (at least a debatable issue).

At the international level, indifference gave way to oblivion. The Turkish government succeeded as a client state in forcing the American superpower to disavow its previous acknowledgement of what happened. From the cold war era till now, Turkey has used its strategic NATO value to coerce the US and other governments into supporting the denial. During the 1980s, Congress abandoned its initial support for some commemoration of those killed, and the Administration agreed not to mention the Armenian matter in the United Nations. The Turkish government uses public relations agencies to produce propaganda and disinformation, instructs diplomats on denial techniques, tries to censor textbooks, closes archives and allegedly forges documents, and pays academics to discredit critical scholarship.

One such bitter episode was the Turkish attempt to cancel the International Conference on the Holocaust and Genocide organized in Tel Aviv in June 1982. The future of Turkish–Israeli relations was at stake; there were vague hints about risks to Jews in Turkey. The Israeli government shamefully co-operated by putting pressure on the organizers to cancel either the whole conference or sessions that mentioned the Armenian issue or to withdraw invitations to Armenian scholars. The government contacted participants to ask them not to come, then suggested moving the meeting to another country, then withdrew financial support and recognition. The conference organizers resisted all these pressures, and the event went ahead as planned.[37]

A new generation of Armenians – especially after 1965, the fiftieth anniversary of the atrocities – began to break the silence and try to reclaim their history. But Armenian churches and monuments in Turkey were destroyed, and in international arenas the Turkish government continues its original denials and attempts to obliterate any commemoration – a double onslaught on the Armenians' existence.

Few denials have been sustained with such determination over such a long period. Typical cases in modern times fit a different pattern: the event takes place in a closed setting; perpetrators set up an internal denial circuit, often maintained by their successors; circles of survivors and bystanders know the truth, but are too weak to break this circle; eventually – because of political change or whistle blowing – researchers, historians, journalists or a Truth Commission begin uncovering what was hidden.

Danner's study of how the truth about the 1981 killing in the remote El Salvador village of El Mozote fared is a detailed micro-politics of this type of denial.[38] Members of the US-trained Atlacatl Brigade systematically murdered some 794 people, many of them small children. The essential facts of the massacre were known and disclosed almost immediately. The *New York Times* published photos and a credible report. Just as immediately, the official denial machine took over. Two local embassy officials crafted reports to the State Department designed (in their own words) to 'have credibility among people whose priorities were not about getting at what exactly happened'. The *New York Times* journalist who broke the story was pulled out of Central America under State Department pressure. US government officials came up with elaborate linguistic tricks and prevarications to deny the whole story: reports, even if based on eyewitness accounts and photos, were discounted as 'unconfirmable' and therefore untrue. The denial was patently constructed to avoid opposition to renewing aid to the El Salvador regime – and was readily 'believed' by collusive politicians. In 1992, eleven years after the massacre, the mass graves were exhumed, and the truth was revealed to the UN Truth Commission set up under the peace accords to investigate past abuses by the government and the opposition.

As a contrast, consider two European welfare states. First, Sweden: from 1935, peaking in 1946 and stopping only in 1976, the Swedish government forcibly sterilized some 60,000 women. This was part of a programme to rid Sweden of 'inferior' racial types and promote Aryan features. The victims included women with learning difficulties, those from poor families or who were not from 'the common Nordic blood stock'. There were no references to this forty-year programme in school or history books. Second, the Netherlands: up till the late 1960s the Dutch Finance Ministry stored a large hoard of gold, silver, jewelry and household valuables looted by the Nazis from Dutch Jews in the 1940s. The owners had been murdered in the death camps, and the property never reclaimed. But instead of tracing or trying to return it, the Finance Ministry organized in 1969 a clandestine internal auction among its employees. So many people wanted to take part – the property was being offered at its 1958 taxation value – that officials drew lots for auction places. These civil servants knew exactly what they were buying: thousands of cash and property deposits had been meticulously filed as 'Unowned Jewish Property'. As the Dutch daily paper *De Volkskrant* wondered, 'Who would give his wife a present of earrings taken from a Jewish woman gassed in Auschwitz?'

Ideological denial

The Holocaust denial movement is the best known, but also most unique, case of organized denial: fully ideological, yet organized by neither the perpetrator state nor its successors. The movement's story and its 'revisionist' history of the annihilation of European Jews have been chronicled in detail.[39] The 'movement' consists of tiny, marginal and unknown groups – anti-Semitic, racist and Fascist – loosely tied into a network of international organizations, publications and internet sites. Besides the occasional media event and court case, their major impact has been on American university campuses. Student newspapers became eager carriers of the denial 'debate' – under the potent joint sponsorship of the traditional liberal value of free speech, post-modern identity politics and dumbed-down multiculturalism.

The meta-message is that every view should be published, and all facts are up for grabs. The revisionist historians' dismissal of the entire Holocaust as a 'hoax' or 'myth' is just another point of view: Jews died from natural causes or overwork in labour camps; there is no evidence for the gas chambers (the gas was too weak to kill and was used only for delousing; the chambers were actually built by Americans and Russians after the war); the Final Solution is a Zionist myth devised to bolster support for Israel. Fanatic and simply insane as this literature might be, it merits attention if only because the logic of all atrocity denials is similar. The techniques of Holocaust denial draw on a standard repertoire found in all forms of propaganda.[40] The partial success of the 'revisionists' in provoking a counter-response and giving even formal respectability to the rhetoric of denial[41] suggests how much easier it is for other far more obscure cases to be forgotten and denied. Or else Holocaust denial is just one among the 'weird things' (UFOs, TV psychics, alien abductions, that Elvis Presley is still alive) that many people, especially Americans, believe.[42]

Other cases of historical denial are ideological in the sense of being patterned, but not having a movement behind them. For years before the 1994 atrocities in Rwanda received media attention, Lemarchand was referring to Western forgetting of previous genocidal massacres in Rwanda and Burundi as 'the politics of ethnic amnesia'.[43] The forgetting of homosexuals and gypsies as Nazi victims are especially egregious cases. The Roma were clear objects of genocidal intent, defined by the same statutes as Jews and destroyed in the same way (20,000 out of the Nazis' 500,000 Roma victims were killed in Auschwitz). But the *Porraijmos* ('the great devouring', the Romani equivalent of *Shoah*) had no cultural capital, literary tradition or powerful sponsor. Other massacres – Uganda, Bengal, the Ache in Paraguay – are more deeply lost to official history.

There are also strategic and ideological shifts to fit different times. During the worst horrors of the Pinochet regime in Chile, well-informed, middle-class people, who must have known about the disappearances and torture, simply denied what was happening. After the transition to democracy, they openly acknowledged that these abuses happened, but switched to justification: current stability and economic success have vindicated the junta; it was necessary to save the country from the chaos that Allende caused.[44]

Cultural slippage

The most profound forms of cultural repression become part of consensual reality: blind spots, shared illusions and zones of tacitly denied information. When the origins of these blind spots are ideological and coercive – the histories that the state prefers not to be known

– then the Freudian notion of 'repression' is curiously relevant. Collective memory is pressed into shape by being repressed.

Uncomfortable knowledge, though, can be forgotten without direct state manipulation. Whole societies have an astonishing ability to deny the past – not really forgetting, but maintaining a public culture that seems to have forgotten. The blind eye is the backward eye. When circumstances change – renewed pressure from victims, the chance opening of an archive – then newspaper editorials (without irony) remind us that this is 'what we always knew'. The dramatic political upheavals in East Timor in 1999 forced an instant acknowledgement of past silence about atrocities. But the sources of this denial are too deep; the Timorese have been reassigned to oblivion.

These forms of knowing shade into the archetypal *open secret*: known by all, but knowingly not known. The denials may be initiated by states that can rely on their citizens to maintain the façade. Or, like Foucault's image of a strategy without a strategist, the collusive wall of silence is built without any agency responsible. Some revelations are too revealing to reveal. 'Washing your dirty linen in public' is a curious metaphor: it concedes, contrary to intention, that there is something dirty to hide.

The Katyn massacre was a state-organized denial abetted by cultural slippage, yet always retained in private memory. In March 1943, Russian soldiers massacred some 14,700 Polish army officers and 10,600 Polish prisoners of the NKVD. The bodies of 4,000 officers were found by the German army in Katyn forest near Smolensk. Only in 1990 did Soviet officials abandon their claim that the Germans were the executioners. This was the classic Stalinist open secret: most Polish children born after the war were told the truth about Katyn and learned to dismiss the Soviet and Polish Communist cover-up. The authorities insisted on the lies, knowing perfectly well that no one believed them. As Havel shows, lies don't have to be believed as long as you participate in public rituals that affirm their acceptance of lies. In October 1992, Yeltsin released to the Polish Government the original top secret order direct from the Politburo.

The recent exposures of Zionist myths about the creation of the 1948 Palestinian refugee problem is another example. The Israeli story – that Palestinians fled their homes because of their leaders' instructions and in expectation of returning after the enemy had been defeated – was always disputed. Arab propaganda made exaggerated claims that all Palestinians were physically driven from their homes. Now, a cohort of Israeli 'new historians' (unfortunately once named 'revisionist historians', the term used for Holocaust deniers) have carefully documented the deliberate Zionist policy of forced expulsion and deportation of Palestinians from their villages. Some 400 villages were depopulated during the war or destroyed in the next five years, and were literally made invisible. The Israeli establishment was outraged that its 'own' intellectuals had so carefully shown what they and everyone else knew from personal memory. The term 'ethnic cleansing' would be anachronistic, but not inappropriate.

In the meantime, Palestinians had carefully compiled 'memory books' about the layers of denial each village passed through before final obliteration from the map. The pre-1948 Arab village of Ein Houd is a trope for the whole transformation: it became Jewish Ein Hod, an Israeli artists' village whose own residents and its cosmopolitan international visitors did not 'know' its history or 'see' the adjacent remnants of Ein Houd al-Jadidah, inhabited by Arab Israeli 'internal refugees' and designated as 'illegal'.[45]

These examples could be multiplied. Historical skeletons are put in cupboards because of the political need to be innocent of a troubling recognition; they remain hidden because of the political absence of an inquiring mind.

6

Bystander States

I now return to my main subject: reaction to knowledge about the suffering of others. My working distinction is between *internal bystanding* – coming to know what is happening around you, in your own society – and *external bystanding* – knowing about other countries. In either case, the term 'passive bystander' (or 'passive bystander effect') refers, strictly speaking, only to people who have already seen, known or heard about the situation – yet have still not reacted. Up to that moment, they are just bystanders. But unlike similar terms – 'onlookers', 'passers-by', 'audiences', 'spectators', 'observers' – the word 'bystander' has acquired the pejorative meanings of passivity and indifference.

Prologue: 'It can't happen to us'

If even potential and eventual victims, despite a clear buildup and warning signs, can deny or minimize their risks ('it couldn't happen here...not to people like us'), not believe that the unthinkable is already happening to them, then surely observers cannot be expected to grasp the truth. This may be a disingenuous denial of responsibility for not inquiring or intervening. But, as we know from many non-political cases, there are indeed cultures of victim denial.

The unfolding perception of the Final Solution by European Jews themselves has become a prototype of collective denial. In the thirties, few people took Hitler's rhetoric seriously. Nazism was seen as a temporary phenomenon, a set-back to be endured till it passed. In Germany each new anti-Jewish measure, each escalation in persecution, was seen as the last. Even as the massacres started, rumours, then confirmed reports and survivor stories, were all disbelieved. Laqueur lists the familiar denials: 'these are like traditional pogroms...just isolated incidents, the work of a local commander...it can't get worse than this...Germans are cultured, this is Europe, not a jungle...this cannot happen to innocent people...common sense tells us that these stories cannot be true.'[1]

At all stages, right up to the end, there was massive deception, secrecy and misinformation – the staggered mailing of fake postcards from the camps, assuring families that all was well; the coded language; the elaborate hoax of the shower rooms. Self-deception and a cruel version of the 'optimistic bias' allowed these deceptions to work and forebodings to be evaded. People were easily taken in, but also took themselves in. The nature and sheer scale of the Final Solution were impossible to imagine. We ask, 'Why didn't they see what was coming?' But expectations for the future are built on familiarity with the past. It was hardly possible to foresee extermination or gas chambers when these had never been heard or conceived of.[2] Arendt's judgement is harsher: 'self-deception had to have been developed to a high art to allow Hungarian Jewish leaders to believe at this moment [after Eichmann's arrival in Budapest in March 1944] that "it can't happen here"...and to keep believing it even when the realities contradicted this belief every day of the week.'[3]

These forms of cultural denial were built on firm historical foundations. Primo Levi often tried to explain why German Jews in the thirties, despite the presence of so many warning signals, still found ways to deny the dangers and to manufacture 'convenient truths'. Like their Aryan counterparts, he writes, 'not only did they not foresee, but they were organically incapable of conceiving of a terrorism directed by the state, even when it was already all around them'.[4] He quotes an old German adage: 'Things whose existence is not morally possible cannot exist.'

In his heart-breaking novel *Badenheim 1939*, Appelfeld conveys the haunting absence of the unthinkable facts.[5] It is spring 1939, and Badenheim, a resort town vaguely near Vienna, is preparing for its summer season. The regular Jewish middle-class visitors arrive. The characters, immersed in their personal lives, manage to misconstrue every signal of their fate. Then more visitors arrive, not the usual vacationers. Slowly, almost imperceptibly, there is awareness of what we, the readers, know from the beginning.

There was also denial and passivity shown by Jews in the *Yishuv* (the pre-state, Mandate period in Palestine) to the unfolding news of the Holocaust.[6] One extraordinary strategy was to displace the present into the past. From the earliest days of the war, the end of 1939, the political leadership began slowly to talk about the Holocaust as if it were already over. Segev interprets this as a way of coping with the terrible news from the countries they came from or knew about – and their own powerlessness to help. So, 'Instead of thinking about the holocaust in terms that would require effective and immediate action, they exiled it from real time into history.'[7] Newspapers worded the story as if it had happened a long time ago. While the massacres were still going on, the leadership had already started to blame one another for their apathy and failure to rescue – as if the event were long over. Some even began thinking about memorials. In September 1942, a proposal was first made to establish a memorial to victims. A committee was set up to discuss this. Soon after, the proposed memorial was given the name it eventually carried, *Yad Vashem*: 'there was no clearer, more grotesque, even macabre expression of the tendency to think of the holocaust in the past tense: while the Yishuv discussed the most appropriate way to memorialize them, most of the victims were still alive.'[8]

Survivors are acutely aware of denial. They remember their *own* inability to believe that what was happening was really happening. Now that atrocities are filmed live and survivors are immediately interviewed in 'real time', we can see that those memories of unreality are accurate. They are not merely cultural suggestions picked up after the event. The faces, voices and gestures of ethnic Albanian women – driven from Kosovo, their menfolk taken away by Serb militias – show fear and shock but also a hallucinatory inability to grasp what has happened to them. They look like figures from their own dreams. This sensation only heightens their fear that even if they do survive to testify, *others* will not believe what happened.

Internal bystanders

The term 'internal bystanders' refers to knowing about atrocities and suffering within your own society. Most explanations of passivity – not noticing, doing nothing, walking by – derive from psychological models inspired by the Kitty Genovese case. This research gains from being 'situational': we can observe and even manipulate variables in the situation (number of bystanders, identity of victim, degree of distress), identify typical bystander scenarios (bullies in the playground, beggars in the street, a neighbour attacking his wife), and identify outcomes (no empathy for the victim, felt empathy but no action, empathy and action).

This situationalism, though, is also the model's weakness: the lack of an outside social context. We use the same concepts to leap from observers of a child being humiliated by her father in a supermarket to witnesses of their friends shooting their neighbours in the village square; from not stopping to help a stranded motorist on the highway to closing the door to a Jewish family in Poland seeking refuge from the Nazis. I have made these leaps too easily myself. After summarizing the situational approach, I will look at some wider political cultures.

Situations

A schoolchild watches his classmates physically bullying another boy; neighbours see a woman in the street screaming and being attacked: these are the prototypes of passivity as not helping, or trying to find out more, or speaking out. Here again are the familiar situational causes: *misperception* – not understanding what is happening; *diffusion of responsibility* – when too many others are present, each person is less likely to help; *fear* – of becoming a victim yourself; *denial* – blocking out any realization of the event's significance; *lack of empathy; boundaries* – victims are beyond your universe of moral obligation; *psychic numbing* – diminishing capacity to feel; *routinization and desensitization* – each further item of suffering becomes predictable, normal and without any special imperative to respond; *no channel of help* – you don't know how to intervene (what to do, whom to tell) in ways that will make a difference; *ideological support* – onlookers who share the world-view of the perpetrators obviously do not intervene.

But how are these disembodied 'variables' experienced subjectively? Do bystanders feel guilt that their passivity helped to allow the atrocity to take place? Most of us can recall the childhood shame as we silently watched a friend being beaten up by school bullies. We are requested now to imagine what we would have done if we had been one of Kitty Genovese's neighbours. When I look at those famous photos of Viennese streets a few days after the *Anschluss*, I examine the faces of the crowd, looking at Jewish women forced to scrub the pavement, a boy painting the word *Jude* on his father's store, elderly religious men humiliated as Nazi soldiers violently cut off their beards. Just what could have been going through the minds of these observers? Some are jeering, some grinning, one group looks like an audience at a street theatre, others look totally blank, eyes barely focused.

Even in these frozen situations, time stopped in a single visual frame, there are infinite gradations of moral responsibility. Bystanders can become, even for an instant, active participants. By applauding, they become helpers or accomplices. But what if they merely look on in total silence? Is this also a blameworthy form of collusion or encouragement? There is too much self-righteous rhetoric about bystanders' blameworthiness. Most victims and perpetrators take passivity as evidence of support and encouragement. But as perpetrators well know – this is what they intend – passivity may result from fear. As the Milgram laboratory studies graphically showed, external compliance does not mean that there is no internal concern or unease. Bystander passivity is not the same as bystander indifference.

Those Vienna street snapshots show onlookers' responses only at that instant of time. We can now interpret these images only because we already know the political narrative and where it ends. As observers of the observers, we can increase the size of the photos' cognitive frame. We extend it outwards: What did the *Anschluss* mean? What was happening in Austria and elsewhere in Europe at the time? And we extend it backward, into history: What preceded these 1938 events? What was the history of anti-Semitism in Austria? (Non-political cases can also be extended: Why are these school bullies predominantly boys rather than girls? Does the ethos of masculinity inhibit boys in the crowd from helping?)

In political conflicts, observers may share the same ideology and identify with the perpetrators; or they may fear and hate the perpetrators and identify with the victim, or belong themselves to the potential victim group. Any of these possibilities may lead to watching in silence. Ordinary Serb families in Bosnia did little to encourage the initial violence, but then silently moved into the houses of their neighbours who had been ethnically cleansed the day before. The moral chains of bystanding are extremely opaque – whether prior states of knowing and not-knowing, or later choice between silence and intervention. It once made sense to think that the further the bystander from the primeval action, the less she is culpable. The witness to a political killing tells her husband what she saw; he tells his workmate, he tells his wife. At each stage, according to one moral viewpoint, the chain of responsibility weakens. But a late-modernist atrocity is different. Scientists design the weapons, and engineers manufacture them; international business cartels run the trade; bankers launder the money from narcotics deals (to which 'liberation' groups may be party); government officials turn a blind eye to export laws; corrupt law enforcement officials take bribes ... and so on. All these people are physically very distant from the killing, but are morally closer to being perpetrators than the chance passer-by who sees it. ·

Slogans about us 'all' being complicit and guilty are too facile. 'Inability to identify with victim' – a standard item on the situational list – is equally complicated. In clichés about bystander passivity, urban anonymity, alienation and anomie, the victim is always assumed to be a stranger. You don't know who he is; you cannot 'identify' with his plight. But internal bystanders to real atrocities are often not faceless strangers at all – they live in 'situations' where they know the victims and could become victims; they know the perpetrators, or could become perpetrators. In settings as different as Rwanda and the former Yugoslavia, people stood by even when their neighbours, schoolfriends and workmates were forcibly expelled from their own homes, hacked to death in front of their eyes, or driven off in buses to be shot.

Chapter 10 provides some consolation from these bleak images. There is no 'situation' of total passivity. Not even fear, ideology, religion or ethnic loyalty can coerce everyone into permanent acquiescence. Commitments and attitudes change over time. Recollections of previous silence and collusion now feel shameful. A sense of human decency or a sudden impulse to help can override, in an instant, the heaviest political pressures to keep silent.

Political cultures

'Bystander' is a convenient enough term to describe people who are neither victims nor perpetrators. It is altogether misleading, however, when applied to cultures of denial that permeate a whole society and are lived through by everyone. Less complicated terms – 'ordinary people', 'citizens', 'the public', 'public opinion' – are quite adequate.

The totalitarian state of Orwell's *Nineteen Eighty-Four* aspired to total control over information about past and present. You don't know, and you don't know what you don't know; you pay a terrible price for too much knowledge or even trying to know more. But no society has ever existed in this pure form. You cannot be literally ignorant of everything unpleasant going on around you. Even the most repressive and closed regime cannot achieve total secrecy or information control. Ordinary citizens come to know some truth, but are terrorized into lying to themselves, as well as to outsiders. Perpetrators and officials 'act' their daily lives, putting on a show that nothing unusual is taking place. Even within the same society, silence and faked normalization (the witnesses who see nothing) can be traced to different sources: direct state coercion, subtle encouragement or self-imposed concern with your country's image.

But how can the impression be sustained that everything is normal when it so manifestly isn't? Imagine that visible evidence and signs surround you; you know the truth from local media, rumour and shared culture; you know what everyone knows, and they know that you know. Telling a foreign visitor that you don't know what's happening is easy, permitted, and encouraged. This is a simple lie, not self-deception. The increasing transparency of all societies to global scrutiny, however – the invention of electronic mail alone – has made literal lying virtually impossible to sustain. CNN footage of soldiers shooting passive demonstrators is seen all round the world.

Literal denial to your fellow citizens – who know that you know – requires further tactical collusion. You have moved from sight to insight, but your meta-insight tells you that it would be wise (for the time being, until things change, until the public wakes up, until things blow over) to play a little dumb in public. Geras nicely captures the nuances of not-knowing, even about mass murder: 'There are the people who affect not to know, or who do not care to know and so do not find out; or who do know or do not care anyway, who are indifferent; or who are afraid for themselves or for others, or who feel powerless; or who are weighed down, distracted or just occupied (as most of us) in pursuing the aims of their own lives.'[9]

More open societies generate looser cultures of selective and self-imposed denial. The soldier who lies to a foreign journalist draws on stock cultural messages: don't snitch, don't blow the whistle, don't give comfort to the enemy, and don't wash your dirty linen in public. There is an unarticulated social contract about what subjects are 'better not spoken about'. Whole societies are constructed around what Havel called 'living in the lie'. The essence of white consciousness in apartheid South Africa was a continuous shutting out of what seemed 'obvious' to any outsider.

This applies even more to interpretive denial. People who readily admit to themselves, their fellow citizens and even outsiders that 'something bad is happening' find it difficult to use the language of genocide, death squads or torture. Some ways of naming reality are not admissible.

In many societies that inflict cruelties on their own citizens, ethnic minorities, occupied or colonized populations, there is little difference between perpetrator and observer accounts. Some regimes prefer active support; others are satisfied with a silence that can be taken as affirmation. Either way, onlookers can be safely offered official justifications rather than apologetic neutralizations. They are not zombies: they know what is happening, but this does not disturb them, either emotionally or morally. They have nothing to 'deny' because they don't care.

The atrocity triangle (perpetrator/victim/bystander) is different when observers are closer to victims. As violence against the original target group widens, observers become more vulnerable. But self-interest, may be counterbalanced by misreading general ('it can't happen here') and personal risk ('it can't happen to me').

Two bystander states look to be universal. The first is *passive support* (or internal collaboration): most South African whites supported apartheid by just 'going along' with their government's policy. The second state is *passive opposition* (or inner emigration). In both Israel and South Africa, pockets of bystanders with liberal values survived the sights and demands around them by retreating into private life. If the society changes, even larger numbers of people claim to have always been opposed to the regime, though they chose not to express this openly or were too frightened. They conformed outwardly, but in their inner psychic space, their oppositional thoughts remained intact ('what I do is not what I think'). The way to sustain this inner/outer split is to cut yourself off from the unpalatable aspects of daily reality: by not watching TV news or reading newspapers, not talking politics with your friends, plus an intense, almost caricatured immersion in private diversions (concerts, cinema, holidays, picnics, sports). In Brazil during the nineteen-seventies, a special term, 'innerism', was coined for the urban middle class who turned inwards and disavowed the political. In the former state Communist societies, inner exile was the defining feature of whole subcultures.

For self-identified liberals this is more than a cognitive retreat to avoid being upset by exposure to disturbing news. They subscribe to universal values, they are uneasy about what they know is happening – but they are reluctant to be too outspoken or to 'get involved'. If the conflict has been protracted, this innerism may be more a sign of burn-out and demoralization. But even if most people 'just don't want to know what's happening', this does not explain why other people in the same culture, sharing the same values, react differently. Nor is this adaptive strategy always healthy. It may create a patho-logical alienation from self and society, or reaction formation in the form of an exaggerated defensiveness about one's country's record, or even a literal rather than simulated blindness to what is happening.

Many societies can be chosen as case-studies, with many gradations between the two extremes of dictatorship and liberal democracy: the traditional authoritarian regimes in the Middle East and South-East Asia; the 'collapsed states' of West Africa, where government author-ity has given way to chaos and permanent violence and ethnic conflict; the violent oscillations between democracies and military juntas in Latin America; societies with relatively democratic internal institu-tions but repressive rule in their colonies, client states or internal

enclaves. I will single out four well-documented cases, on the axis
between coerced and self-imposed silence.

Ordinary Germans

We must repeat the question of how much ordinary Germans knew
during the Nazi years. The simplest answer is that at an early stage, the
majority knew the general outline of the extermination policy, though
not all the details. There is still disagreement about what, when, how
and to whom this information became known. But there can be no
doubt that large sections of the population either knew or suspected
what was happening in the East.[10] The massacres in the Ukraine,
Lithuania, the Baltic countries and Eastern Galicia became known to
millions of Germans almost immediately. Laqueur concludes about
this early period – from June 1941 (the euthanasia programme nearly
over, half a million Jews already slaughtered by the *Einsatzgruppen*) to
the end of 1942 (concentration camps and gassing well under way) –
that although only a handful of Germans knew everything, very few
knew nothing.

Rumours about the death camps came from soldiers on leave and
spread widely; by 1943 the use of gas was discussed by Germans and
even by foreigners; in January 1944, SS men were mailing photographs
of the Auschwitz crematoria and ovens with corpses. Tens of thousands of Germans and many more of the conquered peoples of Eastern
Europe had been actual witnesses: assembling in village squares,
fields, valleys and river banks to watch hundreds of Jews killed in
one operation. Circles of knowing expanded, to families, civil servants,
local politicians, professionals, and people living round the camps.
Despite secrecy and disinformation, the Final Solution was an open
secret. This is a simple conclusion – though the concept of an 'open
secret' is by no means simple. What do 'to know' and 'to believe' mean
in these situations? And know or believe *what*? There were enough
public hints for the millions of Germans who knew that Jews had
disappeared to realize that this was more than 'resettlement'. Yet few
knew the details. 'It is, in fact, quite likely that while many Germans
thought that the Jews were no longer alive, they did not necessarily
believe that they were dead.'[11] This is the type of logical inconsistency
accepted in wartime, reflecting a disintegration of rationality.

The alternatives are not active engagement versus disengagement
with reality, or support versus disagreement. There are states – mental
and political – where denial means *not giving the information much
thought*: 'Mass destruction was accompanied not by the uproar of
emotions, but by the dead silence of unconcern.'[12] Was this silence

knowing encouragement because most victims were Jews, or a general (less ideological) readiness to go along with state authority? Either way, citizens were inured to the unfolding extermination programme. They didn't think or care much about it; it was an awkward, unimportant topic compared to the many other problems of daily life. The leadership was continually disappointed by the regular assessments of public mood prepared by officials. These reports showed a widespread indifference to all events that did not immediately touch personal life. This indifference was the dominant theme. Bankier's description of this prototypical mode of denial echoes in many other times and places: 'they knew enough to know that it was better not to know more.'[13]

People knew vaguely what was happening, but just as vaguely didn't care. This combination does not result in innocence and blind ignorance. As Hilberg notes, 'Even if one looked away, asked no questions, and refrained from talk in public, a dull awareness remained.'[14] Like 'not having an inquiring mind', the phrases 'better not to know more' and 'dull awareness' stand out. They evoke the most resonant of all bystander images: people living next to a concentration camp going about their daily lives. What did they know? Did they try to find out? What did they tell their children? And if they knew, how did they feel?

Horwitz, in his fine study of the people living around Mauthausen, describes the last phase of the camp's existence from the fall of 1944 until the liberation in May 1945. There were too many bodies for the existing ovens in the camp. Some 11,800 corpses were interred in two mass graves near the town. Additional inmates were shot and buried along the route of the evacuation march, all in full sight of the civilian population. Then, in the spring of 1945, 'bystanders to the horror of the concentration camps cautiously slipped from view. To the outside world they have remained invisible ever since.'[15] After the victims and rescuers had left, the bystanders returned to go on with their lives. They never spoke of what they had known of the camps. Surviving inmates, who had acutely sensed the presence of these people, would later ask them: 'What did you see? If you knew, then why did you fail to respond?'

Horwitz describes the topology – the layout of the camp, the contours of the ground, the rock quarries where inmates worked (and were killed), the location of houses in full view of killings. This conveys exactly what Mauthausen residents – 'good Austrians' – *must have seen*. But how did they interpret what they saw? The cumulative exposure to brutalities (the first prisoners had arrived at the camp in August 1938) disturbed some nearby residents. One woman filed a complaint in 1941: because her property was elevated, she was an 'unwilling witness' to such 'outrages' as inmates being shot in the quarries. The badly injured were left lying next to the dead even for half a day. 'I request that it be arranged that such inhuman deeds be discontinued, or else be done where one does not see it.'[16]

The SS warned residents to ignore what they could otherwise not help but notice. 'Citizens learned that if awareness of what was happening in and around the camp was unavoidable, one might still look away. Although cognisant of the terror in the camp, they learnt to walk a narrow line between unavoidable awareness and prudent disregard.'[17] Without such a line – 'unavoidable awareness' on one side, 'disregard' on the other – the concept of denial is useless. Adding the word 'prudent' conveys the political culture of fear, secrecy and insecurity in which these particular bystanders lived.

At Castle Hartman, initially designed to gas the mentally handicapped victims of the (supposedly abandoned) euthanasia programme, the medical staff also 'worked with' sick inmates sent from Mauthausen, eighteen miles away. Despite great effort to hide the evidence, the odour of burning flesh wafted over the surrounding community; residents sealed their windows at night to shut out the smell. Sometimes thick plumes of smoke hovered above the castle and tufts of hair floated on to the street. A closed van known as the 'ash wagon' drove almost daily to the Danube to dump human ashes. The SS quickly responded to the spread of an accurate 'rumour' that people were being killed. The Castle's director, SS captain Christian Worth, convened a meeting of citizens in the local tavern. He gave them an official explanation of the smoke: assorted 'ecclesiastical items' (shoes, images of saints, vestments) were being burned. Anyone who continued to spread the absurd rumour of burning bodies would be severely punished.

In April 1944 another concentration camp was set up in Melk, some forty-eight miles from Mauthausen. In the year of its existence, 5,000 of the camp's 14,000 inmates died from beatings, shootings and work accidents. Each day the inmates were openly marched through the town and put on trains to work: tunnelling underground armament factories. The townspeople believed, as they had been told, that the inmates were hardened criminals; the odour of smoke from the camp crematorium left no doubt that they were being incinerated.

What was done with this knowledge? The following are three women with different memories of what they saw and did and smelt:[18]

- *Frau G. S.* recalls the smoke: 'one smelt the skin, the way it irritates. It has this peculiar odour. And the hair, one smelled that.' Her perceptual tone, records Horwitz, was 'matter-of-fact'. The inmates were criminals; they had died from exhaustion and hunger, not deliberate maltreatment; their disposal in this way was routine. As she strolled along, she could easily explain the odours: 'I said "uh, huh, someone is being burned again." '

- *Frau Maria R.* paid more attention. She started helping the inmates by surreptitiously dropping fruit or potatoes along the route of their march through the town. This got too much for her. She started praying, 'Dear God, an end. Please make an end to it all, because I must never look at that.' Horwitz perhaps awards her too little moral sensitivity: 'the burden of witnessing was itself a form of torment. One simply did not want to look at or think about such things. One "must never look" precisely because to see was to raise unwanted questions of choice and action.'
- *Frau S.* remained silent throughout. She never spoke about, or sought to look at, the camp, even when asked. It was best to pretend it never happened at all. 'I am happy when I hear nothing and see nothing of it,' she said. 'As far as I am concerned, they aren't interned. That's it. Over. It does not interest me at all.' She made a choice: she saw but looked away and ignored what her eyes told her.

The Mauthausen study is a close political analogue of the psychology of denial:

- Bystander awareness is involuntary: the townspeople cannot help but see, smell, sense and know.
- But some people still maintain that they *really* did not see. Others knowingly turn their backs, pretending that nothing is happening.
- This expresses the ultimate wish not to know. Yet you cannot, by an act of will, entirely disengage all your senses: 'one really did not see anything. Only the uncomfortable feeling was present.'
- The townsfolk recognize the smell of bodies burning. But the explanation that people are being deliberately killed is denied. The senses work perfectly, the brain is flooded by all the proper signals: the smoke, the cremation in the camps. 'But the meaningful conclusion is not drawn, cannot be drawn: people are being killed by thousands before one's eyes and ears, under one's nose.'[19]
- The residents did not lack any special cognitive facility. What they lacked was moral recognition, a sense of concern that motivates one to want to know more. Instead, the gaze was straight ahead, the blinkers on, the neck stiff, the angle of vision shutting out the horror.

- The seemingly identical external indifference may not have the same origins. Herr B. was a silent yet attentive observer; he was disgusted by what he saw but 'held his tongue and acted blinded' because of the prevailing climate of fear. By contrast, Frau E. was the type of bystander who, 'though unable not to see what was happening in the nearby camp, chose not to look, or inquire'.
- These choices were not entirely voluntary. The authorities had an unwritten contract with the public. 'The camp administrators would do all within their power to spare the residents direct knowledge of atrocities occurring inside the camp. In turn the residents would make no effort to learn ... To avoid discomforting moral questions it is best to be uninformed. The regime helped people to remain so by warning them against being too curious.'[20]

Living around the concentration camps entailed passive and pro-longed observation, unlike the situation during the early years of the *Einsatzgruppen* in the Baltic states. The spectacles there generated curiosity and knowledge. Local residents could see or hear the stages of each operation: rounding up the victims, herding them into the village square, taking off their clothes, screams of fear, shootings, the bodies being dumped into mass graves. The term 'bystander' is too casual in this case. Some spectators were demonstrably indifferent; this was not their business – 'shrugging the shoulders' is the natural image. More often, they gaped, spurred on, joined in or offered to help. In Kovna (Kaunas), Lithuania, Jews were beaten to death with crow-bars, while the watching crowd cheered and laughed. Mothers held up their children to see the action. German soldiers took photos and stood around like spectators at a football match.[21]

    People came to see things for themselves; they were not chance passers-by. Browning records an execution area 'visited by scores of German spectators from the Navy and the Reichsbahn (railway)'.[22] Many would travel long distances to get the best places at the 'shooting festivals'. Klee describes this as 'execution tourism'. In Zhitomir (Ukraine), on 7 August 1941, some 150 local civilians assembled in the market-place to watch an execution; visiting German soldiers had a better view sitting on the roofs. Two Jews were first hung on the gallows. Another fifty were herded on to a lorry. An announcement came over the loudspeaker that spectators should follow the lorry to the shooting site, some 150 metres away. The Jews were made one by one to jump over a ditch. Most of them fell in. They were then lined up – facing a stack of logs – and shot in the neck. Some visiting soldiers watching by chance were dressed in bath-ing trunks.

Unlike ordinary tourists, local inhabitants actively colluded and helped. Even before the killings, they willingly identified, isolated and helped to transport the victims to the killing sites. They took over jobs, moved into houses, and stole possessions. On the two nights of 25 and 26 June 1940, some 3,800 Jews were killed in Kovna by local Lithuanian partisans. A visiting German officer records that on the next day he 'became witness' to 'probably the most frightful event' he had seen over two world wars: a blond man standing at a petrol station, a wooden club in his hand; at his feet, fifteen to twenty dead or dying people, their blood being washed away by a hose. The man then gives a 'cursory wave' to the next in a line of men guarded by civilians; he clubs the man to death, 'each blow accompanied by enthusiastic shouts from the audience'.[23] A German photographer comes across the same scene: the young Lithuanian has now finished killing forty-five to fifty people; he puts the crowbar aside, fetches an accordion and, standing on the pile of corpses, plays the Lithuanian national anthem; the local people (including women and children) join in singing and clapping. Nearly all the bystanders are German soldiers.

Klee captions some photographs of a similar scene: 'According to their statements the locals and the German administrative officials and police officers did not see anything. Only the photos exist.'[24]

Cultures of fear

The few public scenes in the Latin American 'cultures of fear' decades later were different.[25] Atrocities were directed against highly selected victims, and were supposed to be clandestine. But the public had to be given enough information to be persuaded that the repression was justified. The Argentinian junta generated a richly verbal and sophisticated version of the 'double discourse': the balance between making state terror known, yet hiding or denying its details. The regime would deny (by definition) the existence of disappearances, and simultaneously proclaim that victims got what they deserved. Everything is normal – yet at the same time opponents are demonized, repression justified, and terror heightened by uncertainty. The barrage of communiqués from the junta left Argentinians living in an 'echo chamber', 'hearing the regime use language to disguise its true intentions, say the opposite of what it meant, inspire trust, instil guilt in parents to seal their complicity and spread a paralysing terror'.[26]

In between the constant noise of words, events were staged with an exaggerated theatrical quality: twelve armed men in three cars abduct an unarmed victim in the street. These were 'public' spectacles, but *also* clandestine and later totally denied. Details of the torture, the killings, the disposal of the bodies remained genuinely secret. State violence was enacted behind closed doors, but abstract terror was continually projected on to the public. The representation was coded, but deliberately allowed the junta's agenda to be decoded: 'The eerie, overwhelming silence of the victims – tortured but absent – was paralleled by that of the audience, terrorized by having "witnessed" the abstract spectacle that the Junta at once staged and forbade.'[27] This life in two worlds, public and secret, each with its own encoded discourse was true denial: bystanders recognized what they saw, yet avoided this recognition; knew the general facts, yet would not believe them.

The political split between closed and open created a state of mind – like the Freudian ego split – that was expressed afterwards in the common refrain 'we knew but we didn't know'. And even if you did 'really' know, the price for making public knowledge open was too high. Fear generated a state of self-censorship – you avoided talking in public or even with your friends, you monitored internal thoughts and dialogues. A self-consciously ideological regime like the Argentinian junta wanted more. Media communiqués were aimed at everyone – even the victims' family and friends, who were told to keep quiet about the disappeared person, because news would only cause them dishonour. Parents should reflect on their own responsibility for their children's behaviour. Perhaps their lack of concern had caused this trouble? Did they know what their older children were doing right now? Relatives and friends should make a collective decision to forget this person or consider her as dead. They could even suggest to others that she had voluntarily abandoned them and that, due to this irresponsible attitude, she should be punished by collective indifference.

The 'disappearance' was surely proof of guilt. From your window, you see a Ford Falcon draw up next door; four men in civilian clothes get out; a few minutes later, they emerge with your neighbour's daughter, bundle her into the car, and drive off. According to the authorities, these things do not happen, and surely they are unbelievable. But there must be an explanation. Here the regime exploits your eerie uncertainty: your silenced knowledge cannot be right; only the authorities know the real truth; they must have secret knowledge of the victim's guilt. Hence the refrains: *Por algo sera* ('It must be for something') and *Algo habra[n] hecho* ('He/she/they must have done something'). These are incantations of compliance: 'The refrains were an informal rite of obeisance; they deferred to the military; they conceded in bad faith that the military knew the "something" that the public did not know, the "something" that made atrocity just and necessary.'[28]

Another common refrain at the time was *el silencio es salud* ('silence is health').[29] The phrase was actually coined in 1975 by the Municipality of Buenos Aires in a campaign to reduce traffic noise by limiting the use of car hooters. Only after the *coup* did the phrase take on different meaning – not forced on the public, but a reflex 'bystander sense' of what was required of them.

As time goes on, the state wants more than silent observers. Estranged and under observation themselves, their retreat into silence and private space converts them into victims. Or else, by justifying the repression, they become supporters, at first mystified, then more trusting. In these political cultures, forms of denial oscillate in magical combinations.

Maoist China is an extraordinary case in which witnesses were silenced by a culture of fear not enforced by violence, or even organized by any co-ordinated state disciplinary agency. The art of silencing derived from a highly decentralized coercion and 'psychological totalism', marked by what Tu Wei-ming calls 'the pervasive voluntarism of the victims as well as the victimizers'.[30] Passivity and acquiescence can easily be condemned as political blindness or outright cowardice. But deep layers of self-criticism and a spirit of sacrifice prevented hatred and a sense of injustice from surfacing. The terror inflicted on millions of intellectuals was, in Lu Xun's term, caused by an invisible 'soft knife' that cuts so deeply that society as a whole, rather than any individual, bleeds.

Living in the lie

I will do no more than paraphrase Havel's writings about Eastern European communism in the decades before its collapse. His accounts of everyday denial in these societies apply, uncannily, to places not like them at all.

These were ugly, repressive regimes. Public culture, however, was centred not on fear of the sharp knives of a violent police state but on an all-pervasive dulled anxiety of what might happen if you didn't at least pretend to go along with official definitions of reality. You must sustain an image of a united society supporting its government: 'For fear of losing his job, the schoolteacher teaches things he does not believe; fearing for his future, the pupil repeats them after him; for fear of not being able to continue his studies, the young man joins the Youth League.'[31] Political actions – dummy voting, rigged meetings, staged demonstrations – required people to deny their real opinions, to look like confident, self-satisfied citizens. Everyone was vulnerable because he or she had something to lose (work, status, children's education). Everyone was aware of the invisible web of controls, collaborators and informers, even if this couldn't be seen or touched. Everyone was publicly bribed; no one believed in the official ideology. This hypocrisy, far from being condemned, was encouraged. The only ways to survive were selfishness and careerism. This was a moral climate in which indifference – dismissal of everything that went beyond routine everyday concern – became an 'active social force'.[32] This 'innerism' – escaping from the public sphere into private life and consumer interests – was welcomed by the authorities, who continued with their bombastic slogans about revolution and freedom. Their ultimate message was: avoid politics, leave it to us, keep quiet.

Havel's concept of 'evasive thinking' was the Communist version of cultural denial – and actual party ideology. Phrases and slogans separate thought from reality. Language becomes a ritualized end in itself, gaining 'a kind of occult power to transform one reality into another'.[33] The clichés of the official discourse are reproduced in the wider political culture: 'putting things into proportion', 'in context', 'isolated incident', 'the public interest'. Contextualization becomes another form of evasive thinking: 'What looks like an attempt to see something in a complex way in fact results in a complex form of blindness. For if we can't see individual, specific things, we can't see anything at all.'[34]

The ideology is not internalized by ordinary people. Quite the contrary. Official ideology encourages a collective deception, which everyone knows to be a deception. Havel's famous actor – who should be as well known as Sartre's waiter – is the greengrocer who places in his shop-window the slogan: 'Workers of the world, unite!' He does this not because of any enthusiasm or even thought, but because he's always done it, everyone does it, that's the way it has to be, no point in making trouble. The subliminal message of the slogan is what matters: 'I know what I must do, I am obedient.' He would be ashamed (as Havel cruelly notes) to display the degrading sign 'I am afraid and therefore unquestioningly obedient'. Far better to display his disinterested conviction and maintain the illusion that a system based on hypocrisy and denial is in harmony with human nature. The system works because people are capable and *willing* to live within the lie.

> Because the regime is captive to its own lies, it must falsify everything. It falsified the past. It falsifies the present. And it falsifies the future. It falsifies statistics. It pretends not to possess an omnipotent and unprincipled police apparatus. It pretends to respect human rights. It pretends to persecute no one. It pretends to fear nothing. It pretends to pretend nothing. Individuals need not believe all these mystifications, but they must behave as though they did, or they must at least tolerate them in

silence, or get along well with those who work with them. For this
reason, however, they must live within a lie. They need not accept
the lie. It is enough for them to have accepted their life with it and in it.[35]

Living within a lie is universal. But this was a special version. In an old
Soviet joke a comrade explains why she needs to visit both an ophthal-
mologist and an ear doctor: 'What I see, I do not hear; what I hear, I do
not see.'

Israel: a special case?

The Israeli culture of denial does not derive from state communism or
military dictatorship: Jewish and even Arab citizens of Israel have
most benefits of democracy: the rule of law and space for dissent.
But denial of the injustices and injuries inflicted on the Palestinians
is built into the social fabric. The Jewish public's assent to official
propaganda, myth and self-righteousness results from a willing identification – not fear of arbitrary imprisonment, commissars or secret
police. Many topics are known and not-known at the same time. Israel
is a country full of 'open secrets'. Even those known to the whole
world, like the existence of Israel's nuclear capacity, are protected
with a bizarre tenacity. Official lies are uttered with a straight face,
and received with a knowing wink.

During the decade of the *intifada* from 1987, no one believed official
denials about specific allegations, such as torture, undercover death
squads and killing unarmed demonstrators. But they went on living
'within the lie', exactly in Havel's sense. Most were not ideological
zealots any more than his Communists were Communist zealots.
But they have an unreflective attachment to the pious kitsch of
Zionism and its myths such as 'purity of arms'. There is little hypocrisy or pretence, and none of the irony of Havel's feigned 'Communists'. Unlike the Prague greengrocer, Israeli Jews display flags on
their cars and balconies on every public occasion without any obligation.

There are, of course, good historical reasons why Israeli Jews
should have a defensive self-image and a character armour of insecurity and permanent victimhood. The result is a xenophobia that would
be called 'racism' anywhere else, an exclusion of Palestinians from a
shared moral universe and an obsessional self-absorption: what we do
to them is less important than what this does to us. The close inter-
penetration between civilian and military life (an army drawn largely
from universal conscripts and reservists) means that the public is
less an 'audience' than a reliable source for confirming common

neutralizations. Perpetrators can always assume a populist vindication. The institutions of democratic accountability, however, send out
a more ambiguous message: abuses are authorized (otherwise they
would not happen), but condemned and disowned if they become too
visible or gross. Individuals selected for moral boundary marking
rightly see themselves as victims of a double message: go ahead, we
approve; but remember that we may publicly disavow you.

Two examples from the early months of the *intifada*: on 19 and 21
January 1988, Israeli soldiers entered the two West Bank villages of
Hawara and Beita. Their orders were quite clear – though, since their
origin in Defence Minister Rabin's instructions to 'break the bones' of
suspected rioters, they had been relayed with ambiguity and deniability. The soldiers (using a security service list) pulled twenty young
Palestinian men from their homes, took them to nearby fields, gagged
them, tied up their legs and arms, then threw them on the ground.
They then implemented Rabin's orders: with clubs, stones and by
hand, they systematically broke the arms and legs of each Palestinian
except for one whom they left able to walk for help. A military bus was
left running in the background, revved up by the driver throughout to
muffle the screams.

Public and media reaction kept up for two years, concentrating on
the eventual court martial of the senior officer who gave the proximate
orders. He received wide support from his family, friends and 'bystander' opinion, who all accepted his plea that the higher echelons of the
army had 'thrown him to the dogs'. There was much attention to the
nightmares and traumas of the soldiers; the victims were never mentioned again.

On 5 February, within a few weeks of this incident, a group of
Israeli soldiers entered the village of Kafr Salem, arrested four Palestinian youths, beat them with clubs, and then ordered an army driver
to run them over with his bulldozer. He refused, but instead shovelled
earth and garbage over them until they were almost completely
covered and buried alive. The soldiers departed, and the youths
were dug out by the villagers, unconscious but alive. The overwhelming public reaction was sympathy for the four soldiers who were
arrested. Their families – speaking on behalf of other more detached
bystanders – found the appropriate denials ('A Jewish heart can't
do such a thing') but also the exact sociological explanation: 'Our
brother is the scapegoat who was chosen to prove that there is justice
and democracy in Israel...they'll now set up a show-trial.' One of
the soldiers spent his first days of detention crying; he felt that everyone must be against him. He then began to understand that the other
prisoners, the police and indeed the whole country were behind

him: 'you can feel how their hearts break when they see me crying. Understand, I'm not ashamed of what I did, but what they are doing to me hurts.'

Not everyone, of course, was behind him. For Israeli liberals there is a dissonance between their professed universal values and such events. One resolution is to break ranks and step out of the bystander role into dissent and activism. Another is to return into the safe arms of the consensus. You publicly deny what you privately know and recycle the stock neutralizations. You pretend to believe that dirty work is done by others; your own people surely – sons, husbands, neighbours, friends, colleagues – would surely not have behaved like the Beita soldiers.

We have seen the third solution, 'inner emigration': living in the head, avoiding any more information or confrontation. For some people, this pose is just that: underneath there really is indifference. For others, there is genuine internal opposition: shame about their government, concern for the future, and a deep sense of the power-lessness and fatalism that encourages retreat into private life. When human rights observers exposed another ugly story, liberals would say, 'Thank goodness someone is out there digging out this stuff'; but also, 'Enough stories. Leave us alone, we know already how bad things are.'

Without any serious erosion of its self-image, the political culture came to normalize torture, prolonged administrative detention, death squads, taking civilian hostages, and collective punishments such as curfews, deportations and house demolition. Revelations about these recent abuses are widely acknowledged to be true. But 'revelations' about the past, especially the expulsion of Palestinians in 1948 (and its anachronistic hint of ethnic cleansing), are far more threatening, and are immediately placed in the double discourse of private and public knowledge. Every now and then, a public figure forgets to speak in code. During election campaigns, Yitzhak Rabin (never one for sim-ulation) would reply to right-wing hecklers demanding that Arabs should be expelled ('transferred'): 'Don't tell me about expulsions. No one here has expelled more Arabs than I have.'

Internal denial has another twist: the difference between what can be said inside and outside the country. In Israel, information is quite freely circulated inside, but there are self-imposed inhibitions about being too outspoken outside. Human rights or political activists who go 'beyond the consensus' in criticizing Israel abroad are labelled *malshinim*, the Hebrew word for 'informers', literally those who betray their own people to the enemy.

External audiences

Denial and indifference by external audiences are much simpler to explain. It is quite abnormal to know or care very much about the problems of distant places. You may be deeply affected by a four-minute television report showing yet another trail of refugees in Kosovo – miserable, bewildered, hungry, sick. But channels of information like a TV news item or an Amnesty leaflet can easily be deleted or isolated. We turn off the television, throw away the leaflet and return to daily life. No elaborate edifice of rationalizations is required. Some evasive accounts ('It's too confusing to sort out what's happening') can be put forward in reasonably good faith. But outside perceptions are pre-structured. Before the drama starts, we are cued to recognize the trusted ally who can do no wrong or the 'crazy state' which can only do wrong. This political framing overlays the simple sentiment that this has nothing to do with us.

Using the extreme case of genocide as a backdrop, I will list the four different senses in which the concept of 'external bystanding' has been applied.

External knowing

The concept of cultural denial assumes that we can assess what millions of people actually *do* know despite their denials. We just take for granted or infer what people 'must' have known or know about atrocities elsewhere. The rhetorical phrase 'what the whole world knows' may be nearly true for Bosnia and Kosovo, but not for anywhere in pre-television times, or most places now. Assertions about collective knowledge usually refer to political leaders, elite groups and the media themselves.

Again, the Nazi period has been the most extensively studied. In addition to 'internal bystanders' – ordinary Germans and their allies – information soon reached key outside audiences: the Allied leadership, the British and American media, the Vatican, the Red Cross, world Jewish organizations, the Zionist leadership in Palestine. Was this information discounted, genuinely disbelieved – or was it believed, but its implications denied? The disjunction between 'knowing' and 'believing' appears in the story of Jan Karski, the Polish emissary who in 1942 gave detailed information about the unfolding genocide to a number of Western leaders. The facts were seldom disputed. Justice Felix Frankfurter, however, told Karski, 'I can't believe you.' When assured that Karski was telling the truth, Frankfurter said: 'I did not say this young man is lying. I said that I cannot believe him. There is a difference.'

The difference recurs in this and similar narratives of denial. Powerful people received information whose significance was then discounted. The general truth was eventually accepted, but these audiences either seemed unable to grasp its scale, details and implications, or, for different political reasons, were reluctant to make any public acknowledgement. Their ambivalence was well illustrated by the way other newspapers picked up the June 1942 reports in the London *Daily Telegraph* that 700,000 (then changed to a million) Polish Jews had been slaughtered by the Germans 'in the greatest massacres in world history'. The *New York Times* published its story in the middle of the paper. But, 'if it was true that a million people had been killed this clearly should have been front page news; it did not, after all, happen every day. If it was not true, the story should not have been published at all.'[36] The middle page was a compromise between belief and disbelief.

The Karski and *New York Times* episodes are fables about the differences between information and knowledge, between knowing and believing. These fables could not be repeated today. In the post-modern sensibility, knowledge and beliefs are more easily seen as relative; both are dissociated from action.

Bystander states

The term 'bystander nations' was originally used to describe the seeming indifference of Western leaders to the fate of Jews during the Holocaust. There are numerous controversies about the subject,[37] but clearly the Allies knew *earlier* and *more* about the extermination policy than they conceded officially. Even when the facts became clearly known, believed and acknowledged, the Allied governments either claimed to be unable or were unwilling to help.

The Western reaction to the atrocities in Bosnia and Rwanda is the (partly rhetorical) contemporary equivalent. But the nuances of knowing and not-knowing at the international level are now entirely different: they appear in global media dramas, with live information, press conferences, audio-visual gadgetry. Compared with anything in the last war, the amount of information is extraordinary. How, with intelligence satellites orbiting the space above Bosnia and unmanned drone planes relaying real-time video images, could the USA insist that information about Srebrenica was 'ambiguous'?[38]

Official recognition of the mass of available information has the peculiar post-modern combination of instant transparency and vividness together with instant deniability and disappearance. Now you see it, now you don't. Take the sequence of American reactions to the 1992 revelations about Serbian-run camps, with vivid TV images of emaciated Bosnian Muslims. 'Confronted by the televised faces behind barbed wire, Bush administration officials reacted instinctively: they denied knowing anything about the camps. Or rather, they first said they knew and then, next day, said they didn't.'[39] But soon initial denials were erased from memory; the State Department acknowledged that they had known all along. This was termed 'moving the ball forward one step' – which meant, as Danner explains, reaching the step of knowing, but – because the official policy was to do nothing – stopping well short of the second step of doing something. But if the horrors of Omarska were known about, why didn't the government reveal this?

The role of bystander nations is especially important in the early stages of knowledge, when warning signs can be clearly detected. But if bystander states refuse to take early preventive steps,[40] then perpetrator governments can go safely ahead, relying on their allies, patrons and donors to hold back. In the recent Rwanda case, the buildup was clearly recognized: the local radio broadcast incitements to kill lists of named Tutsi; the diplomatic community and aid workers were fully informed. Although legal application of the term 'genocide' does not ensure intervention, a refusal to use the term makes it easier not to intervene. In May 1994, by which time at least 200,000 people (mainly Tutsi) had been slaughtered in Rwanda, the US government instructed its spokesman 'not to describe the deaths there as genocide, even though some senior officials believe that is exactly what they represent'.[41] The State Department policy was to use the term 'genocidal incidents' or 'events'.

Why do governments turn a blind eye or refuse to intervene in distant conflicts for which they often have indirect responsibility? There are many reasons: national self-interest; the view that the nation-state is not a moral agent with moral obligations; direct involvement and collusion (arms, training, equipment); reluctance to infringe the doctrine of national sovereignty along with the popular sentiment that these are indeed other people's problems. Then there are the varieties of relativism: the right-wing version ('That's the way people like that always behave'); the liberal version ('Respect local culture, don't impose our values; who are we to condemn?'); and the mindless version ('Nothing is absolute, there's no way of knowing what's happening, there is truth on both sides'). The state's right to remain neutral and uninvolved – even not to notice – is a political analogue of the individual's 'right to be an ostrich'.[42]

Like the Argentinian junta's double discourse, patron states send out encoded double messages. In public forums like the UN, they warn, condemn and even threaten to vote for sanctions. In private (and with maximum deniability), they continue military aid and training, instruct their client about how to talk in public, hire PR consultant firms and give the go-ahead nod to invade, stage a *coup*, mop up the opposition – but not too openly, and to limit casualties. This is all more active than 'turning a blind eye'. On 5 December 1975, two days before General Suharto invaded East Timor and began the massacre of some 60,000 Timorese, Henry Kissinger and President Ford arrived in Jakarta on a visit described later by a State Department official as 'the big wink'.

In Chomsky's political economy of denial, the psychological nuances of knowing are redundant. The blatant lies, the double messages and the averted gaze are conscious, intentional and informed by geopolitical interest only. Selective blindsight is always politically calculated. Those countries or ethnic groups designated as worthy or suitable victims are awarded sympathy, but there is no interest in the fate of unworthy or unsuitable victims; there are 'nefarious bloodbaths' versus 'benign and constructive blood baths'. The result is identical to Orwell's conclusions about nationalism: 'the atrocities of official enemies arouse great anguish and indignation, vast coverage and often shameless lying to portray them as even worse than they are; the treatment is opposite in all respects when responsibility lies closer to home. Atrocities that do not bear on domestic power interests are generally ignored.'[43]

Metaphorical audiences

Chapters 8 and 10 deal with the audiences that most interest me: the random consumers of media images of suffering and the more focused targets of Amnesty and Oxfam appeals. Whether factual representation or factoid spectacle, the media's boast that 'the world is watching' turns us all into metaphorical bystanders. We lack the instant and physical immediacy of actual bystanders. But this is replaced by a greater variety and intensity of demands in an average media day than the Good Samaritan would have seen in a lifetime.

Pilgrims, observers and monitors

In the last two decades, there has been a massive increase in the number of international observers whose work or ideological

commitment takes them round the suffering spots of the world. In the
Second World War, the International Committee of the Red Cross was
the only (and limited) neutral observer. There is now a vast network of
monitors and observers – from the UN orbit, supra-national bodies
and humanitarian NGOs – in even the most remote horror spots of the
world. A visible allegiance to human rights rhetoric, the growth of
international humanitarian organizations, democratization of air
travel, and the availability of new communications technologies have
created a global anti-denial elite. They monitor human rights violations, organize disaster relief programmes, advise governments on
everything from fiscal policy to AIDS prevention, make documentaries, and travel around in fact-finding or solidarity delegations. This
is a new cosmopolitan subculture – well informed, articulate and
ideally located to observe the atrocities and suffering which not so
long ago were beyond scrutiny.

Many of these people are 'observers' in a new and special meaning
of the term. They are in the compassion business; they come to know
about the misery of strangers, not as chance passers-by, but as representatives of 'an impalpable modern ideal: that the problems of other
people, no matter how remote, should concern us all'.[44] They live with
a highly attuned sense of acknowledgement. The discourse about
global suffering is largely the product of their moral imagination.
They select and process the information that goes into human rights
reports, documentation for war crimes tribunals, charity appeals and
political briefings.

Local people are sometimes a little cynical about these international
observers. Victims, subordinate and oppressed groups, see these foreigners as not really committed to *their* cause: they flit from one problem
place to another. Governments see them as inherently biased, because
they side with the underdog and represent liberal cosmopolitan values.
Both sides accuse them of blindness to the complexities of the local
problem: 'They see what they want to see, then get the next plane home.'

Other categories of visitors do indeed come with political biases that
cause selective silence and denial about the wrongs inconveniently
committed by the wrong others. Intellectuals have an especially
shameful record of political inhibition against speaking out against
their own friendly or idealized societies on the grounds that this
would damage a good cause. This is what is meant by 'not washing
your dirty linen in public'. This folk injunction becomes more formidable when backed by veiled or actual threats from the state against
giving comfort or weapons to the enemy.

The history of political pilgrims from the Left reveals many dishon-
ourable episodes of willing selective perception, self-censorship and

denial. There is a whole vocabulary to describe dupes, stooges, useful idiots and fellow-travellers. The original and most notorious were the foreign visitors – the pejorative term 'fellow travellers' is surely justi-fied – who went to the Soviet Union on 'study' or 'solidarity' tours while Stalin and his successors were engaged in arbitrary arrests, fake show trials, torture and imprisonment, setting up the gulag systems, and mass killing through starvation.[45] The visitors saw no evil – or rather, they saw, but disavowed the meaning of what they saw. At worst, they were knowingly lying (for a noble cause and higher loyal-ties). At best, they were using the denial logic that Primo Levi identi-fied: if the moral base of communism was the eradication of inequality, injustice and oppression, then how could such phenomena exist? Clearly they could only be the product of capitalist propaganda. Later romantic pilgrims to Maoist China were even more susceptible to being blinded or blinding themselves to the repression and mass suffering all around them.

The Israeli–Palestinian conflict is not symmetrical, but is a striking example of observer denial on both sides at the same time. Two bus loads of bitterly opposed political pilgrims may pass each other at the same tourist site (one of three 'authentic' sites of the Last Supper?). In one bus is a group of Jewish tourists and solidarity delegates from American Jewish organizations, who arrive in tens of thousands each year. Their guide runs through every cliché in the book – draining the swamps, women being equal in the army, Israel never having killed POWs. The 'Palestinian problem' is deliberately obfuscated – starting with the lie about Arab leaders broadcasting instructions to local Palestinians to flee their homes in 1948. The guide talks about 'barren hills' as the bus drives past a site where a Palestinian village, with olive-trees and vines, was totally obliterated from memory by bull-dozers. (The inhabitants, in a perfect idiom of denial, are officially described as 'absentee presences'.) The same American Jews who are outspoken critics of human rights violations everywhere from El Salvador to Tibet now change from sophisticated observers into dumbed-down collective victims. Their fellow Jews who criticize the Israeli treatment of Palestinians too strongly or openly are denounced as 'self-hating Jews' or as having a 'Diaspora mentality'.

Meantime, the Palestinian bus is on its way to a 'settlement tour', guided by an expert Palestinian geographer. The travellers are taken from one Jewish settlement to another, consulting maps showing the exact location and size of Zionist-confiscated land. Each dunam and olive grove is meticulously recorded. The passengers (most of them wearing the obligatory red *keffiya*) are different types of Palestinian sympathizers: knowledgeable and committed radical students from

Palestinian solidarity groups in Europe; free-floating (and ill-informed) 'peace and conflict resolution' activists hopping from one bad scene to another; a few romantic 'Arabists (with a whiff of old-fashioned anti-Semitism); doctoral students working on theses about 'Feminism, Islam and the Post-Colonial Other'. They are known (by Israelis and Palestinians who work together) as 'political groupies'. They seek only information that reinforces the politically correct gaze with which they arrive; many refuse even to visit the Israeli side of the invisible boundary. They are as blind about Israeli political culture as the Zionist tourists from Miami are about Palestinian history.

A model account of these forms of ideological denial is Makiya's controversial study of the silence of Arab intellectuals about the atrocities perpetrated in Sadam Hussein's Iraq: 'Silence is a synonym for the death of compassion in the Arab world; it is the politics of not washing your dirty linen in public while gruesome cruelty and whole worlds of morbidity unfold around you. Silence is choosing, ostrich-like not to know what Arab is doing to fellow Arab, all in the name of a knee-jerk anti-Westernism which has turned into a disease . . . silence in the Arab world is silence over cruelty.'[46]

If the Nazi period created the concept of 'bystander nation', then Serbia, Bosnia and Kosovo transformed it into a whole discourse about bystanding, doing nothing and collusion. Journalists in Bosnia reported atrocities in which bystanders seemed as important as victims and perpetrators. Rohde's chronicle of the fall of Srebrenica, for example, is all about observers: the Dutch peace-keeper force in UNPROFOR; the Dutch government; the UN apparatus; the British, US and French governments.[47] Right from the outset, he claims, everyone from the most junior Dutch soldier to international leaders could see the massacres coming. The official observers and peace-keepers witnessed individual killings and buses being loaded with men; they were actually told what was going to happen and heard the sound of shots; they colluded in drawing up lists and separating men from women and children. Yet they made no attempt to intervene, protest or report. Even afterwards, they tried to deny and conceal evidence of their knowledge. 'Srebrenica was not simply a case of the international community standing by as a far-off atrocity was committed. The actions of the international community encouraged, aided and emboldened the executioners.'[48]

This judgement may be too harsh. These people are not bystanders in any conventional sense of the term, but paid, professional representatives of the so-called international community. Active monitoring, peace-keeping, conflict resolution and armed intervention are part of their job description, not some sort of sentimental, altruistic impulse.

They are supposed to augur a new age of humanitarian intervention, global policing and international jurisdiction. The atrocity triangle – victim, perpetrator and bystander – becomes a square; in the fourth corner the blue-bereted agent of the 'international community'.

As doubly distant observers, we look at visual images or written texts that show others who are looking at the suffering of yet others. But immediate knowing has become democratized and globalized. The ten-second sight of Albanian children packed in a truck leaving Kosovo makes bystanders of us all.

The moral lesson of narratives of social suffering does not become any clearer. The current cultural worship of the confessional mode – telling stories about the suffering of your own special identity group – neither encourages identification with other specific victims nor creates a universal sense of kindredship. It is easy to arouse an immediate consciousness of bystanding. It surely requires very little imagination to see ourselves as Kitty Genovese's neighbours. But how to go further? The charred bodies in the pit on that blurred black-and-white photo from sixty years ago are beyond real seeing. Tonight's prime time news shows us bodies in a pit dug yesterday. The issue, though, is not that one image is more vivid, memorable or 'real' than the other. Building a bridge to the suffering of remote others is a moral, not a technical matter.

In the Holocaust Memorial Museum in Washington, DC, visitors to the 'conceptual museum' are invited to play a game of identifying either with a victim (a Jew in the Warsaw Ghetto), an offender (a German soldier ordered to kill innocent women and children) or a witnessing bystander. The director of the museum comments: 'The understanding of the passive bystander's inadvertent guilt is probably the most important and most relevant moral lesson the museum can teach to its visitors. Its importance lies in its broad applicability to contemporary historical and social phenomena as well as to occurrences in everybody's daily life.'[49]

Yes, the museum is surely right to focus on bystanders; this is what their visitors are. But what is 'inadvertent guilt'? And just how do American teenagers on a high school visit to the Washington museum in the year 2000 'identify' with Lithuanian villagers in 1941, who watched and cheered German police *Aktion* slaughtering hundreds of their Jewish neighbours? Furthermore, what does it mean to 'apply' this identification in their daily lives in New Jersey?

7

Images of Suffering

All readers of this book have known sickness, pain, worry and unhappiness. Many have suffered discrimination because of gender, sexuality, appearance, ethnicity or religion. Many have also been victims of crime; natural disasters or traffic accidents. All have certainly been onlookers and witnesses to the suffering of others – known (family, friends and colleagues) and unknown (beggars on the pavement, disturbed people mumbling on the bus, children abused by their parents in public). They may also have been 'perpetrators' in causing distress to their families and friends.

Since the Second World War, however, most people in most Western democracies have not lived in worlds of mass suffering and public atrocities. We know these worlds only through mediated knowledge. Information has passed through multiple layers of filtering, representation and interpretation – by the mass media, humanitarian organizations, political discourse, high art and mass culture, history and social science – before it reaches the knowing eye. This chapter looks at the two most powerful institutions to have appropriated social suffering[1] – the mass media and humanitarian organizations – and their shared links to denial, especially through the thesis of 'compassion fatigue'.

Appeasing the media beast

The mass media have a near monopoly in creating the cultural imagery of suffering and atrocities. Television is the primary channel through which the agonies of distant others reach the consciences of the more privileged, safe and comfortable. The subject of this book is only conceivable within images generated by the mass media. These images belong to a hyper-reality, a continuous set of paradoxes about the observer's view of what is 'really' happening. There is a real immediacy in the unbearably live sight of a Rwandan mother's face as she searches a refugee camp for her missing children. But there is also a fathomless distance, not just the geographical distance from the event, but the unimaginability of this happening to you or your loved ones. Ignatieff suggests that these effects of television cancel each other out. On the one hand, immediacy breaks down the older barriers to knowledge and compassion, the TV news becoming 'a hopeful example of the internationalization of conscience'.[2] But, on the other, its selectivity, promiscuity and short attention time span, make viewers into 'voyeurs of the suffering of others, tourists amidst their landscapes of anguish'.[3]

We know nothing worthwhile about the cumulative effect of media imagery. Research deals more with the earlier stages: how events are initially selected and presented. The media scan events and places, decide what constitutes 'news', filter and frame the issues, contextualize the problem and set the political agenda. The selection of news about suffering and atrocities fits the classic formula: the media do not tell us what to think, but they do tell us what to think about. As news and popular culture become more globalized, so the format of this 'what' (down to the verbal inflections of the CNN reporter) has become more homogeneous. Human suffering is a commodity to be worked on and recast.

Human rights, aid, development or 'Third World' subjects are usually vaguely classified as 'foreign' or 'international' news: things that happen elsewhere. Humanitarian organizations, in the business of using knowledge to induce compassion, are compelled to adjust their agendas to an increasingly powerful and global media regime. The question becomes: 'how ... the harrowing details of human suffering ... are refracted by modern marketing techniques, broadcasting politics, the cultural styles of national humanitarian movements, the visual imagery and narrative formulae through which disasters and relief are represented, and the peculiar power and enchantment of television.'[4] Coverage is so selective that the media in effect create a disaster when they recognize it: 'they give institutional endorsement or attestation to bad events which otherwise have a reality restricted to a local circle of victims.'[5] These 'bad events' include not just literal events such as a natural disaster or a political massacre, but also unrolling backdrops – infant mortality statistics, the long-time persecution of minority groups and the degradation of women.

The context in which 'bad events' are selected and represented is the steady trend over the last decade for domestic media in the USA, Western Europe and even Britain (once the most global in its coverage) to give far less attention to foreign news. Within the foreign news category (including documentaries) coverage of bad events in distant places has especially declined. Amount of coverage is not the same as amount of *attention*. Even well-covered and dramatic foreign conflicts do not attract high public awareness, especially in the USA. Each month, the *Times Mirror News Interest Index* confirms the obvious in fascinating detail: that domestic stories receive more attention than foreign news, unless Americans are there (usually as soldiers or tourists).[6]

If coverage does not mean attention, neither does attention mean understanding. One study of American university students examined the effects of regular TV watching on awareness of political and social issues.[7] The sample was divided into 'heavy', 'medium' and 'light' TV viewers. All lacked basic knowledge, especially about foreign issues. Most students thought that the US government had condemned dictatorships that it had actually supported. They thought that the Bush administration's response to political killings in El Salvador was pro-human rights (cutting off aid). The opposite and correct answer (continued aid to the Salvadoran government) was picked by only 24 per cent. In reply to the question 'In 1975, which country brutally invaded East Timor, and has occupied it ever since?', four of the five alternatives offered were known Communist 'bad guys' (China, North Korea, Vietnam and the Soviet Union). Every one of these was preferred over the correct answer, Indonesia, the only 'good guy' and ally of the USA listed – chosen last, by only 12.5 per cent. Heavy TV viewers were often less well informed than light viewers. This does not prove the old slogan 'The more you watch, the less you know', but it is not good news for the project of overcoming cultural denial.

Filtering the images

'Out there', bad events are taking place; some events become atrocity stories, and some stories become media events. But why, bombarded with so many alternatives, should a national newspaper or TV network select this particular report, subject, story or event? To understand cultural denial, we must first know *what* the media beast takes in, processes and then represents. This is a subtle operation, precisely because the media filter is so similar to cultural denial itself.

There are three models of media filtering: correspondence, arbitrariness and pattern. In the *correspondence* model, selection is rational and objective. It provides an accurate and reliable reflection of reality, selecting events only according to their seriousness. At the extremes, something like this does happen: a political massacre with 200 victims is more likely to be reported than one with 20 victims. But, as a general rule, nothing like this happens at all. If the 20 people are killed in France, they are given more Western media space than 200 in Algeria. There is no need to labour the obvious. In today's self-reflexive world, no one thinks that the *World News Hour* is a represent-ative and accurate sample of what is happening in the world.

In the *arbitrariness* model, selection is wholly irrational and unpre-dictable. The end result is determined by chance and contingency. Nothing else can explain the unfair ways in which some minor bad events are given sensational coverage and some horribly destructive events are virtually ignored. There is neither correspondence nor any discernible pattern. Legendary cases of famines, political killings or refugee flights are selected only because of the chance contingency of a journalist being on the spot.

Overall, though, chance explains even less than correspondence. The criteria of selection – newsworthiness, ethnocentrism, human interest, political acceptability – are not at all random. In *pattern* mod-els, selection is structured by criteria extrinsic to the event's serious-ness: for example, the victims' ethnic group, the perpetrators' identity, or our social distance from the event. The patterns may be political (selection serves the interests of the powerful, buttresses the dominant ideology, deflects political threats), cultural (shared cognitive schem-ata for constructing social reality) or organizational (the structure of newsmaking, the rhythms of the newsroom, the subculture of journal-ism, and professional folklore about what makes a good story).

These patterns derive from context (geopolitical interest, cultural similarity, ideological affiliation, social and geographical distance) and event (the 'intrinsic' potential for an item to become an event, the event to become news). Like top-down and bottom-up cognitive processes, the two criteria work together. Common rules such as *threshold* (how many deaths, how much suffering) and *unambiguity* (who fired first) are both event- and context-driven. A neat matrix predicts that items more likely to be selected will concern Western and especially American interests; deal with negative matters (violence, crises and disasters); consist of dramatic, sensational events rather than historical and unfolding problems (for example, a *coup* rather than an ongoing guerrilla war). But looking at the potential news-worthiness of atrocities and suffering alone, no matrix can accommo-date the sheer mass of events, political contingency and the vagaries of fashion.

Some conditions are excluded even though massive numbers are involved. These are the invisible atrocities, the silent sufferings that humanitarian organizations or socially conscious journalists try to expose. Conditions that are endemic, widespread and supposedly intractable – hunger, disease, poverty, famine, infant mortality and discrimination – are not newsworthy in themselves. Normalization blocks exposure until opposite social forces become stronger. Collective rape during wars or political massacres was once accepted as spoils of war, like looting. Women were culturally silenced – too ashamed and weak to talk publicly – and double victims, both of the violation and the humiliation of keeping silent. Media reporting of mass rapes in Bosnia broke this wall of ideological normalization.

Other things being equal, the most important determinant of selection is whether the story is already a story. The media's news agenda is self-referential. Early human rights reports about Iraq, Bosnia, Somalia or Rwanda received little attention before these places entered the headlines. In the seventies, stories about death squads in El Salvador met with official US government denial and media indifference. This was not news – just more Latin Americans killing each other. When political attention shifted, the media started recycling old stories and photos to fit the new frame of 'massacres'.

Another strong criterion is whether the event is congruent with the society's political interests. A term like 'American interests' has two different meanings. The more benign, suggested by the phrase 'American angle', refers to whatever will interest American audiences: Do we have some link with the country? Do we have troops, civilians or hostages there? The less benign meaning is that only news that serves American geopolitical and ideological interests will be selected. Violations by friends and allies will not be reported, or will be reported differently from violations by our enemies. 'Interest' means the foreign policy of the US government. Chomsky has documented this master pattern of selection in great detail.[8] Beneath the media surface are layers of every imaginable form of denial: literal cover-ups, double-talk ('quiet diplomacy', 'special relationship'), mindless slogans and deliberate diversions. No esoteric code is needed to figure all this out. Deconstruction is a child's game.

But post-modern news coverage is becoming too arbitrary for such criteria. The new world order, with its shifting alliances and sudden eruptions of political violence, makes it harder to predict the front page of the *New York Times* or the first item on CNN news. Following the State Department's news agenda still helps, but not all the way. Some events are disavowed or never reach the agenda setters. Humanitarian organizations have to decide how to push difficult cases. Even the visually dramatic land-mine issue captured little media attention until it became associated with Princess Diana.

Which country will be chosen? The best bets are those in the news already, those of obvious national interest, or both. Some countries have neither of these. They face the 'Chad rule': no one wants to hear about Chad. Whole zones of the world, like parts of Africa, only have a chance of US or global coverage if the sheer scale of the events, as in Rwanda, becomes newsworthy. There are notoriously stubborn cases: Turkey, despite routine, persistent and well-documented use of torture, has barely appeared on the international news map. The Turkish government – empowered and skilled by its eighty years' practice of denying the Armenian massacres – has perfected a coupling of literal denial with assurances that things are always improving. The reasons for media collusion in this denial are transparent: Turkey is the third largest recipient of US aid; it is strategically important to the USA and NATO; and the West presents it as a model for Islamic countries, rather than Iran.

Other events are difficult to see because the country is *too* prominent. There is always an interest in Israel: information is easy to gather; Jerusalem is a comfortable and culturally familiar city for journalists; there are vigorous domestic media and strong voices on all sides. The problem is too much media noise. Contrast this with Syria: a closed society, no access to information, no lobby in the USA. Countries are selected according to the meta-rule of 'suitable victims'. The best victims are those who are familiar, relatively easy to identify with, and not too responsible for their suffering. Perpetrators should preferably be known baddies, rather than allies.

Other criteria for newsworthiness are less political. Stories have to be presented in a vivid, graphic and dramatic form. Visual images are especially powerful: students in Tiananmen Square, forensic pathologists exhuming mass graves in Ethiopia. Bad events need to be personalized: an ethnic Albanian woman in a truck leaving Kosovo, sobbing as she recounts what happened in her village; a Palestinian family numbly staring at the ruins of their house, just destroyed by an Israeli bulldozer; the kwashiorkor-bellied baby looking hollow-eyed at the camera.

Seeing the images

Some of the images have a dramatic impact at the time and remain unforgettable icons of suffering: the terrified child in Vienna after the *Anschluss*, hands up in the air, a Nazi soldier pointing a gun at him; Don McCullin's 1969 photo of a starving albino boy in the Biafran war; the 1972 AP photo of a naked Vietnamese girl skinned by American napalm; the 1992 ITN film of emaciated Bosnian prisoners behind the barbed wire of Omarska camp. For some people, such images have a nagging, reproachful quality ('I can't get those photos out of my head') as difficult to erase as an advertising jingle running through the mind. But they do leave the mind, and the media regime is ill-suited to remind us of them.

This media-driven cultural amnesia is less fateful than denying future risks. Media narratives are not composed for prevention. Social scientists have created plausible 'genocide early warning systems', but the political buildup and signs (dehumanization, segregation, exclusion) are difficult to depict and easy to minimize. Famine stories tend to be 'creeping disasters' (as opposed to 'quick disasters') whose components (food shortage, crop failure, etc.) are invariably known in advance. Yet, in all major modern famines, even these early predictions and warnings have been denied. Messages about environmental risk are better candidates for selection and harder to block out: they have a certain fuzzy value, and the victims are always suitable. They could be any of us – and if not us, then our children or our grandchildren. Signs (polluted lakes, damaged birds) and preventive action (recycling paper, not using aerosol cans) are easily depicted. Humanitarian agencies have tried using dramatic (and sometimes exaggerated) warnings about the future to overcome current denial: 'Thirty Million People Will Starve to Death in Africa Next Year Unless...'. But this strategy can lay the ground for more denial of the crying wolf variety: 'They are always throwing out numbers like these.'

The problem of 'throwing out numbers' is that attention thresholds are not fixed. Increased receptivity to the humanitarian message means that the subject is routinely inserted into all sorts of other frames – war, foreign news, national conflict, refugees, disasters. The battle for attention intensifies: the globalization of news sources and the sheer accretion of so many horror stories, from so many places for so long, makes it harder for any particular event to be selected. In the whirlwind of struggles against normalization, not all messages get through. Victims, pressure groups and governments have to claim that their social suffering is unique. Human rights stories not only have to push at the same barriers that apply to illness or disasters; they also have to combat strong political denials from official sources, parties to the conflict and their international sponsors. Famine stories do not have a visible other side: famine can be hidden but not defended; torture is always hidden and always defended.

Stories of social suffering have become stories of humanitarian intervention. The visible appearance of workers from familiar international agencies sends the message that something serious is happening.

News coverage of the Somalia or Rwanda tragedies would be unthinkable without images of Oxfam trucks being unloaded, a volunteer nurse holding a starving baby, a doctor from Médecins Sans Frontières bandaging a wound. There are few equivalent images in human rights stories. It's not clear what human rights people actually do. There is a jangle of sound-bites – from journalists themselves, international monitors, government spokespeople, victims, armed oppositional groups, witnesses and political antagonists. The 'hierarchy of credibility' – Becker's term for the unequal moral distribution of the right to be believed – determines which voice is heard.

The content of the news is self-referential. Media coverage of the five-year Sahel drought from 1972 went through a familiar denial/acknowledgement sequence.[9] Basic information about the drought and its certain dangers was well known to international organizations, donor governments and specialist media – and easily available to the general media. When the breakthrough came, following a chance report in *Le Monde*, the media bandwagon moved. The story became attached to visual images of suffering and the (then) newsworthy angle of UN intervention. Only when knowledge became news in the prestigious international media, could serious help be mobilized.

The 1984 Ethiopia famine is a classic story of invisible knowledge – two years of facts and warnings from aid agencies and international bodies – becoming dramatically recognized.[10] The events leading to the original BBC news item were fortuitous, though not exactly random: the right person on the spot by chance, commercial competition between networks, determined reporters, a slack television news pushing the item to the lead story. No one thought that the story would have any continuing impact. Reporters and editors assumed that the public would soon get bored, lose interest and slip into denial. A single narrative or visual image breaks the media and public barrier: suddenly, if briefly, there is deep concern for distant victims.[11]

The formula can also break the other way: the story is selected, but unexpectedly bombs. In 1993, there were spectacular exposures of Iraq's Anfal campaign.[12] All the requirements for a big atrocity story were there: a clear political script, Saddam Hussein an unambiguous villain, no sympathy for Iraq, chemical weapons, helpless victims. But the timing was wrong. These attempts to eradicate the Kurds took place in 1987–9, a distant past for American media culture. The market was sated with Iraq atrocity stories, and this 'exposure' did not seem new enough – despite vivid personalized details and a new dramatic angle of forensic pathologists exhuming graves (with on-site photos of skulls). The horror threshold was raised by using the term 'genocide', and the political stakes were raised by talk about genocide charges against Saddam.

Quality as well as quantity makes information about social suffering newsworthy. Moeller gives detailed case-studies of how narratives of recent famine (Ethiopia, Somalia and Sudan) and atrocities (Bosnia and Rwanda) were carefully composed to get the facts of suffering to reach an 'image-fatigued' American public.[13] To fit the required template for famine reporting, people must already be starving to death; the causes and solutions must be simplified; and the language of a morality play must be used. Mothers and children are ideal victims; men are associated with violent 'factions' or 'war-lords', and seldom appear to be hungry (they are too busy being photographed brandishing guns). And so on. Besides templates, icons and formulae – by definition we know about these – are the unrehearsed scenes, the moments when the iconic reporter finds (or creates) the moment too grotesque to be denied. In Somalia in 1992, Bob Scott, the East Africa correspondent for Voice of America noticed a camera crew at a feeding centre pushing a microphone right next to the mouth of a child who was crawling off to die. Bob: 'When one of the aid workers demanded to know what they were doing, the sound man said "my editor wants us to get the sounds of death".'[14]

Even if a story is deliberately framed to feed the media beast, its eventual impact may be neither instant nor continuous. Cultures of denial are too strong for Brauman's tips on 'How to get on TV with your Disaster':[15] (1) Pictures, not words, turn an incident into an event; they should be available as a continuous flow to be tapped several times a day for cumulative effect. (2) The upheaval must be isolated if it is not to be ousted by another parallel conflict. (3) There must be a mediator – a personality or volunteer from a humanitarian organization – to 'authenticate' the victim, channel the emotion generated, and provide both the distance and the link between the spectator and the victim. (4) Victims must be spontaneously acceptable in their own right to Western viewers. Various ethnic groups have different chances of passing this test, regardless of the amount of hardship they are suffering. They must also be '100%' victims, not active participants. (5) Ideally, there should be a humanitarian volunteer – like the flying French doctor – working and/or being interviewed. This newsworthy figure – neither diplomat nor guerrilla, half amateur and half expert, both hero and narrator – can upstage any other drama by saving a life, live on camera.

Attempts to make an event newsworthy must double-guess the type of story it will make. Responses to distant suffering will depend on how its component images are presented. The *problem* may be framed as foreign news, disaster, ethnic tension or human rights; it may be termed 'mass killing' or 'genocide'; it may be 'naturalized' (the kind of thing always happening out there) or seen as new and specially evil. The *causes* may be hinted to be tribalism and traditional conflict, the legacy of colonialism, or corrupt Third World dictatorships. The *perpetrators* can be depicted as evil, cruel and ruthless, or as ordinary people caught up in a cycle of political conflict or responsible governments defending their citizens against threats to their daily security. The *victims* may be helpless, blameless and passive, or ruthless terrorists who deserve no sympathy, or something in between, responsible in part for their suffering. The *rescuers* may be ranked by credibility. Can we believe this earnest Swiss ICRC official or the young Irish nurse giving vaccines? Are they effective professionals or meddling do-gooders? Finally, there are meta-views about *solutions*. Is this a 'problem without a solution', or can some solutions at least be visualized: internal political change, external intervention, international sanctions, an early warning system?

If the media present a country's violence as just another episode in a centuries-long Darwinian struggle for power, a twist in an endless cycle of retaliation which is beyond any imaginable solution, then bystander 'passivity' is hardly surprising. If victims – whether interviewed in hospital or corpses in hidden graves – are not portrayed as completely blameless, then understanding and empathy are eroded. All the protagonists in many recent conflicts seem to have nuanced (if utterly insane) reasons for killing each other. As Ignatieff notes, the image of both sides being crazy, fanatic and out of control is set against a bleak landscape of chaos and despair, about which nothing can be done. The conscience is comforted (and vocabularies of denial boosted) by a 'shallow misanthropy' and moral disgust.[16] What look like personal rationalizations are clearly refractions from the media.

The truth is that the sheer dimensions of mass suffering are difficult to grasp, and even more difficult to retain. The scale of victimization passes the initial threshold, but interest cannot be sustained; the 'same' story cannot keep being repeated. Ceasing to hold attention is a cultural form of Attention Deficit Disorder. Instant news becomes instant history. The media beast must be continually fed, and is never grateful for your efforts. Prime time news is so Hollywood-ized, that a five-minute meeting in the Oval Office on International Human Rights Day between President Clinton and human rights monitors from Rwanda (a meeting that took an hour's office work to set up) got substantially more media coverage than detailed reports – taking months of time, expertise and careful checking – about the atrocities themselves.

Representation and the starving African child

Within the international humanitarian community, the debate about the politics and ethics of how to represent suffering is more self-conscious than it is in the media world.[17] By the mid-nineteen-sixties, after the Congo and Biafra horrors, the powerful image of the starving African child with haunting eyes and skeletal limbs had become a universal icon of human suffering. The slogan 'A Hungry Child Has No Politics' suggests that visceral emotions can be aroused, uncontaminated by distance or ethnicity. 'As the symbol of common humanity, a child may be the bearer of suffering with no responsibility for its cause.'[18] For most of us, this image was, and still is, irresistible.

In the mid-seventies, radical critics – armed with dependency and neo-colonialism theories – began attacking the traditional 'starving child' appeals used by Oxfam and similar charities. A commitment to long-term structural change called for actively educating donors – not just sentimentally luring them into a guilty gesture of charity. Pathetic images of starving children, helpless and dependent, perpetuated a patronizing, offensive and misleading view of the developing world as a spectacle of tragedy, disaster, disease and cruelty. A mid-sixties photo of the tiny hand of a starving Biafran child being held by the director of Oxfam was denounced as a metaphor of 'the feeble child-like Third World enveloped caringly by the big superior Western man who stoops to meet it out of the goodness of his heart'.[19] The powerful North wants to know and possess the submissive South. The photo shows an object, rather than a knowing subject[20] – not just an allegory of colonialism, but an analogy with pornography: 'The public display of an African child with a bloated kwashiorkor-ridden stomach in advertisements is pornographic, because it exposes something in human life that is as delicate and deeply personal as sexuality, that is, suffering. It puts people's bodies, their misery, their grief and their fears on display with all the details and all the indiscretion that a telescopic lens will allow.'[21] The very sight of a child not ashamed to beg places the photographer and the audience in a position of superiority. 'Third World suffering acts to secure our sense of First World comfort by assuring us that we have the power to help. . . . Their humble and submissive appeal protects our compassion and enables us to give.'[22]

The point of the critique was to give a voice to the represented. Fund-raisers belonged to the old charity discourse of 'pragmatic amorality' – patronizing, ethnocentric, fatalistic (poverty just happens, like natural disasters). They were 'merchants of misery' who would use any images to grab attention and shame audiences into giving money. By contrast, educationalists talked about empowerment, structural causation, political change and social justice. Ideological and intellectual weight moved towards the educationalists; fund raising was just something necessary for survival.

The 1984–5 Ethiopian famine very much influenced this debate.[23] This was a story of denial (initial warning signs ignored, an attempted cover-up by the Ethiopian government) giving way to dramatic acknowledgement (the legendary images on the BBC evening news of 23 October 1984, the massive public response, Bob Geldof and Band Aid, the July 1985 Live Aid concert). Educationalists were both impressed and depressed by the populist power of the media and youth culture. Other disasters had passed virtually unnoticed – yet this had raised consciousness and mobilized compassion on a global scale. And all this because of the visual impact of 'negative imagery' and Michael Buerk's powerful commentary, which was anything but 'educational'.[24]

The public outpouring of emotion, the concerts, the spectacle – even the money raised – deepened the critics' misgivings. For them, Live Aid had undone the educational victories of the seventies; they now attacked what Lidchi calls 'Consumer Aid'.[25] The African subjects of these campaigns had been objectified and then transformed into consumer items. Compassion through consumption: 'People could buy the paraphernalia that denoted that they cared . . . and watch pictures of themselves, or millions like them, caring.' This allowed hedonism with self-delusion, while global television let them witness, and hence 'consume', the suffering and dying of the poor – and weave a message of self-congratulation about their generosity.[26] Post-modernist altruism: the reality of famine turned into a spectacle, image-driven and self-referential.

New concepts, but a familiar debate. On one side: *charity* and *relief* – hand-outs and first aid that encourage dependency and exonerate donors from causal responsibility; attitudes that remain racist, colonialist and Eurocentric; *simplicity* – images of rescuing that ignore the complex causes of Third World poverty; *negative imagery* – decontextualized misery, permanent victims, endless suffering, helplessness, images designed to evoke tear-jerking compassion. On the other side: *social justice* and *complexity* – structural causes, commodity prices, civil wars, Third World debt, the World Bank, IMF stabilization, geopolitics, global power shifts, integrated development, debt adjustment programmes, sustainable health care, world nutritional patterns; *empowerment* and *positive imagery* – community, participation, self-sufficiency, productivity, rights, dialogue, consultation with project partners.

By the 1990s the critique was virtually orthodox. The demand was for fund raising to change and not run on a separate track from education. Codes of practice were drafted for a new 'ethics of representation'. The well-known Save the Children Fund version aims for 'images or words which do not damage the dignity of the children/adults with whom SCF works'.[27] People should not be seen as 'helpless recipients of hand outs. Poverty and dependence are not characteristic of communities.' A photo of four women (one smiling broadly) and two children waiting for food distribution in Ethiopia is praised: 'Misery and resignation are not the sole responses to famine conditions. Poor communities often have considerable strengths and dignity.' There must be no stereotypes and clichés: 'Patronizing, mawkishly sentimental or demeaning words or phrases should be avoided.'

The dispute is about the reality 'behind' the images. Campaigners were instructed not to represent people as suffering and dependent. But isn't this how they 'really' are? And if not, just what is the point of the campaign? Surely being dependent on the help of others is not a shameful state. And if people are portrayed as *not* asking for your help, why then should you offer this help? In fact, there is little ideological variation between the resulting texts. The deep structure of the appeal is an anti-denial message. The variations are in emotional tone and intellectual complexity.

The 1991 Christian Aid week ('We Believe in Life Before Death') combined highly charged emotional images with the message: 'If you don't feel guilty about this, there must be something wrong with you. If you do feel guilty, but don't act, your guilt can't be real.' Television advertisements showed a slow video sequence of an actual foetus in the womb; the voice-over and written text ran: 'For millions of people in the Third World, these will be the best months of their lives.' In a printed advertisement, people were shown scavenging for food on a rubbish dump. Above the photo, was the slogan 'Do You Believe in Life Before Death?' Beneath were eight rhetorical questions, including: 'Do you believe no one should have to scavenge for a living?' 'Do you believe that 40,000 child deaths per day is 40,000 too many?', and 'Do you believe seven years old is too young to work in a mine?' Finally, 'Do you believe these things enough to help us do something about it?' The message is devastating: if you don't do something, you must be 'in denial'; if you are in denial, there are only two possibilities: you don't believe us, or you have deceived yourself into thinking that you *do* believe us.

SCF's successful 1991 campaign, 'Skip Lunch, Save a Life', was quite different. There is virtually no emotion, and the message is cognitively simple, resting on a direct link between problem and solution. Food is the immediate association with 'famine'. This allows an utterly simple way of 'doing something', without moral preaching or psychological techniques to induce 'identification'. The slogan 'Skip Lunch, Save a Life', showed how a mere gesture (not even a change) in your life could save another's life: 'Go without a cheeseburger, then we can supply one person with food for more than a week.' These two campaigns strike a different note – not 'educational' but, for different reasons, difficult to ignore. But what do these images do to you? And will you do anything? Imagine a copy-writer from an advertising agency commissioned to draft a newspaper advertisement for a humanitarian appeal. The format is the standard eleven-inch by seven-inch space, which contains one (only one) black-and-white photo plus a written text. She is briefed about the problem (land-mine injuries in Angola, poverty in Bangladesh), and asked to study 300 campaign advertisements of this kind. She notes:

- Nearly always, there is the Single Unimaginable Fact: *One child dies every minute in Africa*. This fact – in case its significance is unclear – is compared with Imaginable Normality (low infant mortality in Western Europe) or Unimagined Normality (three Barbie dolls sold every minute). The text instructs you that the problem is massive and intractable.
- Despite the unimaginable scale of the problem, though, it can be broken down into manageable parts. There is even a Single Imaginable Person whom you can actually help. Moreover, an action insignificant to you, like not buying a hamburger, will make an enormous difference to this person – even *save* his or her life. Together with others, you can help a whole community. One SCF mailing included a sachet of oral rehydration. This 10p sachet 'is all that keeps Shireena from a death that will claim 5 million children this year'. Over 8,000 children die from dehydration every day; they cannot know how little the 10p seems 'to you and I compared to the value it has in saving a child's life'.
- Better than a one-off gesture to help an unknown person for a short time, you can help an Actual Known Person over the long term. Regular monthly sponsorship payments will provide 'your' child with food, shelter, clothing, medical care and education. This is not inconsistent with general and long-term prevention: 'If you sponsor Shomita, no one will have to sponsor her children.' The politically incorrect image – dependent child/protective parent – is reimagined as the acceptable promotion of social change: village-level projects (literacy, health, farming), continuity, self-reliance, community and sustainability.

- In some adoption and sponsorship appeals (especially those used by American agencies), you are told that this action can also affect *your* life: 'Sponsors discover that writing to their child is a rewarding experience that deepens their relationship.' You receive photos, drawings, letters, and school reports. Christian Children's Fund offers you 'an opportunity to work a miracle in the life of [named child] – and to begin a beautiful new friendship'. Children International offers a Sponsorship Kit, with a frame 'to keep and display your photo of your child'. (British agencies like Action Aid do not use these possessive tones or touchy-feely inducements to feel better about yourself. Contacts between child and sponsor are also limited.)

Our novice copy-writer now consults agency staff members about the campaign. They disagree about four particular issues, and she is struck by both sides: guilt tripping, personalization, vulnerability and identification.

Guilt tripping   Appeals like 'Skip Lunch, Save a Child' look simple, pragmatic and unemotional. But the not-so-hidden subtext is that if you don't comply with this undemanding request, you will feel guilty. How else can you live, knowing that this token amount of money lets you arbitrate between life and death? The more factual and unemotional the tone, the more unwelcome is the precise information about this grotesque disparity between your cost-free gesture and literally saving a human life. The more intrusive the message, the more likely you are to project your resentment on to its senders. They in turn indict you for your selfish refusal to make a sacrifice for others. Your refusal is even more reprehensible when no sacrifice at all is required. Indeed, the easier the effort (sign a petition, buy ethically grown coffee), the smaller the unit sum (£1, the price of a cup of tea), the more you feel guilty for not making it. 'We've got something we'd like you to think about when you're sitting comfortably at home this evening. Oxfam's relief programme for the hungry and homeless of Dacca.' This condemns you, of course, to sitting very uncomfortably: feel guilty if you are too callous to even think of hungry people in Dacca; feel even more guilty if you go on reading about the degradation described.

Personalization   Yes, the subject is far too complex to be reduced to an image of a single child. But what photo would convey the complex causes of poverty in Bangladesh – a board meeting of the IMF? And if the advertisement offers sponsorship of a single child (a successful way of fund raising), surely personalization is the whole point? Yes, these photos lack a context – just the face, neck and shoulders of a crying 'ethnic' child. But what 'context' should be shown? Yes, these images of suffering are 'emotional' – they 'play on' the audience's emotions without offering any rational explanation or solution. But surely there is a rational message: you and others like you help the community through helping *one* person each; *you* are the one to help *this* person; no one gives or can give to *everyone*.

Vulnerability The critique is correct – the children are shown as help-less, weak and vulnerable. Hundreds of photos were rejected to find faces of eighty children who don't smile. And each of them is totally alone. The photo lies – these eighty children, totally alone, never smiling, do not represent all the poor children in this country. But why demand that they are an accurate statistical sample? Surely the point is to represent the problem at its worst. To be sure, this should be done with dignity – but why suppress the fact that the predicament of these millions of people arises entirely from their vulnerability? With-out patterns of vulnerability and dependency, there is no need for political altruism or social justice. True, too *much* vulnerability may leave us feeling hopeless or with a sense of our own vulnerability too much heightened: like the dread we feel so acutely after visiting a seriously ill friend in hospital.

Identification Yes, the average Western observer cannot be expected to 'identify' with a starving African child, in the sense of being able to imagine herself in the place of the other. The text tries to invite this imaginative leap: 'Would you let this child starve to death in front of your house? He is out of sight, thousands of miles away in Africa. But he's as real as your own child, racketing around your own house' (SCF). But is he really 'as real'? Positive imagery hardly makes things easier. Can you really imagine yourself as an 'industrious and resilient Zairian woman learning to construct a sewage system'? And anyway, why should identification be so important? The principle of social justice does not depend on your moral awareness of people like you – but your readiness to extend the circle of recognition to unknown (and even unlikable) people who are not at all like you.

Bogged down in these debates, our copy-writer asks for some hard facts: what appeals actually raise the most money? She is told, incred-ibly, that there is virtually no evidence (or even research) on this subject. The unsurprising consensus is that images of 'active project partners' raise less money than images of a starving child.[28] A study of different images of mental handicap compared the effects of two sets of posters for the charity MENCAP.[29] The traditional 'negative' images of helplessness, pathos and suffering – designed to evoke feelings of guilt, sympathy and pity – elicited more commitment to donate money than 'positive' posters that depicted people with a mental handicap as valued human beings, with the same rights, ideals and capabilities as non-handicapped persons. 'We cannot have it both ways,' the research-ers grimly conclude; 'if people with a mental handicap are perceived as having the same rights, value and capability as everyone else, there is a tendency not to support them with charitable financial donations.'[30]

This simplifies the choice: fund raising versus consciousness raising. All agencies try to do both. But people may not want more informa-tion, positive or negative. Perhaps we *are* like those motiveless deci-sion-makers of cognitive theory. We know that Third World poverty is a complex matter. But cognitive misers as we are, we switch off when people start talking about the debt crisis, the IMF and the price of coffee beans. What matters is not complex education or even subtle pulling of heart-strings. In the peripheral or mindless states that these psychologists unsentimentally assign to us, we pay less attention to the message than to side cues ('What a shy young man to be going around knocking at doors'). As long as the cause is not one that in principle you do not support (for me, anything connected with religion, animals or wildlife) and it does not intrude on your time and space (you're not in the shower when the bell rings), you probably respond.

These heuristics are obviously too amoral to shape social policy. And the representation of suffering is not a mere hermeneutic prob-lem. Political objectives and ethical objections do matter if the starving child and the corpses flowing down the river come to represent 'Africa'. But surely these images cannot be suppressed. Needless mis-ery, sickness and violence, millions of human beings losing their lives . . . : this is the problem, the whole problem and nothing but the problem. No doubt there must be a way to show that atrocities and suffering don't exist and enter the camera lens by chance. Perhaps visual images should only be allowed with textual explanations: that a typical famine affects only 5 per cent of the population; that a typical child is fed by his or her own parents, not by Joan Collins in front of a team of UNICEF photographers; and that nearly all tribal, ethnic, religious and political conflicts are resolved by methods other than genocide. Humanitarian organizations should not use the same filters as the mass media – that is, select the worst (but most accessible) case in the worst village in the worst area. On the other hand, these are not merely 'newsworthy' events: they are the most deserving cases that need urgent help. If the agency had to think each time about repres-entativeness rather than representation, this would undermine – not to say miss the whole point of – their work.

And so the argument goes on. I believe that unless 'negative imagery' is allowed to speak for itself, the universality of suffering will never be acknowledged. The choice is not to give up being 'merchants of misery' in order to become 'salesmen of solidarity'.[31] Why not solidarity with the miserable?

Enlightenment fatigue

Our thirty-something couple are sipping their *cappuccinos* while looking at the morning newspaper. On page five there is an appeal about child soldiers in Sierra Leone. A photo shows a twelve-year-old boy, who has been thrown over the border, both his arms amputated by the rebels. The text explains what has been happening and asks for your help to pay for medical treatment.

Our first question concerns the truth status of this image: is the image itself beyond denial, the facts and their more obvious meanings not open to basic dispute? Our second is expressed in the vague but intriguing notion of 'compassion fatigue': can you be exposed so often to such images that the impact of each subsequent one is dulled and you become too exhausted to respond?

Witnessing the truth

Sophisticated technology can spread images of live atrocities around the world in minutes. But self-evident truth will not be self-evidently accepted. However informative, reliable and convincing they are, accounts of atrocities and suffering do little to undermine overt forms of denial. Humanitarian organizations are living relics of Enlightenment faith in the power of knowledge: *if only people knew, they would act*. Paradoxically, these same organizations know better than anyone how misplaced is a faith that they see undermined by their daily work.

In an electronic age dominated by visual, rather than written, communication, technologies for observing, recording and presenting information have opened extraordinary new opportunities. Electronic mail can bypass most government control; CNN cameras and reporters are on the spot; simple home videos can record vivid, dramatic and incontestable evidence which audiences 'must' believe. The information is immediate and credible. Visual images have a visceral public impact that no other medium can make. The lazy, anachronistic belief in written information ('if only they knew') could become redundant, replaced by 'now they can see'. In this latest round of 'telling truth to power', technology is surely on our side.

In this spirit, the New York-based Lawyers' Committee for Human Rights launched its Witness programme in 1992. The programme distributed video cameras to human rights observers all over the world and trained them to record violations as they happen – for example, peaceful demonstrators being shot. The resulting images would make the facts undeniable: if we have authentic pictures, we have the truth. The rock singer Peter Gabriel cited the El Salvadorian and US cover-up of the 1981 El Mozote massacre: 'The words were not enough. There were no pictures, no videotape. No proof.' It took ten years before the tortured and mutilated bodies were found. He went on:

> We now have pictures. We have the truth.... A camera in the right hands at the right time at the right place can be more powerful than tanks and guns. The power of truth is dangerous ... In Orwell's *1984*, those in power controlled the people by watching every move. Now the people can watch, witness and report on those in power. With *Witness* we are serving notice on governments. We are watching that they can no longer keep their deeds hidden, we are watching.[32]

But life is not so simple when Enlightenment beliefs face late-modern reality. Consider the 'Rodney King effect'.

On a Los Angeles street in 1991, a bystander took out his video camera and recorded – in amateur style, but perfectly clearly – vivid, lengthy images of four police-officers dragging an unresisting black suspect, Rodney King, from his car and brutally beating him on the street. Any viewing of the unedited video – or so it seemed – would yield the same interpretations: 'assault', 'abuse of power', 'violation of civil liberties', 'police violence' or 'racism'.[33] But the raw material of the events (including the video footage) had yet to be processed. The event was immediately slotted into a long-time political discourse about the alleged racism of the Los Angeles Police Department. These organizational and ideological interests were firmly in place when the specially selected jury – suburban, white and angry – heard the evidence and saw the video. They disavowed what they saw (in exactly the way Freud understood 'disavowal'). The law allowed the obvious interpretation to be negotiated, reconstructed and eventually denied. The policemen were acquitted. The bystander had got it wrong: Mr King was perpetrator, not victim.

The implications go far beyond this particular legal verdict. The values of witnessing and telling the truth belonged to a simpler era. They are being inserted into a moral culture too compromised to be rescued by the authentic information relayed by 'electronic witnesses'. The Witness programme claimed that video footage (mass exhumation of graves in Vulkavor, street demonstrations in Guatemala, and evidence of torture in rural Haiti) could be used to 'improve respect for basic human rights by bringing images of brutality to public attention'. But telling the truth, as Jan Karski discovered, is not the same as being believed. And pictures, as Rodney King discovered, can be disavowed as much as words. Furthermore, the transubstantiation of one thing (images of brutality) into another (respect for human rights) can hardly be taken for granted, any more than the iconography of the starving African child can still stand for social injustice.

The increased international awareness of atrocities and suffering, the spread of new information technologies, and the globalization of the mass media indeed mean that sovereign states (or some of them) are being 'watched' as never before. But representing this information is more difficult than ever. There is a profusion of similar images; lines are blurred between fiction and fact (reconstructions, factoids and documentary dramas); 'reality' is always in inverted commas, and multi-culturalism encourages many truths to bloom. Rock stars, more than most people, should know something about images.

The problem is yet more diffuse. Aside from the few thousand academics who take post-modernist epistemology literally, no sane person seriously 'interrogates' truth-claims about, say, infant mortality in Bangladesh. There is no literal denial. On the contrary, the obstacle to action is that you have heard this information so often and have believed it every time. You are tired of being told the truth.

Tired of the truth

Witnessing and reproducing the truth are cognitive projects: how to convey a reality that cannot be denied. But what if continued exposure to this reality eventually deadens our moral and emotional receptivity to further images of suffering? The populist psychology thesis of 'compassion fatigue' is built upon three overlapping concepts: *information overload, normalization, densensitization.*

Information overload, input overload, saturation

The concept of information overload was originally used by psychologists to denote a quantity and intensity of stimuli that exceed our mental capacity to pay attention.[34] The cognitive demands of everyday life overwhelm the mind's ability to deal with each item. Faced by this buzz of stimuli, people slip into what Simmel called an 'urban trance': a self-absorbed state marked by a lack of responsivity. Terms like 'switching off' or 'tuning out' apply to your mind as well as your TV remote control.

Tuning out, though, is not 'shutting down'. Denial theory and common sense recognize that the obvious solution to stimulus overload is *selective* oblivion. If you tune yourself into messages about a particular subject – cricket statistics or movie plots – there is no limit to the amount of information you can receive. Tuning out to avoid troubling or irrelevant information is more difficult. We may indeed 'train' ourselves to walk past homeless beggars as if they were not there. But this means (even the logic and grammar are difficult) that we had once to have known what it is that we don't any longer want to know. The strong thesis suggests that we actually do not notice the beggars' presence at all. In the weaker version, implied by the notion 'as if', we are obviously aware of their presence – but this instant registration is not 'allowed' to occupy, let alone preoccupy, our full awareness. The image does not change the overall cognitive frame. It is relayed to the massive warehouse of stuff designated as either irrelevant or too disturbing to think about or remember.

The overload/shut-down model is applied to media texts and images, as well as sights in the streets. The allied idea of audience saturation is commonly used, especially by media professionals. An audience watches a TV documentary showing children with legs blown off by land-mines; by the sixth child, they feel themselves running out of psychic diskette space; the mind can't cope anymore; they change to another channel. But – to switch from information technology to a more relentless Freudian logic – they can never totally delete what they once knew.

In a purely quantitative sense, the overload thesis is preposterous. It implies that individuals and whole societies have thermostats that switch off when too much information comes in. This is contrary to all theories of cognition and memory. It is not even a good metaphor: baths fill up and overflow; minds and cultures don't.

Normalization and routinization

Normalization is a far richer concept than overload. It suggests that facts and images once seen as unusual, unpleasant, or even intolerable eventually become accepted as normal. The sheer accretion of images leads not to a shutter mechanism, but to a change in beliefs, emotions and perception. What was once seen as disturbing and anomalous – a sense that things are not as they should be – now becomes normal, even tolerable. This is a disturbing and far-reaching idea, going well beyond 'urban indifference' especially when extended to extreme images – a starving child, corpses in a ditch. The potential impact is lost because of familiarity: 'we've seen it all before'. Normalization becomes neutralization, and then indifference: no response is needed after activating the memory trace that 'this is just the sort of thing that's always happening in places like that'.

Some form of normalization is integral to narratives of suffering and atrocities. But the term should not be used too literally. Perpetrators, victims and bystanders can indeed 'normalize' in the sense of 'get used to' the most unimaginable horrors. This progressive accommodation may even be essential for atrocities to take place at all. But even the most active perpetrators and most passive bystanders, however morally or emotionally numbed, do not lose all awareness of conventional definitions of 'normal'. And even if constant exposure to horror images leaves TV viewers in a state of mental inertia, this results more from a sense of helplessness than a perception (either by the sender or the receiver of the message) that everything is just as it should be (in this the best of all possible world orders).

The overload and routinization theses both miss the same point: observers are prone not to information overload, but to *demand* overload. We can receive any amount of information as long as it does not make moral or psychological demands, especially not the nagging demand to 'do something'. As Clarkson notes, the most frequently cited reason for 'bystanding' is the sheer impossibility of being involved with everything which is going wrong with the world: 'There are just too many demands.'[35] But what things are shut out, and just how does this happen? When the need is overwhelming and chaotic, when distant events and statistics are literally beyond comprehension, one obvious solution is to 'conserve' attention by dealing with manageable problems close by. Even – rather, especially – altruists keep going by shutting out demands that they can't meet.

There is one sense, though, in which sheer numbers do matter. There is an invisible threshold at which statistics (and how they are represented) result not in numbness, but in a strange moral dysfunction. What if the text informs us that these exact tens of thousands of children died not every two minutes, but every ten *seconds*. Would this massive statistical change make a difference to anyone's response? Of course not. Take these estimates: 50 per cent of the world's population does not have access to clean water; by the end of the decade, 10 million children in Africa will be orphaned as a result of AIDS; there are over 18 million refugees in the world today. More reliable estimates turn out (really) to be respectively, 46 per cent, 8.5 million, and

16 million. But this will not change our emotional or moral reaction at all. A terrifying thought: are we all such amoral brutes, so pseudo-stupid, that those million or two human lives don't matter a toss?

This is the 'world of infallible logic' that Bruckner ridiculed: statistics so monstrous, quantities of suffering so enormous, that our lives can only be obscene, too insensitive to justify: 'When I eat a half pound steak, I could feed 30 people with the protein that was used to feed the animal.'[36] There is no possible way to 'acknowledge' – let alone do something – about these grotesque inventories. It takes sophisticated denial talk to argue that these numerical comparisons are true – but pointless.

Desensitization, psychic numbing, brutalization

Atrocity statistics and league tables of suffering are collected and presented in order to make a moral point. When you start to see the moral point too often – you must respond to *every* cry of pain, even those you can't hear – you are facing demand overload. It is possible, however, that the message is diverted before moral considerations are even reached. The psychological nerve endings that relay the news are atrophied by a culture of endless and remorseless horror images: a documentary about AIDS in Zambia, more Indian flood victims. No end is in sight; the images become too familiar to retain any visceral power. This is the thesis of 'desensitization' or 'psychic numbing'.

The terms are invariably too melodramatic. No doubt some torturers and terrorists have to become emotionally desensitized. Denial through routinization is essential to crimes of obedience. Trainee torturers learn to experience pain first as simulated victims; then, as guards or observers, they watch the victim being tortured by others; then they graduate to active participation.[37] Once the initial barrier or inhibition is passed, each later step becomes easier to negotiate and harder to refuse. But this is not quite the sequence attributed to the jaded consumer of atrocity images: 'I used to get depressed and all churned up by those photos; now I hardly feel a thing.' This imaginary psychic state is conceived by image producers – journalists, artists, photographers, humanitarian organizations – as a threshold which they must clear to reinduce the 'old' emotions.

Yet even people who deal with death as their daily work – homicide detectives, undertakers, slaughterhouse workers, volunteers in an AIDS hospice, guards on death row – do not go through a uniform and progressive desensitization.[38] And from what are people being desensitized? Compassion is seen as something that has to be taught and learnt – before it supposedly becomes unlearnt. It might, though, be a 'natural' response to the suffering of others, a response which is stifled under certain social conditions, such as Thatcherite individualism. The 'normal' sensation is to feel something. Without having to be instructed, most people can empathize with a baby's crying or a child's distress. As adults, this empathy may evoke (or arise from) visceral memories of our own distress; we go back to childhood pain. Such vicarious distress is surely normal. But whether empathy is primeval or learnt, the brutalization thesis remains the same. The instant, incessant communication of so much suffering eventually creates a moral bluntness, a heightening of our threshold for outrage.[39]

Taken individually, the elements of the desensitization thesis make some sense. But the whole thesis is an urban myth. There is not the slightest evidence for this in personal biography (sensitive souls hardening away with each week of television) or in cultural history (where exactly the opposite could be argued: a heightened emotional sensitivity to the suffering of distant others). Denial cannot result merely from familiarity and repetition. The thesis gives no time span for desensitization, no idea as to *who* is being so brutalized, or how the original compassionate reaction can be made to reappear magically.

Desensitization is a treatment method used in behaviour therapy to gradually induce patients to give up their troublesome phobias. As such, it works with a crude stimulus – response psychology that ignores mental reflection, symbolic meaning and cultural context. It gives rise to the suggestion that making the image of suffering more extreme and painful will re-sensitize people or whole cultures so that they find their lost compassion. But there is no standard, universal response to even the most extreme images of suffering. Strong emotions may just as easily be evoked by familiar images taken out of context, like the posters in the infamous Benetton advertising campaign: a baby with its umbilical cord intact; a dying (or dead) AIDS victim with a startling likeness to the standard Western image of Jesus Christ. The public controversy did indeed mention 'rolling back the frontiers of shock'. But the reaction was less about the images in themselves, than about their (mystifying) use to persuade you to buy a cornflower-blue sweater.

Compassion fatigue, donor exhaustion

Compassion fatigue is the better known of these concepts, embracing all the connotations of overload, normalization and numbing. It is also over-used – vague as a description, and even vaguer as an explanation. At times it means getting used to bad news, at other times a reluctance or inability to respond to demands for help. All the while, the facts are not denied; they are only too well known and their meaning acknowledged. The 'fatigue' refers to burn-out – which may be emotional (a diminished incapacity to feel anything), or moral (a diminished moral sensitivity).

There is also supposed to be an intellectual fatigue that arises from knowing too much about human misery. But this is merely the world-weary sophistication that has long been cultivated by certain classes and subcultures. It is expressed, even by serious people, in recycled clichés: 'Look what happened when we sent money to Ethiopia... in Burundi and Chechnya they killed the very volunteers trying to help them... we can't keep going through this same cycle.' Behind these banalities, there may be something more worrying, a genuine absorption of the meta-image of chaos: things are getting out of control; we can't even understand – let alone solve – these problems.

The compassion fatigue thesis makes some sense. But, like its component parts, it is elusive. Are we talking of reaction to a particular crisis or a more general decline in moral sensibility? Moreover, there is confusion between the psychological language of desensitization or denial and the political reasons for the decline in government aid budgets, tougher international conditionality, greater caution and donor selectivity. According to one distinction, *aid fatigue* is made up of 'donor fatigue' (an objective decrease in government commitment to foreign aid) plus 'compassion fatigue' (a lack of enthusiasm by the mass public to support government aid or to donate money voluntarily themselves).[40]

This is a good distinction. But while many people, especially in the media, public relations and politics, believe that compassion fatigue is a real 'thing' out there, no humanitarian agencies seriously agree. They see not compassion fatigue, but *media fatigue*: the view by the media and cynical elites that no one is interested. This is what may lead humanitarian workers to look for more outrageous ways of getting attention. They are seldom cynical and defeatist themselves. They do not dismiss the idea of compassion fatigue merely to boost their own morale or because of their professional interest in not creating a self-fulfilling prophecy. They argue, correctly, that the political problem is the media's framework of reporting, rather than the public's capacity to keep absorbing.

Agencies and media do, however, share some assumptions, including the patronizing idea that audiences cannot pay attention to more than one big event at the same time. A CARE spokesman explains that fund raising for Somalia was difficult because the Bosnian killings and Hurricane Andrew were 'siphoning off' money and attention: 'We assume it's the psychological interference of all these other disasters.'[41]

Apparently, even people close to suffering cannot cope with too much reality. As the South African Truth and Reconciliation Commission kept on producing – or rather confirming – a regular stream of horrors, some people started talking about 'revelation fatigue'. But this does not mean that the public was so inured to horror that it didn't want to hear more. The media had deemed 'ordinary' revelations as no longer newsworthy, and had decided that only extraordinary exposures would attract public attention.

This causal loop between media and public moves in both directions. Thus Moeller's study is less about the causes of 'Compassion Fatigue', her title, than its effects on 'How the Media Sell Disease, Famine, War and Death', her subtitle. She argues that the American public has slipped into a compassion fatigue stupor. News thought unlikely to receive audience attention has always been filtered out. But the attention threshold is rising so rapidly that the media try even more desperately to 'ratchet up' the criteria for stories to be covered. Moeller's case-studies – such as the Ebola virus epidemic, the Sudan and Somalia famines of 1991–3, the Anfal campaign against the Kurds, death camps in Bosnia, the Rwandan genocide – all show the depressingly formulaic way in which distant mass suffering is represented: the soothing and repetitive chronologies, the sensationalized language, the Americanized metaphors. What causes what? Moeller usually takes compassion fatigue to be a fixed 'thing', to which the media must adjust. They allow compassion fatigue to establish the hierarchy of stories to be covered. But she also argues that compassion fatigue is not an unavoidable consequence of covering the news, but 'an unavoidable consequence of the way news is now covered'.[42] Compassion fatigue may be a media creature, that feeds back into the public's vocabulary of motives. The fact that we can't respond to every appeal is speciously interpreted as a sign that we are too tired to care at all: 'We've got compassion fatigue, we say, as if we have involuntarily contracted some kind of disease that we're stuck with no matter what we do.'[43]

Moeller's analysis of the coverage of the Bosnian and Rwandan tragedies does indeed show the media struggling against palpable audience denial. Atrocity stories sink in response to public mood; Holocaust imagery (death camps, extermination) is explicitly used to capture attention; journalists are frustrated by covering a story that the public is tired of. The coverage of the Rwandan genocide allows Moeller a conceptual change that makes all the difference: what happened was less compassion fatigue than compassion *avoidance*: 'The public flinched when confronted with the images of putrefying corpses or swollen bodies bobbing along river banks. They looked away – even when they believed that the story was important.'[44] This is the essence of denial and bystanding: an active looking away, a sense of a situation so utterly hopeless and incomprehensible that we cannot bear to think about it. She cites (from a *Washington Post* report) just the right metaphor: 'What to do with these pictures, these horrors? Where in our minds do we store the image of bloating bodies floating down a river in Africa?' We become inured to it or try to respond, 'all the while striking bargains with ourselves about how much we will let in'.[45]

Often 'fatigue' is more appropriate than 'avoidance' – but without the connotation of fixed *states* of fatigue 'into' which our bodies fall and our mental facilities begin to numb. These images are too concrete to describe cultural ripples: the shifting thresholds of attention, the bewildering ways in which compassion rises and falls, the blurred boundaries of what is accepted as normal. The sheer repetition of images of suffering, their easy accessibility, or even their intrusiveness need not cause a state of exhaustion. There is, after all, no such thing as love fatigue. And most parents do not become numbed or oblivious to their child's pain and suffering however often she bumps her head or cries. The problem with multiple images of distant suffering is not their multiplicity but their psychological and moral *distance*. Repetition just increases the sense of their remoteness from our lives. These are not our children; we have no bond with them; we can never experience their presence; all we know about them is that they exist for that dislocated thirty seconds during which the camera focused on them. The difference between our own child suffering and not suffering is far more salient than the difference – *a million lives* – between learning that 12 million and not 11 million children under five die every year of preventable diseases.

But we do know these statistics. We don't 'take in' all the numbers, but neither do they pass us by. We can even imagine – an extraordinary possibility only because we have watched so much TV – something of what their mothers and fathers go through. This primordial attachment to their own loved ones does not make people into morally repellent 'bystanders'. Visceral responses to images of suffering can still be as intense as they were in pre-compassion fatigue days – and far more intense than world-weary journalists or sociologists might predict. Take again the 1984 Ethiopian famine story. The reporter, photographer, editors and newsroom staff cried openly as they watched people literally dying on the colour monitor screen. They thought it unlikely that the public would have the same reaction: people would soon get bored and lose interest in the subject.

In 1993 the *New York Times* printed Kevin Carter's famous photo: a desolate Sudan landscape with a vulture perching near a little girl who has collapsed from hunger. The child, more an infant, is naked, bowed over by weakness, totally abandoned and unprotected as the vulture waits, so we imagine, for the final kill. The photo won a Pulitzer Prize, was hailed a classic of photo-journalism and used in many campaigns. The claim was that this extraordinary image 'causes' you to want to know more. Further, 'One cannot look at this picture without wanting to do something to protect the child and drive the vulture away'.[46]

This 'wanting to do something' is, I believe, a universal human response. For reasons that social scientists have not yet discovered – they have hardly even looked – this response is weaker in some people than in others. But if *everyone's* responses become dimmer, we know where to start looking for reasons. These have little to do with fatigue or the sheer repetition of images. The reason is that any dimming of compassion, any decreased concern about distant others, is just what the individual spirit of the global market wants to encourage. The message is: get real, wise up and toughen up; the lesson is that nothing, nothing after all, can be done about problems like these or people like this.

8

Appeals

Outrage into Action

This chapter continues to look at how images of distant suffering are converted into appeals for acknowledgement. Most of the texts cited come from the British and US Sections of Amnesty International over the period 1992–1998.[1] I also draw on some ninety direct mailings received by friends in the USA appealing for liberal causes: human rights, civil liberties, social justice and environment. (These households appear on most such lists and receive on average some 250 appeals each year.[2])

These appeals to recruit new members, supporters or donors are seldom aimed at the whole public. Even the most populist organizations only reach a restricted sector of the population: well-educated, of high socio-economic status, liberal in their political views, already belonging to the 'conscience constituency'. Direct mailings are sent to targets identified by market research profiles and acquired from like-minded organizations such as environmental groups. Advertisements are concentrated in the quality papers which these groups read – in Britain, the *Observer, Guardian* and *Independent*. In bad years these appeals barely break even. Covering the cost of direct mailings, for example, needs at least a 2 per cent take-up rate. In 1993, Amnesty USA mailed some twelve million letters to recruit new members, resulting in only a 0.5 per cent take-up.

Success means 'getting the message across', 'waking people up', or 'getting through to them'; but also 'getting them to do something' – donate money, become active, and be educated. The text is an appeal for acknowledgement: 'Look at this! Listen to what we are telling you. If you didn't already know about it, now you have no excuse for not knowing. If you don't care about it, you should. Something can be done. *You* can and should do something.' The appeal moves through a virtually fixed six-part narrative. The American direct mailings well illustrate this sequence.

Appeal narrative

Who are you?

Existing or lapsed supporters are addressed personally and reminded of their previous commitments and generosity. In the past you made a decision that showed the type of person you are; surely you have not changed; the problem is even more urgent now. 'You have been a wonderful friend of the Salvadorean people throughout the terrible years of suffering, war, "disappearances" and repression by the U.S. armed military forces' (SHARE – Salvadorean Humanitarian Aid, Research and Education). Potential new recruits are identified as part of a like-minded group, defined by ethnicity, religion or shared values; but, as 'people like us', they also belong to a wider moral community. Terms such as 'social justice' and 'oppression' do not have to be explained. The reader is taken to belong to the same enlightened community as the writer. In the wake of the Rodney King event, the Jewish Fund for Justice appeals to a shared history and sense of justice: 'We do this as American Jews . . . as the descendants of immigrants who sought in this country a refuge from injustice and bigotry. . . . We remember the inner cities were our first homes . . . and so we strengthen partnership with those for whom the city has become a deadly trap, rather than an opportunity.'

What is the problem?

The main part of the text describes the problem – whether urban poverty, racial tensions, human rights violations, refugees, famine or homelessness. A case history dramatizes the plight of one individual. A letter by Cesar Chavez for United Farm Workers of America is built entirely around one girl who died of leukaemia after being exposed to pesticides in grape-vines. He describes driving at 5.30 a.m. along a Californian highway, past fields of farm workers: '*Suddenly, I realized something. In the dim light, I was looking at rows of children working quietly beside their parents. Picturing them at the end of their day, tired and dirty, I wondered: What does the future hold for them? . . . And then I thought of Mirian Robles . . . Mirian is a little girl who haunts the memory. Once you see her face, you can't get her out of your mind.*' We then read Mirian's story through the eyes of her family: the diagnosis, her ten-year struggle and her death.

In addition to the specific problem, there are background details and contextual explanations about human rights issues. Why can we not relax our vigilance, given the collapse of communism, military juntas in Latin America and apartheid? A list of horrors is then presented to convince readers that nothing has changed or that changes have been for the worse ('new ominous forces'). '[E]ven though the Cold War has ended, the world remains as terrifying, violent and deadly as ever. And human rights are no more respected nor better enforced by most governments than before.... In some places, it's far more threatening – the *nature of government threats against human rights is changing . . . all too often for the worse.'*

Who are we? What do we do?

The text now describes the organization, its programmes and what it could do with more money. Readers are reassured about accountability: the money will be spent only where needed and will not be deflected either to corrupt Third World leaders or to bolster the expense accounts of agency bureaucrats. There is no equivalent of the starving African child at a clinic; the text seeks to explain just how the organization can 'make a difference'. Amnesty has its own images: 'voices raised in defence of those who have no voice'; 'bringing light into the shadows'; 'a candle of hope in a circle of barbed wire'; 'giving freedom to people who have been consigned by government to oblivion . . . abandoned to die in an unknown cell, unseen and unremembered by the outside world'. Methods of work are described (the urgent action network mobilized, thousands of letters written), followed by claims of success. This prisoner is no longer being tortured, he has been removed from solitary confinement, and is now seeing a doctor or a lawyer. A dramatic claim: 'A former torturer in El Salvador says it makes the difference between life and death: "If there's an appeal from a foreign government or Amnesty International, they will live. Otherwise, they are dead."'

The text explains how overall government policy can be changed, as well as individuals helped. For example, prevent further disappearances by identifying people at risk ('We are trying to find them before the government murders them'); expose governments to international censure and isolation; bring individual perpetrators to justice, end official denials. Amnesty may save individuals, but can't stop civil wars, change governments or establish democracies. Readers are assumed to be pessimistic, but not cynical: they have to be persuaded that something can be done, even though the overall situation is bleak.

What can you do?

Now comes the message of empowerment: 'You can do something.' An existing commitment may need reinforcement: 'Of course, you also helped make possible the dramatic return of thousands of Salvadoran refugees to their bombed and abandoned village. After they resettled you continued to support them ... You have been a steadfast partner to the Salvadorean people ... What a tragedy it would be if we were to stop our support for the Salvadorean people just when they have a real chance to recover from the terrible wounds of a decade of war' (SHARE).

For new audiences, the text tries for a delicate balance: the problem is enormous, but individual action can have some effect. A specific amount ($15) is needed for one case (measles inoculation in this village). The problem is urgent; terrible tragedies lie ahead if no action is taken now. The text refers less to general principles (justice and human rights) and more to personal identity: you have certain values, you know the scale of the problem, you've seen what we can do. Here are a few simple steps for you to take.

Why should you do anything?

Readers are assumed to be discriminating in allocating their limited resources. They are bombarded by endless appeals of this type and are prone to compassion fatigue. It is not enough to persuade them to pay attention and do something – they must select *this* particular appeal. The letter now confronts denial. The *negative* impulse must be overcome (another letter for the trash can) and the *positive* reinforced (the sort of person you are, your values, your capacity for empathy – and the satisfaction you will receive from acting accordingly). The text anticipates common denials and rationalizations for doing nothing – then tries to counteract them. No, it's not true that the problem is so enormous that a few dollars won't make a difference. No, the money won't go to bolster a corrupt regime. No, we are not hostile to this particular country.

The 'problem' is not just the human rights violations themselves (the reader knows all about these), but public apathy, silence and indifference. '*In 1993, the constant barrage of horror from Bosnia was so visceral as to challenge our capacity to acknowledge the pain and sustain moral outrage. Its continuing story is so disgraceful that most of us do not even want to think about it. But that is part of Amnesty's challenge – to overcome the psychic numbing in the face of such tragedy.*'

One entire four-page US mailing was built around Rev. Martin Niemoller's famous text. The text is reproduced ('In Germany they came first for the Communists, and I didn't speak up because I wasn't a Communist...'). Then follows the moral lesson from the Nazi case: *'Today, just as it was in the darkest depths of the 1930s and 1940s, there are millions of people waiting to see if the world – people like you and me – will speak out ... or if they, too, will have to pay the ultimate price for our silence.'*

The themes of denial and forgetting appear in numerous texts. One report is 'a powerful indictment of forgetting and resignation'. There are references to the 'world's fatalism', how 'we simply cannot stand silent and do nothing'. Ordinary people must speak up. The text confronts the readers' sense of helplessness and anger: *'But today you can do something about it. I want you to join me and thousands of others in saying "Enough is enough – it's time the world became a better place."'*

The final pitch

Letters usually end by dramatizing the importance and urgency of the message, sometimes returning to the personal case: *'It's too late for Mirian Robles, but thousands of other lives can be spared.... Without your support, we can never win against the powerful, greedy growers who are defiling the bodies of our children with their toxic pesticides.... Please help assure that Mirian's death was not in vain.'* The final pitch reminds people who they are ('principled people') and stresses the urgency of the appeal. In 'a chaotic new world racked by vicious and escalating human rights emergencies', this is a 'critical moment to help'.

Amnesty Britain's regular full-page newspaper advertisements – visible trademarks since 1990 – are condensed formats of the same six-part sequence. They have attracted bitter attacks by target governments and consistent praise from advertising agencies for their extraordinary impact.[3] In content and style, they look like an exact application of theories of denial and acknowledgement.[4] Four distinctive features stand out:

Immediacy   The most striking feature is a sense of urgency and what the director of one advertising agency called their 'consistently nagging, compulsive, harrowing quality'. They literally grab your attention and do not allow you to slip away. Three methods are used to achieve immediacy and assign an emotional priority to 'what matters': the visual impact of an emotional or intriguing *photo*; a shocking *slogan*, headline or caption; a *text* that holds the reader's attention right through to the final call for action.

The headlines are particularly compelling and memorable – using complex variations of irony, sarcasm and bitter understatement. This effect is often achieved by juxtaposing the banal and the shocking:

- *The Spanish police didn't like the colour of his skin. So they changed it.*
- *Brazil has solved the problem of how to keep kids off the streets. Kill them.*
- *You may well be tortured or killed when you return to Sri Lanka. But that's no reason to feel persecuted.*

Outrage into action   The driving emotional message is 'a quiet rage'. The advertising agency described its brief as converting 'outrage into action'. The Amnesty promotions officer noted that the copy-writers of an Iraq advertisement 'are continually striking a nerve – it uses rage, but it is controlled and directed rage'. There is a consistent sense of anger, indignation and despair at the silence of the public and the hypocrisy of political leaders. After a neutral travelogue opening, the images of Iraq become horrible; the tone turns to outrage: '*Now you have to harness outrage into action: if you know about these horrors and the hopeless indifference of governments, then you must help us. The only way to make a gesture towards acknowledging this obvious madness is to join Amnesty.*' As Sinha summarizes the message: 'You have a choice. Get offended or get involved.'[5]

Reason   Alongside the emotional message of outrage, the advertisements also call for thought and reason. The Iraq/Kurds, November 1990 advertisement presents the reader with dense information – a collage of eyewitness accounts, press reports, official documents, direct quotes, borrowed headlines. As the trade journal comments, 'You never once feel that the person quietly winning you over is anything other than the voice of reason.' The literary style, though, is complex, literate and self-conscious. The reader is credited with being too intelligent and too reasonable to be converted by crude emotional appeals. The text is full of knowing post-modernist allusions to its own failures at representation:

- *The fine words we honour don't serve us. In fact they subvert our message. They make it philosophical when it's about real pain.*
- *Words fail us. As T. S. Eliot said, they slip and slide beneath the strain.*
- *Well-meaning adverts like this one can never begin to succeed.*

The onslaught on denial   The 'problem' is not just what is happening, but public denial, apathy and moral weakness in the face of 'what everyone knows' – hence the heading of the Bosnia advertisement:

'Take a good look. Don't ever say, "I didn't know it was happening."' There is a nagging, insistent quality about the messages:

- *Year after year we shout and scream – and people turn away.* (East Timor)
- *For years we have been exposing atrocities committed by the Iraqi government ... Why should you now be surprised? ... Yes, we told you so. In '80, '81, '82, '83, '84, '85, '86, '87, '88 and '89. And you did nothing effective to help.*

This time, you must convert your acknowledgement into action:

- *When our pity and anger can alter nothing; when we see pain we cannot heal, grief we cannot confront; when our generosity is as useless as indifference – what should we do then? Should we despair and do nothing?* (Myanmar)
- *If the news stories upset you, don't just weep. For God's sake get angry. If enough of us around the world make our outrage heard and felt, governments will have to listen.* (Yugoslavia)

The text attacks not just the silence of ordinary people, but the hypocrisy, indifference and collusion ('official denial') of politicians, governments and the international community. Together with self-referential reminders about previous knowing and not-knowing, the denial paradox is even used as a trick: a UNHCR poster displayed on the London Underground read simply: 'DON'T LOOK ... DON'T READ ... WALK AWAY.'

Issues

Students of persuasion, marketing, advertising, political discourse and attitude change still use Lasswell's classic four-part communication formula: *who* says *what* to *whom* with what *effect*. The standard requirements for persuasive communication remain: the *source* must be trustworthy; the *message* must follow certain rules of logic and attract attention; the *audience*'s feelings must be understood.[6]

Psychodynamic models of persuasion appeal to unconscious motivation (denial in the emotional sense). Learning and rational choice theories deal with incentives to accept the message. Cognitive models see audiences as active thinkers who interpret messages and make inferences, but are 'cognitive misers': their ability to process information is limited, so cognitive energy is preserved by shutting out certain items and oversimplifying messages. Twenty direct mailings a week, all requesting help for causes that sound deserving, cannot be processed rationally.

Attention

The appeal must attract and then retain the audience's attention. We see many similar images of horror and suffering. Why pay special attention to this advertisement, pamphlet or letter? And why should we continue reading it? There are three related methods to fix attention: *drama, shock*, and *vividness*.

Drama   Appeals draw on a series of fixed dramatic narratives. In the background is a world stage of chaos, horror and suffering. In the foreground is this particular drama – say, death squad killings in Colombia. There are agents of evil, innocent victims and indifferent bystanders. We – the rescuers who can break this atrocity triangle – represent the forces of good, which you are invited to join. '*The great mass murderers of our time have been responsible for the deaths of no more than a few hundred victims. In contrast, states that have chosen to murder their citizens can usually count their victims in the thousands. As for motive, the state needs little excuse, for it will kill its victims for a careless word, a different viewpoint, or even a poem.*' (AmB, 1993)

Shock   Communications are often discussed in terms of their 'shock value' or their use of 'shock tactics'. The concept of shock is difficult to define: it can be neutral (a sense of surprise at the unexpected) or carry negative, disturbing or unpleasant emotions. Both kinds apply to many appeals. Shock may be achieved by jarring and unexpected juxtapositions. And the information conveyed is meant to be literally 'shocking'. A controversial example was the AmB 1993 'Holiday Snaps'. This used shock in both senses of the unexpected and the disturbing. A direct mailing was sent in a yellow envelope captioned '*Your holiday photos are enclosed*'. A reader opening the envelope found six black-and-white postcard-sized photographs of victims, each in a different country. Three of the photos were 'ordinary': an Islamic militant under police arrest in Egypt, children walking in a street in Brazil, and a Moroccan woman's face. Three were 'gruesome': a dead Indian man lying in the street with gunshot and torture wounds on his body, a Turkish youth lying on his stomach exposing wounds or burns on his back, and seven or eight dead bodies of Chinese students lying next to their mangled bicycles in Tiananmen Square. The text on the

back of five of the photos was straightforward and unemotional. On
the Turkish photo were graphic descriptions of torture: the boy was
'made to lie over the embers of a fire until he began to burn'; ' "They
raped me with a truncheon" – pregnant nurse'. The accompanying
letter starts:

Dear...
Have you had your summer holiday yet? Or are you still looking forward to
getting away? That's one of the advantages of living in a free society. As long
as we can afford it, most of us get the chance to recuperate in the sun....
   But for thousands of victims of inhumanity there is no sunshine. Their idea
of a holiday is for the guards to stop torturing them for just one day... I really
don't want such thoughts to taint your visions of your holidays. But I do ask
you to give a thought to Prisoners of Conscience and victims of human rights
abuses who are suffering around the world. Take a look at the enclosed picture
cards. If you recently have visited or will be visiting any of these countries,
spare a moment to think about the people they describe...

Vividness   Vivid information attracts attention by standing out in a
message-dense environment: it is emotionally engaging, allows pictorial images, and conveys immediacy.[7] A visual personalized image is
far more easily coded and retained. You find yourself thinking about it
afterwards: 'I can't get those pictures of starving children in Somalia
out of my mind.' This is not neutral vividness, but 'negative imagery'
that is meant to be disturbing.
   On the cover of an AmB leaflet 'Children and Repression' is a photo
of a uniformed man pointing a gun at one of three frightened children;
the caption reads 'Street Scene in São Paulo, December 1990'. In an
AmU recruitment leaflet we read: '*Children doused with gasoline and set*
afire. People dunked in barrels of human excrement. Women raped in deten-
tion by their captors. In Iran, parents have been forced to watch while their
children were shot and then asked to pay for the bullets. In Bangladesh a
prisoner was beaten on the soles of his feet and genitals, whipped with electric
cable and kicked.' Texts can be vivid and attention-holding but not
obviously shocking or gruesome. The cover of another insert shows a
photo of single baby shoe. The caption reads: '*One day in September, 3*
year old Mariana Zaffaran mysteriously "disappeared". Help us keep more
than just her memory alive.'
   The vivid/gruesome issue draws on the general debate about the
representation of atrocities and suffering. Critics are uneasy about
exploitation, voyeurism or 'the pornography of violence'. But which
images are too shocking, graphic or disturbing? Human rights
violations such as censorship, unfair trials, administrative detention

or religious coercion can indeed be described in ordinary terms. But other violations are intrinsically disturbing. Take the widely reported news about business people in Bogotá and elsewhere in Colombia hiring killers to dispose of street children regarded as a nuisance. It is difficult to see how this story could be made to sound anything other than 'vivid': $5,000 fees to clean up a neighbourhood, death notices inviting the local community to attend funerals of street children, the imagery of 'social cleansing'.

This raises three issues: *effectiveness, counter-productivity* and *ethical limits*. We simply don't know whether appeals about atrocities and suffering are more effective if they use shock/vivid tactics. Claims of dramatic success – like the spectacular publicity stunts by animal rights activists who go way beyond the ethical limits of aid and human rights agencies – are impossible to prove. AmB carried out one controlled evaluation in 1993. It sent 98,000 letters to lists obtained from two market research data bases, Oxfam and Friends of the Earth. Two random mailings consisted of a new version of the 'generic' Amnesty appeal letter and (as a control) an older version of this letter. The third mailing included the new letter, but also an envelope containing a package titled *Amnesty International Case File*. On the cover was the warning: 'This envelope contains a small selection of the type of cases that Amnesty faces every day. Many of our cases include harrowing details of human suffering and torment. Please do not open if you are likely to be distressed by such details.' The four cards were indeed harrowing, showing graphic examples of torture, ethnic cleansing, street children and disappearance. Adding the cards elicited a larger response and income than the other two mailings. The average response rate to the cards mailing was 4.34 per cent; to the new text alone, 3.28 per cent, and to old text, 3.05 per cent. Considering that the break-even response for new mailings is taken as 2 per cent, the effect of the cards in producing an extra 1 per cent response (and an income of £17,500 compared to £12,000) is quite striking. These findings, however, are too isolated for generalization.

The counter-productivity thesis is that people turn off in disgust if images are made *too* vivid: the 'severed head rule' is not to show severed heads. Information may become so disturbing that it actually facilitates denial. Most of us have experienced the feeling of being literally unable to continue processing further pieces of information. Like 'compassion fatigue', however, the counter-productivity theory is difficult to prove. Further, many people stop reading the text and throw the letter in the rubbish bin – yet still take some action: 'I renew my membership every year, but I can't bear actually reading the stuff they send me.'

The turn-off effect may be stronger among people who have already accepted the general message and object to their emotions being manipulated further. Existing members of Amnesty sometimes complain about the disturbing images used to attract new members. Referring to the 'Holiday Snaps' mailing, one member wrote: 'I already care about human rights. I therefore do not need to be shocked from a state of apathy or ignorance, which I assume was the intention in designing such an envelope.' Deep empathy can be too uncomfortable: seeing a victim who is the same age as your own child. Focus group research among American Amnesty members, however, found that horrendous images are experienced as too repetitive rather than too offensive.[8] People who are not yet committed may find this tactic distasteful, while existing supporters are accustomed to it. The 'severed head rule' refers not just to pragmatic considerations of what works – certain images are just too gruesome to use – but to ethical limits: self-imposed or from external advertising and marketing codes. Humanitarian organizations have to ask themselves, 'How far can you go?'

Negative or positive imagery

The human rights community did not pass through a crisis of representation. There has been no push from negative to positive imagery, or from passive, pathetic victim to empowered, dignified survivor. The notion of 'empowerment', in fact, has a quite different meaning in this context. Instead of referring to the 'objects' of the appeal, it refers to giving the 'subjects' (the Western public) a sense of their power to act. The aim is to overcome the *audience's* passivity and helplessness. Victims may be mostly portrayed as innocent and passive, the arbitrary objects of brutal state power, but many are attacked precisely because they are active agents, fighters for social justice and political change. Both kinds of victims need fair representation. A recent Amnesty campaign about women highlighted this opposition between positive/strong/active and negative/weak/passive. One pamphlet shows a photo of a woman with her two children (her husband was a community activist disappeared in Colombia). The general caption is: '*Women on the front line of human rights abuses.*' After examples of state violence towards women, there are two parallel columns which follow these stories of helplessness and passivity. The left side is headed **STRONG**:

> *Many women are targeted because they are strong – because they are political activists, community organizers or because they persist in demanding that their*

rights and those of their relatives are respected. As more women reach out for equality and participation in the governance of their society, they become more visible in that society and so more vulnerable.

The right column is headed **WEAK**:

Many women are also targeted because they are weak – gender difference causes women to be perceived as easy targets for both physical and psychological abuse; young women who can easily be sexually abused; frightened mothers desperate to protect their children; pregnant women fearful for their unborn babies; women who can be used to get at male relatives; refugee women isolated in an alien environment at the mercy of authorities with the power to grant them necessary food or documentation.

There is no evidence, though, that this balancing evokes more acknowledgement. The problem to be overcome here is the lack of vivid images of the *alleviation* of suffering. The image recently engraved on public consciousness – bodies being dug out of mass graves – does not allow for much distinction between passive victim and active fighter. And it is hardly an image of success.

Simplicity versus complexity

Simplicity in this context is a vivid story of atrocity followed by an appeal for immediate help. Complexity refers to the wider educational and political goals demanded by the nature of the problem. The pragmatic case is that communication must be as simple as possible to overcome audience indifference. The message must create a connection between 'what you need to know' and 'what you should do'. To make this link, people need not really know very much. Too much information blurs the message. The more complexities you introduce – the historical context, that victims are not always passive, that the government is faced with a security threat, the nuances of international law – the more difficult it becomes to elicit support. Complexity may give an alibi for passive bystanding: 'It all looks so complicated ... Who can tell if this is what's really happening? ... Who are the good and the bad guys in the story? No one can make an informed judgement about what's going on.'

Standard human rights texts – their distinctive style, the citation of all sources, the legal dialect of international conventions – are clearly unsuited to a wider public audience. The original report typically passes through four or five distillations before reaching the public as a one-page leaflet. At each stage, information is flattened out and simplified. An international campaign against disappearances and political killings eventually focuses on one country. By the time the information reaches a children's group, it is reduced to the bare dramatic minimum – a quote on the cover of a children's magazine: '*To those who stole my daddy: I ask God to tell these men to let you come home*' (twelve-year-old girl).

Accessibility entails costs and compromises: details (names, dates, statistics, and sources of information) disappear; there are no nuances of 'allegedly' or 'reportedly' or 'according to most sources'; contextual information is lost. This may be noticed only when the country is familiar. An Amnesty campaign about racism in Europe – with vivid material about police ill-treatment of ethnic minorities and migrant workers – was criticized by European members: Why the focus on the police, instead of racism in general? For them, the material was not complex enough. Southern sections, however, were enthusiastic – for them, the simplicity (the same 'simplicity' with which their problems are viewed by the North) was enough.

Not much crucial information is lost in the strategic link between *what you need to know* (recent political history) and *what you need to do* (write a letter to the authorities). A typical simplified text is a poster about India. About 40 per cent of the page is taken up by a peaceful photo of peasants and bullocks in a field, entitled 'Rural scene, Gujerat, India'. The heading is 'India – Torture, Rape and Deaths in Custody'. The full text reads:

> *Torture in custody is a daily routine in every Indian state. Many hundreds, if not thousands, of people have died as a result of torture during the past decade, and since 1985 Amnesty International has recorded 415 such deaths.*
>
> *Judges, journalists, lawyers, civil libertarians, politicians and police officers themselves have openly expressed concern about the widespread occurrence of torture including rape and deaths in custody. Many Indians, notably civil libertarians, have for years urged the government to halt police violence against detainees. A major cause for the persistence of widespread torture in India is that successive Indian governments have failed to acknowledge that torture exists at all, let alone that it needs to be vigorously tackled....*
>
> *By denying that torture occurs, by failing to condemn it, by failing to bring torturers to justice and by failing to uphold human rights safeguards, successive Indian governments must take responsibility for the persistence of torture and deaths in custody.*

Such texts may not be complex enough. But is the information simple enough to arouse an active, engaged response? A comedian from Comic Relief (a group of British entertainers who raise money for aid/relief and human rights) suggested a pragmatic guide-line: 'You have to give people enough information about the complexity of the issue so that they have all the reasons for avoiding their inclination not to give – even though five minutes later, they don't remember the information or the reasons.'

Virtually all appeals, whether from old-fashioned charities or from sophisticated humanitarian organizations, use an individual case to represent complex information. This is how the situation touches the lives of individual people. These are the 'lives behind the lies': the stories (in first or third person) of a prisoner of conscience, a torture victim, a sentenced prisoner waiting on death row or family members who witnessed their loved one disappear. Personalization has two advantages. First, drama and comprehensibility: complex information can be expressed in clear, vivid forms that attract and sustain attention. Second, identification: however remote and complex the situation, you find a personal link by grasping the predicament of another individual. This is heightened by Amnesty's original trademark style of working with prisoners of conscience. Members write directly to individual prisoners (and/or their families and the authorities) and receive letters in reply. This creates a sense of personal involvement. Not only do you know about this person, but he or she will come to know about you.

But while cases are cited in the original report to illustrate the bigger story, a more concise format requires them to carry the load of actually *telling* the bigger story. The temptation is to use cases that are dramatic, vivid or sensational, rather than representative. The tragic narratives of individual victims may obscure the complexities, and distract from the political issues. If the organization already has a credible brand name and the public has some idea what it does, then detailed information is unnecessary. Sad cases and success stories are enough.

Countries or issues?

Should appeals concentrate on a particular country or frame a general issue, such as impunity, torture or political killings? The consensus is that the country focus works better for recruiting new members. A country that is visible, in the news and the 'cause of the moment' presents strategic opportunities that even the most dramatic issue lacks. Issues or themes, especially complicated ones, are more suited to existing members or in raising general awareness. Issues – torture, children's rights, and women's rights – attract people who want to solve problems, rather than think about Sri Lanka or support the Kurds.

To answer the question 'Which countries?', we need to place personal and cultural maps alongside media maps and the real geopolitical atlas of atrocities. Nothing like this information exists. An American-based organization, we know, will get virtually no response to appeals regarding countries that are off the public map, unknown and uninteresting: Sri Lanka, Chad, Togo or Uganda. Often – like East Timor and Zaire – they were deliberately removed from the map because of American interests. Geopolitical interests select suitable victims and suitable enemies. They also influence the fickle dependence on the international news agenda.

Which issues? Torture is probably the single best issue to use, both in recruiting new supporters and in retaining existing members. No one is 'in favour' of torture; the practice can be easily described; there is an individual victim with whom to identify; intervention (like a letter-writing campaign) may have some effect. A 1993 AmB survey ranked torture as the problem that most concerned members. Racism in Europe and political asylum for refugees, two issues closer to home, were ranked lowest in concern. An equivalent AmU survey showed the opposite: out of five general issues, the two more domestic issues – linking US aid policies to a country's human rights record and aid to political refugees from oppressive regimes – were ranked as most important.

Last, a long way behind, was the most unpopular of issues: eliminating the death penalty. Campaigns in non-abolitionist countries like the USA, where there is strong support for the death penalty, are avoided, so as not to alienate members. Publicity material has to be more vivid (emotional descriptions of last hours of death row inmates, graphic details of the effect of electrocution on the body) and more 'intellectual' by anticipating and refuting common sentiments. A death penalty campaign concerning another country (for example, Saudi Arabia) is easier than a universal prohibition that applies to your own country. For other issues, the opposite is true. Campaigns on indigenous people make more sense in Canada and the USA, where the issue is relevant to Native Americans.

The sheer scale of atrocities like the Rwanda genocide obviously overrides any country or issue variation. But differences in actual or perceived severity are less important lower in the scale. In one study run against common-sense expectations, American and Australian undergraduate students were presented with a list of three scenarios, each with two variations, depicting various human rights violations. Imaginary names of countries were used, but the descriptions were based on events that actually occurred (such as the Holocaust, Uganda in 1976–8, and Argentina in the 1970s). The differences manipulated were (i) type of human rights violation, (ii) number of victims, and (iii) category of victims (ethnic, religious, racial or political groups or gender). Respondents were asked to rank the severity of the cases on a scale from 'most appalling' to 'least appalling'. The vivid scenario of the torture to death of 'dozens' of political opponents each week tended to be ranked as more severe by most respondents than the wholesale shooting of 'thousands' of members of religious minorities. The sheer number of deaths seemed less important and inspired no greater empathy than the death of far fewer people from bloodier methods. (It made little difference whether victims were 'innocent' or political dissidents taking calculated risks.)[9]

Intellectual denial

Implicatory denial consists of arguments, reasons or rationalizations for not responding sympathetically to distressing information. Human rights appeals, in particular, may need a written text condensing arguments that anticipate and then try to counteract standard modes of intellectual denial. These can be tricky arguments. Unlike health or environmental causes, there can be no appeal to self-interest. Unlike famine relief or natural disasters, there is no simple humanitarian appeal, or any obvious symbolic equivalent of a starving child. The nature and context of the suffering have to be carefully explained. Opinions, values, beliefs and political ideologies are more salient. The basic principles of universal rights and international legal standards are not at all self-evident. All this leaves the 'grey areas' that the AmB advertising agency reported from its market research: 'Cruelty to children, poverty, people dying of cancer or multiple sclerosis could not be argued with. The freedom of choice for a communist sympathizer to speak out against his country's government, or the sanctity of the life of a mass murderer condemned to death require more thought for people to agree with.'

Appeals try to counteract both *official denial* and *bystander passivity*.

Countering official denial

Accounts circulate swiftly in the global market-place. Appeals have to address the public versions of virtually all the official denials listed in chapter 4. *Non-partisan*: we are neutral and non-political; we do not take sides in the conflict or prefer any particular political solution. *Violence by the other side*: we condemn violence and violations (torture, hostage taking, killing prisoners or suspected collaborators) committed by armed oppositional groups (liberation or nationalist movements, terrorists, guerrillas, etc.). *Death penalty*: long texts have to set out the standard abolitionist arguments: no, the death penalty is not a deterrent; yes, innocent people are executed, etc. Information has to break conventional frames: 'With the exception of Iran and Iraq, the USA has executed more juvenile offenders than any other country in the last decade.' Sympathetic cases are selected: a seventeen-year-old mentally retarded black offender. The human rights angle (violation of the right to life) needs argument and dramatic imagery: 'If hanging a woman by her arms until she experiences excruciating pain is rightly condemned as torture, how does one describe hanging her by the neck until dead?' *Hypocrisy and foreign policy*: another complicated argument is the connection between Western foreign policy and human rights violations in the target country. This means addressing issues such as arms sales, trade policy, alliances, geopolitical interest, etc. Entire appeals are structured around charges of double standards and hypocrisy ('human rights' invoked to attack enemies, downplayed to defend allies). *New world order*: why, despite the end of the cold war and the collapse of notorious dictatorships, has a more benign world order not materialized. The text has to convey some sense of the chaotic forces of nationalist conflict, ethnic tension, religious intolerance, disintegrating governments, apathy, helplessness, confusion about international intervention – and hence, the even greater need for you to respond to this appeal.

These and other arguments (our organization is independent, and does not take government funds; our research is accurate; we do not rank or compare governments; we do not single out particular governments) are part of the standard repertoire of counter-responses to anticipated objections. They are listed as 'Commonly Asked Questions' in *The Amnesty Handbook*. Aid agencies produce guide-lines to counter popular denial techniques. *Save the Children* has a list of 'Famine Myths' such as 'Famine is caused by over population', 'There's nothing you can do to avoid famines. They are inevitable', 'There is no point in giving any money because nothing is ever done to deal with the root causes'.[10]

Countering bystander passivity

The appeal must draw the audience into a shared moral community ('inclusivity') with at least some common values and obligations. Even for torture, genocide and other gross atrocities, this cannot always be taken for granted. It is even more difficult (and in a sense quite unreasonable) to require concern about administrative detention, political imprisonment, women's rights, death penalty, censorship – all happening in far distant places. A few lines in a newspaper advertisement are unlikely to persuade people to extend the boundaries of their moral community.

The appeal to 'do something' about 'distant' and 'big' problems of visually represented suffering is difficult enough, but is even more so if based on abstract universal values. I can see why truth, justice and accountability should be important to me in my own society, but why should I care about them in Zaire or Peru? Using logical reasoning and good evidence to persuade people to change their strongly held positions is no guarantee of attitude change. Research is not very consoling to those who have faith in the power of rational argument. Opposing partisan groups tend to respond to the same mixed and inconclusive evidence by increasing the strength and polarization of their initial beliefs.

For instance, proponents and opponents of the death penalty were shown the same package of mixed evidence and arguments; each group emerged with its views not only intact, but strengthened.[11] In a study of the 'hostile media effect' two groups of respondents, one pro-Israeli and the other pro-Arab, were shown identical TV coverage of the 1982 Sabra-Shatilla massacre of Palestinians in Lebanese refugee camps by Israel's Phalangist allies.[12] Each group was convinced that the *other* side had been favoured by the media and their side treated unfairly, and that these differences reflected the interests and ideologies of the media. They disagreed totally not just on interpretation, but on the facts of what they had seen.

People stick to their preconceived beliefs despite evidence and arguments that ought rationally to weaken or even reverse them. The more people are committed to a particular opinion or action, the more they resist information that threatens those commitments. Under certain conditions, of course, opinions do change, ideological conversions do occur. Should you present the arguments in their most extreme form or moderate the message by presenting it as not too different from the audiences' own position? When the communicator has high credibility, then a larger discrepancy will be more persuasive; when the credibility of the source is doubtful, then moderate discrepancies work better. Is a two-sided communication – raising the opponents' arguments and then attempting to refute them – more effective than a one-sided communication which ignores the opponents' arguments? The more informed the audience, the less likely it is to be persuaded by one-sided arguments. Thus appeals concerning your own society need two-sided communications more than do appeals about outside countries.

Emotional denial

If, in Arthur Miller's words, human rights information is a regular 'assault on denial', what is the emotional drive behind this assault? If neither the information itself nor the weight of intellectual argument is convincing, what emotions are meant to be aroused?

The information should be potent enough to speak for itself: this is so outrageous that you cannot be indifferent. But this emotional chain does not come easily. Appeals like Amnesty's are more explicitly 'psychoanalytical'. They anticipate defence mechanisms and recognize the deep and understandable reasons for denial in the sense of either blocking off information or staying silent. The audience must be reassured: yes, we are aware of these reasons; yes, your responses are quite normal; a powerful emotional effort is needed to break through the barriers of denial. Appeals, that is, cannot assume that the information speaks for itself. They keep repeating: 'you must be tired of the same old things', 'you've all seen these images before', 'you must want to look away' – but we have to keep telling you the horrible truth. There are three emotional constellations: anger, guilt and empathy.

Anger, rage, outrage

The anger felt by the producers of the message should be an emotion that you obviously share, a feeling so strong that you will feel compelled to do something. 'Outrage into Action' was Amnesty Britain's trade mark strategy. One leaflet is entitled 'Oppression is a locked door, your outrage is a key'; a 1991 file on 'What Amnesty International Does' was subtitled 'Thirty Years of Outrage'. But is anger actually aroused by this information? And anger about what: that these things happen? That people get away with it? That governments collude and ordinary people are silent?

We cannot assume a connection between anger and the desired response of altruistic action. Indeed, anger may be deflected on to the *organization*, for bombarding you with material that only makes you feel miserable and guilty.

Guilt, responsibility, shame

Three varieties of guilt appear in human rights appeals. First is the vague sense in which the information and visual images leave you 'feeling bad'. This sense is induced by the implicit contrast between your easy, comfortable life – and the horrors out there. This contrast is manipulated explicitly and routinely by some aid agencies: 'While you are having your breakfast, ten children in Somalia are starving to death.' Even if the contrast is not made explicit, atrocity images evoke an inchoate sense of discomfort and unease, close to guilt.

Second is the more explicit sense of being made to feel guilty for continuing with your life as if you did not know what you obviously do know. The text of the Amnesty 'Holiday Snaps' letter claims: 'I really don't want such thoughts to taint your visions of your holidays.' But this is precisely what the subtext is meant to do. You *should* feel guilty if you do not change your behaviour. How can you still go to Turkey?

Third is the principled moral appeal to conscience and responsibility. You are invited to join a network which AmU calls 'Partners of Conscience'. Your sense of duty and inner moral imperatives are at stake. You are being asked, to make a moral declaration of where you stand, what sort of person you are. *'It is up to us – you and me – to find out what happened to those who have "disappeared" and to free those prisoners of conscience and thousands like them around the world and to stop torture and execution.'* To do anything less would be to let yourself down, to be unfaithful to your inner convictions – and hence to feel guilty.

The weak link in the guilt-induction chain is the imputation of personal responsibility. In the sense of *original* or *proximate causation*, can it be your fault that street children are being killed in Brazil? You may be deemed to have some personal responsibility to intervene even if you have not caused the suffering. But if you don't have a current causal role, you still have a moral responsibility. These last two senses are often confused. The Niemoller appeal may mean that by the time he spoke, it was too late; if you don't speak up now, you will be responsible for horrors continuing. This is not quite the same as saying that joining Amnesty is 'morally necessary for anyone who is moved by the words of Martin Niemoller...and recognizes what they say about personal responsibility'.

Most student group participants report that the advertisements did make them feel guilty and threatened by the fact that they were not doing anything. So they just skimmed past the text. Why should they continue reading about what they already know to be true? They resent the imputation of guilt. One participant reports first feeling compassion on reading the advertisement, then getting annoyed, 'because you're almost being told that if you're not doing anything, go away...It's your fault that this has happened'. Anger is then directed towards Amnesty, rather than the source of the suffering.

The political cliché about silence making you an 'accomplice' is stretched by implying that you are as morally blameworthy as the perpetrators. An AmU letter showing the faces of fifteen torture victims around the world surely exaggerates the moral symmetry between bystander and perpetrator: '*So take another look at the faces on these pages. And as you do, remember this: To know of their suffering, and to do nothing about it, is a wrong that differs only in degree – not in kind – from the wrong of the torturer himself.*'

Many appeals have refined the theme of 'feeling guilty'. You can overcome emotional denial because 'you should care, you are a caring person, you have a sense of what is fair and unfair', and 'we know that you have an emotional need to show that you care'. This does not impute a lifelong guilt (children are being killed while you eat your croissant) that can only be slightly alleviated by filling out the membership coupon. The message is rather: guilt will come only if you *don't* fill out the coupon. We address your emotional need to do something about cruelty and suffering.

The appeal to shame is used much less. Shame is a more social emotion than guilt – it appeals to a sense of community and moral interdependence rather than to personal responsibility. Being ashamed is also a disreputable state; you cannot feel proud to be ashamed. Asking a liberal Western audience to feel guilty about street kids in Bogotá being killed by death squads makes no sense. More intellectually convincing, morally manageable and an easier task is to ask them to feel ashamed – about passively accepting a world in which these things happen. As Marx wrote, 'shame is a revolutionary emotion'.

Whether guilt or shame, though, there is a peculiar sense in which the *more* you acknowledge all this distressing information, the more responsible and 'bad' you feel for not doing anything, so the *less* you feel motivated to absorb more information – that is, the more likely you are to shut out and switch off. Jane, one of the student group, saw the guilt spiral lying ahead: 'We all feel uncomfortable reading it. And so if we send *more* money, then we're going to have to read *more* of it and feel *more* guilty and going through the whole thing again and again . . . paying fifteen pounds isn't going to stop the guilt next time you read it.'

Sympathy, empathy, identification

The emotional constellation of sympathy, empathy and identification is central to all discussions of the bystander effect and altruism. To simplify, *sympathy* means feeling sorry for victims; *empathy* means feeling what their suffering must be like to them; *identification* means imagining yourself in their position. Each emotional state implies seeing the 'other' as part of your shared moral universe.

All humanitarian messages rely on arousing these feelings. This is not easy. Geographical and social distance, media stereotypes, lack of knowledge, and the sheer scale of many horrors give a sense that these events belong to another world. Can I really imagine what it would feel like if one afternoon, a car were to pull up outside my house, two men were to enter, and my daughter were 'disappeared' into the void? Two equally difficult strategies try to overcome such obstacles: first, a moralistic appeal to enlarge the boundaries of your universe of obligation; second, a personal appeal to identify with specific victims.

The moralistic appeal is to your membership of a universal community not bounded by ties of nationality, ethnicity, religion or politics. Passivity in Germany in the thirties because you were not a Communist or a Jew becomes the same as refusing help today because you are not a Tutsi in Rwanda or a Kurd in Iraq. More sentimentally, the appeal is to *'the hope and love that people in need share with people who care. We are these people and they are us'*. Lapsed members are reminded that *'When you first became a member of AI, you clearly recognized the inextricable bond between yourself and those people suffering under ruthless oppression, physical torture or political violence. You knew that when the human rights of one individual are abused, your human dignity also suffers.'*

A more personal appeal to identify with individual, specified victims is different. One AmU mailing about torture shows fifteen photos of named victims. Then: *'Look around you. The faces on these pages are victims of torture, imprisonment or "disappearance". And despite their having different names and coming from far away homes, they are flesh-and-blood people just like you and me. They have families. They have children. They feel pain. And they suffer.'*

Victims are portrayed as ordinary people. The appeal also tries to normalize the way violations occur: perhaps this couldn't happen to you, but it could happen to people like you and for reasons you can imagine. An AmB mailing on racism in Europe tries to shift the reader from familiar to more improbable identifications: most of you have experienced some form of discrimination (even based on accent or physical appearance); you have different ethnic, religious and sexual identities. So many of you know what it's like to be different. *'But can you imagine your first thoughts each morning when you wake wondering if you and your family will still be alive at the end of the day?'* At this point you are asked to imagine yourself as a Bosnian Muslim or an ethnic Albanian.

Appeals to particular audiences can be more focused: women (imagine yourself as a potential victim of rape) or journalists (imagine being arrested for writing an article). The cover of a 'Youth Action' leaflet reads: 'Would you be put in prison if you complained about your school?' The text tells of a girl in Albania arrested for forming a 'Freedom Society' to protest a decision to withdraw Albanian language lessons. The case of a twelve-year-old Iraqi boy follows: 'Would you be tortured because of your parents' views? Ali was.' A short story competition asked teenagers to *'try to put into words what it would feel like to have your freedom being taken away from you, imprisoned for your beliefs . . . Imagine yourself as a prisoner of conscience: the loneliness, fear and misery of being imprisoned without having committed a single crime.'*

We know very little about the effect of such appeals. Hypothetical atrocity scenarios can arouse empathy for the victims, support for intervention, and a willingness to make personal sacrifices to defend other people's rights.[13] Distress and empathy correlated with the strengths of the remedies they would endorse. But images intended to produce empathy may be seen as too depressing and likely to deter donors. In one study, the simple logo of the charity's name was enough; situational pressures (image, social pressure) worked irrespective of whether there was an empathy photo or message.[14]

Inducing empathy is a complex matter. *Victim-oriented* appeals stressing the victims' urgent personal needs differ from *target-oriented* appeals, which stress the responsibility of the person asked to help. Victim appeals elicit more, but only if the need seems genuine. *Empathy-induced altruism* and the desire to uphold a *moral principle of justice* are independent pro-social motives that may coincide but sometimes conflict. In one study, participants not induced to feel empathy acted more according to the principle of justice; those induced to feel empathy were more likely to violate this principle and act unjustly. In preferring to help the person with whom they empathized, they recognized that they were being unfair.[15] We hardly need social psychologists to tell us that the people or causes for which we feel special emotional concern are often not those in greatest need. But we do need reminding about the myopia of empathy-induced altruism, the random compassion resulting from one country being more photogenic than another.

Just as there are no foolproof intellectual arguments, so there is no emotional mixture – this much anger, that much guilt, that much empathy – guaranteed to produce the desired response. Studies of altruism show that the dominant reason people give for helping – their sense that they just 'had' to do something – is far too intangible to reduce to such formulae. This response of one Amnesty member is common: 'Let's say you get a letter, and it talks about human rights. I have a gut feeling about what I need to do.'

Action, empowerment and making a difference

'Gut feelings' may be a pre-condition for responding to an appeal ('this is the sort of person I am') rather than the effect produced by the appeal. Complex emotions such as guilt and empathy may be as redundant as complex intellectual arguments. Much passivity results not from lacking the right feelings, but from perceiving that an ordinary person like me can do nothing about such a monstrous problem.

Successful appeals depend on the empowering assurance that you can indeed do something simple to help – hence the success of 'Skip Lunch, Save a Life'. One study compared different Red Cross mail campaigns to raise money for the victims of war-induced famine in Sudan.[16] Empathy induced by 'cognitive perspective-taking' (you can imagine yourself in the same situation as the needy person) produced a *lower* response rate than 'perceived effectiveness of helping' induced by seeing the need as deserving and amenable to short-term help. (The fact, though, that the *total* donations from 2,648 respondents was only $390, not even meeting the mailing cost, does not say much for the overall success of the appeal.)

But a message like 'Skip Lunch, Save a Life' hardly applies to the world of atrocities. How do you demonstrate an empowerment chain? As Charny notes, the psychological principle that channelling people to act on information leads to better assimilation of knowledge than passive reception is even more relevant when the information itself is a reminder of the audience's impotence.[17]

There are three links in the empowerment chain: (1) *Something can be done.* (2) *We can do it.* (3) *You can make a difference; here is what you can do.*

These examples from AmU show the first and third stages:

'*a weapon forged not of sharpened steel, but of the* consciences of ordinary men and women like you *wielded in the form of letters, postcards and a bright unyielding spotlight that permits an oppressive government* no place to hide...'
'the truly extraordinary power ordinary people possess *when they stand* together in a mission of conscience *with the bright light of truth and world opinion as their only weapons.* A mighty voice for justice before which even the worst tyrants have repeatedly given way, *unwilling to bear the damage to their image and the threat of their international relationships.*'

The message is: 'By joining AI and condemning the ill-treatment of such people, you can help expose corrupt government, secret police, torturers and murderers.' You join, you condemn, you help expose, you show your commitment – but what does the organization do? 'Your Letter Can Save Lives,' but how? This missing second stage needs to appear at two levels: *micro-power* (how individuals are helped) and *macro-power* (the organization's overall record).

Micro-power

The iconography of the original Amnesty appeal – free an individual prisoner of conscience – remains a strong form of empowerment. One leaflet asks: 'What's the best way to free an innocent victim of brutal injustice?' The method is described with drama and emotional intensity. 'Daily monitors' all over the world tell Amnesty about the plight of a particular victim of injustice; the facts are checked by skilled researchers in the sophisticated nerve centre of the organization; the Urgent Action Network is 'alerted' and set into motion within twenty-four hours of the person's arrest; thousands of letters, faxes, postcards are sent from all over the globe. The result: many of the thousand Amnesty prisoners released each year would not be free but for (the organization and) you: '*Remember and cherish this accomplishment when you hear the cynics say that an individual cannot make a difference in this world. You can. You did!*'

'Making a difference' refers to two claims. One is sentimental – a prisoner in a dark cell awaits your help; she knows you are out there, she is not alone – whereas the other promises concrete results – 'Your Letter Can Save Lives.'

Macro-power

In addition to helping one prisoner, can the organization achieve long-term changes in a particular country or on a particular issue? What is the organization's cumulative record in defending human rights? These achievements are important, but not pictorial enough to contrast with the rather bleak picture that the organization has given (and the informed public knows) about the state of human rights. The unstated message may only be: 'without us things might be much worse: so you should help.' The paradox is that you have to arouse concern by claiming that the problem is deep-seated and intractable ('things are getting worse'), but simultaneously elicit support by claiming that your work has led to some improvement ('we have made things better').

'*We know Amnesty works, but its work is not yet over*' resolves the paradox. But the textual balance is tricky: 'If nothing is getting better, why give? If everything is better, then you don't need to. Somewhere in the middle you need a sense that there are grounds for hope but that there is still work to be done.'[18]

Becoming involved

Most activists, however – as opposed to the unconverted – may not need any utilitarian empowerment to keep them motivated. They are less interested in effects, goals, successes or results, it is enough to know that they are acting in keeping with the sort of person they are. Empowering the individual by stressing the pooled, cumulative effect of all their tiny contributions may be seen as pandering to an undesirable attachment to results: 'Unless they can have the narcissistic gratification of participating in the success, they are unwilling to engage in the struggle.'[19]

A vision of altruism for its own sake appeals to many ordinary people who do not have time, resources or opportunities to be dedicated activists. An Amnesty member writes about why she became involved: 'For me, human rights work isn't a case of "is it effective?" but rather "can I live any other way?"' A renewal letter to lapsed members, reminds them to think back to the reasons why they joined: 'Whatever it was, you suddenly knew that you could not sit by and watch.'

This primeval sense of not being able to live another way must not be confused with another psychological appeal: 'becoming involved' as a way of gratifying your need for personal satisfaction, self-fulfilment, meaning, self-esteem, wholeness, growth or whatever. This – far more than utilitarian success – is the 'narcissistic gratification' to be warned about. The appeal to relieve other people's suffering in order to make you emotionally 'whole' and discover your true self is repulsive. 'Why Volunteer at the Canadian Centre for Victims of Torture?' asks the Centre's leaflet. The last two of its five answers refer to supporting newcomers in their transition from 'refugee to Canadian'. But here are the first three: 'Gain personal satisfaction through helping newcomers adjust to life in Canada . . . Gain personal growth in multicultural awareness and experience . . . Make new and lasting friendships.'

Involvement is a matter of integrity, good faith and being able to face yourself in the mirror. If they were motivated only by results, most human rights activists would have given up long ago. And if motivated only by the quest for self-realization, they do eventually give up.

9

Digging up Graves, Opening up Wounds

Acknowledging the Past

Chapter 10 returns to the question of how images and appeals about current suffering are acknowledged. Before this, I detour backwards in time to review modes of acknowledging past atrocities.

For the collective, as for the individual, 'coming to terms with the past' is to know (and admit to knowing) exactly what happened. Overcoming repression – the conscious cover-up or the gradual slippage – is supposed to be traumatic (opening up graves and wounds) before it becomes liberating. The public and political discourse about acknowledgement (as about denial) draws heavily on metaphors from personal life. Virtually all the objectives of Truth Commissions – overcoming denial, facing the truth, coming to terms with the past – can be expressed in psychological as well as political language. In German, the particular Freudian derivation and meanings of these political concepts are quite explicit. The terms *Aufarbeitung der Vergangenheit* and *Vergangenheitsbewaeltigung* mean something like 'working through', 'coming to terms with', 'reckoning with' or 'overcoming' the past. They also have connotations of treatment and catharsis. The terms *Bewaeltigung* and *Aufarbeitung der Vergangenheit* referred in West Germany to the Nazi past. Soon after 1989, they were also being used to describe the (much more rigorous) policing of the East German Communist past.

Whether there is acknowledgement and what forms it takes depend on the nature of the previous regime, its residual power, how the transition happened, and the character of the new society. The current government may have collusive reasons to suppress the past and encourage cultural amnesia; or, on the contrary, it may have a strong interest in differentiating itself from the past and reaping some of the benefits of truth telling as a way of increasing its legitimacy. In some cases, events are readily recoverable because they were meticulously recorded at the time. In other cases, even with the best political will, past events are unrecoverable because their traces were obliterated at the time. Sometimes the previous regime knew that it was only temporary and would later have its record examined. In other all too well-known episodes, the powerful – Stalin, Mao or Pol Pot – never anticipated that there would be an 'afterwards' when their actions might be judged from a vantage-point that was different from their own.

There are no historical cases of total regime change, complete displacement of every agent of power and influence. The search for knowledge is thus always compromised by the fact that many powerful people in the transitional or new leadership were involved in past atrocities or (more commonly) colluded in them by their silence. Revelations may prove politically embarrassing for those with something to hide and may open a past too dangerous to acknowledge today.

Taking its cue from long reflections on the Nazi case, the discourse has long since moved to meta-questions of representation: not what is known, but how to know, remember and imagine; how to create novels, poetry and films; how to construct memorials, oral histories, testimonies and documentaries. Combating denial is itself subject to forgetting by dealing only with those emblematic cases engraved on Western consciousness. There are places in the world where not only is the past apparently unretrieved or unretrievable, but where the present immediately slips down a black hole. Who remembers political massacres in Liberia? Even international projects to uncover past atrocities leave some cases forgotten. In 1994 a team of Argentinian forensic experts arrived in Ethiopia to exhume the mass graves of victims of Mengistu's former Communist regime, which was overthrown in May 1991. Some 50,000 people were summarily executed during the seventeen-year dictatorship, but neither the original atrocities nor their uncovering received any attention.

There are also obstacles from forces in the old regime which remain close to power. This is evident when the change is not dramatic, sudden or revolutionary, but the result of a slow unfreezing: a new political climate, dissidents released from prison, media censorship relaxed, archives opened. This fits the slow buildup, then sudden final collapse, of state Communist regimes. In the former Soviet Union the terrible legacy of the past has hardly been explored at all – or only gradually and grudgingly. There have been admissions of the official lies about individual incidents (like the Katyn massacre), but no general government inquiries or disclosures. No political force has any interest; a long time has past since the worst horrors, and current problems are more pressing.

In East Germany, the former Czechoslovakia and Romania, know-ledge was initially tied more to demands for individual punishment or the purgative policy of lustration. Truth telling took the dramatic form of 'opening files'. In East Germany, angry crowds stormed the Stasi (the former Communist secret police) headquarters early in 1990. Files were seized, exposed and publicized; the former Ministry of Security office was opened as a 'Stasi Museum'. A January 1992 law granted all citizens access to the dossiers. Controlled revelations con-tinued regarding one of the most spied-on societies ever: some 100,000 full-time agents; some 300,000 informal informers; betrayal by friends, colleagues, close family (wives and husbands spying on each other); millions of individual dossiers.

Most of the Latin American cases, in which military juntas handed over to civilian rule, resulted in more organized, ritualistic searches for knowledge. Official and highly publicized investigations were set up, with names such as 'Commission of Truth'. Each has its own fascinating story:

• In Brazil there was the extraordinary underground project, kept totally secret for five years, to document every single violation by the military regime between 1964 and 1979.[1] This was carried out by a volunteer team under the direction of church organizations, and culminated in the publication *Brazil: Nunca Más* ('Never Again') in 1985. All information derived from official records of the regime itself, verbatim transcripts of military trials never intended to be read by the public. The sheer amount of document-ation – stories of 17,000 victims, details of 1,800 torture episodes, all gathered on a million pages – raises an issue dramatized at the end of President Stroessner's brutal thirty-four-year regime in Paraguay. When human rights groups and lawyers broke into central police headquarters in 1992, they found records of every torture and every disappearance. The 'dossier society' has its progressive uses: without this compulsive bureaucratic urge to record every detail, however loathsome, full knowledge would never be possible.

• In Argentina, immediately on assuming office in 1983 after the collapse of the military junta, President Roul Alfonsin set up a civilian commission (CONADEP, the National Commission on Disappeared Persons) to investigate the 'disappearances' during the preceding eight years, when some 20,000 people were abducted, tortured, murdered and their bodies secretly disposed of. The commission's report (subsequently published as a best-selling book, *Nunca Más*, named after the Brazil case) describes the junta's machinery of terror, the abductions, torture, clandestine imprisonment and murder.

- In Chile, the National Commission on Truth and Reconciliation was set up by President Alwyn's new democratic government in April 1990. Its report investigated 4,000 cases and accounted in detail for each of the 2,000 killings and disappearances perpetrated by the previous government. All victims, though not the perpetrators, were named. The report also described the precise political context and methods of repression used by the military regime. The findings were widely publicized, and were presented individually to all the victims' families.[2]

Why is this collective truth telling seen as so important? What drives a quest so persistent that for more than twenty years the Mothers of the Plaza de Mayo have walked around this Buenos Aires square, demanding information on the fate of their loved ones 'disappeared' during the dirty war? There are three major reasons.

First, for survivors of the old regime, there is the value – old-fashioned as this sounds – of truth in itself. After generations of denials, lies, cover-ups and evasions, there is a powerful, almost obsessive, desire to know exactly what happened. For torture victims, the demand for truth may be more urgently felt than the demand for justice. People do not necessarily want their former torturers to go to prison, but they do want the truth recognized. This, Weschler writes, is 'a mysterious, powerful, almost magical notion, because often everyone already knows the truth – everyone knows who the torturers were and what they did, the torturers know that everyone knows, and everyone knows that they know. Why, then, this need to risk everything to render that knowledge explicit?'[3]

His answer – attributed to the philosopher Thomas Nagel[4] – is precisely the distinction between *knowledge* and *acknowledgement*. Acknowledgement is what happens to knowledge when it becomes officially sanctioned and enters the public discourse. In the former Communist Eastern European states there was little need for 'new' historical revelations. Most people knew what happened in the past and retained this information intact in private memory; no one really believed the official lies. But this information now had to be converted into official truth.

Second is the special sensitivity of victims. This is particularly acute for families and friends of people who were 'disappeared'. Even if you have given up hope of finding your loved ones alive, you desperately want to know what happened to them. The unknown bodies in unmarked graves need a symbolic burial. As Archbishop Tutu states, 'I recall so vividly how at one of our hearings a mother cried out plaintively, "Please can't you bring back even just a bone of my child so that I can bury him". This is something we have been able to do for some families.'[5] For victims of torture, the need is equally dramatic. They have to overcome a double denial: to prove what happened and disprove that this was justified because they had done terrible things.

A final justification for truth-telling lies in the sentiment 'never again': the eternal hope that exposure of the past will be enough to prevent its repetition in the future. Surely, past and future potential miscreants are more likely to offend if no one even bothers to find out and record what they did, let alone bring them to justice. But the principles of deterrence cannot supply a strategy for 'learning from history'. It may seem plausible that the cycle of political violence will never be broken under a regime of impunity. But the deterrent value of knowing that others have been punished elsewhere is uncertain. The same, of course, can be said about the presumption that pardons and amnesties promote reconciliation.

Leaving aside today's scepticism about the Enlightenment faith that learning from the past is possible, there is the brutal political reality that, despite all this knowledge, the same institutions of repression keep returning. Some denials of past atrocities cannot be undone; they might even suggest techniques that will be used later. This dark possibility, though, should restore, rather than weaken, our faith in the preventive potential of truth telling. 'Who, after all', asked Hitler in August 1939, 'speaks today of the annihilation of the Armenians?'

So there are Truth Commissions, government investigations, human rights reports, academic research and teams of forensic experts now travelling the world, exploring the dark secrets of mass graves. These enterprises face profound obstacles: technical problems of memory, political opposition by those who have something to hide, and the sometimes genuine, but often disingenuous, sentiments that old graves should stay unopened and that wounds should be left to be healed by time.

The following are ten methods – used in many different combinations – for converting the information exposed about the past into modes of current acknowledgement.

Modes of acknowledgement

Truth commissions

The Truth Commission, an institution created only in the last two decades, is the most resonant symbol for the uncovering and acknowledging of past atrocities. There is already a substantial literature comparing its powers and its solutions to the vexing problem of the link between truth and justice. In theory, three such links are possible. First, the commission is empowered only to search for the truth; this is a self-contained exercise with no linkage to the implementation of judicial punishment. Second, the determination of truth is directly tied to accountability – by identifying suspected perpetrators or explicitly referring prosecution to another agency. Third, the commission is authorized to implement or recommend policies such as reconciliation, compensation, mediation and – most controversially – amnesty and indemnity. The South African Truth and Reconciliation Commission (TRC) can facilitate amnesty for those who make 'full disclosure', prove that their crimes were politically motivated and demonstrate remorse.

The TRC's report is one of the great moral documents of our time, because of its commitment to truth as a moral value in itself. As a 'historic bridge' to the new society, the commission saw its role as establishing as 'complete a picture as possible' of past injustices, coupled with a public, official acknowledgement of the untold suffering that resulted from these injustices.[6] 'Untold' means vast, but also, literally, 'untold'. The public hearings (and the intense media coverage) offered a stage for people to tell stories that had never before been told. The commission knew that it had to arrive at a version of the past that would achieve some common consent: 'We believe we have provided enough of the truth about our past for there to be a consensus about it.'[7] But whose truth? The report switches to a version of truth telling far more complicated than that of 'consensual truth'. The 'life of the Commission' revealed four notions of truth: factual or forensic; personal or narrative; social or 'dialogue'; healing and restorative.[8]

- *Factual or forensic truth*: legal or scientific information which is factual, accurate and objective and is obtained by impartial procedures. At the individual level this means information about particular events and specific people: what exactly happened to whom, where, when and how. At the societal level, it means recording the context, causes and patterns of violations: an interpretation of facts that should at least erode any denials about the past. Disinformation once accepted as truth must lose its credibility.

- *Personal and narrative truth*: the stories told by perpetrators and (more extensively) victims. This is an opportunity for the healing potential of testimony, for adding to the collective truth and for building reconciliation by validating the subjective experience of people who had previously been silenced or voiceless.
- *Social truth*: the truth generated by interaction, discussion and debate. The hearings provide transparency and encourage participation. Conflicting views about the past can be considered and compared. It is the process that matters, rather than the end result.
- *Healing and restorative truth*: the narratives that face the past in order to go forward. Truth as a factual record is not enough: interpretation must be directed towards goals of self-healing, reconciliation and reparation. This requires the acknowledgement that everyone's suffering was real and worthy of attention.

The report repeats obsessively its driving metaphors of scars and wounds, opening and healing. The past left 'indelible scars' on the collective consciousness; these scars often concealed 'festering wounds'; these wounds must be 'opened up' for the 'cleansing and eventual healing' of the body politic; it is not enough, however, simply 'to open old wounds and then sit back for the light of exposure to do the cleansing'.[9]

This is my entire subject: why is it not enough to sit back waiting for the light of exposure to work?

Criminal trials

From the Nuremberg trials fifty years ago to the current International Criminal Tribunals (for Rwanda and the former Yugoslavia) to the future International Criminal Court, the standard issues of justice and retribution are the same. Two sub-issues are relevant here.

First, must collective truth-telling always lead to justice because individual moral responsibility is essential to this truth? Mainstream human rights policy is clear: we investigate the past in order to identify those responsible and bring them to legal account. We know that this seldom happens. There has been no historical episode where anything remotely like a full policy of criminal accountability has been implemented. Amnesties are granted (secretly or openly) as a condition of regime change. Truth telling is not the *beginning* of coming to terms with the past, but all there is. There is no political will to go further; the enquiry drags on endlessly; evidence is destroyed; witnesses somehow lose their memory; investigators turn out to be corrupt, intimidated or connected to the security forces; the criminal justice system is hopelessly weak and inefficient. And hovering above is the residual power of the old regime, the risk that prosecutions would jeopardize fragile democratic gains.

There is a second, less familiar, issue: not whether recovering the past 'must' lead to legal accountability, but whether the criminal law is at all helpful in this recovery. To convert private knowledge to public acknowledgement, are the rituals of accusation, proof, attribution of blame and punishment necessary? These, after all, are the central rituals of political trials, whether the explicitly staged Stalinist show trials or the other famous Durkheimian boundary-setting trials of history – Jesus, Socrates, Dreyfus, Sacco and Vanzetti, the Rosenbergs, Nuremberg, Eichmann.

The trials (and Truth Commissions) of recent transitions, have raised familiar problems:

- *Time* How far back should they go? For a military junta which lasted for five years after seizing power from a previous democracy, this is not a problem. But for South Africa, post-Communist societies, the Israeli–Palestinian conflict or hypothetical future democracies (China? Iraq?) there is no consensual year zero from which to start accountability for atrocities.
- *Authority and obedience* Who gave what orders to whom, and who obeyed? The conditions under which crimes of obedience occur and the nature of administrative massacres are formidable obstacles to acknowledgement. Faced with the traditional problems of individual moral responsibility, ambiguous orders, blurred and multiple command structures, neither judicial justice nor narrative truth are easily served.[10]
- *Degrees of involvement* How do we identify the different modes of involvement in keeping the old regime going? Occupied Europe is the standard historical precedent, raising the difference between commission and collusion, between active and passive collusion, between deliberate silence (inner exile) and wilful ignorance (turning a blind eye), and the morally repellent but historically accurate idea of collective responsibility. There is a wide range: from the military elite running a Latin American junta to the nuances of involvement, collusion and silence that characterized – in different

ways – South Africa and the former Communist regimes.[11] Everybody grasps the distinction in South Africa between police-officers carrying out a death squad execution and low-level government clerks signing 'passes' which restrict blacks' freedom of movement. But the territory in between is not at all clear.

These three ways of 'drawing the line' – moral history, biography and geography – pose obvious problems for using legal strategies to arrive at the truth. Osiel usefully reviews further problems.[12] Rights of defendants may be sacrificed for the sake of social solidarity. Historical perspective may be lost. Citing faulty precedents or false analogies between past and future controversies may foster delusions of purity and grandeur. The admissions of guilt and repentance required may be too extensive: more people required to admit more responsibility and to break too strongly with the past. Legal blueprints are ill-suited to evoke and construct a consensual collective memory. Even if the collective memory can be deliberately constructed by the law, this may be done dishonestly.

Two recent French cases illustrate these problems. The 1987 trial of Klaus Barbie (the former SS officer, 'the butcher of Lyon') was explicitly justified in pedagogic terms: an opportunity for self-improvement, a history lesson for the new generation. Its failure as a method of generating relevant knowledge is hardly disputed.[13] Finkelkraut argues that the baggage from the long-distant past was too heavy. The defence strategy was to exploit this time gap by running together too many historical issues: the meanings of Nazism, anti-Semitism and racism; the uniqueness of the Holocaust; the character of the Occupation of France; collaboration and resistance; the French record in Algeria and Vietnam; even the nature of Zionism. The result was a post-modernist trial – a text from which no one could learn very much.

The 1997–8 trial of Maurice Papon resulted in yet further frustration with truth telling.[14] Papon, a high-ranking former civil servant (ex-prefect of the Paris police, ex-cabinet minister, close to Mitterrand), was sentenced to ten years for complicity in crimes against humanity. After 1940 he helped organize the deportation of 1,500 Jews (about half the city's total) from Bordeaux to Drancy concentration camp near Paris for shipment to the gas chambers. The trial was intimately linked with the entire post-war denial of collaboration. Ever since the myths of resistance were challenged after 1968, France has gone through binges of feverish self-scrutiny about the whole structure of occupation, collaboration and resistance.[15] The trial could hardly produce a consensual version of this history. To be proved guilty anyway, was it enough that Papon had to have understood the purpose of the deportations, even if he had not 'agree [d] with it ideologically'? Why had the prosecution loaded all the guilt onto one man, who was only a middle official at the time?

The trial revealed neither Papon's moral character nor whether the (young) jurors were more in tune with the new historiography (which acknowledges the choice of Vichy officials in collaborating) or stuck in the old reading: reluctant bending to Nazi coercion to shield their fellow French citizens from something worse. By trying to serve simultaneously justice, history, pedagogy and commemoration, the trial ended up serving none.[16]

The doubts that Nuremberg raised about justice and truth remain exactly the same – though they matter less today simply because there are so many alternative modes of acknowledgement.

Mass disqualification

Lustration is a mode of accountability that bypasses the criminal law by removing or disqualifying whole categories of people from government jobs. (The term derives from the Latin *lustratio*: purification by ritual sacrifice.) The precedent for this mass purging was the de-Nazification policy applied (very partially) by the Allies and the purification of collaborators in Occupied Europe. In recent transitions, it has been used almost exclusively by some post-Communist states in Eastern Europe, especially Czechoslovakia and former GDR (where de-Communization was considerably more thorough than the original de-Nazification).

On the face of it, this looks a suitable way to deal with gradations of mass collusion, silence, informing and collaboration. The nuances of collaboration under state communism were surely too devious, complex and ambiguous to be slotted into any known version of individual legal culpability. And, for a while at least, this looked like some attempt to face up to knowledge about the past.

The unfair implementation of the policy has been widely criticized on civil liberties grounds. But the principle itself does confront responsibilities that would otherwise remain denied. Nevertheless, besides its legal flaws, lustration is a poor method of truth telling. Truth lies in the accumulation of individual details – who did what to whom, when, where and how – not in a blanket disqualification of anyone tainted by association with the old system. Even the sheer fact of collusion has never been properly acknowledged. As the Czech opposition journalist Jan Urban wrote: 'The silence was what mattered, not any individual bastards... And all the current noise surrounding lustration is simply a way of keeping silent about the silence.... We are not looking for facts but hunting for ghosts.'[17]

Compensation

Forms of mass compensation and restitution, the best known being the German policy of reparations to victims of Nazism, have not received much attention in recent transitions. Acts of individual reparation – financial compensation to families of the disappeared, paying for the rehabilitation of torture victims – are surely more important to many survivors than the unwieldy and selective procedures of criminal justice. Others may be repelled by the idea that their suffering can be 'compensated', and may see this as paying people off to keep quiet. There is no evidence though, that this has ever happened. In meeting the victims' need for acknowledgement, publicly organized reparation can make the symbolic link between individual suffering and state accountability. None of this can repair the deeper damages from the past. But the direction is right: victims and survivors see the ledger balanced not (or not only) by humiliating the perpetrator, but by replacing their own physical pain and loss with some political dignity.

Naming and shaming

'Naming and shaming' has become a popular and populist slogan in recent years, referring to a vague notion of accountability by the public exposure of named wrongdoers of all sorts: negligent doctors, corrupt government officials, racist police or careless social workers. In the case of past atrocities, ritual ceremonies of public naming, shaming and denunciation call for official recognition by perpetrators and their political masters that what they did was wrong. The prospect of shaming is a low-risk form of accountability that answers some of the need for truth. If carried out fairly, the public identification of perpetrators marks them with a stigma that is a punishment in itself, as well as a mode of truth telling.

Most of us can sympathize with Nadezhda Mandelstam's response to meeting a woman who had been a paid informer during the Stalin years. People whom she had denounced now came to get revenge, but on seeing her pitiful reaction to the confrontation, the victims lost interest in revenge. Still, Mandelstam reflects, something must be done to make it more difficult to recruit people for such jobs in the future: 'They need not be imprisoned or killed, but a finger should be pointed at them, and they should be named.'[18]

Criminalizing denial of the past

The Holocaust denial movement opened a question (to which I return in chapter 10): Should, and can, a society legally require people to acknowledge a particular past? Most liberals find this a distasteful strategy – a form of censorship that raises the spectre of thought control. In response to the deliberate attempt to deny and obliterate the past by 'revisionist historians' of the Holocaust, some countries have made denial of the Holocaust and other genocides a punishable criminal offence.

The civil liberties protection of free speech is balanced by the symbolic functions of law in clarifying moral boundaries, the special feelings of the victims, and the possibility of deterrence. The renaissance of Fascist, racist and neo-Nazi groups in Europe has given this debate a revived political relevance. Could this have been prevented by a more rigorous (and even legally enforced) attempt to know about the past?

Commemoration and memorialization

The oldest way of acknowledging past suffering is to commemorate the victims by building statues, naming streets and city squares after them, poetry and prayer, vigils and marches. For many reasons – transitions from repressive regimes, the empowerment of marginal and forgotten minorities, political pressures to remember – there has been an exponential increase in the structures (memorials, museums, archives) and rituals (ceremonies, memorial days, standing in silence) of commemoration. Behind the memory industry is a meta-memory, cultural industry concerned with iconography, collective memory, memorialization and representation of the past.

Young's study of the iconography of monuments examines how we remember the past, for what reasons, to what ends, in whose name.[19] His images – as a 'memory tourist' himself – of the European 'landscape of memory' are unforgettable. Much work on this subject, however, is stuck in the gnostic discourse of representation, texts and hyper-reality. The issues raise higher stakes, as revealed in the bitter debates about the US Holocaust Museum in Washington, DC. The museum tries to create a living memorial. Interactive technology and the personalization of history allow visitors entering the museum to punch into a computer, receive an identity card for an actual person of the same age and gender who lived in the period, then learn whether the 'twin' survives or perishes.

These and similar populist methods attract much fashionable criticism about exploitation, sentimentality, dumbing down, death camp chic, etc. The worries underlying such criticism are valid when linked to a wider critique of subjects such as kitsch[20] and the place of the Holocaust in American public life.[21] But qualms about using gimmicks to attract attention and facilitate some education are less important than doing justice to the contested political meaning of the event itself. In the case of Holocaust museums, for example, a major debate is about the historiography of 'uniqueness'. The extreme position is that the attempted extermination of Jews was quite different from the fate of other Nazi victims (such as gypsies and homosexuals) as well as other attempted genocides anywhere before or since – so unique that it was 'out of history', and including other cases is a 'denial of specialness'. Supporters of this position are in turn accused of denial, exclusivity and a racist indifference to the suffering of others. Many advocates of 'uniqueness' are not interested in any serious comparisons. They appeal to a mystical notion of a special Jewish fate which has no conceptual room (let alone physical museum room) for the modest claim that documenting the unique features of each case (Cambodia and Rwanda were also 'unique') is compatible with assembling cases sufficiently similar to be placed alongside them in a general category such as genocide.

The conceptual architecture of a museum, though, is less important than the exploitation of its historical narrative to support current xenophobia and nationalist exclusivity. The 'Museum of the Potential Holocaust' in Jerusalem exhibits contemporary anti-Semitic photos and texts, with warnings about where this might lead without resistance ('Don't let it happen again').[22]

All over the world, commemorations of atrocities have turned into memory wars, the forces of denial and acknowledgement literally battling it out over territory. With each political oscillation, statues are pulled down, street names changed, and public holidays abolished. Some unkempt graveyards in remote villages in Lithuania and Latvia have changed their identity three times over the last decade. In one such graveyard, before the collapse of communism, a small hand-painted sign marked the 'Victims of Fascism' in the unmarked graves; the fact that nearly all the dead were Jews from the village was not mentioned. In the first wave of re-remembering, signs were changed to identify 'Jewish Victims'. The re-ascendance of nationalism then gave semiotic priority to 'Lithuanian Victims', all brave fighters against the Nazis and the Stalinists. As long as there is no literal denial of the historical record of any group's suffering, disputes about interpretation can make a useful education. As Young suggests, we should not just commemorate but do 'memory work', not just build monuments but argue about them, change them and reinterpret them.

This is easier when we commemorate with real live people rather than plaques or statues. In April 1977, the Madres de Plaza de Mayo, the Mothers of the Disappeared, began their first silent procession in the Plaza de Mayo, the main square of Buenos Aires. They demanded to know the exact fate of their loved ones, disappeared by the junta during Argentina's dirty war between 1976 and 1983. Twenty-three years later, they are still walking round the square, joined by the Grandmothers and now the Children of the Plaza. Right from the beginning, during the junta rule, they grasped just the right way to confront the instant historical denial intended by the term 'disappearance'. They named the names and held up photos, thus rendering personal and knowable what the official discourse could not allow. But by carrying their message in a public square, the most open space in the city, they shifted clandestine practices and personal fears into the realm where they should have been denied.

Because the regime was so intensely ideological, this was not a 'simple' breaking of silence, a retrieval and reconstruction of a destroyed memory. As Taussig notes, assassinating and disappearing people, then denying this and enshrouding it in clouds of confusion, does not aim to destroy memory, but to relocate collective memory elsewhere.[23] The state's interest was to keep alive memories of brutal repression – but to remove this entirely from the public sphere (that is, never to acknowledge the truth officially) and deflect it into personal and family memories. There, in the quiet of domesticity, the fears and nightmares are supposed to remain, stifling any opposition. This is what the Mothers still challenge: 'they create a new public ritual whose aim is to allow the tremendous moral and magic powers of the unquiet dead to flow into the public sphere.'[24]

Expiation, apology and exorcism

For many people, the most profound way to acknowledge the past is beyond truth telling or even justice. There is an inchoate sense that the enormity of what happened in the old regime calls for something more radical than appointing a commission of inquiry, punishing a few selected offenders, or demoting them from their jobs. Some kind of ritual cleansing is needed to remove impure elements or ways of thinking, so that they lose their power. At the mundane level, this is merely a demand for apology, admission of guilt, or 'coming clean'.

But these secular terms are elevated into an explicitly religious world-view and language: *expiation* – making amends for previous sins; *exorcism* – expelling evil forces by invocation of the good; *expurgation* – purification by removing objectionable matter; and the many variations of *contrition, confession, atonement* and *repentance*. This religious vocabulary does not sit easily in the modern discourse of 'rights'; the only equivalent secular vocabulary comes from psychoanalytical ideas such as catharsis. Nevertheless, secular participants appear to go along with the religious rhetoric. There was some unease in South Africa about the prospect of immunity for offenders who publicly expressed remorse. But the desirability of repentance was taken for granted: the only question was whether these public accounts of remorse were 'genuine'. Archbishop Tutu continually referred to the cleansing power of truth and warned that if truth does not emerge, it will come back to 'haunt' the society.

Truths about moral responsibility do not need supernatural blessing; they should be directed towards exoneration of the victims: secular rituals to cleanse the identity and reputation of victims, searching police files to find the falsely accused, the arbitrarily arrested, the tortured – and then publicly reminding people of what was done to them. 'Freeze-dried' stigmas can thus be unfrozen: a gesture of reparation to living victims and the families and friends of the dead. This secular version of expiation is directed towards others, not turned inwards. It must allow that former victims and enemies were heroes. This politics of vindication may or may not ease the pain of survivors or reach the inner demons of perpetrators.[25] South Africans asked the old regime to make two difficult acknowledgements.[26] First, to admit that apartheid was not just a 'mistake', 'irrelevant', 'coming to a dead end', a 'closed book' or what ex-President de Klerk referred to (as late as March 1992) as something that 'started in idealism in the quest for justice'. These are wholly inadequate expressions of regret for the deliberate suffering that was caused. Second, to concede that the opposition's cause was justified: that is, people were victimized not because they were wrong or bad, but because they were right and good.

Few of those fallen from power can be expected to make such acknowledgements or express much genuine regret. They are more likely to feel that any 'transitional justice' is merely revenge. They can also accuse the new regime of scapegoating: a logical extension of earlier denials of responsibility (and justified when the selection of perpetrators is tendentious or random). Most leaders see themselves as forced by circumstances ('history') to adjust to change. Other less powerful participants give voluntary testimonies that sound more like attempts at exorcism or catharsis: a tormented Graham Greene-type character tells the awful truth to rid himself of the burden of living too long with too many bad secrets. In March 1995 – well after the Truth Commission and the trials of the junta generals – Adolfo Scilingo chose to divulge his secrets. For eighteen years, he had lived with nightmares about realities that the Truth Commission had not uncovered. He had been an officer at ESMA, the Navy School of Mechanics in Buenos Aires – a centre where thousands of people had been kidnapped, tortured and disappeared. Scilingo recounted that he had personally murdered thirty political prisoners, throwing them alive from an aeroplane into the ocean. Every Wednesday for two years these routine flights took place: the prisoners (some 2,000 just from ESMA) were placed in a room with soothing music; injected with sedatives by a doctor; driven to the airport and stripped naked; then placed in the plane for dumping. Catholic Church leaders, Scilingo claimed, had been consulted and approved the murders 'as a Christian form of death'. The Church denied these charges; President Menem denounced Scilingo ('Scilingo is a crook. He is rubbing salt on old wounds'); a campaign was begun to discredit him (he had been convicted in 1991 of car theft and stripped of his officer rank). A retired senior army officer stated: 'It was a civil war that happened 19 years ago. It's stupid to continue reopening old wounds.'

The 'Scilingo effect' did more than authenticate the worst rumours and fears. His public appearances and obsessive stories were reminders of what most people preferred to forget. Mignone optimistically argues that 'the society was forced to confront its own denial, its tacit approval during those years of clandestine crimes'. Public reaction was subdued during the commanders' trials, and the proceedings were not allowed to be shown on television. Seeing faces 'is the only way for them to realize that nice-looking, well-dressed, articulate Mr. Scilingo, that gentleman who could be your next-door neighbor, is the very embodiment of the Process ... and here he is addressing you in your living room night after night'.[27]

Other tales of expiation sound less purgative than Scilingo's and closer to the secular notion of apology as reparative and remedial device – as in Goffman's fine definition:

> In its fullest form, the apology has several elements: expression of embarrassment and chagrin; clarification that one knows what conduct has been expected and sympathizes with the application of negative sanction; verbal rejection, repudiation and disavowal of the wrong way of behaving along with vilification of the self that so behaved; espousal of the right way and an avowal henceforth to pursue that course; performance of penance and the volunteering of restitution.[28]

An example is the public letter written by the South African doctor, Benjamin Tucker, in 1991. In 1977, Dr Tucker had behaved in a grossly negligent and unethical way by failing to treat properly the black consciousness leader Steve Biko in prison. He also credulously accepted the Security Police version of Biko's injuries. The truth came out about Biko's killing, and in 1985 Dr Tucker was made accountable and shamed (barred from practice for 'disgraceful conduct' by the disciplinary committee of the South African Medical Council). He was then reintegrated: his medical licence reinstated after he sent a letter of apology to the council. He then wrote a public letter which does not simply admit negligence, plead unthinking obedience, or claim that he was only doing his job. He makes the crucial admission: that he had become too closely identified with the security interests of the state rather than to medical and personal ethics.

Few statements of regret or acts of penance meet Goffman' stringent criteria. Furthermore, these rituals may be performed without touching the political causes of past atrocities or contributing to the prevention of future episodes. For this reason, the goals of *reconciliation* and *reconstruction* have now come to the fore.

Reconciliation

The voice of reconciliation starts with the tone of gentle reason: 'Why live in the past?...You have to draw a line somewhere...Close the book on the past...Time to turn a new page...What's over is over...We must learn to live with each other...No one has clean hands...Let's look forward to a new future for our children instead of looking backwards.' This voice, however – especially under the slogan of 'national reconciliation' – may be bogus and self-serving, a strategy to evade accountability and perpetuate historical denial. People who set neighbours, friends and families against each other as informers, now preach reconciliation. They pardon themselves, give themselves the right to be magnanimous, and take the prerogative on closing the book on the past.

When the rhetoric of reconciliation is genuine, it looks for tolerance, forgiveness, social reconstruction and solution of social conflicts in ways other than punishment. If made in good faith, such appeals do not call for denial of the past. On the contrary, they assume that perpetrators and bystanders have already acknowledged what happened. Victims and survivors cannot be expected to forgive without full knowledge: 'Father, I am ready to forgive, but I need to know whom to forgive and for what.'[29] Again, this is not just a matter of factual knowledge: 'It is impossible to expect "reconciliation" if part of the population refuses to accept that anything was ever wrong, and the other part has never received an acknowledgment of the suffering it has undergone or of the ultimate responsibility for that suffering.'[30]

Reconciliation is a radical way of confronting the past. It demands the greatest struggle in the personal lives of victims, survivors and their families, especially if coupled with a demand for forgiveness. Mathew Kondile's mother listens to a session of the South African TRC. Her son was killed by the infamous Dirk Coetzee, one of the most savage leaders of the South African Police death squads. Mrs Kondile refuses to forgive him. Mandela and Tutu, can forgive she says, because they live 'vindicated lives'. But, 'In my life nothing, not a single thing has changed since my son was burnt by barbarians. Nothing. Therefore I cannot forgive.'[31]

In the cultural space between public pronouncements and private torment, indices of reconciliation are hard to detect. I will argue later that becoming reconciled to the changes is enough, even if this is not 'genuine', 'sincere' or 'from the heart'. But even this criterion is ambiguous, especially after a long record of atrocities and widespread collusion. South African whites are 'reconciled' in the sense of accepting that they have no choice, but not in the sense of accepting responsibility for past injustices inflicted by a regime which they overwhelmingly supported. A recent survey suggests that the majority of whites are unconvinced that they played a role in apartheid abuses.[32] Some 44 per cent thought that the former system was not unjust and that apartheid was a good idea, but badly implemented. Proportionately more responsibility for past atrocities was assigned to anti-apartheid activists and 'troublemakers' in the black communities (57 per cent) than to the security forces (46 per cent) and former nationalist government (46 per cent). Some 60 per cent felt that victims of apartheid should not be compensated for the ills they suffered in the past. A hopeful finding, however, was that younger whites were consistently more supportive of the transition.

Reconstruction

The most politically fitting way to acknowledge past injustices and suffering is to rebuild (or build from scratch, if there is no democratic tradition to fall back on) the foundations necessary to maintain the new democracy. Atrocity is neither a concept nor a state of mind, but an institution and a concrete set of social practices. 'Human rights education' is not a matter of telling more atrocity stories, but of explaining why a particular practice began and was sustained. Acknowledging the realities of torture needs far more than collating the screams of victims or the justifications used by torturers. What needs dismantling is the entire 'torture regime'.[33] Torture used for a long period of time in any society must have its own laws, jurisprudence, bureaucracy, education, language, cultural representations and political justifications.

The need for reconstruction is obvious: creating the conditions for democracy and legality, restoring a decent public life, advancing social justice. After the first thrill of opening the secret casket, people are more interested in policies that address the present and the future rather than looking back. But there must be room for 'negative' reconstruction: looking back not just to acknowledge, but to undermine the public discourse which allowed for collusion, silence and indifference. Civic education should include a discussion course on linguistic morality. This would scrutinize the public denials from the past: all the techniques of neutralization, rationalizations, excuses, justifications and bystander clichés. Some of these accounts should at least be censured.

Acknowledgement and social control

'Who controls the past ... controls the future; who controls the present, controls the past.'[34] We have learnt that this applies not just to Orwell's Nineteen Eighty-Four, in which the Ministry of Truth rewrote the past, but to daily life in very different political conditions: 'the control of the past depends above all on the training of memory. . . . It is necessary to *remember* that events happened in the desired manner. And if it is necessary to rearrange one's memories or to tamper with written records, then it is necessary to *forget* that one has done so. The trick of doing this can be learned like any other mental technique. . . . It is called *doublethink*.'[35] The denial paradox is identical to 'doublethink' – and hence part of the state's task of creating and enforcing the sense of temporal continuity needed for public order.[36]

To escape state-centred social control is to establish some break between present and past, becoming a permanent fugitive from one's own past.[37] People all over the world live with dreadful memories – as victim, survivor, perpetrator, bystander. They see themselves trapped in the past; they talk of escaping it, or try to forget the suffering. Others seem unable to remember. Like Oliver Sacks's patients, they need the psychological equivalent of L-DOPA to be awakened.

Memories of living through a political history ('this is what it must have been like during the junta') are not subject to such unitary, neurological processes. There is more than one perception of past suffering; perception is always distorted to meet the agenda of the present. Personal memory is contaminated by the passing of political time. Memory is a social product, reflecting the agenda and social location of those who invoke it. This is yet another memory war: those trying to suppress versus those trying to resurrect what has been or what potentially might be forgotten. But when you say that you were 'just doing your duty' or 'only a cog in the machine' or that 'others have done much worse', was this true at the time, or only fabricated, then made true, by later political history?

Even without verbal accounts, the torturer from last year's military junta does not seem to quite belong to today's time. Rosenberg, writing about Marcel Ophuls's film *The Memory of Justice*, meditates on the profound discontinuity resulting from the fact that the accused is tried for an act he committed in a very different past. At the time of his trial, he seems to be another person. 'In some degree, punishment is always meted out to a stranger who bears the criminal's name.'[38] This is true for all criminals. But the political perpetrator appears before a tribunal that represents no less than the 'judgement of history'. Project time from the offence backwards: during the early trials of French collaborators, Sartre and de Beauvoir were troubled by the biographical question: they had known this fellow in school, a bright friendly boy. What did he have to do with this nasty informer in the dock? Or project time from the offence forward: would this harmless-looking bumbler in court – Eichmann peering through his spectacles – be capable of committing these atrocities *now*? A survivor of Auschwitz walks past the Nuremberg prisoners' box and suddenly sees the accused as human beings:

> A metamorphosis had taken place. The real criminals have been carried off by history and will never return. In their place has been left a group of ageing stand-ins, sick and trembling with fear. Judgement will be pronounced on a round-up of impersonators, a collection of dummies borrowed from the wax-works museum. At worst, these feeble mediocre fellows, 'just like other people', could only have been, as they claim, cogs in the death machine somehow fashioned by history.[39]

Of course, not all state criminals present themselves as pathetic mediocrities. They can just as easily be arrogant, bullying and self-righteous. Like the Argentinian generals or Ceauşescu in Romania, they justify their actions, condemn their judges, and refuse to recognize their legitimacy. In the Argentinian junta trial, General Videla announced his self-sacrificial martyrdom; like Christ, he was putting himself at the mercy of a court with no authority: 'Your Honours of this Court: You are not my natural judges. And for that reason you lack jurisdiction and legal authority to judge me.' They may even assert that no amount of information recorded by Truth Commissions, no details revealed in criminal trials, will detract from the historical justice of their cause. This is what another convicted Argentinian ex-junta commander, Emilio Massera, meant by his chilling words in court: 'I am responsible but not guilty. *My judges may have the chronicle, but History belongs to me* and that is where the final verdict will be decided.'

These appeals to higher loyalties or evasions of responsibility (just following orders) are attempts to deny history, to become fugitives from time and, above all, to be judged not by standards of today (legality, human rights, justice) but by the standards of the past. This 'denial of time' is surely the most powerful of all justifications, the most difficult for their ahistorical judges to refute – not because its ideology is coherent, but quite the reverse. They kept silent in the immediate post-war period, because 'the new generation would not have understood those times'. Their claim now is infinitely more radical (and terrifying because we cannot be sure that it is totally impossible): 'If you were there then, you would have done exactly the same.' So set me free, cut me loose from history. The voice of the present refuses to accept these pleas for historical relativity. It echoes the cry from the balcony during the Eichmann trial: 'But ah! You should have seen him in his colonel's uniform.' The trial is about that other – the creature empowered to dispatch millions to death, not the balding old man listening through the headphones.

So much for individual acknowledgement. But what refuge is there for the collective, for the whole society? To be free from social control means to be without any repository of historical knowledge. There is no need for collective rituals of expiation or reparation, because nothing has happened, there is nothing to be sorry about. Some social suffering is not remembered at all. Whole societies slip into mass denial – with terrible consequences, especially for victims and survivors who find themselves literally dislocated from historical time. Given the pace of events and the proliferation of instant media facts, this slippage is now normal.

Social control may be achieved not just by relentlessly confronting the past – opening the last archive, punishing the last offender, compensating the last victim. The ideal of an International Criminal Court assumes that social control is inextricably tied up with accountability. You discover the truth about the past in order to achieve justice in the present. But social control is also possible by transforming or obliterating the past, especially by weakening or redefining the relationship between what has gone before and what currently exists: not by opening the past to scrutiny, but closing it and deliberately setting up barriers to memory. This mode of policing the past calls not for the recovery of memory, but its eradication.

All societies use both strategies – recovery and eradication. But perhaps particular societies, at particular times, slip into one or other of these modes – control by opening or by closing. Spitzer compares regimes of continuity with regimes of discontinuity. In *regimes of continuity*, selective amnesia is induced by eliminating certain elements of the past and preserving others. The past has to conform to the present to establish a version of history (a master narrative) to legitimate current policy. The Stalinist form of controlling the past – the deliberate suppression and distortion of history – is the classic type. (But, as Havel notes, its rewriting of history was never very effective: 'It is truly astonishing to discover how, after decades of falsified history and ideological manipulation, nothing has been forgotten.'[40])

By contrast, there is the selective forgetting of *regimes of discontinuity*, where the multiple narratives of the market dominate. Here, forgetting is the by-product of rapid social change, a post-modern Disneyland 'history', an inability to assimilate the present. The past is not deliberately obliterated or rewritten in the Orwellian sense; instead, it evaporates and disintegrates in the cacophony of the present.

Regimes of continuity, Spitzer notes, tend to be centripetal. In state Communist or classic totalitarian societies, the truth is shaped in relation to a single centre, a homogeneous core of beliefs not to be questioned or disturbed. The past is continuously adapted and revised to reflect shifts in belief and the current political agenda. Some events are, in Kundera's memorable phrase, 'airbrushed' out of history – but they may also be restored when previously unacceptable ideas or persons are rehabilitated. This is why lustration is so characteristic of societies like these. This is just the type of policy to be expected in regimes familiar with the business of rewriting history – and which have gone through previous sequences of upheaval, followed by purges, followed by rewriting history.

The process is different and more subtle in post-modern market societies. In these regimes of discontinuity, knowledge disintegrates and is subject to scepticism, revision and irony. The truth dissolves in an implosion of too much information or quasi-information, facts or factoids, documentaries or dramatic reconstructions. The movement is centrifugal rather than centripetal. Information and memory simply fall away. It becomes difficult to establish the connection between what is and what has gone before. The past is erased without need for censorship, propaganda or a Ministry of Truth. Repression of the past (slippage from memory and history) merges into denial of the present (losing phenomena in the implosion of information). How many people who were adults in 1960, can list the massive political massacres since then: the Ibo in Nigeria, the southerners in Sudan, the Ache in Paraguay, the East Timorese by Indonesia, the Kurds in Iraq, the Hutus in Burundi, the Tutsis in Rwanda, the Cambodians by the Khymer Rouge, the Ethiopians by the Mengistu regime, the Ugandans by Idi Amin, the Bosnian Muslims by the Serbs ...

These are not two different types of society, corresponding to Communist and market, each with its own mode of repressing the past. Despite their post-modern, centrifugal forgetting, Western democratic market societies still encourage the more traditional rewriting of history. The astonishing shifts in American foreign policy are textbook Orwellian: last year's ally and favoured arms customer becomes today's enemy; today's 'emerging democracy' was last year's terrorist state. The only post-modern feature of these shifts is that the state does not even attempt any principled justification; a total transformation is merely a 'change of course'.[41] An invasion of Zaire does not even need to mention previous support for the same regime.

The global movement to the free market – the other face of democratization – allows post-modern forgetting to supplement these older more ideological forms. The very traditional (continuous, linear, centripetal) Turkish denial of the Armenian genocide has thus been supplemented by a contemporary, post-modern version. This is a discourse of mindless relativism, a mechanistic repetition of the stupid idea that there must always be another point of view.[42] In the name of 'looking at both sides', the massive historical record of the massacres now becomes a series of 'allegations', 'feelings', 'claims', or 'rumours'.

Over-acknowledgement

Long before the era of Truth Commissions, we heard the platitude that societies which failed to remember their own past would be doomed to a terrible fate. Today it is *impossible*, we are told, for a society to deny or evade the discreditable truths of its recent history; past demons will always return. This is the political version of Freud's haunting idea that the neurotic is doomed to repetition. Acknowledge now, or the same horrors will keep on happening.

Still, we vaguely disapprove, or even mock, people who 'live in the past', who insist on 'dragging up the past'. From our cosmopolitan heights, deracinated lives and faith in reconciliation, we fail to understand the depths of historical grievance. (As a small child, I once showed my father a tiny toy car I had bought. He looked at the label, then crushed the car in his hands. All he said was, 'Remember next time: we don't buy anything made in Germany.')

The opposite of amnesia is a literal inability to forget anything. The Russian neuro-psychologist, Luria, studied the famous mnemonist, Shereshevski, who had an extraordinary capacity to remember any data or lists and fully recall this information a decade later.[43] Shereshevski's acute sensory perception allowed him to remember all images and facts, but he lacked the capacity for abstraction. He entertained audiences with his memory tricks, but could never live an ordinary life. 'Tormented by a clutter of facts that he could forget only through an enormous effort of will, he found his gift a burden.'[44]

More onerous are the burdens of memory carried by millions of people who – as victims, observers and perpetrators – have lived through the most awful experiences imaginable. They survived, but are condemned to remember and relive. The clinical term 'Post Traumatic Stress Disorder' is hopelessly bland to describe their thoughts and feelings, as they endlessly replay the events that have marked their lives forever. Even 'through an enormous effort of will' they cannot forget. Some are compelled into giving public testimony, others remain in an internal theatre, hidden – sometimes for a lifetime – from even their families and loved ones. In Freudian theory, all life's memories are retained; the unconscious has no sense of time. Painful pasts are assigned to the unconscious, covered up and warded off by more benign screen memories. The analyst deciphers this 'reverse mnemonics' – and recollection starts again.

These private torments cannot easily be relieved, not by grief counsellors or by memory workers. You cannot make people forget. But strong political action is needed to prevent the more virulent forms of over-acknowledging the past from becoming the driving force of political cultures. Collective memories become programmes for revenge and hatred directed even against screen targets.

Historians have well exposed the 'imagined communities' and 'invented tradition' which drive today's ethnic nationalist violence. The litany of memory is endless – martyrs, revenge, feuds, shame, redemption, sacrifice, grudges and the suffering of ghosts. The language of collective denial combines with the rhetoric of 'blood and belonging' to offer two attractions: settling accounts with the past and shaking off any residual restrictions on present brutality.[45]

When General Ratko Mladic entered Srebrenica, his first public statement was a vow to take revenge on the 'Turks' for the Serbs they had killed in the area. 'Here we are in Srebrenica on July 11, 1995. On the eve of yet another great Serbian holiday...we present this city to the Serbian people as a gift. Finally after the rebellion of the Dahijas, the time has come to take revenge against the Turks in this region.'[46] Mladic referred to today's Muslims as if they were the Ottoman Turks; the 'rebellion of the Dahijas' was a Serb uprising that the Turks crushed in 1804. Nearly two centuries later, he was still seeking revenge. The memories 'recovered' by the Serbian ideologues are even older, repressed for six centuries of suffering (the historical equivalent of repressed memories of Dr Karadic's psychiatric patients?) since the primal defeat in the Battle of Kosovo in 1389.

Post-modern acknowledgement

Historical accountability is now an item on the international agenda. Countries which did not even pay lip-service to democracy a decade ago are now lining up to sign human rights declarations and adopting the rhetoric of accountability for past abuses. And more stable democracies are being pushed to acknowledge their own historical victims, like indigenous peoples, or their proxy support of distant atrocities. All history has become revisionist. The notion that current political agendas influence how the past is viewed is now banal – and dangerously close to the thesis that no objective record of past events is possible. Like collective forgetting, today's collective acknowledgements of the past retain traditional along with post-modernist modes. Historical denial now is 'coming to terms' with a past episode by denying its continuity with what came before or what exists now. History was ruptured; something happened; it no longer happens; so there is no point in talking about it too much.

For two decades after Morocco's annexation of Western Sahara in 1975, hundreds of Sahrawi people were arrested and 'disappeared'. Their relatives were too scared to speak openly; the authorities denied all knowledge of detention, disappearance or tortue. Tazmament was a secret fortress detention centre in southern Morocco. For eighteen years from 1973 to 1991 fifty-eight political prisoners were detained there in appalling conditions. Half died from their treatment; all suffered terribly. All along, despite frequent allegations by human rights organizations, the Moroccan government totally denied the prison's existence. As late as July 1991, King Hassan said in a public statement that 'Tazmament existed only in the minds and imaginations of ill-intentioned people'. At about this time, the last inmates died or were released; their families were never notified of their fates; the place that never existed was closed. In July 1992, King Hassan stated: 'It was a place used to keep persons administratively assigned there . . . it has no further reason to exist. The chapter is closed. It existed. It no longer does. That's all.'[47] Knowledge without acknowledgement; suffering without compensation; violation without accountability; horrors that are not exorcised; history without continuity – perfect post-modern events.

But alongside such instant 'forgetting' – the past erased with a few inappropriate words – there is instant remembering. This is a virtual-memory industry, trading in kitsch cultural products and instant memorialization. It is impossible to convey the particular combination of the pious, the fake and the sheer tacky in these ceremonies, films, novels, poems and art. I started a long analysis of this genre, but gave up when I heard of a case beyond all analysis: the US team for the 1996 Olympic Games in Atlanta chose the Holocaust as the subject of its synchronized swimming performance. (The routine was rehearsed, but later withdrawn on grounds of 'bad taste'.)

Going further than virtual commemoration, these are political times for instant virtual apology, guilt, regret and exorcism. The Japanese government apologizes to Korea for the comfort women and is asked to apologize for its treatment of British POWs; the New Labour government apologizes for the Irish potato famine; Yeltsin apologizes for the murders of the Romanovs; the Queen signs a New Zealand act of parliament apologizing to the Maoris; the USA is busy apologizing for everything – the eradication of Native Americans, slavery, drug experiments on black prisoners; Clinton tours Africa and apologizes for slavery the minute he arrives at a former slave-state; and Suharto steps down and asks Indonesians to forgive him.

These spectacles of remorse are harmless enough. At least they do not invent a mythical past to justify future revenge and hatred. But acknowledgement of a collective narrative (or confirmation of collective memories of this narrative) should be done for its own sake. That is, we must know at all costs and without compromise, but not insist on drawing a 'lesson'. Any principled lessons about moral accountability will always be compromised by political reality. Zalaquett's slogan – 'All the truth and as much justice as possible' – is good advice, not because the truth heals, but because no political institution, least of all the state, can be entrusted with rationing the amount of truth. As for justice, nothing can be done to put right the residues of previous atrocities. The choice is not between truth and justice, but between the amount of past injustice that is and is not tolerable. Forgetting is not possible. Yet to live 'on' these terrible memories, the whole society eaten up by hatred and desire for vengeance, must be wrong. 'You have to remember', writes Michnik, 'but you have to be able to transcend the frontier of your own suffering, you must not insist on remaining in the world of your own suffering.'[48]

At the personal level, this sounds right. But which of us is arrogant enough to give this advice to someone who has personally suffered? We should have no moral unease, though, in advising people who were not victims themselves, but have so deeply absorbed the collective survivor mentality, that surrogate memories of past suffering become the only thing that gives meaning to their lives. To them, we can appeal without any apologies: Instead of remaining locked in the very loyalties that caused the suffering, look for some cosmopolitan identity.

To deny past horrors is immoral, but to make collective apologies for the past to whole groups (or their representatives on earth decades or even centuries later) is preposterous. In July 1999, the Florida-based Lutheran Orient Mission Society went on a Reconciliation Walk through the Middle East, tracing the path of the Crusaders from Cologne to Jerusalem. The 400 apology hikers ended up praying in Jerusalem to mark the 900 years since the Crusaders slaughtered Jews, Muslims and Eastern Rite Christians. Instead of being solemnly greeted and *thanked* by religious and political leaders, they should have been treated with total derision and told to pack their crosses and go back home.

10

Acknowledgement Now

In populist psychology, denial is an aberrant state, something to be exposed, confronted and undermined. People must face up to their 'troubling recognitions'. Then everyone, from the alcoholic in denial to the passive bystander, can join the rest of us in accepting reality. In Amnesty or Oxfam appeals, the world looks different. Denial – in the sense of shutting out awareness of others' suffering – is the normal state of affairs. This is precisely why so much effort has to be devoted to breaking out of this frame. Far from being pushed into accepting reality, people have to be dragged out of reality.

The Amnesty–Oxfam world-view is better social science. Instead of agonizing about why denial occurs, we should take this state for granted. The theoretical problem is not 'why do we shut out?' but 'why do we ever not shut out?' The empirical problem is not to uncover yet more evidence of denial, but to discover the conditions under which information is acknowledged and acted upon. The political problem is how to create these conditions. This reframes the classic studies of obedience: instead of asking why most people obey authority so unthinkingly, let us look again and again at the consistent minority – nearly one-third, after all – who refuse to obey.

By taking denial as normal, I am being neither moralistic nor ironical. This just makes it easier to see 'acknowledgement' as the active and infrequent opposite of denial: When do people pay attention? When do they recognize the significance of what they know? When will they be aroused to act, even at personal risk? The emotional logic of the Amnesty–Oxfam agenda applies to all human life: how to transform ignorance into information, information into knowledge, knowledge into acknowledgement (cognition into recognition, sight into insight), and finally acknowledgement into action.

The *cognitive* demands are to know what is happening, to retain the information in a zone of awareness not easily blocked off, and to find an appropriate frame – whether vernacular terms like 'atrocity', the pre-modern frame of 'evil', or the legal frame of 'human rights viola-tions'. Above all, the list of acceptable vocabularies of denials must be shortened by refusing to give credibility to the more meretricious items. The *emotional* demand is for feelings – empathy, outrage, shame, compassion – to be widely shared, expressed and culturally available. *Moral* sentiments – this is wrong and cannot be tolerated – should be known and accessible in the form of vocabularies of acknowledgement ('We must not let this happen again'). Appeals must reach this threshold: 'I cannot keep silent; I must do something about it.' And finally, cultural channels should be visibly in place: to validate the sense that something *can* be done, inform you *what* this something is and enable you to do it. There must be easily recognized paths between, on the one side, general support and vague intentions to 'do something' and, on the other, a starting point for what the professionals term 'consequential social action'.

If the call to acknowledgement comes from Oxfam or Amnesty, various 'consequential social actions' are made clear – signing a bank-er's order, adopting a child, joining the organization, attending a vigil. Mass media images of atrocity and suffering, however, seldom suggest a channel for action. They are random texts about random horrors. In 1995 the media reported Saddam Hussein's policy of mass mutilation of army deserters, draft evaders and petty offenders. They were branded on the forehead, and their hands and ears cut off. An official decree specified the exact size of the X brand, seared into the flesh with a hot iron placed between the eyebrows. Baghdad television showed a terrified-looking man whose hand had been cut off and forehead branded for stealing a television set and 250 *dinars* (about 30 pence). A neatly dressed newsreader, wearing a suit and tie, recites a verse from the Koran, then reads out an account of the crime and punish-ment. There is no expression on his face. The offender's surgically removed hand is displayed for viewers and reproduced in the inter-national media. A colour photograph shows him holding the stump of his arm and screaming in agony.[1]

What exactly would it mean to 'acknowledge' this type of informa-tion? Everyone knows that it is true; nearly everyone, surely, will feel an instant repugnance. But to live daily with this repugnant truth is neither desirable nor possible. Not only is such 'acknowledgement' unhelpful, but it immediately mutates into the feeling that 'nothing can be done about things like this'.

Collective acknowledgement is another matter: the transformation that makes previously normalized conditions into social problems. This carries radical implications for victims, offenders and bystanders.

Social institutions, policy strategies, and, even a new language are in place to undermine denial and to encourage and channel individual acknowledgement. Things are different when individual acknowledgement is expressed without cultural support or even runs *against* the cultural ethos.

The meanings of acknowledgement

The term 'acknowledgement' is routinely used in public discourse to describe official confirmation that a previously denied allegation or suspicion is indeed correct. 'Yes' some hapless official announces at a press conference, 'we retract our previous denials ... we confirm that it did happen ... it shouldn't have happened ... we acknowledge that the claims were substantially correct ... we will set up a commission of inquiry.' Last month's baroque edifice of official denial is not mentioned again – as if it never existed. Such narratives of official acknowledgement are now commonplace. A regular ritual of public life consists in government inquiries to investigate abuses that were previously denied to have happened. Just as regular are stories of public figures coming clean about their denied involvement in corruption, sleaze or sexual scandals.

My interest is more in ordinary people who come to acknowledge the suffering of others and then find the right channel of action or improvise their own. These are like folk-tales of conversion: the slow buildup or the sudden epiphany, then a lifetime's selfless dedication. Here are four such mundane tales of acknowledgement: fables about *opening your eyes* or *not turning the other way*. The first is my favourite – simple, but rich enough to cover the whole sequence. The second suggests the paradoxical and unintended effects of official knowledge. The third is a typical media story of 'outrage into action'. The fourth tells of an altruism that runs determinedly against the political current.

Mrs Agnes Buys

In 1991 Mrs Agnes Buys was a housewife living in Kuils River, a small town close to Cape Town and a solid Afrikaner and Conservative Party neighbourhood.[2] This was a time of massive political violence ('unrest') throughout South Africa. Mrs Buys had seen newspaper reports about whites and policemen provoking or carrying out violence in the townships, but didn't believe what she read. One Wednesday in September, she noticed that her black domestic servant Eunice

Sindizi, was 'out of sorts': late for work, nervous and not concentrating. Mrs Buys asked her what was wrong, and Mrs Sindizi said that she'd slept in the bush.

Later that day, Mrs Buys went to the supermarket and picked up a newspaper. There was a report about a Democratic Party MP alleging that whites were involved in local violence. Again she didn't believe it, but on returning home: 'I asked Eunice whether it was true but she didn't want to talk. I said if she won't talk, how can anybody do anything and then she told me what happened.' After hearing the story, Mrs Buys phoned the Democratic Party, got through to an Unrest monitoring organization, which sent a field-worker to take a statement from Mrs Sindizi. This was her story.

On the Monday, Mrs Sindizi had been at home in Khayelitsha Township with her two children and two friends. A car drew up, a type like those used by the police. Two men in ordinary clothing, heads covered in balaclavas, got out. They began firing in the direction of her house. One gun 'threw a long fire flame', which hit the window, setting the house on fire. (Flame-throwing guns had been used in the Angolan war.) The trapped occupants screamed for help, and the neighbours broke down a door. Mrs Sindizi and her children slept in another part of the township. Next midnight, the same thing happened. They ran to the police station – where they were chased away. They spent the night in the forest behind one of the township blocks. Mrs Sindizi said that a friend had seen that one of the men was white when he pulled down his balaclava.

Mrs Buys at first didn't want to believe Eunice's story. Then 'she said to me: "That's why there's no point in telling you", and I realized that it was true. I have been making enquiries, talking to people, trying to find out things. There must be records of things like who uses police vehicles, who is on or off duty, but I keep coming up against a brick wall...Something, somewhere is terribly wrong. Who is doing this?' Mrs Buys thinks that the men were either policemen or whites involved in the local taxi wars.

The realization of what was happening had been a shock to Mrs Buys. Attempts to solve the country's problems were useless, she began to think, while this sort of thing was happening. 'I put myself in Eunice's shoes and I know that if black people came roaring up to my house with science-fiction weapons like those and burnt down my house, I would be very unhappy. But would I have the right to be angry? How can we expect black people to treat us fairly if this is what we do to them?'

Mrs Buys realized that she could be exposing herself to much trouble from her neighbours. 'That's fine. What is right is right. You can't put a blanket over your head and pretend it's not happening.'

Lena

'Lena' was an Indonesian student of a colleague of mine.[3] She went to school and then university in Jakarta during the late 1980s. In 1994 she obtained a scholarship to study at an American university. In the first few weeks of the term, she joined the Indonesian students' association. Among the hand-outs that she was given was a pamphlet prepared by the Indonesian Foreign Ministry and distributed by the Embassy. The pamphlet contained detailed guide-lines on how to counteract any criticisms of Indonesia that the students might hear, particularly about its human rights record. Two 'allegations' received most attention. The first was about the mass slaughter of Communists and other political opponents during 1964–5, when President Suharto seized power. The second was about the genocidal massacres that occurred during and immediately after the Indonesian invasion and occupation of East Timor in 1975. Some 60,000 East Timorese were killed in the first year. Appropriate denial techniques (all appearing in the official discourse described in chapter 5) were suggested to counter these two claims.

Lena was astonished to read all this. Although she was aware that there was criticism of Indonesia's foreign policy, she had little idea about these particular claims. She knew, of course, that there had been some sort of *coup* in 1965, but had heard nothing about mass killings. As for East Timor, she recalled that her school history textbooks had given the impression that the island had always been another province of Indonesia. She had heard something about troubles from Communist guerrillas – but certainly not that some 10 per cent of the Timorese population had been wiped out.

Like Mrs Buys, Lena had an 'enquiring mind'. She went to the library and read what she could find about these episodes. She tracked down more material. After a short time, she became convinced that the allegations were substantially correct. The official denials had opened her eyes.

Nikki du Preez

One night in the first week of 1993, Nikki du Preez, a management consultant living in Edinburgh, watched in horror a Channel 4 News item. It suggested that the Serbian forces in Bosnia had raped thousands of Muslim women. (The figures are still disputed.) 'It really blew my mind, I felt outraged,' she recalled a few weeks later.

As a Jew, she immediately saw parallels between the Muslims in Bosnia and the Jews in Nazi Europe. She also thought that Muslim women would have a particular horror of any form of sexual assault. She still felt angry the next morning, and wanted to do something. She was haunted by the story, and read more material that convinced her that the facts were not exaggerated and that the rapes were deliberate policy. She contacted the senior reporter of Channel 4 News, who encouraged her to travel to London on a fact-finding mission. Within two weeks, she founded a charitable organization, BOSNIA NOW, to help the Bosnian women. Two of the committee members were Muslim women from Edinburgh's Asian community.

Jean Baptiste Nteturuye

In early 1994, Jean Baptiste Nteturuye was an old man living in the Songa district of Burundi.[4] He was looking after thirty-eight people living in his house, all women and children. This was not so strange in itself. In the previous months of horror in Burundi, at least 100,000 people had been slaughtered, and nearly a million had lost their homes. In the Songa district alone, twenty-four people had been killed the week before, and 150 houses burnt down. The homeless would crowd into the houses of relatives until they felt safe enough to go back to their villages.

What was strange was that all the guests in Mr Nteturuye's house, were Hutu – and he was a Tutsi. They had been attacked by a group of Tutsis from the next hill. Four members of one woman's family had been killed, the house burnt down, and the children had fled to the forest to hide until Mr Nteturuye gave them shelter. He knew this was dangerous; why had he taken them in? 'Because they are my friends.' He was old enough to remember the genocidal massacres of 1965, 1969, 1972, 1988, 1991 and 1993.

These four stories raise all the questions I posed in the Preface. I approach the end of the book with the same questions. Take Mrs Buys. Why did she open her eyes when the overwhelming majority of her neighbours, friends, family and fellow citizens had done something else with their sight for so long: kept their eyes closed, turned a blind eye, averted their gaze, looked away, seen nothing?

Yes, we can talk about History: these were the dying years of apartheid, when whites were more open to change. But why *Mrs Buys* and not others like her, or more others? Some would propose that she was psychologically different all along: she had a loving, caring childhood;

a socialization into values of inclusivity; an ego not threatened by anomalous cognitions...and so on. But this does not even look like an 'explanation'.

Telling the truth

Before looking at theories of altruism, let me review four quite different senses in which acknowledgement is opposed to denial: *self-knowledge, moral witness, blowing the whistle,* and *living outside the lie.*

Self-knowledge

The opposite state of psychological denial is *self-knowledge*. To be whole and healed, you must face the truth about yourself. The early history of this ideal state of mind, Foucault showed, goes back to the confessional. Its modern history starts from another religious image: the early nineteenth-century penitentiary, each prisoner alone, confined in his cell, with only the Bible as an aid to contemplation. He eventually reaches self-insight, realizes the error of his ways, and emerges as a moral being. The secular, therapeutic version is part of popular culture: the patient patient who lies and lies on the psychoanalyst's couch, day after day, year after year. Eventually, with the help of the wise Herr or Frau Doktor, she reaches self-insight, realizes the neuroticism of her ways, and emerges as a healthy being.

Without self-knowledge there can be no healing; indeed, selfknowledge *is* healing. We must give up our defensive strategies and distorted sense of reality, and face up to what is really happening. The initiate into Alcoholics Anonymous offers the primal utterance of acknowledgement: 'I am Susan and I am an alcoholic.' All else follows – as it does for every other psychological problem. We live in cultures of denial about others, but cultures where knowledge of the self is unambiguously valued.

Self-knowledge, insight, self-actualization and integration: these were the Freudian versions of the Enlightenment faith that the truth will set you free. Freud, though, never departed from his ironical insight that *what holds you together is a split*. New Age psychologists have dispensed with irony. In their populist psychic democracy everyone must overcome denial: break the conspiracy of silence, admit the inadmissible. The cult Swiss therapist Alice Miller attacks the 'monstrous consequences' of the denial of child abuse:[5] Nazism and Romanian communism could have been prevented if only the destructive family upbringing of Hitler and Ceauşescu had been recognized. Whole bookshops are stocked with this sort of psychic junk food. Salvation by truth telling has become dumbed down and speeded up – not a lifelong spiritual quest, not a fifty-minute hour five days a week for three years, not even a weekly *Deniers Anonymous* meeting. All you need is a self-help book that opens with a twenty-item insight scale. You first tick off your score, read the book, carry out some mental plumbing, then return to the scale to see your progress – that is, how many more bad things about yourself now need to be acknowledged.

But self-acknowledgement is not enough. We are encouraged (when not actually compelled) to announce to others – preferably in public – that we have reached this state. This announcement (testimony, confession, admission) is real proof of acknowledgement. We first had to 'come in'; now we must 'come out'. We do this willingly, even enthusiastically: let it all hang out, tell it how it really is. This, however, is not the path recommended by the intelligentsia *for themselves*. They have reached the post post-Freudian discourse in which self-knowledge is a wholly ironical concept. There is neither 'a' self to know nor 'a' knowledge beyond dispute. But as post-modern intellectuals settle into their disintegration and fragmentation, middle-brows are still reassured that liberation for them means wholeness; wholeness means 'know thyself'; 'know thyself' means 'show and tell thyself'.

Collective knowledge, especially of others *like you* and where you stood in the social universe, once offered quite different prospects: political liberation, social justice. This was the Marxist ideal of combating 'false consciousness'. To the Frankfurt School the façade of denial was maintained by repressive tolerance: something far more complicated to expose than obvious lies and mystifications.

Moral witness

Moral witness looks for the quiet but certain knowledge of what the powerful deny and would rather not have witnessed. In the original Quaker ideal, knowledge and truth telling were values in themselves. The idea of distributing video cameras to human rights observers is more utilitarian: recording evidence to achieve accountability. A row of silent witnesses – VCRs in hand or not – watching wrongdoing, often putting themselves at risk, is a powerful image. They are *active* bystanders – powerless to intervene, but a reminder to perpetrators that not everyone approves or colludes, and that their future denials will be countered by another testimony.

Besides the ideal of deliberate witness as a moral act in itself was a more ambitious hope that the organized presence of others would shame the perpetrators. This faith should not be abandoned. On many such occasions in Israel, though – watching soldiers blow up Palestinian houses or bulldoze their olive orchards to make way for a settlement – I cannot remember seeing shame in any soldier's face. Even when witnesses are noticed and allowed, they can be ignored. Further, they may be incorporated as a fixed part of the scene, even as proof that the authorities have nothing shameful to hide.

Blowing the whistle

The idiom of 'blowing the whistle' is too banal to describe either the agonies behind this type of acknowledgement or its dramatic consequences. Academic definitions are worse: 'organization members' disclosure of illegal, immoral or illegitimate practices under the control of their employers to persons or organizations that may be able to take action to stop the wrongdoing.'[6] The term 'employers' does not fit superior army or police-officers; disclosures may be aimed at truth telling, without much hope of stopping the wrongdoing. But we get the point.

Here is a composite example. A junior reserve soldier does his army service in a detention centre for suspected political offenders awaiting trial. His duty is to escort them to the Secret Service interrogation wing and then back to their cells. After some period of ambiguity – half-knowing, not knowing, not wanting to know – he realizes that the detainees are being physically abused (he may or may not have the word 'torture' in his mind). He hears them scream, sees them bleeding; once he has to drag a prisoner who cannot walk. But he keeps quiet and does nothing. Perhaps he never questions the authorities; the detainees belong to a debased ethnic group; their suffering means nothing to him. Or he has moments of unease, but feels bound by old loyalties, and is reluctant to bring shame to himself and his family. Or else he is miserable and morally repelled all the time – but doesn't know what to think or do, and is unaware of cultural accounts supporting dissent. The denial circuit remains intact.

But something might trigger acknowledgement: a detainee dies under interrogation; the soldier's girl-friend tells him of a newspaper article describing allegations of torture and praising an army doctor who has leaked information; a human rights organization distributes leaflets giving an anonymous hot line (the 'pathway to disclosure'). Our soldier contacts the journalist; this results in a more detailed article. If the army traces the soldier's identity, they may try to discredit him or punish him. He may withdraw back into silence or, on the contrary, amplify his story.

We have no idea why these different pathways are followed. No doubt social psychologists are correct that situational differences are important. Unremarkably, whistle blowing is more likely when the wrongdoing is clear, and less likely when many other observers are present. No, there doesn't seem to be anything like a whistle-blowing personality.[7] We don't know whether whistle-blowers have 'an extended sense of responsibility'. We do know that their stereotype as disgruntled employees or ex-employees is wrong: according to the evidence, they are more satisfied with their jobs, earn more and are higher performers than other organization members.

Although the information disclosed by whistle-blowers was sometimes secret and its revelation astounding, more often it was an 'open secret' or belonged to the twilight zone of half-knowledge. The effect of disclosure is to 'arouse an apathetic public to dangers everyone knows about but does not fully acknowledge'.[8] A long period of normalization and denial is often broken in a sudden moment of acknowledgement: 'Enough is enough... I couldn't keep quiet any longer... This was more than I could take... I couldn't live with this knowledge.' Previously silent observers who reach this epiphany may be people already ideologically primed to be uneasy about what is happening, but too anxious to talk out. Alternatively, they are people who never saw anything wrong and even colluded, but then suddenly had their eyes opened. The latter types are seen as more credible: they cannot be discredited for deliberately 'looking out' for something.

The pathways to whistle-blowing, especially for people vaguely sympathetic, are similar to those of humanitarian appeals. About seven or eight hits (a stable if apocryphal rule) will be shunted out of consciousness or rationalized away. Then one more photo or story – no better or more heart breaking than the others – gives the final nudge.

Living outside the lie

There are those personal moments when you can't stand yourself any more; you have made too many compromises, pretended too long that things were okay; your bad faith has to end. There are also those periods of history that begin imperceptibly, when some impersonal momentum magically allows many personal moments to coincide, when a whole society 'comes out' and acknowledges the truth. This is what Havel calls 'living outside the lie'.

I remember a less dramatic individual story. Naomi was a woman in her late forties, a member of a progressive Jewish discussion group in San Franciso to whom I talked in 1991 about the Israeli–Palestinian conflict. Ever since her student days, she had been active in progressive or leftist causes. But she found that her Jewish roots and her inchoate Zionist sympathies made it impossible for her to apply the same moral standards to Israel. The *intifada* became headline news from 1988, TV screens showing Israeli soldiers beating Palestinians in Gaza. Naomi found this impossible to watch. These images were too upsetting; they did not fit what she had always believed. In her heart she knew that the criticisms of Israel were true, and found government denials unconvincing. But she was unwilling to break the silence. She began to feel perpetually ashamed and stopped talking to her former political comrades as well as her more conservative Jewish friends and family. She felt sick – physically and emotionally. Gradually she was drawn back to watching TV, and then started obsessively reading sources more critical of Israel. After an arduous two years, she joined this discussion group. Naomi knew that she was still not 'taking in' everything, but felt 'morally cleaner' because she had stopped lying to herself and others.

Remember Havel's greengrocer placing in his window the slogan 'Workers of the World, Unite!' He never thinks about the meaning of the slogan; that's the way it has to be. He has become a player in a collusive game of denial, a political version of the Laingian or the alcoholic family. Everyone is living in a lie. But imagine, Havel suggests, that something in the greengrocer 'snaps'.[9] He stops putting up the slogan. He begins to say what he really thinks and to support people according to his conscience. The system now has to punish him. He has committed something more serious than an individual offence: he has broken the rules of the game by exposing it as a game: 'He has demonstrated that living a lie is living a lie.'[10] The emperor, as everyone knew all along, has no clothes. People discover that it is possible to live inside the truth, to find a repressed alternative to the inauthentic, to expose a 'hidden sphere of life'. Havel's 'power of the powerless' is the force of truth that may break out at any time. Then individual people like the greengrocer may find themselves part of a sudden explosion of unrest by a whole society.

For these people – Naomi, the greengrocer, Mrs Buys, Lena – acknowledgement is a potent conjunction between 'something snapped' and an 'enquiring mind'. A one-off intervention may now become a way of life. People become committed, driven, unable to return to their old lives or shut their eyes again. On the contrary, they need to repeat their atrocity stories. They become full-time moral witnesses – telling their tales like the Ancient Mariner.

There are some people who, often from a very early age, seem unable to deny. Their moral and emotional sensitivities are so finely tuned, their membranes so thin, that they recognize everything, acutely pick up and even 'feel' the agonies of others. The very thought that someone else is suffering is literally unbearable. Moreover, they seem unaware of the usual boundaries of blood and belonging. They will give priority to family and friends, but the suffering of distant others is equally felt. If they see a child humiliated by his mother and crying in public, this registers an emotional trace that runs through the whole body and remains as an after-image.

These are people overwhelmed by information; they cannot filter the horrors to which they are exposed; their attention is indiscriminate. Unless they find some socially acceptable way to channel or muffle their acute sensitivity, they live in an enclosed space filled with images of atrocities. Their enveloping identification with the suffering of others is combined with a perpetual sense of their own helplessness. Some can organize their public lives around their inner preoccupations. As artists, journalists or photographers, they create representations of suffering. Or else as professionals or volunteers, they spend much of their lives trying to alleviate the suffering of others. This does not mean that all humanitarian workers are dedicated altruists. Supposed over-acknowledgers are figures of folk ridicule, secular versions of Mother Teresa. To cynical conservatives, these are 'bleeding heart liberals'. To smart-arsed radical sociologists they are voyeurs of suffering, pornographers of violence, exploiters of exploitation, merchants in misery. To smart-arsed psychoanalysts they are sublimating, projecting, repressing, masochistic and, of course, 'in denial' about their own immersion in suffering. Theirs is not a happy time.

In fact, I have never met or heard about a real person like this. The gullible sentimentalist who only sees good and is always being conned is a figure of the past. Even more misleading is the idea that humanitarian workers feel responsible for solving every bit of misery in the world. On the contrary, the really effective people are self-consciously selective about which problems they take on. 'Doing something' is possible only if they do not allow themselves to be overwhelmed – or take on a romantic identification with their chosen victims that blurs their judgement and sense of justice.

There is a paradoxical risk of denial: you cannot bear hearing another horror story, you skip through case notes without reading the details, you dread the phone call about another detainee being tortured. This is a genuine burn-out, a numbing from being too long on the job, seeing the same things too often. The opposite hazard is a chronic heightening of sensitivity. The war photographer

Don McCullin insists that his sensitivity has remained the same or even increased: 'Having done all these wars, instead of hardening me up, it's softened me up. What happened to people like me is that we became psychological cripples. We put ourselves in these awful situations, and every time we went there another small layer of skin was taken away. All my nerve ends are hanging out.'[11]

There is no easy way to get it right: nerve endings dulled or continually sensitive. But there are easy ways to get it wrong. An American Jewish Zen abbot leads 150 associates of his Peacemaker Order on a field trip of 'bearing witness' and 'engaged spirituality': a week's 'retreat' at Auschwitz-Birkenau.[12]

Intervention: pro-social behaviour and altruism

The opposite reactions to passive bystanding appear under the rubrics of *altruism* (helping someone else without expecting to be rewarded), *pro-social behaviour* (any act that helps or is designed to help others) and *positive morality*.[13] Is altruism inherently rewarding and satisfying? Are there just altruistic actions, or are there consistently altruistic personalities? Why are some people more likely to help than others? Do some societies encourage more pro-social behaviour than others? Can we create the conditions for more altruism?

To begin with, let me supplement my original four fables with a better known hero, Hugh Thompson.[14] On 16 August 1968 the My Lai massacre – as it became known later – is well under way. Led by Lieutenant Calley, under the command of Captain Ernest Medina, the platoon is slaughtering some 350 civilians: children, women and old people. They were ordered to wipe out the enemy in the village, but the Vietcong had already disappeared. Nevertheless, they continue, some claiming that the order was ambiguous. Chief Warrant Officer Hugh Thompson and his door gunner arrive in their observation helicopter and start hovering over the village. Thompson notices something peculiar: there are dead bodies all over, and they appear to be women and children. He circles around again: 'I'd seen some things that at the time I couldn't understand why they'd happened . . . *I couldn't understand.*' No explanation makes sense – why are the bodies stacked up like that? He flies lower and sees a captain walking up to a dying woman with a wound on her stomach. He nudges her with his foot, steps away and then shoots her. Thompson lands and remonstrates with Calley. He then begins the first of his rescue lifts, picking up wounded villagers, and flying them to hospital.

The disturbing fact, McCarthy notes, is that to an ordinary man of Thompson's 'ordinary intelligence', the sight of the bodies raised questions that ordinary people would want answered. 'Thompson's density, his puzzled inability to *"understand"*, were a sort of saving slow-wittedness.'[15] Everyone else, from Calley and Medina up to the generals, knew the score in Vietnam. This incident didn't surprise them; everyone knew this was not a clean war; atrocities just as bad as My Lai were frequent. Thompson's indignation and his appeals to higher authority to stop the slaughter showed just how little he grasped. 'His disbelief in what his eyes were showing him was companioned by a touching belief in the willingness of his superiors to correct what in his view *had* to be a ghastly mistake.'[16] Thompson's rural background – a conventional southern boy with a conventional faith in the war – had made him 'culturally retarded', unable to wise up to what was happening. Neither he nor his nineteen-year-old gunner Larry Colburn (who reacted like him) was opposed to the war on moral or political grounds. They were two 'ordinary men' who imagined that something extraordinary was happening.

This has some strange implications for denial theory. The conventional interpretation is correct: Calley, his men in Charlie Company and his immediate officers were certainly doing some instant denial; they did not have very enquiring minds. But denial means disavowal, a refusal to believe what is happening. The archetypal denier is an imbecile who seems unable to see, let alone accept realities obvious to everyone else. But this is just what *Thompson* does: his acknowledgement is precisely his refusal to believe what he sees. His pseudo-stupidity is his 'touching belief' that this is not the way things should be. Denial is not a neurotic defence mechanism, but a sane recognition that everyone else around is utterly insane. In this sense, a statement like 'I can't believe what is happening' is, paradoxically, not an expression of denial, but a signal that something disturbing or special has been recognized.

But why, living within and knowing about the same injustice, are most people passive and only a few aroused to help? Studies have compared the social conditions that produce active helping (or less collusive silence) in some societies rather than others – for example, the very different degrees of collaboration in the occupied countries of Europe.[17] Some explanations are obvious (such as an anti-Semitic tradition), yet cannot account for differences between Latvia, Lithuania and Poland, where some 90 per cent of Jews were killed, and Denmark, where 90 per cent were saved. And why do Norway, the Netherlands, France, Bulgaria and Hungary appear at different points on this index of collusion?[18] Then there are the differences within the same society: the dismal Vichy record of collaboration compared with the remarkable story of Le Chambon, a small Huguenot village where, under the direction of its pastor, hundreds of Jews were saved and sheltered.[19]

There are motivational differences even within the same groups of rescuers.[20] Many are responding to their influential group; others react more empathetically, overcome by the pain of those they help; only a small minority arrive at their decision because of a set of autonomous moral principles. There is little evidence that an 'altruistic personality' exists. The main differences between rescuers and a control group of non-rescuers from the same country was the rescuers' 'extensivity'. They were more likely to attach themselves to others, to assume responsibility for them, and to act inclusively towards a wide range of people. 'Involvement, commitment, care and responsibility are the hallmarks of extensive persons. Dissociation, detachment, and exclusiveness are the hallmarks of constricted persons.'[21] The 'constrictedness' of passive bystanders comes from a self that does not see most of the world beyond its own boundaries. Less conscious of others' needs, they distance themselves from the demands of wider relationships. By contrast, the 'extensivity' of rescuers meant caring for others beyond immediate family and community, feeling part of a common humanity, being sensitive to moral violations, even seeking out opportunities to help. 'Already more deeply and widely attached to others, they find it difficult to refrain from action. Already more inclined to include outsiders in their sphere of concern, they find no reason to exclude them in an emergency.'[22]

They found no reason to exclude them: this, I believe, is crucial. These people reacted instinctively: they did not look for accounts or neutralizations for why *not* to help. They were rather confused about other bystanders. Rescuers knew that most of their fellow citizens were apathetic or had actually refused to help. Yet, to play down their own uniqueness, they claimed that most people requested to help would respond in the same way: 'I did nothing unusual; anyone would have done the same thing in my place.' Yet experiencing themselves as unable not to help is their special personal character. Fogelman's interviews with some 300 rescuers – covering altruistic action from a single, one-time gesture (giving good, offering shelter for a night) to years of belonging to a resistance and rescue network – reveal a similar ambivalence in comparing them with others.[23] On the one hand, there is the recurrent sense of the 'banality of goodness'. Most rescuers never thought of themselves in heroic terms; they were just ordinary people doing what had to be done at the time. They seemed bewildered later that such a fuss was made of them. But looking back, they themselves could not quite understand their behaviour – how could ordinary people like them have taken such risks? On the other hand, they appear to be rather extraordinary people. The act of rescue is 'an expression of the values and beliefs of the innermost core of the person. . . . This rescuer self was, and over the years has continued to be, an integral part of their identity.'[24] This is not an adaptable, situational self – merely the opposite of the self that adapts to horrible situations by indifference and obedience – but rather an intrinsic self.

Other motivations have been mentioned, such as sympathy, ties of friendship, political or religious belief, or ethical judgements about the value of life. But *banality of virtue* is the most constant theme: acting with 'common-sense' human decency; not thinking of themselves as doing anything special; seeing the situation as giving them no choice; helping because this was simply the obvious thing to do and continuous with the routine morality that they learned and practised in their communities and families.

Any transformation from bystander to rescuer is far more demanding than in the Good Samaritan parable. In Occupied Europe, the punishment for helping Jews was severe. The rescuers took risks with their own and their families' lives that were never asked of the Good Samaritan (not to mention research subjects whose 'helping behaviour' is to give street directions to a lost stranger). Like Jamesian religious conversion, there are different narratives of transformation: a long, gradual process; a dramatic, transforming encounter; a sudden epiphany; a special 'ability'. There is often a peculiar sensation of seeing familiar objects with new eyes. One woman interviewed, Gitta Bauer, had private reservations about the regime over a long period. She then saw *Kristallnacht*. 'Before, all this had been in her peripheral vision, now she really saw it. The ability to see clearly, to strip away the gauze of Nazi euphemisms and recognize that innocents were being murdered, is at the heart of what distinguishes rescuers from bystanders.'[25] Like having an enquiring mind, this 'ability to see clearly' – the move from peripheral to central vision, seeing through the 'gauze' of euphemism – makes all the difference.

Altruism is an anomaly to rational choice theory in the obvious sense that altruists are defined precisely as people who act without expecting rewards. The theory's response is that the rewards are merely hidden: the cost–benefit calculus takes in rewards of psychic gratification, reciprocity and peer-group approval. But the model simply does not fit rescue in Occupied Europe. A recent study (of a small group of thirteen rescuers) finds no sign of self-interested rational actors.[26] The rescuers' individual decisions to help Jews were not the result of any conscious calculation of costs and benefits. The rescuers followed a consistent life pattern that did not fit any rational choice explanations: they had no need to atone for past wrongs; there was no evidence of either 'goods altruism' (action undertaken for material gains or honours) or 'participation altruism' (action undertaken to feel good about yourself); there was no expectation of reward.

Altruism resulted rather from a particular cognitive outlook – a sense of self as part of a common humanity ('inclusivity') rather than tied to specific interests of family, community or country. The recognition of who you are was more important than allegiance to any abstract moral or political agenda: help whomever you can, when you are asked. With this strong sense of identity, the rescuers did not need to make a considered decision by assessing options and choosing the best one. They acted spontaneously, as if no alternative response were possible. Every study records the same accounts: 'One cannot really act otherwise'; 'What else could I do?' Further, 'It was not a question of reasoning. . . . There were people in need and we helped them . . . People always ask how we started, but we didn't start. It started . . . very gradually. We never gave it much thought.'[27] As Badhwar points out, though, 'rescuers' claims that they had no choice but to help must be taken to mean that they felt that other choices were not possible *for them*, and not that they believed that other choices did not *exist*.[28] This perception continued: 'Even after they had been forced to evaluate the costs, there was still no conscious choice for rescuers to make; rather it was a recognition that they were a certain kind of person and that this meant that they *had* to behave in a certain way.'[29]

This recognition fits nearly all activists whom I have known. Nothing explains its biographical origins, or why some people rather than others have this 'instinctive extensivity'. At the sociological level, we don't know whether this state is fostered more by some political cultures than others; or, at the psychological level, why it appears in this particular minority within the same culture. Might women be different from men in this respect? Does this reaction transfer consistently to other situations? Some inconsistencies are well known: people who in the public realm are altruistic and deeply compassionate about humanitarian causes, but in their private lives are neglectful parents, narcissistic friends and indifferent to all others' need. And we need not go so far as Lifton's 'splitting' (the Nazi doctors who are so loving to their children and dogs) to find the opposite: people who are caring parents, selfless friends, sensitive and rooted in their own community – yet utterly indifferent to appeals from outside their immediate circle.

This raises a disturbing question. Do survivors and victims, people who have suffered terribly themselves, have a special sensitivity to the suffering of others? Or, on the contrary, was their experience so engulfing that they have little sympathy for others whose plight is less serious? There is no hard evidence either way. Some early studies of Holocaust survivors living in America depicted people who could not avert their gaze, however much they wanted to, when images of Biafra and Vietnam were on the television screen.[30] Like rescuers, they felt that they had no choice but to respond. They seemed incapable of indifference; whether they wanted to or not, they saw what they would rather not see, felt what was not comfortable to feel. This did not necessarily make them more virtuous or humane, however, and they had little sympathy for anti-war and other political causes of the sixties. There may be greater inconsistency – even a dichotomy – between 'our' and 'their' suffering.

Creating more acknowledgement

Any child understands that in a better world, Mrs Buys, Gitta Bauer and Hugh Thompson would not stand out. We must hope that the many good people paid good salaries to think about these problems – in United Nations agencies, think tanks, universities, governments, peace research institutes, conflict resolution projects – also understand the point. We must also assume that they are serious, decent people who know what they are doing.

In the meantime, the less ambitious programme is to overcome the more noxious forms of cultural denial and to encourage more acknowledgement. We already know the bad news: that just giving people more information will not help. But how to bridge the gap between what people know (and profess to believe) and what they do. The social-scientific lesson (once called 'cognitive dissonance theory') is not reassuring. If there is a conflict between inconsistent self-images – I am a decent human being, but I live and believe in a country which is acting in a way opposed to all my values – then change of attitude and corresponding action are only one way of searching for congruity, balance or consistency. The other two ways of reducing psychological discomfort are more frequent. The first is to restore equilibrium – or at least relieve tension – by ceasing to think about the subject: 'removal from the field' or 'internal exile'. The second is to change, twist or distort the information by drawing on culturally approved denials: things are not as bad as they look; there are worse places.

Changing attitude and behaviour – especially under conditions of threat, insecurity, terrorism and risk – is much harder. As political leaders well know, it is never enough to present the facts or invoke moral arguments, or even to be patient with deep insecurities and fears. All this should be done – but for its own sake rather than in expectation of immediate results. Let me set out four political strategies: *education and prevention, legal compulsion, appeals* and *channelled acknowledgement*.

Education and prevention

The human rights community is divided between two views of education. One stresses the virtues of human rights values: the Universal Declaration is the 'positive imagery' – rights as attainable conditions for a dignified life. The other ('negative imagery') is the reproduction of more atrocity stories and images of suffering. Both are needed to encourage acknowledgement and are linked to policy agendas (little more than liberal prescriptions) for transforming passive bystanders into active, socially responsible agents.[31] These include child-rearing practices that stress values of moral inclusivity and personal example; tolerance for those who are different and widening the boundaries of your moral universe; public education about the limits of obedience and the role of passive bystanders in allowing atrocities to be perpetrated; the virtues of mobilizing people into 'caring networks'.

But how exactly can this be done? Clarkson suggests that just as the Ambulance Service runs first aid classes for ordinary people, so we should conceive of 'bystander intervention training'.[32] The syllabus should include detailed and vivid accounts of atrocities, suffering, denial and complicit bystanding. These are not for moral indignation or voyeuristic contemplation. The lesson must concentrate entirely on exposing and undermining the accounts given by perpetrators and bystanders. The narratives of altruism and intervention must provide an alternative set of motivational accounts to be encouraged. Look how they explain what they did. Can you imagine using the same words?

The motivational models should not only be legends and Nobel Peace Prize-winners, but ordinary people. An instructive example is the Right Livelihood Award, presented annually since 1985 in Stockholm, the day before the Nobel ceremony. The awards go to individuals and organizations – united by 'a vision of an indivisible humanity' – working for social justice and human rights, peace and disarmament, protection of minorities, women's rights, environmental issues. They come from all over: a community organizer in Burkina Faso; a lawyer working voluntarily for Ogoni rights in Nigeria; a campaigner for Roma rights in Hungary; a technician (Mordechai Vanunu) who revealed details of Israel's secret nuclear weapons plant. On another tier from these partially known people are people like Mrs Buys, Lena, Jean Baptiste Nteturuye, Nikki du Preez and Hugh Thompson.

Besides ideals and role models, people must know how and where they can follow through on their desire to help. There are handbooks listing these opportunities,[33] but these do not link acknowledgement with action. The victim's need for a channel to disclose his or her suffering also applies to the bystander. One therapist proposes designing 'pathways' for victims of family violence.[34] These pathways must precede disclosure, and victims must have prior awareness of them. The pathways for victims (and bystanders) must be reachable, walkable, interconnected and worth walking.

Legal compulsion

At first sight, the law looks too crude an instrument to either prevent states of denial or compel forms of acknowledgement. But if action can be influenced, as it surely can, without trying to change hearts and minds, then why not use the normative and coercive powers of the law? Regulation and control are used in other equally complex areas of social life. There are four possibilities: *denial as a crime* and *duties* to *remember, rescue* and *know*.

Denial as a crime

A number of countries – Austria, France, Canada and Switzerland in the nineties, Israel and Germany earlier – have passed legislation against denial of the Holocaust and/or genocide and other crimes against humanity.[35] This derives from the more general use of the criminal law against incitement to hatred and discrimination. The target is sometimes called 'hate crime': crimes committed for ethnic, racial or religious reasons. Other laws prohibit the dissemination of views based on claims of racial superiority or expressions of contempt that imply racial inferiority.

The political reasons behind Holocaust denial laws include sensitivity to victims, the (correct) perception that neither denunciation nor scholarly argument will prevail against revisionist and other historical denials, and concern about the revival of the far Right, especially in Europe. Claims that the 'so-called Holocaust' was a hoax fabricated by Jews to extort compensation from Germany are obviously linked to inciting hatred and violence against Jews. Under some laws, though, literal denial of the extermination as a historical event is not in itself grounds for conviction. There must also be intent to incite or allegations that Jews were responsible for the hoax. Under Israeli law, 'denying or diminishing the proportions of acts' during the Nazi regime ('crimes against the Jewish people or against humanity') requires proving intent to defend the perpetrators or express sympathy with them.

Some Western European legislation comes closer to prohibiting atrocity denial in itself, without requiring intent or incitement. French law refers to anyone who *contests* the existence of specified crimes against humanity. All three classic forms of denial are covered: denying of facts, their interpretation and their justification. Anyone is liable to punishment who publicly *denies, grossly trivializes, approves or seeks to justify* the national socialist genocide or its other crimes against humanity (Austria); *grossly minimizes or seeks to dispute* genocide and other crimes against humanity (Switzerland). The offence in German law prohibits the *attempt to approve, deny or make appear harmless* within the framework of laws against 'insult'.

The argument for special laws against the denial of crimes against humanity is that general provisions against incitement, spread of falsehood, glorification of crimes, or protection of honour cannot be relied upon. There are obvious freedom of speech and other civil liberties objections. Other critics argue that this sort of trial would only create martyrs. It is difficult to know whether these laws have any deterrent or preventive effect.

The duty to remember

It is assumed that Truth Commissions, political trials and inquiries – and attempts to establish and publicize details about past abuses – will reduce the likelihood of future abuses: 'Never Again.' If so, might not governments have some legal 'duty to remember'? I believe that the absolute and symbolic value of collective acknowledgement of the past would justify making a Truth Commission – with specified aims, minimum standards and codes of conduct – a legal requirement during transitional regimes.

The UN Subcommission for the Prevention of Discrimination has already included a duty to remember in its Draft Principles:

> A People's knowledge of the history of their oppression is part of their heritage and, as such, shall be preserved by appropriate measures in fulfilment of the State's duty to remember. Such measures shall be aimed at preserving the collective memory from extinction and, in particular, at

guarding against the development of revisionist and negationist arguments.[36]

The duty to rescue

The social-scientific work on the bystander effect and the biblical
parable of the Good Samaritan are intended to convey an unequivocal
moral lesson. We are meant to conclude that Kitty Genovese's neighbours and the priest and the Levite who passed by the injured man
failed to live up to elementary standards of moral decency and citizenship. But can there be a legally enforced duty, obligation or requirement to intervene on behalf of strangers, especially to save their lives?
Can we 'enforce' acknowledgement?

The legal concept of the 'duty to rescue' is the subject of a complicated jurisprudential debate.[37] There are civil or criminal statutes that
create an affirmative duty for citizens to intervene or at least notify
authorities when they witness emergencies, especially where life is at
stake. Typical situations include lost children, rape, assault and
domestic violence. 'Rescue' or 'duty to assist' laws have a long history
and are more common in the continental European legal tradition than
in Anglo-Saxon common law systems.[38] Bystander intervention laws,
though, have been increasingly debated in the USA – with the Kitty
Genovese case the most cited prototype.

The debate is not about the moral virtue of rescue, but about the
desirability and feasibility of using the law to enforce certain standards. Many people dislike the idea of a legal obligation making it an
offence not to try to help someone in danger. They argue that virtue
cannot be legislated; this is an infringement of civil liberties; conscience cannot be legally controlled; and that in any case such laws
are unenforceable. These objections are even stronger when moral
culpability and the notion of 'immediate danger' are extended to
victims living in distant situations which you clearly know about,
even if you do not physically witness them. Is a moral obligation to
do something about this suffering the equivalent of requiring help in a
visible bystander situation? If not, and if the moral obligation applies
only to visible, specific and known dangers, then appeals to 'do something' about hunger in Bangladesh or extra-judicial killings in Sri
Lanka lose their universal moral status.

The duty to know

An even more radical requirement than the duty to act is the legal duty
to know, to keep informed about suffering and atrocities. No one can

question our genuine ignorance of some facts. But what if we have *chosen* to ignore them, deliberately turned a blind eye, stopped watching or reading the news? Are we not morally culpable for our lack of attention? Does reluctance to stay informed and to acknowledge others' suffering carry some moral blameworthiness?

The ethics of lying, secrecy and self-deception tries to identify situations in which pleas of ignorance may acquit you of moral responsibility. Bok asks: What is the moral status of strategies of avoidance used to claim ignorance of avoidable cruelty or suffering?[39] Self-imposed ignorance, she concedes, may differ from other forms of ignorance; under certain circumstances 'deliberate blindness' may be morally culpable. It would be excessive, though, 'to stretch the notion of moral responsibility so far as to cover all that individuals ignore or fail to notice, or all the situations in which we perceive some rationalization or strategy of avoidance'.[40]

The opposite thesis is the idea of an 'obligation to keep informed about distant atrocities'.[41] On one side, ignorance of major atrocities cannot be a legitimate moral excuse if one deliberately keeps oneself uninformed; on the other, ignorance is a quite legitimate excuse if one lacks the means or opportunities to be informed. The more familiar cases fall in between. Felice argues that for 'average' Westerners such as US citizens (exposed to CNN?), ignorance about distant atrocities is not excusable, and hence does not excuse their doing nothing about atrocities. If the legal obligation to prevent major harm is accepted, then the duty to make serious attempts to become and remain informed about distant atrocities (particularly in your country's sphere of influence) follows, and can be realistically adhered to. Felice tries to dismiss these obvious objections to his proposal:

1 Ordinary citizens are too politically ignorant and naïve to be really informed, especially about atrocities ignored or played down by the mainstream media. To search for information beyond this, would require prior commitments and background knowledge that would be unreasonable to expect.

2 Even if citizens decide to seek out the relevant information, they would be too unsophisticated and powerless to know how to use all this.

3 You should help only those whom you can. Intervention by a single individual in these distant human rights problems is unlikely to prevent any harm. It makes more sense to help those close to home – your neighbours, your own community. So why waste time and effort in trying to keep informed about distant atrocities?

4   The individual cannot prevent or delay events such as massacres in East Timor because such periodical horrors are necessary products of the present world order. Historical forces beyond anyone's control shape human rights violations.
5   'Yes, it would be great to help, but is it wrong not to help?' There is a distinction between acts that are commendable and those that are obligatory.
6   By the time the average citizen finds out about a major atrocity, it has already occurred and hence nothing can be done to prevent it. Knowledge should be pre-emptive to allow prevention.

Few will be convinced by Felice's responses to these objections, and fewer would support his virtually unenforceable legal proposals. Most people would prefer to invoke what Daniel Elsberg nicely called their 'right not to know'. These six objections, however, are precisely those addressed in standard Amnesty-like appeals. In that context, most of us would dismiss them as clichéd denials and rationalizations that deserve rather patronizing replies.

Appeals

Rational choice theorists seize on the idea that altruism is intrinsically rewarding, and thus part of the cost–benefit calculus. But getting a 'reward' from acting in keeping with your integrity is far less tangible and predictable than this formula suggests. The only stable effect is reinforcement through repetition. Once people start helping, they continue. Initial commitment, however, is reinforced in different ways: some people need results, others a sense of empowerment; yet others are content to be faithful to their self-image and values.

Appeals, as we saw, use quite different – and even theoretically incompatible – messages. The old-fashioned guilt and shame messages (the starving child) can be reframed in the unemotional discourse of rational choice and marketing. The target group consists of individual 'consumers': each is a caring person, endowed with a sense of what is fair and unfair, and looking to satisfy the need to help others. The message 'you should care' is not meant to induce guilt about yourself. You are offered, rather, a consumer choice to avoid the guilt – or shame – which will come *only* if you don't respond. There is no need to feel guilty about your life-style – unless you don't acknowledge (think about, do something about) these other realities of the world.

Channelled acknowledgement

Like nearly all charities, humanitarian organizations are expanding their use of what I call 'channelled acknowledgement'. This is a form of fund raising in which donors (however much they contribute) are not required to make a major investment of thought, time or energy. They don't even have to write a cheque, sign a petition or drop coins into a box. Their acknowledgement that the cause is worth supporting – feeding starving children or destroying land-mines – is conveniently channelled into the patterns of regular life. The commitment becomes institutionalized and ritualized. Here are some examples.

Ethical wills   The ancient practice of leaving an inheritance to your favourite good cause has now become professionalized in the form of ethical wills. Full-time consultants and experts work, in a highly competitive market, to encourage and allocate legacies: acknowledgement beyond the grave.

Ethical investments   Using such slogans as 'Profit with a Conscience', investment consultants offer advice on ethical pensions, mortgages, savings and life insurance. Most advice is negative: not to invest in companies, corporations or banks that have a clearly blemished humanitarian record (unfair trading, land confiscation from indigenous peoples, exploitation of child labour, unjust employment of women). Other advice is positive: to invest in companies with explicit 'ethical business' practices or groups working on issues of fair trade and debt payment. Some savings accounts offer the option of donating all or some of the interest to a linked charity.

Fund-raising credit cards (also billed as the 'guilt-free credit cards') The basic idea is that a regular percentage of your credit card payments goes to a charity. A few years ago, American Express card members were informed that when they took a one-hour cocktail cruise on New York's Seaport Line, half the fare would be donated to cancer research. 'Womankind World-wide' recently linked up with the Bank of Scotland to produce a card in which the organization gets 25p from the bank for every £100 spent on the card. A spokeswoman for Womankind said, 'For three suits, or £900, Womankind would receive enough to pay a community worker in India for a month or buy a milking goat and two chickens in Africa.' She asserted that women normally feel terrible when they go out shopping; this would make feel better about themselves.

'*Change For Good*' is the clever slogan on the UNICEF (United Nations Children Fund) envelopes that have been distributed on international flights over the last decade. The envelope is entitled 'Here's a Better Place to Put your Foreign Change'. It gives the standard pitch: *Did you know that* ... 'each day, 40,000 children die needlessly from causes such as malnutrition, dehydration and infectious diseases?' Then, *for as little as* ... $5.00, 'You can immunize a child against the major childhood diseases'. There is sometimes an accompanying video (Audrey Hepburn or Geri Halliwell with pathetic children in Somalia); the captain or purser announces that the staff will be coming around to collect the envelope in which you drop all foreign money (you still have too many junk pesetas and are only too pleased to get rid of them).

Politically correct consumption   The consumer boycott – often associated with the anti-apartheid campaign – is the most familiar method of channelled acknowledgement: 'Don't buy South African (Spanish, Israeli) oranges.' The method is now widely used in the environmental and animal welfare movements: injunctions not to buy ecologically unfriendly products or products tested on animals. Negative appeal plus guilt plus abstemious denial of pleasure tell women that chocolate is a cash crop in which inequities specially affect women workers.[42] The positive message is to selectively buy products or services that you would anyway enjoy, knowing that the profit goes to a good cause. A British travel agent advertises: 'Book your holiday with us and we'll donate £50 to ACTIONAID.' A percentage of profits from Ben and Jerry's ice cream goes to good causes (buying special nut flavour will save the rain forests). Buying the Body Shop's 'environmentally friendly' products ensures more profit for workers. The Fairtrade Foundation awards logos to endorsed companies, allowing the consumer to identify goods produced and marketed without exploiting workers. The Ethical Consumer Research Association produces detailed product guide-lines, rating tables and company profiles, uncovering all sorts of hidden connections to help you weed out your own most 'unprincipled' buys.[43] Organizations sell ethnic objects (bags, cushion covers, scarves, carpets) listed in lavish catalogues (with a code to identify whether produced in Bangladesh or Nepal plus an instant empowerment message, 'Every time you buy, X per cent goes to ... '). In 1992 Café Direct started a campaign (sponsored by organizations like Oxfam and Christian Aid) to sell 'ethically sound coffee'. The money paid for Café Direct coffee goes directly to coffee-growers in Latin America; this coffee is traded so that producers and their families benefit directly from the purchase. The publicity slogans were simple, easily identifiable and empowering: 'You Discover Excellent Coffee. They Discover School' and 'You Get Excellent Coffee. They Get Vaccines'. This campaign was highly effective, with sales quickly established and continuing evidence that people welcome – and are even prepared to pay more for – ethically traded products.[44]

Feel-good and do-good   The basic scenario: Hollywood celebrities publicly eat meals of rice and water to symbolize their solidarity with the world's poor. At the annual Oxfam America Hunger Banquet, guests are randomly picked to receive a gourmet meal, or beans and bread, or rice and water.[45] In Britain, the charity War Child organized a 'Feast for Peace' in which guests eat at a hundred restaurants that agreed to donate 25 per cent of their takings to charity. The more you eat, the more they'll give. A spokesman for War Child explained the principle: 'To do good, while having a good time'. In organizations like 'Dieters Feed the Hungry', on the other hand, dieters give to others the food they would otherwise be overeating. Its founder claims that 'The purpose of *Dieters Feed the Hungry* is to bring a deeper meaning to the dieting experience by encouraging dieters to focus some of their time and energy on feeding those who really need food.'[46] This sounds like a gimmick for fat, rich people to lose weight. But no, donating food 'in honour' of your own diet – putting aside a can of tuna or a jar of peanut butter or making a casserole to take to a soup kitchen – is a path towards deep acknowledgement. 'For many people, the act of writing a check is a quick escape from confronting the underlying issues, whereas hands on involvement in feeding others has a deeper and more immediate meaning.'[47]

At best, these are like the methods of parents persuading their children to eat because the children of Africa are starving. (As Allan Sherman said, 'So I ate my food, got fatter and the children of Africa went on starving'.) Growing up in post-war South Africa, the actual starving children around us were never mentioned; we were induced to eat thinking of the poor children of *Europe*. At worst, these methods are self-serving evasions. The donor finds a cheap way to deny and look good at the same time – culturally approved bad faith. The corporations pay guilt money but get good cheap publicity.

My own view of these methods of fund raising (rather than the general politics of acknowledgement) is benign. As long as the source is not itself involved in dirty business, there is no need to call the Mind Police to scrutinize and censor peoples' motives for donating money. Let them give in peace.

It would be nice to assess the amount of acknowledgement in any society. We could then compare changes over time or between societies. It would be even nicer to have a formula to determine the 'appropriate level' of social reaction to horrors. An international Commission of Good People chaired by the Dalai Lama and Nelson Mandela would devise universal scales of atrocities and suffering. Like judicial sentencing formulae, each point on the scale would be allocated an appropriate (mandatory) response. An Atrocity at Level A2 (10 to 15 peaceful demonstrators killed, 5 to 10 blinded by tear gas, at least 30 arbitrary arrests) or Suffering at Level B3 (200 people in a refugee camp dying each day of dysentery) should result in Acknowledgement and Action at 6 points on the Richter Scale of Decency.

This project, alas, cannot be taken seriously. These are subjective and political judgements; well-intentioned people with similar values may reach very different conclusions. Moreover, they may judge the threshold of denial very differently.

There might be some common ground in Arendt's minimalism. Discussing a German sergeant who helped Jewish partisans (and was arrested and executed), she asks: Why were there so few people like him, and what difference would it have made if there had been more? 'Under conditions of terror most people will comply but *some people will not*, just as the lesson of the countries to which the Final Solution was proposed is that "it could happen" in most places but *it did not happen everywhere*. Humanly speaking, no more is required, and no more can be reasonably asked.'[48]

Other political philosophers aim for more. Geras takes the rescuers in Occupied Europe as an image of an alternative ethical landscape: envisage, he asks, a moral culture imbued by a sense of responsibility for the safety of others.[49] Could there be a global community in which the obligation to assist others in danger or distress was a powerful imperative? And where a deep shame of passivity becomes an 'effective mobilizing norm of social life'?

We need to envision these practical utopias. But in the meantime, our criticisms of denial may be too harsh and self-righteous. And our expectations of acknowledgement – get informed, open your eyes, don't pass by, don't conform, do something, blow the whistle – are too high. If evil people – those who plan and implement atrocities or deliberately let others suffer – are a small minority, so too are those who have the time, energy and commitment to devote their lives to the cause of defending human rights or alleviating human suffering. In between are the vast majority of ordinary people. In many societies, public engagement is difficult simply because of the mundane pressures of daily survival. Most people, at most times, in most societies, are more interested in 'making life' than 'making history'.[50] Their sustaining ideology is what Israelis nicely call a *rosh katan* (literally, a

'small head'): keep a low profile, and don't let yourself get too bothered by big problems. People fortunate enough to make a life working
for humanitarian causes (and being paid reasonably for an interesting
and rewarding job) can ask others to 'do something'. But they (and
their academic fellow-travellers, like me) should not ask much more.

But how much is 'something'? Zalaquett says: 'The law can only
demand from the ordinary citizen to be a law-abider, not to be a
hero.'[51] But surely social justice deserves more than law. There are
states of being such as good citizenship, which are less than heroic but
more than mere law-abiding. They do not demand extraordinary
heroism, but they do discourage ordinary silence.

11

Towards Cultures of Denial?

The project of 'overcoming denial' is more complicated and stranger than I imagined. 'And ye shall know the truth, and the truth shall make you free' (John 8:32). But what is this truth to be acknowledged rather than denied? And how exactly will it make us free? And what about the difference between the absolute value of truth telling, as an end in itself, and its instrumental value as a means to achieve social justice?

We already know some of these complications: the idea that personal denial may be functional and healthy. The healthy denial thesis, however, can hardly apply to whole societies facing risk and danger. There is nothing positive about a society denying that it has an AIDS problem or the failure of the international community to recognize early warning signs of genocide and other mass disasters.

But all this is obvious. Far more interesting is the very idea of a unitary self that underlies both the therapeutic and the political critique of denial. Persistent denial is taken to indicate personal pathology (dissociation, disintegration, splitting) and political atrophy (living in the lie, cultural amnesia). But it only makes sense to see denial as a problem if we retain the modernist assumption of unity. The post-modern self, by contrast, is fragmented and accepts fragmentation.

The political consequences are far-reaching. We can condemn passivity, indifference and bad faith only from within the meta-psychology of the targeted and desirable Amnesty/Oxfam self. Without this, we cannot speak of audience denial; nor can we say, 'If you know this and believe that, then you must do this'. As this meta-psychology fades, so does its dependent ideals of truth, integration and commitment. In the post-modernist landscape, ends and means, landmarks and destinations, bear only an ironical relationship with each other. There is little point in 'exposing' normalized denial, splitting or dissociation, let alone hinting at their immorality. There are too many confusing signals and meta-signals to 'react' to messages about twelve-year-old children being killed in Angola. We always knew about the gap between knowledge and acknowledgement, the split between what you know and what you do. Those who remind us of this message now are just seen as irritating.

This is what happened to Teiresias, 'the prophet in whom, of all men, lives the incarnate truth'. At first, when Oedipus senses that bad news is in the air, he merely says to him: 'It seems you bring us little encouragement.' As the message becomes clearer, Oedipus starts raging wildly against Teiresias – he curses and threatens him, accuses him of having a hand in the plot, and finally banishes him. Poor blind Teiresias could see this coming; far from setting him free, the truth was his burden:

> when wisdom brings no profit,
> To be wise is to suffer. And why did I forget this
> Who knew it well? I should never have come.

But he has the last laugh on Oedipus: 'When you can prove me wrong, then call me blind.'[1]

Truth and wisdom are no longer the burdens they once were. We hardly believe that only full knowledge about the past or present can guarantee 'never again'. Introducing his history of the Nazi 'euthanasia' programme, Burleigh notes: 'It goes without saying that I do not expect this book to promote enhanced democratic awareness, or even more sensitive treatment of the disturbed and disabled.'[2] Referring to people in Europe trying to subvert democracy or those deliberately cruel to the disabled, he writes: 'Attempts to convince such people of what "actually happened" are faintly ridiculous, since denial of reality is bound up with their political agenda.'[3]

Despite widespread recognition of lying as a tool for political ends, we hardly understand 'the nature of our ability to deny in thought and word whatever happens to be the actual fact. This active aggressive capacity of ours is clearly different from our passive susceptibility to falling prey to error, illusion, the distortions of memory.'[4] The Pentagon Papers revealed that the planners (and their tamed intellectuals) were playing a bizarre game of 'fool yourselves' – acting as if hardly aware of the massive gap between the known facts and the hypotheses according to which decisions were made. So befogged did their minds become, that they no longer knew or remembered the truth behind their concealment and lies: 'the trouble with lying and deceiving is that their efficiency depends entirely upon a clear notion of the truth which the liar and deceiver wishes to hide.'[5]

Intellectual denial

'A clear notion of the truth' is not quite the message of today's intellectuals. In the past, their treason was to help create and dignify the vocabularies of denial required by 'true believers' and fellow-travellers. Otherwise well-functioning minds become closed, and the gaze is averted from the uglier parts of their ideological blueprints and experiments. Or they allow themselves – for tangible rewards or an eagerness to please the powerful – to be duped into pseudo-stupidity. These shameful records of collusion go way back.

Over the last two decades, though, a smaller, but very articulate and elegant, section of the Western intelligentsia has been marketing – mostly with good intentions, indeed usually in the name of 'radicalism' – a very different form of denial. Their leading product is brand-named deconstructionist and post-modernist theory in which 'truth' and 'reality' are always placed in ironical (rather than grammatical) inverted commas. They profess to believe that old-fashioned exposures of literal or interpretive denial lack any 'privileged' authority. All counter-claims about the denied reality are themselves only manoeuvres in endless truth-games. And truth, as we know, is inseparable from power. Nor can any sensible moral implications be drawn from particular information: morality and values are relativistic, culturally specific, and lacking any universal force.

Many of these ideas are simply ludicrous. And as long as they remain in seminar rooms, conferences and *curricula vitae*, they are harmless fun. But when they circulate noisily in middle-brow and even mass culture, they begin to supplement the inventory of denials available to the powerful. This was not intended. Nor, of course, do tyrants have to read post-modernist philosophy to get the moral go-ahead for doing what they have always done. But tyrants too live today under the meta-rules of globalization and reflexivity. They need new and better stories – designer accounts to offer in the General Assembly, to visiting plenipotentiaries from the IMF, the World Bank and WHO, and even to the fact-finding mission from Human Rights Watch.

Narratives and truth-games

The most pernicious element in the critique of what is variously called 'positivism', 'rationality', 'science' or 'the Enlightenment' is the idea that there can be no access to current or historical reality from outside a vantage-point of power. Ultimately, there is no way of determining that one version of reality is more valid than any other. All of us who carried the anti-positivist banners of the sixties are responsible for these philosophical high jinks. When contemplating the versions of epistemic relativism favoured by the cultural Left, we should, at the very least, have the grace to say, 'That's not what we meant'.

In March 1991, shortly after the end of the Gulf War – thousands dead and maimed in Iraq, the country's infrastructure destroyed by 'smart bombs', and the Kurds abandoned to their fate – Baudrillard published his article 'The Gulf War Has Not Taken Place'.[6] The 'true belligerents', he argued, were those who thrived on the ideology of the truth of this war. His earlier prediction that the war would never happen had been correct.[7] 'War' was a free-floating signifier, devoid of referential bearing. What had happened was only a figment of media simulation, a series of imaginary scenarios that exceeded all limits of real-world facticity. The 'thing' existed in the mind of its audience, an extension of the video games that had filled the TV screens for so long. Everyone – not just prime-time viewers but five-star generals – had become dependent on these computer-generated images. We might as well drop all self-deluding distinctions between screen events and 'reality'.

Baudrillard and others have brilliantly criticized the presentation of spectacles such as the Gulf War by political spin-doctors and the mass media. I understand this critique as an *exposure* of denial: the dazzling uses of meaningless statistical data to create the illusion of factual reporting; the euphemisms about 'precision targeting', 'smart bombs', and 'collateral damage' to convince us that the mass destruction of civilian lives was either not happening (literal denial) or was accidental (denial of responsibility); the war reporting in which no bodies appear, except the endangered CNN reporter. (General Schwarzkopf promised that there would be no body counts or body bags, only 'human remains pouches'.) The high-tech images of aerial reconnaissance, electronic mapping and cartoon simulations were weapons in a war of representation. The corporate media colluded with the State Department to deny reality, injury and dissent.

This war of representation was, however, deliberate, not just a reflection of the post-modern *geist*. The USA did not want another Vietnam – that is, a war in which the TV images were so realistic that they were widely credited with the demoralization that fuelled opposition to the war. But even if a war between images in cyberspace monopolized our consciousness, down on the ground a war between bodies did take place. None of these theorists, so I have been patronizingly assured, 'really' thinks that this 'real' war didn't happen; I had missed the meta-ironies.

Christopher Norris explains how the bland assumption arose that, because every text involves some kind of narrative interest, there is no way to distinguish factual, historical or documentary material, on the one hand, from fictive, imaginary or simulated material, on the other.[8] If there can be no access to truth or historical record, Norris shows, this leaves a realm of unanchored persuasive utterances, where rhetoric goes all the way down, and where nothing could count as a demonstration of the falsity of what media or governments would have us currently believe.

This is just the right theory for boosting even the most untenable forms of denial, like that of Holocaust deniers, 'for whom it clearly comes as good news that past events can only be interpreted according to the present consensus values, or ideas of what currently and contingently counts as "good in the way of belief"'.[9] Even the crudest deniers can exploit the current intellectual malaise to claim that they are simply offering an alternative version of history.[10] Lipstadt is rightly appalled at the willingness of academics, university students and the media to see Holocaust denial as simply 'the other side' or a 'different' version of the truth.[11] You cannot appeal to the relativism of knowledge in order to turn 'Holocaust assertion' and 'Holocaust denial' into positions of equal currency in a high school debate. This is not how we regard views that the earth is flat or that slavery never existed. These are not two 'points of view' – one position is simply a fanatic rejection of evidence and a refusal to abide by the rules of rationality and logic.

I have often cited the Armenian case: the eighty-year evolution of an indisputable genocidal massacre of more than a million people into an 'issue' in which 'the other side', the Turks, must be given their rightful hearing. Des Pres asks, 'What has happened to the argument that there are two sides to everything which once worked to foster truth but now works against it?'[12] What happened was an old-fashioned victory of power over truth: client state offers political loyalty to persuade superpower to deny its indisputable earlier knowledge. At its best, Enlightenment scepticism could undermine official discourse and fake scholarship. At its worst, empty talk of 'multiple narratives' leaves only a void: 'the kind of care for truth that insisted on reviewing the evidence has given way to a bewildered scepticism that ends up accepting official positions.'[13]

Thanks to survivors, whistle-blowers, historians, journalists and human rights organizations, previously denied histories are being uncovered, and current denials rendered transparent. But, as the volume of documentation increases, so too does scepticism about the existence of objective truth. According to this epistemic relativism, established scientific facts are merely social constructions. Narratives compete equally and openly in indeterminate truth-games. One day, perhaps, all those tiresome debates about what can be learnt from the past will become less acrimonious. After all, if one story is as good as another, why bother to fight for your version? Instead of instructive acrimony, we will have the unresolved insanity of a mental hospital in which more than one patient claims to be Jesus Christ.[14]

A sign that this insanity is already with us is that *lawyers*, of all people, are called upon to arbitrate on historical narratives. In enforcing laws against the denial of genocide, courts will increasingly have to adjudicate these epistemological battles. When legal discourse coincides with common sense, this may not be such a bad thing. Note, for example, the simple words of the Los Angeles Superior Court judge, ruling in the 1981 case of 'Mermelstein versus the *Institute of Historical Review* [a fake academic institute in the Holocaust denial industry]': 'This court takes judicial notice of the fact that Jews were gassed to death at Auschwitz Concentration Camp in Poland.' The existence of the Holocaust is not reasonably subject to dispute: 'It is capable of immediate and accurate determination by resort to sources of reasonable indisputable accuracy. It is simply a fact.'[15]

It is simply a fact. Such facts, of course, may be elusive, and their details impenetrable. Even a fully televised atrocity, each recorded frame repeated on each news hour – as many invisible slaughters never were – is seldom totally unambiguous. All sides in the wars of the former Yugoslavia will deny the reality, interpretation and implications of each such image. Each has convinced itself that it is blameless. But this is only their *conviction*. Somewhere there is an elusive vantage-point that is not on the side of either side, but just a little beyond both sides. From here, routine exaggeration and manipulation of the facts can be observed; cover-ups can be photographed (secret graves, destruction of evidence, cleaning up a previously photographed burial site), and the voices of Karadic-equivalents recorded on tape ('So-called massacre'; 'no order to kill them'; 'atrocity stories part of an international conspiracy against the Serbs, led by Middle Eastern countries who control the West and CNN oil markets'; 'the bodies were Muslim soldiers killed in legitimate fighting'). From this vantage-point, observers could agree on at least one truth-claim: that in five days Bosnian Serb soldiers killed at least 7,000 mostly unarmed Bosnian Muslim men. When an International Criminal Court is set up, then – for all the defects of judicial discourse as the repository of truth – a conclusion like the Los Angeles judge's will be *able* to be reached: 'It is simply a fact.'

Concepts like 'cover-up' assume that what is being covered up is not another rhetorical device, but a narrative truth with moral implications. Some people gave the orders; others obeyed them; others were indifferent bystanders. This does not mean that the texts and representations of events like these have a single meaning to everyone. My whole book tries to show the opposite. The despair of Brecht, Benjamin, Levi, Orwell and Steiner comes from their sense of being unable to represent the uniqueness of a particular atrocity and also convey a universal meaning. This was the same despair of journalists in Rwanda in 1994: how to describe the hacking to death of people with machetes, clubs and kitchen implements; 800,000 killed in a hundred days, five people killed each minute – three times the rate of Jewish dead in the Holocaust, a rate that would have left ten million dead in four years. The Associated Press's West African correspondent writes: 'I doubt if there is any other place in the world where so many people who write for a living have used the phrase, "Words cannot describe...".'[16]

Those writers reflecting on the Holocaust and these journalists reporting on Rwanda are expressing exactly the same frustration: a paralysis of language, an unbridgeable gap between language and the event it is supposed to describe. This has nothing, nothing at all, to do with 'proving' the event's existence. You cannot talk about 'inadequacy' or appeal to poetic silence without knowing where the inadequacy is or what you are being silent about.

This is not a subject to be 'problematized' or 'situated' in some T-shirt slogan about the 'fictionality of the factual'. Friedlander patiently explains the problem as he reads a standard historical book describing the massacres and deportations at Chelmo.[17] The text, he notes, is scholarly and factual, just the right source to use in combating denial. But the very factuality blocks the emotional appeal. The text has, as it were, two halves. Part A records that 'The Jews of some transports... were not assigned to the local ghettos or camps'. Part B notes that 'These Jews were shot on arrival'. There is a disparity, an unreality here: part A describes administrative matters in normal speech; part B suddenly describes mass murder. But the style does not, and cannot, change: 'It is in the nature of things that the second half of the text can only carry on the bureaucratic and detached tone of the first. That neutralizes the whole discussion and suddenly places each one of us, before we have had time to take hold of ourselves, in a situation not unrelated to the detached position of an administrator of extermination.'[18]

This dreadful conclusion is not a tired aesthetic gesture. It comes from engaging with the despair of representation: the sense that conventional modes of truth telling cannot convey the truly atrocious, let alone elicit an 'appropriate' response. This thesis is utterly different from asserting that there can be no access to truth – the idea now peddled in the cultural market-place. Tyrants who have never heard the word 'narrative' do recognize a good story. They can rely on cultural entrepreneurs to dumb down the message to MTV level. Literary figures are just right for this. As the novelist E. L. Doctorow kindly explains, 'There is no longer any such thing as fiction or non-fiction; there's only narrative.'

Moral relativism

Respectable ideas about moral and cultural relativism have also become cultural commodities. The game is up for universality, we are told. If there is no foundational base for morality, then it is impossible to stake out universal values such as those enshrined in human rights declarations. Not only is the ideal of universality undesirable and unattainable, but it reflects values that are Western, ethnocentric and individualistic. The Universal Declaration of Human Rights was the product of a particular moment in Western (European, White) history. These alien values were imposed globally and with typical colonialist zeal. They are now used selectively – especially to denigrate societies where communal responsibilities are more natural than individual rights and where social and economic rights must take precedence over civil and political rights. Even within the liberal democracies of the West, there can be no core values. These are multi-cultural societies in which each identity – ethnicity, gender, sexuality – carries its own world-view, each one as valid as the other.

The historical part of this tale may be incomplete, but is certainly not wrong, and some other claims are plausible enough. Its political implications, though, detached from its meta-theory, are utterly pernicious. As we saw, an automatic fall-back in the official discourse of denial is the government's 'principled' rejection of the applicability of international human rights norms: we are different; we face special problems; we have our own culture; this is the Asian way, the African way, Islam or the Jewish tradition; the world does not understand us. These disingenuous denials now look respectable, even intellectually dignified: a sophisticated vocabulary for 'condemnation of the condemners'.

In the nuttier North American versions of multi-culturalism and identity politics even what used to be called 'sub cultural' groups do not share any core (that is, 'dominant' or 'hegemonic') values. If on a single California college campus every such group proclaims its difference, how then can Indonesians, Libyans and Ukrainians be bound by the same values? Unlike epistemic relativism, which is only recognized tacitly, avant-garde theories of cultural specificity are explicitly co-opted. The powerful go on doing what they have always done, while intellectuals supply them with what Wole Soyinka nicely calls 'cultural alibis'.

The universality/cultural specificity debate is, of course, far more complicated than my caricature. Human rights advocates cannot possibly be (or want to be) insensitive to local values. They are indeed at the forefront of attempts to reconcile universal norms with traditions such as Islam. Local workers themselves represent the specific and the general; they struggle every day with the accusation that they are imposing alien values. But what they expect from progressive intellectuals is a recognition of their dilemma and some help in undermining their government's cultural alibis. Instead, they hear that local struggles for social justice are losing their meaning because they are informed by universal foundations and master narratives that have now been discredited. Goodbye the Enlightenment.

These confusing times invite some thinking about 'the role of the intellectual'. My inverted commas recognize the term's old-fashioned– even faintly ridiculous – ring. We indeed have to go back to anachronistic figures such as Orwell. The nearest contemporary voice is Chomsky's. To him, the intellectual responsibility of the writer as a moral agent is obvious: to try to find out and tell the truth *as best one can* about *matters of human significance* to the *right audience* – that is, an audience *that can do something about them.*[19] Finding out and telling the truth are redundant only in the sense that 'the facts are known and not denied, but considered a matter of no concern, given the targets'.[20] There are no psychological subtleties: people know, but they don't care. Chomsky disagrees with the old Quaker slogan 'Speak truth to power'. It is a pointless waste of time to 'speak truth' to the Kissingers of the world, who already know the truth very well. The people who matter belong to 'a community of common concern'. They want to hear the truth not for self-enlightenment, but 'for guiding the best policy to help alleviate suffering and distress'.[21] Intellectuals who keep silent about what they know, who ignore the crimes that matter by moral standards, are even more morally culpable when their society is free and open. They can speak freely, but choose not to.

To Chomsky, the post-modern cultural Left is not even interesting enough to criticize. But their theories *are* interesting. It's just that as a citizen of South Africa, Ethiopia, Cambodia or Zaire, I would prefer not to have a deconstructionist appointed to be chairperson of our Truth and Justice Commission. The resulting text would be interesting, but not in my interests.

More or less denial?

In the half-century since the end of the Second World War, some 25 million people have been killed, mostly civilians and by their own governments, in internal conflicts and ethnic, nationalist or religious violence. Civilian fatalities have climbed from 5 per cent of war-related deaths at the turn of the century to more than 90 per cent in the 1990s. About 50 million people were forced to flee their homes. In 1998, more than 2,000 people every month were killed or maimed by land-mine explosions. It is impossible to even estimate the numbers injured and disabled, tortured and raped, during these conflicts. The statistics on poverty, hunger, and children dying from preventable diseases continue to defy the imagination: 17 million people a year die from infectious and parasitic diseases such as measles, diarrhoea and malaria; 600 million are chronically undernourished; 3 million die of TB; if everyone had access to safe water and basic sanitation, 2 million young lives would be saved each year. Large parts of the world are ravaged and depopulated because of the AIDS virus: 16,000 people become infected with HIV each day.[22]

How will we react to the atrocities and suffering that lie ahead? The political changes of the last decade have radically altered how these issues are framed. The cold war is over, ordinary 'war' does not mean what it used to mean; nor do the terms 'nationalism', 'socialism', 'welfare state', 'public order', 'security', 'victim', 'peace-keeping' and 'intervention'. The dismantling of communism and apartheid, the collapse (mainly in Africa) of some nation-states, and the fragmentation of the new world order have given rise to an intensification of lethally violent ethnic, separatist, religious and nationalist conflicts. Inequality within advanced stable democracies has increased: the gap between the richer North and poorer South countries has increased even more. Pre-modern practices – piracy, 'war-lords', machetes, torture, kidnapping and mercenary armies – continue, using modern gadgetry and being represented by post-modern information technology. The beginning of 1999 saw atrocities never reported before: in Sierra Leone twelve-year-old child soldiers, their arms amputated by rebel fighters as a warning, were crawling into UNHCR refugee camps.

Assuming that more knowledge of this kind lies ahead, will it be received with more denial or more acknowledgement? Both cases can be argued.

More denial

However elusive are concepts like overload or fatigue, the sheer accretion and repetition of horror images must have some cumulative effect. Imagine what has been seen by a sixty-year-old person today who has watched forty years of television news. It is difficult enough to absorb and retain these sights now. New communications technology will make each problem more visible, but less comprehensible. Context questions will matter even less: What did the colonial power do here? Historically, who are the victims, and who are the oppressors? Did that massacre really happen? Where are the refugees? It will become harder even to *conceive* of effective intervention. Still harder to comprehend will be the catalogue of reasons for 'why isn't something being done?': the state of the UN, the complexity of the conflict, the dangers of humanitarian interventions, semi-legal and illegal arms dealing, trade agreements and geopolitical interests. There will also be more competition for the scarce resources of attention and compassion. Demands are already overwhelming: each week sees more appeals, news stories and documentaries about distant suffering, as well as domestic troubles. Why should the target for these appeals be extended beyond its small liberal audience? In Britain, all humanitarian agencies together receive some 4 per cent of total charity donations (the rest going to health, animals, religion, environment, education and the arts).

The success of the environmental movement has been striking. Its initial rise, till the end of the eighties, was partly achieved at the expense of humanitarian causes. Its message is safer, virtually non-political and easily appeals to self-interest (if not your health, then your children's). Even if the agenda is long-term and complicated, tangible successes can be shown – air pollution lowered, a nature zone preserved, dolphins rescued. The media, especially television, can make connections between global problems such as pollution, acid rain, greenhouse warming, disposal of toxic waste, wildlife preservation and rain forests and the way we live our life in the industrial North. 'Think globally, act locally' is a vivid media message. Such immediacy and implied causality are far more difficult to establish in the human rights area. There are no images equivalent to the visual connection between recycling your garbage and protecting world resources.

The concept of compassion fatigue may be a little shaky. But each new moral demand makes coping harder: yet another filter or priority to be set up. I have tested this by looking at my own reactions to environmental and animal rights issues. I cannot find strong rational arguments against either set of claims. But emotionally, they leave me utterly unmoved. I am particularly oblivious – in total denial – about animal issues. I know that the treatment of animals in cruel experiments and factory farming is difficult to defend. I can even see the case for becoming a vegetarian. But in the end, much like people throwing away an Amnesty leaflet, my filters go into automatic drive: this is not my responsibility; there are worse problems; there are plenty of other people looking after this. What do you mean, I'm in denial every time I eat a hamburger?

As for the suffering of our fellow humans, the bind and boundary of this 'fellowship' will always be at issue. How far does our compassion extend beyond our families, friends and intimate circle? Where is the line between domestic problems and those of the distant other? If there is a meta-rule of looking after your 'own people' first, has the threshold for responding to the plight of distant strangers been reached? We cannot be confident that more information (or more dreadful information?) will change the threshold. People resent being told what they already know; they dislike the preachy and exaggerated tone of appeals. But they do feel horrified, upset, guilty and compassionate. They *are* concerned about human suffering, they do not regard it as normal and tolerable. The gap is between concern and action.

Changes in the world order over the last decade look unpromising. International intervention, like the Kosovo bombing, may create a political backlash in favour of more isolationism. There is already an obvious trend to write off as basket cases whole parts of the world, like West and Central Africa. Isolationism may seem strange in a world of globalization, transnational corporations and federal structures like the EU. In these mammoth institutions, however, structures of responsibility and accountability are more difficult to find – thereby allowing more deniability.

Changing political culture *within* Western democracies also invites pessimism. In Britain, new sectors of the population are born-again free-market individualists and chronically infected by the selfishness of the Thatcher years. On the Left, the 'new social movements' from the early seventies have been drifting away from internationalist commitment. These movements were built around shared identity, separatist interest and preoccupation with the daily issues of 'self-realization', 'the personal is the political' and 'quality of life'. None of these encourages much thinking about famine in the Sudan or massacres in Algeria. Current versions of identity politics, moreover, are based on collective identity as *victims*. Some notions about the 'culture of complaint' and a 'nation of victims' may be overstated, but there is a trend that encourages competition about which group has suffered the most.

The sixties' ideal of a general activist who can be mobilized for all sorts of progressive causes is far removed from activism built around the exclusive subjective experiences of special groups. The doctrine of multi-culturalism reinforces this politics of separate and special identities. This is not fertile ground for asking people to mobilize on behalf of distant others. Human rights appeals derive from the anachronistic ideals of public life, fraternity, solidarity, universality and common citizenship. The ideal of world citizenship, once a respectable idea, sounds merely flaky when even national citizenship has become outmoded.

More acknowledgement

A far more hopeful narrative can be told: the quite recent and long-term evolution of a more universal, compassionate and inclusive consciousness. Television viewers' impulse 'to do something' about the sights of suffering (or say to each other that 'something should be done') signals an increasing sense of moral obligation beyond nation and family.[23] Fragile and ambiguous as this narrative of compassion looks, subservient as it must be to the primeval bonds of human attachment, its presence has to be recognised. A new moral imagination has grown perceptibly over the last fifty years, thanks to the visible efforts of international humanitarian agencies and the inescapable presence of global televised news. Everything is coming closer and faster: the faces of people in agony, the space and time it takes to reach them, the life-saving work of doctors or engineers. The boundaries of 'moral impingement' have been widened – along with the sense that something, after all, can be done.[24]

In this long-term history, the claims that floods of new information will lead to over-stimulation, compassion fatigue or donor burn-out are ephemeral clichés. Journalists and humanitarian agencies may worry that the same old images will bore their audience, but there is no evidence that this happens. Nor is there some finite pool of compassion that has now been exhausted. The quick and massive mobilization for humanitarian emergencies shows how readily altruistic responses can be invoked. The three-month story of genocide in Rwanda hardly touched the public, but immediately the story switched to Goma, refugees, children dying, cholera and dysentery, the donor response was massive. Contrary to the rational self-interest model, people *continually* respond – not just to mass disasters, but by supporting traditional charities, development/aid agencies and other causes (such as animal rights) where no self-interest is at stake.

Nor is there evidence for Sunday supplement clichés about the 'me-generation', 'looking after number one' or yuppie narcissism. It may not be translated into action, but there is widespread support for basic human rights principles. Furthermore, although domestic problems retain priority international causes such as environmentalism, human rights and aid/development have each built up their own constituencies. In their shared transcendence of national boundaries, they hardly compete with each other. The same people subscribe to a cluster of organizations (moral investment in a balanced portfolio?), such as Amnesty International, Greenpeace and Oxfam.

Global communications technology gives instant access to live news and to 'real-time' scenes of people directly caught up in horrors. Standard criticisms of images of suffering as normalized, stereotyped and restricted are becoming out of date. Media exposures on subjects like illegal arms deals go well beyond any sixties radicals' expectations and knowledge. Pressure groups, humanitarian organizations, and victims are becoming exponentially more sophisticated in increasing public awareness of human suffering.

The globalization of information networks and the creation of universal cultures such as rock music allows the rapid transmission of humanitarian appeals. The astonishing successes of Bob Geldof's Live Aid and the Human Rights Now world tour show that universal altruistic messages can motivate wide audiences. Geldof's vision should not be denigrated: music as a symbolic vehicle to bypass conventional structures and reach potential supporters with disposable income, and a reservoir of undirected passion not usually targeted by charitable organizations.[25] The immediate enthusiasm soon wore off, but these events rekindled an awareness of Third World issues that had disappeared along with the rest of the sixties.

Yes, new social movements are infected by the politics of special identity. But they also show an encouraging ability to capitalize on disenchantment with party politics. This generation of activists is not searching for the numinous spot beyond Left and Right. They are attracted to single-issue causes *because* these do not have a general programme.

As the old structures of loyalty and identity – nation, class, religion, trade union, the military – lose their binding authority, so movements based on more universal identities may emerge. The environmental model of 'think globally, act locally' adapts to other issues. A healthy distrust of authority encourages these more egalitarian commitments. So does a moral empathy with victims of violent authority whatever its ideological flavour – exactly the human rights conception of victims. The stress on transparency and accountability, the greater scrutiny of public figures, and the regular exposures of their private lives could, no doubt, turn into a corrosive cynicism about any prospects of change. It could, also, encourage an involvement in limited-issue humanitarian causes. At the very least, it should create a reflex suspicion of official denials.

Thresholds

And so on. These optimistic and pessimistic predictions are unstable, and each could be projected further. Ignatieff's optimistic narrative of an expanding moral imagination – driven by the universal immediacy of TV images and the interventionist dramas of the early 1990s – has transmuted, not even a decade later, into isolationism and pessimism. The moral reflex of 'something must be done' was based on the illusion that 'something could be done'. The failure of most interventions – the continuing low-level violence in the same old places (and high-level violence in newer places like Chechnya) – feeds into something uglier than helplessness or compassion fatigue. There is a palpable impatience – even *moral disgust* – with societies that seem not only unable to benefit from outside help, but degenerate further into inexplicable chaos and cruelty.[26] This is the cue for the passive bystander's lament 'You can't do anything about places like that'.

As if to compete with the horrors out there, an extraordinary media culture is being created around the private suffering of ordinary people. On Oprah, Phil, Sally and Jerry, the art of confession and testimony is being perfected. Everyone can be a victim; nothing is private or unmentionable. Far from being 'in denial', the victim is 'in exhibition'. In one episode, Sally Jessy Raphael thanks a serial rapist for confessing that he, too, is a victim of bad upbringing and abusive parents. But 'serial rapist' is already too common a signifier. The categories of exhibited deviance must become even more refined; the vacuous injunction to 'let your feelings come out' is focused only on the immediate situation. The remote tragedies of famine and political massacres cannot compete on the same ground.

The free market of late capitalism – by definition a system that denies its immorality – generates its own cultures of denial. More people are made superfluous and marginal: the deskilled, unskilled and sinking poor; the old, who no longer work; the young who cannot find work; the massive shifting populations of migrants, asylum seekers and refugees. The 'solution' to these problems now physically reproduces the conditions of denial. The strategy is *exclusion and segregation*: enclaves of losers and redundant populations, living in the modern version of ghettos, remote enough to become 'out of sight, out of mind', separated from enclaves of winners, in their guarded shopping malls, gated communities and retirement villages.

The professionalization of helping is a double-edged victory. The old experts in domestic suffering (social workers, priests, doctors and therapists) now have counterparts at the international level. These experts do care and help; they need special skills and deep knowledge of local cultures. The technical term 'complex emergencies' understates the complexity of this work. But there is too much pressure for cost–benefit accounting, too much monitoring and evaluation, and far too much Thatcherite gibberish about 'performance indicators'. This creates professional monopolies that exclude volunteers and amateurs, and can stifle a sense of collective responsibility among ordinary people.

Can we expect more moral acknowledgement from ordinary people? Bauman suggests that all the 'natural' moral reflexes we have are inherited from the pre-modern era. This 'is a morality of proximity, and as such woefully inadequate in a society in which all important action is action at a distance'; we have to stretch our imagination beyond its limits to grasp the chains of causation and possible intervention applicable to somewhere like Rwanda. 'We do not "naturally" feel responsibility for such far-away events, however closely they may intertwine with what we do or abstain from doing.'[27] For a pre-modern 'morality of proximity' to acknowledge the plight of distant strangers demands some leap of identification. This, in turn, as Ignatieff reminds us, assumes a natural or universal human identity, at least 'in the basic fraternity of hunger, thirst, cold, exhaustion, loneliness or sexual passion'.[28] But our responsibilities, obligations and feelings are shaped by the social rather than the natural. Even basic bodily needs are marked by social differences: 'The identity between such hunger as I have ever known and the hunger of the street people in Calcutta is a purely linguistic one.'[29]

There is only one way to include the distant stranger: to define the threshold of the intolerable as *exactly the same for everybody*. The starting point is not pseudo-universalism or touchy-feely empathy, but a recognition of the radical and irreducible differences that do matter. These differences derive not from my ethnicity, culture, income, world-view, age, sexuality or gender, but from the primeval facts that *my children have not and will not die from hunger* and that *I have not or will not be forced from my home after watching my wife hacked to death with a machete.* It is precisely because these differences are so profound that the most ignored of revolutionary principles has to be invoked: not liberty, not equality, but *fraternity.*

'Turning a blind eye' does not literally mean not looking – it means condoning, not caring, being indifferent. Physical vision is a metaphor for moral vision. Some moral fields resemble physical vision by only 'taking in' the suffering of restricted and selective groups of people. Yet other fields instead of ending somewhere, only start at a certain point: beyond this point, you can't 'go along' with things, they 'go too far', you cannot tolerate them. Some fields are defined more emotionally ('Beyond that point my stomach turned, I couldn't take it'). The purely cognitive blind eye is the least important ('There's too much going on. At this point, I stop taking in any new information'). These visual fields are also manipulated by the powerful: there are no 'natural' points, no neuro-physiological barriers where the horrors can be normalized or moral proximity reaches its outer edges. Of course, the scale and seriousness of the suffering matters: yes, it makes a difference whether 50 or 5,000 people are slaughtered. But even a perfect empirical matrix of all those fields of vision could not predict how the mere volume of the suffering would affect the social reaction.

The reason is that we are moved by the utterly unreasonable, unpredictable, even bizarre: the source of the information, the method of slaughter, even the mood we are in. The world of suffering makes moral imbeciles of us all. McCarthy gives a fine example. Why, she asks, was the My Lai massacre – the deliberate killing, one by one, of unresisting women and children – viewed as more repugnant than achieving the same results by the standard mechanical means of smart bombs dropped invisibly from a distance? Perhaps because knowledge of impersonal mass killing is much like the background knowledge that children are starving while you eat.

> If one and the same person can condemn Calley and still 'live with' the B-52 raids in Laos and Cambodia, which he *knows* must be killing an unknown number of peasants on a daily basis, this only means that he is not totally callous. He knows if he stops to think, but mercifully he is not obliged to think twenty-four hours a day. There are knowledge and inescapable knowledge. Somewhere in between lies the toleration threshold, differing, obviously in different people.[30]

Every personal life and every society is built on denial. Only an over-riding principle – like social justice – can determine which forms of denial matter, which can be left alone. We then try to lower the toleration threshold by transforming knowledge into *inescapable know-ledge*. There are unpredictable moments when a particular image of suffering cuts right through us: a literal *wrenching* of the heart, a silent tear, that 'sees' the desperation on a child's face. But these moments cannot be programmed in advance. Nor will anyone be persuaded by tacky sermonizing about the Good Samaritan. As a religious parable about virtue and compassion, this is just as inappropriate as the Kitty Genovese episode is as a secular parable to encourage 'intervention'. In the post-modern world, there are not many one-off encounters with mugged strangers lying in the road, unexpected 'moments of truth' in which your moral instincts are tested. Our knowledge is not depen-dent on chance. It is permanent and continuous; those single moments when a crying Rwandan orphan appears on the screen are reminders of what we already know. The test of acknowledgement is not our reflex reaction to a TV news item, a beggar on the street, or an Amnesty advertisement, but how we live in between such moments. How we do we carry on with normal life, knowing what we know?

This is a rhetorical question, a tendentious bit of moralistic nagging. But I mean it also in an empirical sense. What is the space between us and the collective suffering of others? In Auden's poem, the architec-ture of detachment is fixed: the 'human position' of suffering is that it always takes place when we are busy somewhere else: eating, opening a window, just walking along. The subjects of the Old Masters have not deliberately turned a blind eye. Their and our detachment is the outcome of a structural position, a built-in estrangement from the world of other people's suffering.[31] This space is even vaster than the ideological gap between people like us and those who belong to other moral communities.

Personal denial can be tolerated, because dignity and privacy are also important. Compromises are possible; no one else may be harmed; knowing (and telling) the truth does not set you free. It is your human right not to have to face the truth about yourself; you can create your favourite fiction and live in blissful self-deception and bad faith. At the political level, though, we simply cannot tolerate states of denial. There is no room for compromise. Even if truth telling is not a value in itself, denial *must* always affect others.

Despite the complex obstacles between information and action – the entire subject of my book – no humanitarian, educational or political organization should even consider limiting its flow of knowledge. But the sheer volume and reflexive character of knowledge call out for some disinterested moral filtering. If only there were an International Commission of Good People to sort out atrocities and suffering, rank their demands in a principled way, then set up filters and channels. Trusting some well-meaning and informed people with news filtering must be better than allowing the market to choose which information to sell and the state to choose which information to deny.

But only our own internal psychic antennae can pick up different kinds of suffering. Whether the truth 'sets you free' is neither here nor there. The choice is between 'troubling recognitions' that are escapable (we can live with them) and those that are inescapable. This is not the 'positive freedom' of liberation, but the negative freedom of being given this choice. This means making *more* troubling information available to more people. Informed choice requires more raw material: statistics, reports, atlases, dictionaries, documentaries, chronicles, censuses, research, lists. Someone has to inform us *exactly* how many children in the world (and just *where* and *why*) are still dying of measles, are conscripted as twelve-year-olds into killer militias, are sold by their families into child prostitution, are beaten to death by their parents. This information should be regular and accessible: rolling in front of our eyes like the news headlines on the screens in Times Square.

I return, for the last time, to these eyes.

The photo never lies

There is no innocent eye. The photos of a starving Somalian child and the report of a massacre in Algeria come from and bring with them points of view. This is obvious, even if the critique of innocence has become exaggerated: the child existed, the massacre happened.

Curiously, we know more about visual representation than about verbal reception, the meaning attributed to what is perceived. Famous war photos and images, like that of the starving African child, are often taken to 'speak for themselves'. This assumes some degree of congruence – if not full symmetry – between the intentions of the sender and the perception of the viewer. A far more fateful assumption is that, despite each viewer's idiosyncratic sensibility, there is a common vulnerability to the raw sight of extreme human suffering: truths no one could deny, universal feelings of pity.

But, of course, none of this is self-evident. I tell a friend that I was 'deeply moved' by an exhibition of war photographs. She goes to the exhibition, but she is not moved at all. 'It left me cold,' she says. Our views and tastes are so similar that this complete divergence is puzzling. I will conclude with an allegory of the puzzle: a review written twenty-five years ago by a youngish female New Yorker of a collection of photos taken by another youngish female New Yorker.

The photographer is Diane Arbus, the first 'art' photographer who left an impression on me. When I first saw her work at the beginning of the seventies, I was stunned, totally mesmerized. Her photos have always stayed with me, her people gazing at the absent camera as I gazed on them. I knew nothing about Arbus then, but I deeply identified with her work. I could sense that she was tuned into the denial problem. Her subjects (pejoratively and wrongly called 'freaks') make two powerful but contradictory demands: to acknowledge their utterly disturbing difference from us and also their common humanity with us. They were not attractive people; you would be embarrassed to be seen in public with most of them; you could not easily 'identify' with them. But they could move you; you had to admire their fortitude.

I was astonished then to see Susan Sontag's hostile review in 1973 of the retrospective exhibition, two years after Arbus's suicide.[32] *Every one of her* reactions was the opposite of mine. I forgot about the review and only read it again twenty-five years later. I now disagree even more. She describes Arbus's 112 photos as 'assorted monsters and borderline cases – most of them ugly; wearing grotesque or unflattering clothes; in dismal or barren surroundings'.[33] I wouldn't use the term 'monster' even ironically; about a quarter of the photos, anyway, are of quite 'normal' people, not freaks in any sense. Look at 'Woman with a veil', 'Woman on a park bench', 'Woman with a locket', 'Four people at a gallery opening', the nudists and the topless dancer. None of them is remotely monstrous. And what are 'borderline cases'?

Sontag's literal descriptions are recognizable; we both saw the same photos. But from this point, the divergence is total. I will give four examples.

'Arbus's work does not invite viewers to identify with the pariahs and miserable-looking people she photographed. Humanity is not "one". Her message is anti-humanist.' This is incredible. In my view, Arbus's photos not only clearly 'invite', but also instantly achieve this identification. And she does this, most extraordinarily, with the full awareness 'that it's impossible to get out of your skin into somebody else's . . . that somebody else's tragedy is not the same as your own'.[34] True, some of the people look miserable, but many do not at all. One of the twins on the cover looks altogether content; two sets of 'Untitled' mentally handicapped young women are laughing; most of the nudists look stupid but happy; two of the transvestites are smiling; the lovely 'Jewish Couple Dancing' are radiant with happiness. Arbus saw and showed some-

thing quite stunning: 'Most people go through life dreading they'll have a traumatic experience. Freaks were born with their trauma. They've already passed their test in life.'[35] They have reached a strange tranquility; the awful has already happened. I see this in the photos every time, but Sontag never does. Yes, I agree that Arbus is non-political. But 'anti-humanist'? Surely the message is altogether 'humanist'.

'The ambiguity of Arbus's work is that she seems to have enrolled in one of art photography's most visible enterprises – concentrating on victims, the unfortunate, the dispossessed – but without the compassionate purpose that such a project is expected to serve. Arbus's work shows people who are pathetic, pitiable, as well as horrible, repulsive, but it does not arouse any compassionate feelings.'

The photographs may not elicit *Sontag's* compassionate feelings. But such feelings hit me instantly and remain just as strong twenty-five years later. I don't see the slightest trace of 'ambiguity'.

'Far from spying on freaks and pariahs, catching them unawares, the photographer has gotten to know them, so that they pose for her . . . A large part of the mystery of Arbus's photographs lies in what they suggest about how her subjects felt after consenting to be photographed. Do they see themselves, the viewer wonders, like that? Do they know how grotesque they are? It seems as if they don't.'

Is Sontag saying that she would have *preferred* these subjects to have been spied on and secretly photographed? Her rhetorical 'mystery' about how these people see themselves is preposterous and degrading. These are not wolf-people from the forests: they are social beings; they see and know other people; they have mirrors; they have brothers and sisters, parents and children, and neighbours; they watch cinema and television. Sontag's supposition that they are unaware of their supposed ugliness is grotesque. So too is her meaningless accusation that Arbus's work 'excludes sufferers who presumably know they are suffering, like victims of accidents, wars, famines and political persecution'.

'In so far as looking at most of these photographs is, undeniably, an ordeal, Arbus's work is typical of the kind of art popular among sophisticated urban people right now: art that is a self willed test of hardness. The photographs offer an occasion to demonstrate that life's horror can be faced without squeamishness . . . Arbus's work is a good instance of a leading tendency of high art in capitalist countries: to suppress, or at least reduce, moral and sensory queasiness. Much of modern art is devoted to lowering the threshold of what is terrible.'

For myself, I have never found looking at these photos an 'ordeal'. By 'lowering the threshold', I assume that Sontag means including in the definition of human, people who are ugly, deformed, sexually weird or perform very badly on IQ tests. If so, then we must be eternally thankful for Diane Arbus and other sophisticated urban capitalists.

I have listed my disagreements with Sontag not to denigrate her critical faculties as compared with mine. On the contrary, there is absolutely no doubt that she is far better informed than I am about aesthetics, photography and Arbus. I cite this as a painful example of how people living within the same moral world see the same images in radically different ways. I belong to the same tiny subculture as Sontag: middle-class, intellectual, English-speaking, culturally Anglo-American, similar generation, left-liberal political views, cosmopolitan, deracinated. Yet every Arbus photo that impressed me with its integrity, humanity and compassion, she saw as lacking all these qualities.

I could reverse direction by borrowing her criticisms to describe my own reaction to another photographer of suffering. There are many people in the aid and human rights world, whose judgement I respect, who greatly admire the work of Sebastiao Salgado. His instantly recognizable photos – fleeing refugees, workers, peasants – are widely praised for their social documentary and 'artistic' realism. But whatever Salgado's impeccable intentions, I find his work a wholly aesthetic response to suffering. The photos are beautifications of tragedy, with gratuitous hints of religious symbolism – the Madonna-like woman refugee holding the Christ-like child. These images leave me altogether unmoved: some I find offensive, others just embarrassing. To me, these are photos to be collected in a coffee-table book or pinned on an undergraduate's wall-board.

Aesthetic relativism, though, does not mean that there can be no universal response to suffering. This response may be (and needs to be) no more than the UN Secretary-General, Kofi Anan's irritated reply in 1998 to a journalist's question about whether 'Africans' shared the same human rights values as Europeans: 'Why don't you ask a mother in Rwanda what she feels about her child being killed by a death squad?'

I once thought that I had found an ur-image, something impossible to deny. This was Don McCullin's unforgettable 1969 photo of an emaciated albino boy in the Biafran War. This image has stayed with me for thirty years. It was reinforced by McCullin's memoirs of what he felt at the time. He walks into a mission school turned into a hospital for 800 war-orphaned children.

> As I entered I saw a young albino boy. To be a starving Biafran orphan was to be in a most pitiable situation, but to be a starving albino Biafran was to be in a position beyond description. Dying of starvation, he was

still among his peers an object of ostracism, ridicule and insult. I saw this boy looking at me. He was like a living skeleton. There was a skeletal kind of whiteness about him. He moved nearer and nearer to me. He wore the remnants of an ill-fitting jumper and was clutching a corned beef tin, an empty corned beef tin.

The boy looked at me with a fixity that evoked the evil eye in a way which harrowed me with guilt and unease. He was moving closer. I was trying not to look at him. I tried to focus my eyes elsewhere. Some French doctors from 'Médecins sans Frontières' were trying to save a small girl who was dying.... They were trying to revive the little girl by thrusting a needle in her throat and banging her chest. The sight was almost unendurable. She died in front of me. The smallest saddest human being I had ever, in all my grim experience, seen die.

Still in the corner of my eye I could see the albino boy. I caught the flash of whiteness. He was haunting me, getting nearer. Someone was giving me the statistics of the suffering, the awful multiples of this tragedy. As I gazed at these grim victims of deprivation and starvation, my mind retreated to my own home in England where my children of much the same age were careless and cavalier with food, as Western children often are. Trying to balance between these two visions produced in me a kind of mental torment.

I felt something touch my hand. The albino boy had crept close and moved his hand into mine. I felt the tears come into my eyes as I stood there holding his hand. I thought, think of something else, anything else. Don't cry in front of these kids. I put a hand in my pocket and found one of my barley sugar sweets. Surreptitiously I transferred it to the albino boy's hand and he went away. He stood a short distance off and slowly unwrapped the sweet with fumbling fingers. He licked the sweet and stared at me with huge eyes. I noticed that he was still clutching the empty corned beef tin while he stood delicately licking the sweet as if it might disappear too quickly. He looked hardly human, as if a tiny skeleton had somehow stayed alive....

It was beyond war, it was beyond journalism. It was beyond photography, but not beyond politics. This unspeakable suffering was not the result of one of Africa's natural disasters. Here was not nature's pruning fork at work but the outcome of men's evil desires. If I could, I would take this day out of my life, demolish the memory of it.[36]

McCullin's camera (which he likened to a tooth-brush, just something that does the job) gave us eyes not easily blinded, or even turned. If only for an instant, we have to look. John Berger, reviewing McCullin's work, describes how this happens: these photos 'bring us up short'; they are literally 'arresting'; we are 'seized by them'; 'the moment of the other's suffering engulfs us'.[37] The result may be *despair* (which takes on some of the other's suffering to no purpose) or *indignation* (which demands action). We sense a radical discontinuity as we leave the frozen 'moment' of the photo to go back into our own lives: 'the contrast is such that the resumption of our lives appears to be a hopelessly inadequate response to what we have just seen.'[38] The moment of agony was isolated, discontinuous from normal time and space.

This discontinuity is not, however, our personal response or responsibility: *any* reaction to such photographed moments is bound to be felt inadequate. Those moments of agony exist by themselves; they *must be* discontinuous with other moments in our own lives. We know, however, that images of suffering are meant to evoke shock, acknowledgement, concern and action. This is how we are supposed to feel. But, argues Berger, as soon as we sense the discontinuity as being our own moral inadequacy – and either shrug it off as just part of the human condition or perform a kind of penance, by giving money to UNICEF – we deflect the issue inwards. We worry about our own moral inadequacy or our psychic tendency to deny – *instead* of turning to a political critique of the atrocities.

I often think of that albino boy. Berger describes how people are 'seized' by such images. But he casually and parenthetically notes: 'I am aware that there are people who pass them over, but about them there is nothing to say.'[39]

I would not like to believe this.

Notes

Preface

1 Stanley Cohen, *The Impact of Information about Human Rights Violations: Denial and Acknowledgement* (Jerusalem: Centre of Human Rights, Hebrew University, 1995).
2 Arthur Kleinman et al. (eds), *Social Suffering* (Berkeley: University of California Press, 1997).

Chapter 1 The Elementary Forms of Denial

1 Gordon J. Horwitz, *In the Shadow of Death: Living Outside the Gates of Mauthausen* (London: I. B. Tauris, 1991), 178.
2 In 1999, the original *New York Times* articles were reprinted as a book: A. M. Rosenthal, *Thirty-Eight Witnesses: The Kitty Genovese Case* (Berkeley: University of California Press, 1999).
3 Daniel Goleman, *Vital Lies, Simple Truths: The Psychology of Self-Deception* (New York: Simon and Schuster, 1985).
4 Robert Jay Lifton and Eric Markusen, *The Genocidal Mentality* (New York: Basic Books, 1990).
5 Arthur Miller, Foreword to Amnesty International, *Thoughts on Human Dignity and Freedom* (New York: Universe, 1991), 5.
6 Michael R. Marrus, *The Holocaust in History* (Harmondsworth: Penguin, 1987), 157.
7 Leo Kuper, Preface to Israel Charny (ed.), *Genocide: A Critical Bibliographical Review*, vol. 2 (London: Mansell, 1991), xiv.
8 Michael Ignatieff, *The Needs of Strangers* (London: Vintage, 1994).
9 'Death of a Nation', directed by John Pilger on Channel Four, Feb. 1994. See also John Pilger, 'Journey to East Timor: Land of the Dead', *Nation*, 25 Apr. 1994, 550–2.

Chapter 2 Knowing and Not-Knowing

1 Israel W. Charny, ' "Innocent Denials" of Known Genocides: A Further Contribution to a Psychology of Denial of Genocide (Revisionism)', *Internet on the Holocaust and Genocide*, 46 (Sept. 1993), 23–5. But no dedicated Holocaust deniers are 'innocent' in this sense – unlike people who genuinely have never heard about the Armenian genocide.

2 Leon Wurmser, 'Blinding the Eye of the Mind: Denial, Impulsive Action and Split Identity', in E. L. Edelstein et al. (eds), *Denial: A Clarification of Concepts and Research* (New York: Plenum Press, 1989), 175–201.

3 George E. Vaillant, *Ego Mechanisms of Defence: A Guide for Clinicians and Researchers*, Appendix 5: 'Ego Defence Mechanisms Manual' (Washington, DC: American Psychiatric Press, 1992), 272.

4 Christopher Bollas, *Being a Character: Psychoanalysis and Self Experience* (London: Routledge, 1993), 167.

5 J. Laplanche and J.-B. Pontalis, *The Language of Psycho-Analysis* (London: Hogarth Press, 1973), 118–21.

6 Ibid., 118.

7 S. Freud, 'The Neuro-psychoses of Defence' (1894), in *Standard Edition*, III (London: Hogarth Press, 1961).

8 Freud, 'The Infantile Genital Organization' (1923), in *Standard Edition*, XIX, 143–4.

9 Freud, 'Some Psychical Consequences of the Anatomical Distinction between the Sexes' (1925), in *Standard Edition*, XIX, 248–58.

10 Ibid., 252.

11 Ibid., 253.

12 Ibid.

13 Freud, 'The Loss of Reality in Neurosis and Psychosis' (1924), in *Standard Edition*, XIX, 183–7.

14 Ibid., 185.

15 Ibid., 187.

16 Freud, 'Fetishism' (1927), in *Standard Edition*, XXI, 350–7.

17 Ibid., 352.

18 One critic, however, compared the virtual inability of the American public to 'see' the damage to Iraqis during the Gulf War with the scotomas experienced by victims of certain neurological disorders. These are peculiar occlusions of the visual field: patients find themselves staring at a face but unable to see it. Stranger still, they are momentarily unable to remember the idea of a face. By analogy, the public could not see or imagine what the Iraqis had been living through (Lawrence Wechsler, 'Notes and Comments', *New Yorker*, 25 Mar. 1991, 25–6). Other neural analogues of denial include a cerebral lesion that causes anosognosia, a syndrome in which patients are unaware of damage such as hemiplegia or deny that illness has occurred. A rare variant, 'Anton's syndrome', is the denial of blindness. 'Visual anosognesics' act as if they could see, and persist this way despite

all evidence to the contrary. 'They obstinately refuse to learn to accept blindness, even though this incapacity is disorienting' (Ruth Shalev, 'Anosognosia: The Neurological Correlate of Denial of Illness', in Edelstein et al., (eds), *Denial*, 123). Other forms of visual-perceptual damage, or hemianopsia, suggest unawareness rather than 'denial'; patients claim that they 'see just fine' (see David N. Levine, 'Unawareness of Visual and Sensorimotor Defects', *Brain and Cognition*, 13 (1990), 233–81).

19 Freud, 'Fetishism', 355.
20 Ibid., 356.
21 Quoted by John Steiner, 'The Relationship to Reality in Psychic Retreats', in *Psychic Retreats: Pathological Organizations in Psychotic, Neurotic and Borderline Patients* (London: Routledge, 1993), 88–115. This paragraph of mine draws heavily on Steiner.
22 Eugene E. Trunnel and William E. Holt, 'The Concept of Denial or Disavowal', *Journal of the American Psychoanalytic Association*, 22 (1974), 771.
23 Freud, *An Outline of Psychoanalysis* (1940) and 'Splitting of the Ego in the Process of Defence' (1940), in *Standard Edition*, XXIII.
24 Freud, *Outline*, 203.
25 I came across this quote attributed to Freud many times, but citations were incorrect and I could never locate its source. The phrase certainly sounds Freudian.
26 Trunnel and Holt, 'Concept of Denial', 775.
27 Ibid.
28 Anna Freud, *The Ego and Mechanisms of Defence* (New York: International Universities Press, 1966), ch. 7; and Anna Freud and Joseph Sandler, *The Analysis of Defence: The Ego and Mechanisms of Defence Revisited* (New York: International Universities Press, 1985).
29 A. Freud, *Ego and Mechanisms of Defence*, 95.
30 Anna Freud, in Freud and Sandler, *Analysis of Defence*, 351–3.
31 Theo L. Dorpat, 'The Cognitive Arrest Hypothesis of Denial', *International Journal of Psycho-Analysis*, 64 (1983), 47–57.
32 Martin Wangh, 'The Evolution of Psychoanalytic Thought on Negation and Denial', in Edelstein et al. (eds), *Denial*, 5–15.
33 Ibid., 12.
34 H. Samuel Ehrlich, 'Adolescent Denial: Some Psychoanalytical Reflections on Strengths and Weaknesses', in Edelstein et al. (eds), *Denial*, 144.
35 Michael Frederic Chayes, 'Concerning Certain Vicissitudes of Denial in Personality Development', in Edelstein et al. (eds), *Denial*, 87–105.
36 John Steiner, 'Turning a Blind Eye: The Cover Up for Oedipus', *International Review of Psycho-Analysis*, 12 (1985), 163. See also *idem*, 'The Retreat from Truth to Omnipotence in Sophocles' "Oedipus at Colonus"', *International Review of Psycho-Analysis*, 17 (1990), 227–37. For Steiner's new integration of these papers see his *Psychic Retreats*, ch. 10, 'Two Types of Pathological Organization in *Oedipus the King* and *Oedipus at Colonus*', 116–30.
37 Steiner, 'Two Types', 120.

38 Steiner, 'Turning a Blind Eye', 161.
39 Ibid.
40 Ibid.
41 Steiner, 'Retreat from Truth', 228.
42 Ibid., 233.
43 Ibid., 233–4.
44 Michael A. Milburn and Sheree D. Conrad, *The Politics of Denial* (Cambridge, MA: MIT Press, 1996).
45 Ibid., 3.
46 American Psychiatric Association, *Diagnostic and Statistical Manual of Mental Disorders*, 4th edn [DSM – IVtm] (Washington, DC: American Psychiatric Association, 1994), 751–3.
47 Harold I. Kaplan et al., *Kaplan and Sadock's Synopsis of Psychiatry, Behavioral Sciences, Clinical Psychology*, 7th edn (Baltimore: Williams and Wilkins, 1994), 249–53. There could hardly be anything *more* immature than denial, which pops up on their 'developmental table' as an ego defence used between birth and the oral stage *just before age one*. Altruism is up at the top, ranked as a *Mature Defence* along with sublimation, asceticism and humour.
48 The opposite is true. The reason why you bought this book – on obesity rather than sado-masochism – is that you are *unable* to shut out your anxieties about this condition. Far from being in denial, you are obsessed with the subject.
49 R. D. Laing, *Knots* (London: Tavistock, 1970), 5.
50 J. A. Barnes, *A Pack of Lies: Towards a Sociology of Lying* (Cambridge: Cambridge University Press, 1994), 11.
51 W. Peter Robinson, *Deceit, Delusion and Detection* (London: Sage, 1996), 33.
52 Barnes, *Pack of Lies*, 87–98.
53 Herbert Fingarette, *Self-Deception* (London: Routledge, 1969), 67, and (summarized) *idem*, 'Self-deception and the "Splitting of the Ego" ', in R. Wollheim and J. Hopkins (eds), *Philosophical Essays on Freud* (Cambridge: Cambridge University Press, 1982), 212–27.
54 Sisela Bok, *Secrets: On the Ethics of Concealment and Revelation* (New York: Vintage Books, 1982), 60.
55 Ibid., 61.
56 Jean-Paul Sartre, *Being and Nothingness* (New York: Philosophical Library, 1956), 50.
57 Ibid., 49.
58 Ibid.
59 Jon Elster, *Ulysses and the Sirens: Studies in Rationality and Irrationality* (Cambridge: Cambridge University Press, 1984), 172–9.
60 Ibid., 178.
61 Brian P. McLaughlin and Amelie Oksenburg Rorty (eds), *Perspectives on Self-Deception* (Berkeley: University of California Press, 1988), 1.
62 Amelie Oksenberg Rorty, 'The Deceptive Self: Liars, Layers and Lairs', in McLaughlin and Rorty (eds), *Perspectives*, 10–28.

63 Ibid., 17.

64 Elster, *Ulysses*, 172.

65 In jettisoning all superfluous Freudianism, cognitive psychology picked up new pseudo-scientific baggage to explain some rather simple matters. Many 'cognitive errors' (and some motivated denials) arise, as Sutherland nicely shows, from stupidity, vanity, folly or just plain *daftness*. These include wishful thinking; avoiding exposure to awkward evidence, rejection or distortion of contradictory information; selective memory; misinterpreting evidence; false inference; over-confidence; faulty risk assessment, etc. (Stuart Sutherland, *Irrationality: The Enemy Within* (Harmondsworth: Penguin Books, 1992)).

66 For a review of these fields, see Robert J. Sternberg, *Cognitive Psychology* (Fort Worth, TX: Harcourt Brace, 1996).

67 For a convenient summary, see Michael W. Eysenck and Mark Keane, *Cognitive Psychology: A Student's Handbook* (Hove: Lawrence Erlbaum, 1990), ch. 3: 'Theoretical Issues in Perception'.

68 Lawrence Weiskrantz, *Blindsight: A Case Study and Implications* (Oxford: Oxford University Press, 1986), and *idem*, 'Blindsight', in M. W. Eysenck (ed.), *The Blackwell Dictionary of Cognitive Psychology* (Oxford: Blackwell, 1994), 44–6.

69 Daniel Goleman, *Vital Lies, Simple Truths: The Psychology of Self-Deception* (New York: Simon and Schuster, 1985), 67.

70 F. Christopher Kolb and Jochen Braun, 'Blindsight in Normal Observers', *Nature*, 377 (Sept. 1995), 336–9.

71 The classic account was Elliott McGinnies, 'Emotionality and Perceptual Defense', *Psychological Review*, 56 (1949), 244–51.

72 Matthew Erdelyi, 'A New Look at the New Look: Perceptual Defence and Vigilance', *Psychological Review*, 81 (1974), 1–25.

73 Duncan Howie, 'Perceptual Defense', *Psychological Review*, 59 (1952), 311.

74 Clearly set out in Richard Nisbett and Lee Ross, *Human Inference: Strategies and Shortcomings of Human Judgment* (Englewood Cliffs, NJ: Prentice-Hall, 1980).

75 Goleman, *Vital Lies*, 19.

76 Ibid., 43.

77 Ibid., 61–6.

78 Laing, *Knots*, 1.

79 See Sternberg, *Cognitive Psychology*, ch. 3: 'Attention and Consciousness'.

80 Ibid., 95–100.

81 Ibid., 109.

82 Ibid., ch. 12: 'Decision Making and Reasoning'.

83 Susan T. Fiske and Shelley E. Taylor, *Social Cognition* (Reading, MA: Addison-Wesley, 1984), 88.

84 See John Searle's accessible and (to me) convincing account of the current debates: *The Mystery of Consciousness* (New York: New York Review of Books, 1997).

85 Daniel C. Dennett, *Consciousness Explained* (Harmondsworth: Penguin, 1992). On Orwellian versus Stalinesque models of the mind, see esp. 116–24.
86 Ronnie Janoff-Bulman, 'Assumptive Worlds and the Stress of Traumatic Events: Applications of the Schema Construct', *Social Cognition*, 7/2 (1989), 113–36.
87 Shelley E. Taylor, 'Adjustment to Threatening Events: A Theory of Cognitive Adaptation', *American Psychologist*, 38/11 (Nov. 1983), 1161–73; Shelley E. Taylor and Jonathon D. Brown, 'Illusion and Well-Being: A Social and Psychological Perspective on Mental Health', *Psychological Bulletin*, 103/2 (1988), 193–210.
88 Anthony G. Greenwald, 'The Totalitarian Ego: Fabrication and Revision of Personal History', *American Psychologist*, 35/7 (July 1980), 603–18.
89 Saul Bellow, *Mr. Sammler's Planet* (London: Weidenfeld and Nicholson, 1970), 81.

Chapter 3 Denial at Work

1 Nadera Shalhoub-Kevorkian, 'Tolerating Battering: Invisible Methods of Social Control', *International Review of Victimology*, 5 (1997), 1–21.
2 Shlomo Breznitz, 'The Seven Kinds of Denial', in *idem* (ed.), *The Denial of Stress* (New York: International Universities Press, 1983), 185–235.
3 M. J. Horowitz, 'Psychological Responses to Serious Life Events', in Breznitz (ed.), *Denial of Stress*, 129–59.
4 Sydney H. Croog et al., 'Denial among Male Heart Patients: An Empirical Study', *Psychosomatic Medicine*, 33/5 (Sept. 1971), 385–97.
5 An earlier study reported that 19 per cent of a sample of cancer patients denied that they had cancer only a few weeks after being given the diagnosis. Other recorded denials include not seeking treatment for a visible disfiguring illness; denying the existence of pregnancy, even after giving birth, and doing push-ups next to the bed in a coronary unit while recovering from a heart attack. For reviews of these and similar studies, see David Ness and Jack Ende, 'Denial in the Medical Interview', *Journal of the American Medical Association*, 272 (Dec. 1994), 1777–81, and Jacob Levine et al., 'A Two Factor Model of Denial of Illness', *Journal of Psychosomatic Research*, 38 (1994), 99–110.
6 Levine et al., 'Two Factor Model'.
7 Karen G. Langer, 'Depression and Denial in Psychotherapy of Persons with Disabilities', *American Journal of Psychotherapy*, 48/2 (Spring 1994), 191.
8 Summarized by Paul Martin, *The Sickening Mind: Brain, Behaviour, Immunity and Disease* (London: Flamingo, 1998), 229–34.
9 Timothy R. Elliott et al., 'Negotiating Reality after Physical Loss: Hope, Depression and Disability', *Journal of Personality and Social Psychology*, 61/4 (1991), 608–13.
10 My own common-sense, 'deep' reading of such research. No human being coping with personal devastation is visible. Simple findings are buried

under tacky theory and pretend scientism (the *Correlation Matrix of Variables Used in Hierarchical Regression Analysis* contains the Hope Scale, the Inventory to Diagnose Depression and the Sickness Impact Profile).

11 Shelley E. Taylor, 'Adjustment to Threatening Events: A Theory of Cognitive Adaptation', *American Psychologist*, 38/11 (Nov. 1983), 1161–73.
12 Neil D. Weinstein, 'Unrealistic Optimism about Susceptibility to Health Problems: Conclusions from a Community-Wide Sample', *Journal of Behavioral Medicine*, 10/5 (1987), 481–500, and *idem*, 'Why it Won't Happen to Me: Perceptions of Risk Factors and Susceptibility', *Health Psychology*, 3/5 (1984), 431–57.
13 Note Sontag's critique of illness as metaphor, from TB to cancer to AIDS: Susan Sontag, *Illness as Metaphor* and *AIDS and Its Metaphors* (New York: Anchor Books, 1989).
14 Eva Lowy and Michael W. Ross, ' "It'll Never Happen to Me": Gay Men's Beliefs, Perceptions and Folk Constructions of Sexual Risk', *AIDS Education and Prevention*, 6/6 (1994), 467–82.
15 Elisa J. Sobo, *Choosing Unsafe Sex: Aids-Risk Denial among Disadvantaged Women* (Philadelphia: University of Pennsylvania Press, 1995).
16 Cited in Shelley E. Taylor, *Positive Illusions: Creative Self-Deception and the Healthy Mind* (New York: Basic Books, 1989), 4.
17 Christopher Layne, 'Painful Truths about Depressives' Cognitions', *Journal of Clinical Psychology*, 39/6 (Nov. 1983), 848–53; this evidence is reviewed by Shelley E. Taylor and Jonathon D. Brown, 'Illusion and Well Being: A Social Psychological Perspective on Mental Health', *Psychological Bulletin*, 103 (1988), 193–210.
18 Taylor, *Positive Illusions*.
19 C. Wright Mills, 'Situated Actions and Vocabularies of Motive', *American Sociological Review*, 15 (Dec. 1940), 904–13.
20 Marvin B. Scott and Stanford M. Lyman, 'Accounts', *American Sociological Review*, 33 (Feb. 1968), 46–62.
21 Ibid., 47.
22 Gresham Sykes and David Matza, 'Techniques of Neutralization', *American Sociological Review*, 22 (Dec. 1957), 664–70.
23 Laurie Taylor, 'The Significance and Interpretation of Replies to Motivational Questions: The Case of Sex Offenders', *Sociology*, 6 (1972), 23–39.
24 Scott and Lyman, 'Accounts', 47.
25 On the distinction between act and actor adjustment (and defensive and offensive accounts) see Jason Ditton, *Part-time Crime: An Ethnography of Fiddling and Pilferage* (London: Macmillan, 1977).
26 Charles H. McCaghy, 'Drinking and Deviance Disavowal: The Case of Child Molesters', *Social Problems*, 25/2 (1968), 43–9. The concept of 'deviance disavowal' appears in the classic study by Fred Davis, 'Deviance Disavowal: The Management of Strained Interaction by the Visibly Handicapped', *Social Problems*, 9 (Fall 1961), 120–32.

27 Diana Scully and Joseph Marolla, 'Convicted Rapists' Vocabularies of Motive: Excuses and Justifications', *Social Problems*, 31/5 (June 1984), 530–44.
28 The example and theory derive from Cressey's classic paper about 'compulsive' and 'impulsive' crime: Donald R. Cressey, 'Role Theory, Differential Association and Compulsive Crimes', in Arnold M. Rose (ed.), *Human Behaviour and Social Process* (Boston: Houghton Mifflin, 1962), 443–67.
29 Robert J. Kearney, *Within the Wall of Denial: Conquering Addictive Behaviors* (New York: W. W. Norton, 1996).
30 L. Charles Ward and Paul Rothaus, 'The Measurement of Denial and Rationalization in Male Alcoholics', *Journal of Clinical Psychology*, 47/3 (May 1991), 465–9.
31 Daniel Goleman, *Vital Lies, Simple Truths: The Psychology of Self-Deception* (New York: Simon and Schuster, 1985), 17.
32 See Stephanie Brown, *Treating Adult Children of Alcoholics: A Developmental Perspective* (New York: John Wiley and Sons, 1987), esp. 33–57, and *idem*, 'Adult Children of Alcoholics: The History of a Social Movement and its Impact on Clinical Theory and Practise', in Marc Galanter (ed.), *Recent Developments in Alcoholism*, vol. 9 (New York: Plenum Press, 1991), 267–85.
33 Christopher Bollas, 'Violent Innocence', in *Being a Character: Psychoanalysis and Self Experience* (London: Routledge, 1993), 165–92.
34 Ibid., 168.
35 Ibid., 180.
36 Ibid., 183.
37 Ibid., 184.
38 Summarized in Goleman, *Vital Lies, Simple Truths*, 180–93.
39 My sources on the Scott Inquiry are Richard Norton-Taylor, *Truth is a Difficult Concept: Inside the Scott Inquiry* (London: 4th Estate, 1995), and B. Thomson and F. Ridley, *Under the Scott-Light* (Oxford: Oxford University Press, 1997).
40 Richard Norton-Taylor et al., *Knee Deep in Dishonour: The Scott Report and its Aftermath* (London: Gollanz, 1996).
41 I. F. Stone, 'It Pays to be Ignorant', *New York Review of Books*, 9 Aug. 1973, 6–9. All my other quotes about Watergate are from this classic piece.
42 Bib Latane and John M. Darley, *The Unresponsive Bystander: Why Doesn't He Help?* (New York: Appleton-Crofts, 1970).
43 Petruska Clarkson, *The Bystander (An End to Innocence in Human Relationships?)* (London: Whurr Publications, 1996), xi, emphasis original.
44 Ibid., 6.
45 Melvin Lerner, *The Belief in a Just World: A Fundamental Delusion* (New York: Plenum Press, 1980).
46 See N. Eisenberg and P. A. Miller, 'The Relation of Empathy to Prosocial and Related Behaviors', *Psychological Bulletin*, 101 (1987), 91–119; Lauren Wispe, *The Psychology of Sympathy* (New York: Plenum Press, 1989).
47 Latane and Darley, *Unresponsive Bystander*, 125.
48 Pat Carlen, *Jigsaw: A Political Criminology of Youth Homelessness* (Milton Keynes: Open University Press, 1996).

49 Cathryn A. Christy and Harrison Voigt, 'Bystander Responses to Public Episodes of Child Abuse', *Journal of Applied Social Psychology*, 24 (1994), 824–47. (The authors list a bibliography of 47 bystander studies.)
50 Ibid., 844.
51 Stuart W. Twemlow et al., 'A Clinical and Interactionist Perspective on the Bully–Victim–Bystander Relationship', *Bulletin of the Menninger Clinic*, 60/3 (Summer 1996), 296–313.
52 See Diana E. H. Russell, *The Secret Trauma: Incest in the Lives of Girls and Women* (New York: Basic Books, 1986); R. L. Scott and J. V. Flowers, 'Betrayal of the Mother as a Factor Contributing to Psychological Disturbance in Victims of Father–Daughter Incest', *Journal of Social and Clinical Psychology*, 6 (1988), 147–54.

Chapter 4 Accounting for Atrocities

1 On the distinction between ordinary and ideological crime, see Stanley Cohen, 'Crime and Politics: Spot the Difference', *British Journal of Sociology*, 47 (1996), 2–21.
2 Daniel Jonah Goldhagen, *Hitler's Willing Executioners: Ordinary Germans and the Holocaust* (London: Little Brown and Co., 1996).
3 Zygmunt Bauman, *Modernity and the Holocaust* (Cambridge: Polity Press, 1989).
4 The American psychologist who observed the defendants behind the scenes of the trial describes how these accounts were collectively negotiated: G. M. Gilbert, *Nuremberg Diary* (New York: Farrar Straus, 1947).
5 Yisrael Gutman, *Denying the Holocaust* (Jerusalem: Institute of Contemporary Jewry, Hebrew University, 1985), 14.
6 Israel W. Charny, 'The Psychology of Denial of Known Genocides', in *idem* (ed.), *Genocide: A Critical Bibliographical Review*, vol. 2 (London: Mansell, 1991), 3.
7 Documented in standard work and summarized by Michael Marrus, *The Holocaust in History* (Harmondsworth: Penguin Books, 1989). The quote is from another useful summary: Michael Berenbaum, *The World Must Know: The History of the Holocaust as Told in the United States Holocaust Museum* (Boston: Little, Brown & Co., 1993), 106–7.
8 Hannah Arendt, *Eichmann in Jerusalem: A Report on the Banality of Evil* (New York: Penguin USA, 1994; original edn, 1965), 84–6.
9 Ibid., 85.
10 Ibid.
11 Clearly summarized in Berenbaum, *The World Must Know*, 112–17.
12 Ibid., 115.
13 See Frank Graziano, *Divine Violence: Spectacle, Psychosexuality and Radical Christianity in the Argentine Dirty War* (Boulder, CO: Westview Press, 1992), and Marguerite Feitlowitz, *A Lexicon of Terror: Argentina and the Legacies of Torture* (New York: Oxford University Press, 1998).

14 Feitlowitz, *Lexicon of Terror*, 65. It is uncertain, she notes, whether continued use of perverted words like *parrilla* long after the junta 'is a deliberate effort to salvage earlier, untainted meanings, whether it is a sign of denial or whether it is a sign that, come what may, life goes on' (ibid., 61).
15 Ronald D. Crelinsten, 'In Their Own Words: The World of the Torturer', in R. D. Crelinsten and A. P. Schmid (eds), *The Politics of Pain: Torturers and Their Masters* (Boulder, CO: Westview Press, 1995), 34–64.
16 Ibid., 39.
17 Graziano, *Divine Violence*, 8.
18 *El Libro de El Diario del Juicio*, cited by Graziano, *Divine Violence*, 45.
19 Michael Taussig, 'Terror as Usual: Walter Benjamin's Theory of History as a State of Siege', in *The Nervous System* (London: Routledge, 1992), 11–35.
20 Ibid., 21.
21 Ibid., 'Talking Terror 4', 26–30.
22 Michael Burleigh, *Death and Deliverance: 'Euthanasia' in Germany, 1940–1945* (Cambridge: Cambridge University Press, 1994), 150.
23 Gitta Sereny, *Albert Speer: His Battle with Truth* (London: Picador, 1996).
24 Dan van der Vat, *The Good Nazi: The Life and Lies of Albert Speer* (London: Phoenix, 1997), 2. This is a crude, badly written book, but is correctly sceptical of Speer's 'carefully cultivated self-image as the apolitical Nazi functionary who redeemed himself by owning up' (364). He was not just a functionary; nor did he ever own up.
25 Sereny, *Albert Speer*, 167.
26 Ibid., 340.
27 Ibid., 690.
28 Ibid., 115.
29 Ibid., 115–16.
30 Ibid., 161.
31 Ibid., 164.
32 Ibid., 175.
33 Ibid., 379.
34 Ibid., 200.
35 Ibid., 148.
36 Ibid., 707.
37 Van der Vat, *Good Nazi*, 24.
38 Albert Speer, *Inside the Third Reich* (London: Weidenfeld & Nicholson, 1970), 113.
39 Quotations in remainder of this paragraph are from Sereny, *Albert Speer*, 707–8.
40 Ibid., 222.
41 Ibid., 706.
42 Ibid., 707.
43 Ibid., 222.
44 Bauman, *Modernity and the Holocaust*, 163.
45 Most commentators over-simplify this great experiment. The differences Milgram observed by varying the experimental conditions are ignored,

along with his acute insights into obedience to authority. See Stanley
Milgram, *Obedience to Authority* (New York: Harper and Row, 1974).
46   Herbert C. Kelman and V. Lee Hamilton, *Crimes of Obedience* (New Haven:
      Yale University Press, 1989).
47   Crelinsten, 'In Their Own Words', 48.
48   Gordon Horwitz, *In the Shadow of Death: Living Outside the Gates of
      Mauthausen* (London: I. B. Tauris, 1991), 80.
49   Ibid.
50   The classic analysis remains Everett C. Hughes, 'Good People and Dirty
      Work', *Social Problems*, 10 (1962), 3–11.
51   Robert Jay Lifton, *The Nazi Doctors: Medical Killing and the Psychology of
      Genocide* (New York: Basic Books, 1986), and *idem*, 'The Genocidal Men-
      tality', *Tikkun*, 5 (June 1990), 29–32 and 97–9.
52   For a convincing study of how German lawyers acquiesced in terrible
      crimes by invoking denials embedded in mainstream legal ideology, see
      Ingo Muller, *Hitler's Justice: The Courts of the Third Reich* (Cambridge,
      MA: Harvard University Press, 1991).
53   Burleigh, *Death and Deliverance*, 154.
54   Ibid., 252.
55   Melvin Lerner, *The Belief in a Just World: A Fundamental Delusion* (New
      York: Plenum Press, 1980).
56   Michael Ignatieff, *Blood and Belonging: Journeys into the New Nationalism*
      (London: Vintage, 1994), 6.
57   Ibid.
58   See 'Moral Inclusion and Injustice', Special Issue of *Journal of Social
      Issues*, 46 (1990). I draw extensively from two papers: Susan Opotow,
      'Moral Inclusion and Injustice: An Introduction', 1–20, and Albert
      Bandura, 'Selective Activation and Disengagement of Moral Control',
      27–46.
59   Michael Ignatieff, 'The Narcissism of Minor Difference', in *The Warrior's
      Honour: Ethnic War and the Modern Conscience* (London: Chatto & Windus,
      1998), 60.
60   Ignatieff, *Blood and Belonging*, 30.
61   Ernst Klee et al., *'Those Were the Days': The Holocaust through the Eyes of the
      Perpetrators and Bystanders* (London: Hamish Hamilton, 1991), 220.
62   From a report by Obersturmbannführer Dr Strauch, cited in ibid., 193.
63   Ibid., 197.
64   Ibid., 69.
65   Mary McCarthy, *Medina* (London: Wildwood House, 1973).
66   Ibid., 44.
67   Arendt, *Eichmann in Jerusalem*, 287.
68   Arendt, *Eichmann in Jerusalem*, 116.
69   Ibid., my emphasis.
70   For a longer version of this section, see Stanley Cohen, 'Government
      Responses to Human Rights Reports: Claims, Denials and Counterclaims',
      Human Rights Quarterly, 18 (1996), 517–43.

71 Noam Chomsky, *The Culture of Terrorism* (London: Pluto Press, 1989), and *idem*, *Necessary Illusions: Thought Control in Democratic Societies* (Boston: South End Press, 1989).

72 See Elaine Scarry, *The Body in Pain* (Oxford: Oxford University Press, 1987), and Crelinsten and Schmid (eds), *Politics of Pain*.

73 Ariel Dorfman, 'Political Code and Literary Code: The Testimonial Genre in Chile Today', in *Some Write to the Future* (Durham, NC: Duke University Press, 1991), 141.

74 Feitlowitz, *Lexicon Of Terror*, 22.

75 Mark Danner, *The Massacre at El Mozote: A Parable of the Cold War* (New York: Vintage Books, 1994).

76 Graziano, *Divine Violence*, 41–5.

77 Feitlowitz, *Lexicon of Terror*, 49.

78 George Orwell, Appendix to *Nineteen-Eighty Four* (Harmondsworth: Penguin, 1954 [1949]), and *idem*, 'Politics and the English Language', in his *Selected Essays* (Harmondsworth: Penguin, 1957), 143–58. On euphemism and other techniques of 'control-talk' see Stanley Cohen, *Visions of Social Control* (Cambridge: Polity Press, 1985), 273–81.

79 Orwell, 'Politics and the English Language', 362.

80 See Robert Jay Lifton and Eric Markusen, *The Genocidal Mentality* (New York: Basic Books, 1990).

81 Cited by Feitlowitz, *Lexicon of Terror*, 50.

82 These terms were used in the 1955 Wuillame Report, the French government's response to allegations of torture – a word that only appears twice in a report that actually describes some twenty-five techniques of torture. See Rita Maran, *Torture: The Role of Ideology in the French-Algerian War* (New York: Praeger, 1989).

83 The term 'moderate physical pressure' was invented by a 1987 Judicial Commission that allowed the Israeli General Security Services to continue the regulated use of certain interrogation practices (listed in a secret appendix) against Palestinian detainees. On the debate and evidence of torture, see Stanley Cohen and Daphna Golan, *The Interrogation of Palestinians during the Intifada: Ill-treatment, 'Moderate Physical Pressure' or Torture?* (Jerusalem: B'tselem, March 1991), and *idem*, *The Interrogation of Palestinians during the Intifada: Follow-up Report* (Jerusalem: B'tselem, March 1992). On reactions to the original report see Stanley Cohen, 'Talking about Torture in Israel', *Tikkun*, 6 (Dec. 1991), 23–32.

84 Leo Kuper, *Genocide* (Harmondsworth: Penguin, 1981), 161.

85 Ibid., 39.

86 This and many other techniques on my list appear in Bandura, 'Selective Activation'.

87 In response to international criticism after the 1982 invasion of Lebanon and bombing of Beirut, the Prime Minister, Menachem Begin, said in the Knesset: 'No one, anywhere in the world, can preach morality to our people.'

88 Kanan Makiya, *Cruelty and Silence: War, Tyranny, Uprising and the Arab World* (London: Jonathan Cape, 1993).

89   Indeed, the likeliest result is an even more sophisticated circuit of responses. The exchanges – allegations, government reply, counter-response – may go on for years. The growth of human rights bureaucracies guarantees that the circuit of paper work will be prolonged. Israel not only has civil servants who construct replies to allegations, but it recruits volunteers to reply to letters from Amnesty's volunteers. A busy little denial industry.

Chapter 5 Blocking out the Past

1   Vaclav Havel, 'Dear Dr. Husak', in *Open Letters: Selected Writings, 1965–1990* (New York: Vintage Books, 1992), 50–83.

2   Sigmund Freud, *The Interpretation of Dreams* (1900), in *Standard Edition*, IV (London: Hogarth Press, 1953), 600.

3   Freud, 'Repression' (1915), in *Standard Edition*, XIV.

4   Or rather, our Inner Dummy keeps doing them: David L. Weiner, *Battling the Inner Dummy: The Craziness of Apparently Normal People* (Amhurst, NY: Prometheus Books, 1999).

5   The original criticisms remain the best guides: Richard Ofshe and Ethan Waters, *Making Monsters: False Memories, Psychotherapy and Sexual Hysteria* (Berkeley: University of California Press, 1996), and Mark Prendergast, *Victims of Memory: Sex Abuse Accusations and Shattered Lives* (Hinesberg, Va.: Upper Access Books, 1996). Note also Frederick Crews, *The Memory Wars: Freud's Legacy in Dispute* (New York: New York Review of Books, 1995): a fine introduction to the controversy, despite his excessive vitriol and the rather pathetic defences from Freudians.

6   Ellen Bass and Laura Davis, *The Courage to Heal: A Guide for Women Survivors of Child Sexual Abuse* (New York: Harper Perennial, 1988), 42. This was the prototype of the first wave of guidebooks. The most influential theorizing was Judith Herman's *Trauma and Recovery* (New York: Basic Books, 1992). These are the main (and easy) targets of all critics.

7   Ofshe and Waters, *Making Monsters*, 33.

8   Jody Davies, quoted by Crews, *Memory Wars*, 25.

9   Nicholas P. Spanos, *Multiple Identities and False Memories* (New York: American Psychological Association, 1996). MPD was later renamed DID, Dissociative Identity Disorder.

10   For the links between MPD, childhood sexual abuse and the Recovered Memory movement – and a rich account of the social construction of these categories – see Ian Hacking, *Rewriting the Soul: Multiple Personality and the Sciences of Memory* (Princeton: Princeton University Press, 1998).

11   Accused perpetrators receive theoretically symmetrical, but politically opposite, treatment. A therapist (who later retracted her belief in RMS and became herself a 'retractor therapist') recalls working with a mid-thirties patient who had just written to her father accusing him of incest when she was three: 'He called her and completely denied everything, but

we took that as evidence that he was in denial' (cited in Prendergast, *Victims of Memory*, 237).

12 The phrase is Renée Fredrickson's, one of the more extreme Recoverers. Referring to patients' 'crippling disbelief' about their newly recovered memories, Fredrickson notes that 'The existence of profound disbelief is an indication that memories are real' (quoted by Ofshe and Waters, *Making Monsters*, 108).

13 Lawrence L. Langer, 'The Alarmed Vision: Social Suffering and Holocaust Atrocity', in Arthur Kleinman et al. (eds), *Social Suffering* (Berkeley: University of California Press, 1997), 47–65.

14 Ibid., 55.

15 'Avoiding the Truth Trap': the heading of a case-study in a 1994 *Family Therapy Newsletter*, cited in ibid., 512. Crews makes the interesting claim that Freudianism itself has forsaken its more ambitious pretensions and retreated into 'hermeneutic perspectivism' – that is, 'towards abandoning truth claims and recasting the therapeutic goal as mere reconciliation of the client to a less punitive myth about his or her identity' (*Memory Wars*, 20).

16 Ofshe and Waters, *Making Monsters*, 110–11.

17 Dan Bar-On, *Legacy of Silence: Encounters with Children of the Third Reich* (Cambridge, MA: Harvard University Press, 1989).

18 Besides acknowledgement as truth, I deal with justice, reconciliation and other issues in a fuller review: Stanley Cohen, 'State Crimes of Previous Regimes: Knowledge, Accountability and the Policing of the Past', *Law and Social Inquiry*, 20 (1995), 7–50.

19 When Waldheim was rumbled in 1988, many commented not just on the former UN Secretary General's original literal denial ('frailty of memory'), but on his failure to grasp its significance. He seemed to think that deliberately obscuring details of his German army record was like a student slightly fudging an item on a CV.

20 Andrew Gumbel, 'Touvier Retreats into Forgetfulness', *Guardian*, 3 Mar. 1994.

21 Marguerite Feitlowitz, *A Lexicon of Terror: Argentina and the Legacies of Torture* (New York: Oxford University Press, 1998), 151.

22 Ibid.

23 Hannah Arendt, *Eichmann in Jerusalem: A Report on the Banality of Evil* (New York: Penguin USA, 1994; orig. edn 1965), 52.

24 All quotes are from David Beresford, 'Vlok "Knew Nothing" of Police Abuses', *Guardian*, 16 Oct. 1997, and checked with South African newspapers.

25 Raul Hilberg, *Perpetrators Victims Bystanders: The Jewish Catastrophe, 1933–1945* (New York: Harper Collins, 1992), 26.

26 Michael Burleigh, *Death and Deliverance: 'Euthanasia' in Germany, 1940–1945* (Cambridge: Cambridge University Press, 1994), 125.

27 Timothy Garton Ash, *The File: A Personal History* (New York: Random House, 1997), and *idem*, 'Bad Memories', *Prospect*, Sept. 1997, 20–3.

28 See Michael Lynch and David Brogen, *The Spectacle of History: Speech, Text and Memory at the Iran Contra Hearings* (Durham, NC: Duke University Press, 1996), and Richard Norton-Taylor et al., *Knee Deep in Dishonour: The Scott Report and its Aftermath* (London: Gollancz, 1996).

29 Extracts from testimonies at the South African Truth and Reconciliation Commission, quoted by Antjie Krog, *Country of My Skull* (London: Jonathan Cape, 1998).

30 Lawrence L. Langer, *Holocaust Testimonies: The Ruins of Memory* (New Haven: Yale University Press, 1991), 40.

31 Ibid., 9. See ch. 1: 'Deep Memory: The Buried Self'.

32 Dori Laub, 'An Event without a Witness: Truth, Testimony and Survival', in Shoshana Felman and Dori Laub, *Testimony: Crises of Witnessing in Literature, Psychoanalysis and History* (New York: Routledge, 1992). This book, alas, is a typical (though mild) example of how humanistic insights, become fashionable academic junk. After some good sense about the difficulties of witnessing, we are told: 'One might say that there was, thus, historically no witness to the Holocaust, either from outside or inside the event' (p. 81). Really? And 'This collapse of witnessing is precisely, in my view, what is central to the Holocaust experience' (p. 80). Really? Most of us think that the mass slaughter of six million people was what was 'central to the Holocaust experience'.

33 Ibid., 81.

34 Arendt, *Eichmann in Jerusalem*, 126–7.

35 Israel W. Charny, 'The Psychology of Denial of Known Genocides', in *idem* (ed.), *Genocide: A Critical Bibliographical Review*, vol. 2 (London: Mansell, 1992), 3–37.

36 For an early account of how the Turkish genocide of Armenians became denied and forgotten, see Leo Kuper, *Genocide* (Harmondsworth: Penguin, 1981). The most up-to-date reviews are Richard Hovannisian, *Remembrance and Denial: The Case of the Armenian Genocide* (Detroit: Wayne State University Press, 1999), and Vahakn Dadrian, *Warrant for Genocide: Key Elements of Turko-Armenian Conflict* (New Brunswick, NJ: Transaction Publishers, 1999).

37 Details are chronicled in the conference programme published by the Institute of the International Conference of Holocaust and Genocide, Jerusalem 1983. Only the conference's president, Elie Wiesel (after being approached by the Israel Foreign Ministry) was prepared to make a deal to cancel the conference, and did not himself attend.

38 Mark Danner, *The Massacre at El Mozote: A Parable of the Cold War* (New York: Vintage, 1994).

39 Deborah Lipstadt, *Denying the Holocaust: The Growing Assault on Truth and Memory* (New York: Free Press, 1994).

40 Roger Eatwell, 'The Holocaust Denial: A Study in Propaganda Technique', in Luciano Cheles et al. (eds), *Neo-Fascism in Europe* (London: Longman, 1991), 120–46.

41 Much attention was given to the astonishing finding of an April 1993 Roper Poll that some 22 per cent of a US public opinion sample thought it possible that the Holocaust never happened. It emerged later that the questions were badly worded, and grossly overestimated the extent of actual denial. An analysis of twelve further polls concludes that some 2 per cent are consistent and committed deniers; another 2 per cent think it either possible or probable that the Holocaust did not happen; somewhere between 1 and 8 per cent are unsure, but express ignorance rather than doubt. Most uncertainty and doubt result from general historical ignorance, not from absorption of neo-Nazi ideology. See Tom W. Smith, 'Poll Review: The Holocaust Denial Controversy', *Public Opinion Quarterly*, 59 (1995), 269–95.

42 Martin Shermer, *Why People Believe Weird Things: Pseudoscience, Superstitions and Other Confusions of Our Time* (New York: W. H. Freeman, 1998).

43 Rene Lemarchand, 'Burundi', in Helen Fein (ed.), *Genocide Watch* (New Haven: Yale University Press, 1992), 70–86.

44 Some Chileans, of course, use both strategies at once – nothing happened, and it was justified. Few, however, would dare to add the third account that Lady Thatcher invoked in 1999: that we should be grateful to General Allende for *restoring* democracy to Chile.

45 On the intricacies of these dual histories of Ein Hod, the Zionist and Palestinian narratives, see Susan Slyomovics, *The Object of Memory: Arab and Jew Narrate the Palestinian Village* (Philadelphia: University of Pennsylvania Press, 1998). She is a bit heavy on the 'contradictions' between the Dadaist identity of Marcel Janco, the artist-founder of Jewish Ein Hod in 1953, and his Zionist nationalism: 'Dada provided Zionism with a cultural and intellectual alibi, a kind of absurdist cynicism and an aesthetic veneer to disguise the implacable disenfranchisement of all that was and is Arab' (p. 7). It is unlikely that much Dada was needed for Zionism in general, or for the conversion of Ein Houd's mosque into a bar-restaurant.

Chapter 6 Bystander States

1 Walter Laqueur, *The Terrible Secret: Suppression of the Truth about Hitler's Final Solution* (Boston: Little Brown, 1980), ch. 5. See also Raul Hilberg, *Perpetrators, Victims, Bystanders: The Jewish Catastrophe, 1933–1945* (New York: Harper Collins, 1995).

2 Lawrence L. Langer, *Holocaust Testimonies: The Ruins of Memory* (New Haven: Yale University Press, 1991), 20–2.

3 Hannah Arendt, *Eichmann in Jerusalem: A Report on the Banality of Evil* (New York: Penguin USA, 1994; orig. edn, 1965), 196.

4 Primo Levi, 'Beyond Judgement', *New York Review of Books*, 17 Dec. 1987, 14.

5 Aharon Appelfeld, *Badenheim 1939* (Boston: David Goine, 1980).

6 Well documented in Tom Segev, *The Seventh Million: The Israelis and the Holocaust* (New York: Hill and Wang, 1993).

7 Ibid., 103.

8 Ibid., 104.

9   Norman Geras, *The Contract of Mutual Indifference: Political Philosophy after the Holocaust* (London: Verso, 1998), 96.
10 David Bankier, *The Germans and the Final Solution: Public Opinion under Nazism* (Oxford: Blackwell, 1996), ch. 6: 'Awareness of the Holocaust'.
11 Laqueur, *Terrible Secret*, 201.
12 Zygmunt Bauman, *Modernity and the Holocaust* (Cambridge: Polity Press, 1989), 74.
13 Bankier, *Germans and the Final Solution*, 115.
14 Hilberg, *Perpetrators*, 195.
15 Gordon J. Horwitz, *In the Shadow of Death: Living Outside the Gates of Mauthausen*, (London: I. B. Tauris, 1991), 2.
16 Ibid., 35. In 1941, a group of 348 Dutch Jews arrived, transferred from Buchenwald. All died in the quarry, most shot or their skulls crushed by the guards. Others killed themselves by jumping into a pit. The civilian employees at the quarry who saw all this requested the authorities to stop these suicides, 'since the fragments of flesh and brains clinging to the rocks afforded too gruesome a sight' (p. 53).
17 Ibid.
18 Ibid., 110–14.
19 Ibid., 120.
20 Ibid., 175.
21 These and similar scenes are memorably recorded in the photographs, diaries and letters discussed by Ernst Klee et al., *'Those Were the Days': The Holocaust through the Eyes of the Perpetrators and Bystanders* (London: Hamish Hamilton, 1991). *Schöne Zeiten* ('Those Were the Days') was the heading of a page in the commemorative photo album of Kurt Franz, the last commandant of Treblinka.
22 Christopher R. Browning, *Ordinary Men: Reserve Battalion 101 and the Final Solution in Poland* (New York: Harper Collins, 1992), 112.
23 Klee et al., *'Those Were the Days'*, 28.
24 Ibid., 6.
25 The term was originally applied to juntas from the late sixties to early eighties: see Juan E. Corradi et al. (eds), *Fear at the Edge: State Terror and Resistance in Latin America* (Berkeley: University of California Press, 1992).
26 Marguerite Feitlowitz, *A Lexicon of Terror: Argentina and the Legacies of Torture* (New York: Oxford University Press, 1998), 20.
27 Frank Graziano, *Divine Violence: Spectacle, Psychosexuality and Radical Christianity in the Argentine Dirty War* (Boulder, CO: Westview Press, 1992), 73. See the whole chapter, 'The Strategic Theatrics of Atrocity', 61–106.
28 Ibid., 77.
29 Feitlowitz, *Lexicon of Terror*, 34.
30 Tu Wei-ming, 'Destructive Will and Ideological Holocaust: Maoism as a Source of Social Suffering in China', in Arthur Kleinman et al. (eds), *Social Suffering* (Berkeley: University of California Press, 1997), 162.
31 Vaclav Havel, *Open Letters: Selected Writings, 1965–1990* (New York: Vintage Books, 1992), 52. What follows on Czechoslovakia and other Com-

munist states, is drawn from the 1975 paper, 'Dear Dr. Husak' (pp. 50–83); the 1965 'On Evasive Thinking' (pp. 10–24) and the wonderful 1978 'The Power of the Powerless' (pp. 125–214).

32 Ibid., 58.
33 Ibid., 12.
34 Ibid., 13.
35 Ibid., 136.
36 Lacqueur, *Terrible Secret*, 74.
37 Discussed most recently in Richard Breitman, *Official Secrets: What the Nazis Planned, What the British and Americans Knew* (Harmondsworth: Penguin, 1999).
38 See Mark Danner's seven-part *New York Review of Books* series, especially 'America and the Bosnian Genocide', Dec. 1997.
39 Ibid., 57.
40 Helen Fein (ed.), *The Prevention of Genocide: Rwanda and Yugoslavia Reconsidered*, Working Paper (New York: Institute for the Study of Genocide, 1994).
41 'Officials Told to Avoid Rwanda Killings Genocide', *New York Times*, 10 June 1994.
42 Michael Stohl, 'Outside of a Small Circle of Friends: States, Genocide, Mass Killing and the Role of Bystanders', *Journal of Peace Research*, 24 (1987), 151–66.
43 Noam Chomsky, 'Human Rights: The Pragmatic Criterion', in *Year 501: The Conquest Continues* (Boston: South End Press, 1993), 120.
44 Michael Ignatieff, *The Warrior's Honour: Ethnic War and the Modern Conscience* (London: Chatto & Windus, 1998), 5.
45 For a justified, if too jaundiced, critique, see Paul Hollander, *Political Pilgrims: Travels of Western Intellectuals to the Soviet Union, China and Cuba, 1928–1978* (New York: Oxford University Press, 1981).
46 Kanan Makiya, *Cruelty and Silence: War, Tyranny, Uprising and the Arab World* (London: Jonathan Cape, 1993), 325.
47 David Rohde, *Endgame: The Betrayal and Fall of Srebrenica, Europe's Worst Massacre since World War II* (New York: Farrar, Straus and Giroux, 1998).
48 Ibid., 350.
49 Jeshajahu Weinberg, 'From the Director', in Michael Berenbaum, *The World Must Know: The History of the Holocaust as Told in the United States Holocaust Museum* (Boston: Little, Brown & Co., 1993), xv.

Chapter 7 Images of Suffering

1 Arthur Kleinman and Joan Kleinman, 'The Appeal of Experience, The Dismay of Images: Cultural Appropriations of Suffering in Our Times', in A. Kleinman et al. (eds), *Social Suffering* (Berkeley: University of California Press, 1997), 1–24.
2 Michael Ignatieff, 'Is Nothing Sacred? The Ethics of Television', in *The Warrior's Honour: Ethnic War and the Modern Conscience* (London: Chatto & Windus, 1998), 11.

3 Ibid., 10.
4 Jonathan Benthall, *Disasters, Relief and the Media* (London: I. B. Tauris, 1993), 3–4.
5 Ibid., 11.
6 See *Studies of Public Awareness: Times Mirror News Interest Index* (Washington, DC: Times Mirror Center for the People and the Press). In December 1993, the story of Lenore Bobbit cutting off her husband's penis was followed more closely than the Bosnian war.
7 Summarized by Justin Lewis, 'What Do We Learn from the News?' *Extra*, Sept. 1992, 16–17.
8 Noam Chomsky, *Necessary Illusions: Thought Control in Democratic Societies* (Boston: South End Press, 1989); *idem, Year 501: The Conquest Continues* (Boston: South End Press, 1993); *idem, Secrets, Lies and Democracy* (Tucson, AZ: Odonia Press, 1994), and *idem, Media Control* (New York: Seven Stories Press, 1997).
9 James W. Morentz, 'Communication in the Sahel Drought: Comparing the Mass Media with Other Channels of International Communication', in Committee on Disasters and the Mass Media, *Disasters and the Mass Media* (Washington, DC: National Academy of Science, 1980), 158–83.
10 Paul Harrison and Robin Palmer, *News out of Africa: Biafra to Band Aid* (London: Hilary Shipman, 1986). On media denials imposed by the state, see Alex De Waal's studies of the 1980s famines in Ethiopia and the Sudan and the story of the Chinese government's massive lies about the country's 1959–61 famine in *Starving in Silence: A Report on Famine and Censorship* (London: Article 19, April 1990).
11 Benthall, *Disasters, Relief and the Media*, 8.
12 *Genocide in Iraq: The Anfal Campaign against the Turks* (New York: Human Rights Watch, July 1993).
13 Susan D. Moeller, *Compassion Fatigue: How the Media Sell Disease, Famine, War and Death* (London: Routledge, 1999).
14 Ibid., 102.
15 Rony Brauman (then head of Médecins Sans Frontières), 'When Suffering Makes a Good Story', in Francis Jean (ed.), *Life, Death and Aid* (London: Routledge and Hachette, 1993), 149–58.
16 Ignatieff, 'Is Nothing Sacred?', 25.
17 I am indebted to Henrietta Lidchi for much help on this subject. What follows draws on her review of the debate and her close observations of two campaigns (Action Aid and Save the Children): ' "All in the Choosing Eye": Charity, Representation and the Developing World' (Ph.D. thesis, School of Education, Open University, Oct. 1993).
18 Patricia Holland, *What is a Child? Popular Images of Childhood* (London: Pandora Press, 1992), 157.
19 *New Internationalist*, 228 (1992), cited in Lidchi, ' "All in the Choosing Eye" ', 4.

20 See Bill Nichols, *Representing Reality: Issues and Concepts in Documentary* (Bloomington: Indiana University Press, 1991).
21 Jorgen Lissner, 'Merchants of Misery', *New Internationalist*, 100 (1981), 23.
22 Holland, *What is a Child?*, 150.
23 See Harrison and Palmer, *News out of Africa*, and Peter Burnell, *Charity, Politics and the Third World* (Hemel Hempstead: Harvester Wheatsheaf, 1992).
24 Harrison and Palmer, *News out of Africa*, 122.
25 Lidchi, ' "All in the Choosing Eye" ', 119–20.
26 Jon Bennett, *The Hunger Machine: The Politics of Food* (Cambridge: Polity Press, 1987).
27 Save the Children Fund, *Focus on Images* (London: IMG, Sept. 1991).
28 Some of this evidence is cited (in a review of the more interesting general issues) by Maggie Black, *A Cause for our Times: Oxfam, the First Fifty Years* (Oxford: Oxfam, 1992).
29 Caroline B. Eayrs and Nick Ellis, 'Charity Advertising: For or Against People with a Mental Handicap?', *British Journal of Social Psychology*, 29 (1990), 349–66.
30 Ibid., 362. There are a few bits of counter-evidence. In one study, potential donors who were sent fund-raising appeals with positive images (like a photo of a smiling child) donated more than prospective donors sent the same literature illustrated by negative photos. See Evelyne Dyck and Gary Coldevin, 'Using Positive and Negative Photographs for Third World Fund Raising', *Journalism Quarterly*, 69 (Fall 1992), 572–9.
31 Lissner, 'Merchants of Misery', 24.
32 Peter Gabriel, launching the Witness programme at the Reebok Human Rights Awards Ceremony, 10 Dec. 1992 (press release).
33 But not 'violation of human rights' – the obvious label if this event had occurred in Zaire and not North America or Western Europe.
34 See Daniel Goleman, *Vital Lies, Simple Truths: The Psychology of Self-Deception* (New York: Simon and Schuster, 1985), 216.
35 Petruska Clarkson, *The Bystander (An End to Innocence in Human Relationships?)* (London: Whurr Publications, 1996), 11.
36 Pascal Bruckner, *The Tears of the White Man: Compassion as Contempt* (New York: Free Press, 1986), 63–6.
37 The training method developed during the Greek junta from 1967 to 1974. See Mika Haritos-Fatouros, 'The Official Torturer: A Learning Model for Obedience to the Authority of Violence', in R. D. Crelinsten and A. P. Schmid (eds), *The Politics of Pain: Torturers and Their Masters* (Boulder, CO: Westview Press, 1995), 129–46.
38 Michael Lesy, *The Forbidden Zone* (New York: Anchor Books, 1989), discusses each of these groups.
39 Clarkson, *Bystander*, 31.
40 Peter Burnell, 'Aid Fatigue: Concept and Methodology', Working Paper no. 51, Department of Politics and International Studies, University of Warwick, 1991.

41 'Crisis after Crisis Tiring Aid Donors', AP, cited by Moeller, *Compassion Fatigue*, 141.
42 Ibid., 2.
43 Ibid., 9.
44 Ibid., 306.
45 Ibid., 283.
46 Arthur Kleinman and Joan Kleinman, 'Appeal of Experience', 4. But see their account of the photographer's moral relationship with the dying child, pp. 3–7. Carter killed himself a few months after the Pulitzer Prize announcement.

Chapter 8 Appeals

1 For all detailed sources and citations, see Stanley Cohen, *The Impact of Information about Human Rights Violations: Denial and Acknowledgment* (Jerusalem: Centre for Human Rights, Hebrew University, 1995). Unless otherwise indicated, all quotations in italics are from texts of Amnesty International, British Section, (AmB) or USA Section (AmU). I refer to Bruna Seu's focus groups (London university students) as 'student groups'.
2 There are interesting cultural differences between these texts. The American style and tone is mock-personal, sentimental, cloying and somewhat kitsch. The British texts are confrontational and aggressive, more politically explicit and verbally complex, using tropes of irony, sarcasm, cynicism and deliberate understatement.
3 See reviews of the advertisements in the weekly trade journal, *Campaign* (16 Nov. 90; 14 Dec. 90; 14 Dec. 94).
4 The most influential creator of this style is Indra Sinha, the agency's copywriter for most of the advertisements. See Diana Allard, 'A Quiet Rage', *Campaign*, 3 May 1991.
5 Ibid., 29.
6 On the social psychology of persuasion, see Anthony Pratkanis and Eliot Aronson, *Age of Propaganda: The Everyday Use and Abuse of Persuasion* (New York: W. H. Freeman and Co., 1992). On using advertising techniques to overcome resistance to human rights messages, see Israel W. Charny, 'Innovating Communication Initiatives for Human Rights' (Amnesty International Conference on Extra-Judicial Executions, Amsterdam, 1982).
7 Richard Nisbet and Lee Ross, *Human Inference* (Englewood Cliffs, NJ: Prentice-Hall, 1980), 44. On research on the vividness effect, see Pratkanis and Aronson, *Age of Propaganda*, ch. 18.
8 'Findings from Focus Groups Conducted among Current Regular and Lapsed High Dollar Donors for Amnesty International' (Washington, DC: Peter D. Hart Research Associates, June 1992), 10–11.
9 Barbara Harff, 'Empathy for Victims of Massive Human Rights Violations and Support for Government Intervention: A Comparative Study of American and Australian Attitudes', *Political Psychology*, 8/1 (1987), 1–20.

10 *Famine Myths: Setting the Record Straight* (London: Save the Children, first pub. 1991).
11 R. Lord et al., 'Biased Assimilation and Attitude Polarization: The Effect of Prior Theories on Subsequently Considered Evidence', *Journal of Personality and Social Psychology*, 37 (1979), 2098–109.
12 R. P. Vallone et al., 'The Hostile Media Phenomenon: Biased Perception and Perceptions of Media Bias in Coverage of the Beirut Massacre', *Journal of Personality and Social Psychology*, 49 (1985), 577–85.
13 Harff, 'Empathy for Victims'.
14 Bill Thornton et al., 'Influence of a Photograph on a Charitable Appeal', *Journal of Applied Social Psychology*, 21 (1991), 433–45.
15 C. Daniel Batson et al., 'Immorality from Empathy-Induced Altruism: When Compassion and Justice Conflict', *Journal of Personality and Social Psychology*, 68 (1995), 1042–54.
16 Peter E. Warren and Iain Walker, 'Empathy, Effectiveness and Donations to Charity', *British Journal of Social Psychology*, 30 (1991), 325–37.
17 Charny, 'Innovating Communications Initiatives', 21.
18 Amnesty member, quoted in 'Findings from Focus Groups', 26.
19 Petruska Clarkson, *The Bystander (An End to Innocence in Human Relationships?)* (London: Whurr Publications, 1996), 74.

Chapter 9 Digging up Graves, Opening up Wounds

1 The story is dramatically told by Lawrence Weschler in *A Miracle, a Universe: Settling Accounts with Torturers* (New York: Penguin USA, 1990).
2 See the English version: *Report of the Chilean National Commission on Truth and Reconciliation* (South Bend, IN: University of Notre Dame Press, 1993), especially the introduction by José Zalaquett, a member of the commission and a central figure in the debate about justice in transition.
3 Weschler, *A Miracle*, 4.
4 *State Crimes: Punishment or Pardon?* Papers and Report of Conference organized by Justice and Society Program (Queenstown, Md.: Wye Centre, Aspen Institute, 1989).
5 Archbishop Desmond Tutu, 'Chairperson's Foreword', *Truth and Reconciliation Commission of South Africa Report*, vol. 1 (London: Macmillan, 1999), 8. (Tutu unfortunately chooses to continue: 'and thereby enabled them to experience closure'. This psycho-babble not only adds nothing to his perfectly clear account, but is wrong. There is no such thing as 'closure' for parents whose child is killed.)
6 *Truth and Reconciliation Commission*, 104.
7 Tutu, 'Chairperson's Foreword', 18.
8 See *Truth and Reconciliation Commission*, ch. 5: 'Concepts and Principles', 103–34.
9 Ibid., 115.

10   For a comprehensive overview, see Mark Osiel, *Obeying Orders: Atrocity, Military Discipline and the Law of War* (New Brunswick, NJ: Transaction Publishers, 1997).

11   Julian Barnes's satirical version of the trial of 'Stoyo Petkanov' (based loosely on Todor Zhivkov, the former ruler of Bulgaria) is a fine account of the ambiguities of the 'truth' revealed by trials in the former Communist states: Julian Barnes, *The Porcupine* (London: Picador, 1992).

12   Mark Osiel, *Mass Atrocity, Collective Memory and the Law* (New Brunswick, NJ: Transaction Publishers, 1997).

13   Alain Finkelkraut, *Remembering in Vain: The Klaus Barbie Trial and Crimes against Humanity* (New York: Columbia University Press, 1992).

14   On the current French debates, see Robert O. Paxton, 'The Trial of Maurice Papon', *New York Review of Books*, 16 Dec. 1999, 32–8.

15   See Henry Rousso, *The Vichy Syndrome: History and Memory in France since 1944* (Cambridge, MA: Harvard University Press, 1991).

16   Paxton, 'Trial of Maurice Papon', 7, citing Eric Conan's detailed *Le Procès Papon: un journal d'audience*.

17   Cited in Lawrence Weschler, 'The Velvet Purge: The Trials of Jan Kavan', *New Yorker*, 19 Oct. 1992, 82.

18   Nadezhda Mandelstam, *Hope Abandoned* (New York: Athenaeum, 1972), 572.

19   See James E. Young, *The Texture of Memory: Holocaust Memorials and Meanings* (New Haven: Yale University Press, 1993).

20   For a serious analysis of kitsch, see Saul Friedlander, *Reflections of Nazism: A Essay on Kitsch and Death* (New York: Harper and Row, 1984).

21   See Peter Novick, *The Holocaust in American Life* (Boston: Houghton Mifflin, 1999).

22   The museum (as some innocent tourists never discover) is operated by the late Meier Kahane's Fascist Kach and its American partner, the Jewish Defense League.

23   Michael Taussig, 'Violence and Resistance in the Americas: The Legacy of Conquest', in *The Nervous System* (London: Routledge, 1992), esp. 48–51.

24   Ibid., 48.

25   On the uses of vindication in the former GDR, see John Borneman, *Settling Accounts: Violence, Justice and Accountability in Postsocialist Europe* (Princeton, NJ: Princeton University Press, 1997).

26   Kadar Asmal et al., *Reconciliation through Truth: A Reckoning of Apartheid's Criminal Governance*, 2nd edn (Cape Town: David Philip, 1997).

27   Mignone, a well-known Argentinian human rights intellectual whose own daughter was a *desaparecida*, quoted by Marguerite Feitlowitz, *A Lexicon of Terror: Argentina and the Legacies of Torture* (New York: Oxford University Press, 1998), 195. For details, see her ch. 6: 'The Scilingo Effect', 193–255.

28   Erving Goffman, *Relations in Public* (London: Allen Lane, 1971), 113.

29   The response of a woman in Uruguay being counselled by a priest about the disappearance of her child; quoted in Alex Boraine et al. (eds), *Dealing with the Past: Truth and Reconciliation in South Africa* (Cape Town: IDASA, 1994), 121.

30 Letter from Human Rights Watch to President de Klerk, in 'South Africa: Accounting for the Past', *Human Rights Watch Africa* (newsletter), 4 (23 Oct. 1992), 2.

31 Quoted in Antjie Krog, *Country of My Skull* (London: Jonathan Cape, 1999), 109.

32 Gunnar Theissen and Brandon Hamber, 'A State of Denial: White South Africans' Attitudes to the Truth and Reconciliation Commission', *Indicator South Africa: The Barometer of Social Trends*, 15 (1998), 7–12.

33 Ronald D. Crelinsten, 'The World of Torture: A Constructed Reality', unpublished paper, 1993.

34 George Orwell, *Nineteen-Eighty Four* (Harmondsworth: Penguin, 1954; first pub. 1949), 31.

35 Ibid., 170–1.

36 My discussion on social control draws heavily on Steven Spitzer, 'Policing the Past', unpublished paper read at the Law and Society Association, Amsterdam, June 1991. I am indebted to Steve for these and other stimulating discussions.

37 Martin Amis's novel *Time's Arrow* (New York: Vintage, 1991) is an original meditation on this subject: an escaped Nazi war criminal now in the United States lives his life backwards till the moment he became an Auschwitz doctor.

38 Harold Rosenberg, 'The Shadow of the Furies', *New York Review of Books*, 20 Jan. 1977, 47.

39 Ibid., 48.

40 Vaclav Havel, 'The Post-Communist Nightmare', *New York Review of Books*, 27 May 1993, 10.

41 Noam Chomsky, *The Culture of Terrorism* (London: Pluto Press, 1989), esp. 74–111.

42 Terence Des Pres, 'On Governing Narratives: The Turkish–Armenian Case', *Yale Review*, 75 (1986), 517–31, and Gregory F. Goekjian, 'Genocide and Historical Desire', *Semiotica*, 83 (1991), 211.

43 Alexandr R. Luria, *The Mind of a Mnemonist* (Cambridge, MA: Harvard University Press, 1968).

44 Patrick H. Hutton, 'The Art of Memory Reconceived: From Rhetoric to Psychoanalysis', *Journal of the History of Ideas*, 48 (Sept. 1987), 372.

45 Michael Ignatieff, *Blood and Belonging: Journeys into the New Nationalism* (London: Vintage, 1994), and *idem, The Warrior's Honour: Ethnic War and the Modern Conscience* (London: Chatto & Windus, 1998).

46 Cited in David Rohde, *Endgame: The Betrayal and Fall of Srebrenica, Europe's Worst Massacre since World War II* (New York: Farrar, Straus and Giroux, 1998), 167.

47 See Amnesty International, 'Morocco: Tazmament: Official Silence and Impunity' (London: Amnesty International, Nov. 1992).

48 'More Humility, Fewer Illusions: A Talk between Adam Michnik and Jürgen Habermas', *New York Review of Books*, 24 Mar. 1994, 29.

Chapter 10 Acknowledgement Now

1　For details, see Patrick Cockburn, 'Campaign of Mutilation Terrorizes Iraqis', *Independent*, 13 Jan. 1995.
2　All direct quotes are from Linda Galloway, 'Domestic Worker Opens Madam's Eyes On Violence', *Cape Argus*, 14 Sept. 1991, 4.
3　I have changed her name and identifying background details.
4　Most details are from Richard Dowden, 'A Glimmer of Hope Flickers in the Wake of the Carnage', *Independent*, 15 Feb. 1994.
5　Alice Miller, *Breaking Down the Wall of Silence: The Liberating Experience of Facing Painful Truth* (New York: Meridian, 1993).
6　Marcia P. Miceli and Janet P. Near, *Blowing the Whistle* (New York: Lexington Books, 1992), 45.
7　Ibid., 133–5.
8　Sisela Bok, *Secrets: On the Ethics of Concealment and Revelation* (New York: Vintage Books, 1982), 211.
9　Vaclav Havel, 'The Power of the Powerless', in *Open Letters: Selected Writings, 1965–1990* (New York: Vintage Books, 1992), esp. 146–8.
10　Ibid., 147.
11　Interview in *Signature*, Jan. 1992, 10.
12　Bernie Glassman, *Bearing Witness: A Zen Master's Lesson in Making Peace* (New York: Bell Tower, 1998). Highpoints included sleeping in the Auschwitz Museum, meditation at the camp, saying Kaddish at the execution wall, walking on the railway tracks, chanting 'peacemaker vows' (such as 'I vow to heal myself and others' and 'I vow to be oneness') and putting slips of paper with the names of people killed there (from the death books) in a red lacquered box on the ground of the selection site.
13　See Ervin Staub et al. (eds), *Development and Maintenance of Prosocial Behaviour: International Perspectives on Positive Morality* (New York: Plenum Press, 1984).
14　All direct quotes from Mary McCarthy, *Medina* (London: Wildwood House, 1973). For a more detailed account of the My Lai massacre and the consequent trials, see Michael Billington and Kevin Sims, *Four Hours at My Lai* (Harmondsworth: Penguin, 1993).
15　McCarthy, *Medina*, 77.
16　Ibid., 78.
17　See Helen Fein, *Accounting for Genocide* (New York: Free Press, 1979).
18　For a useful summary, see Raul Hilberg, *Perpetrators Victims Bystanders: The Jewish Catastrophe, 1933–1945* (New York: Harper Collins, 1992), 75–86, 212–24.
19　Philip Hallie, *Lest Innocent Blood be Shed: The Story of the Village of Le Chambon* (New York: Harper and Row, 1979).
20　Samuel P. Oliner and Pearl M. Oliner, *The Altruistic Personality: Rescuers of Jews in Nazi Europe* (New York: Free Press, 1988), and *idem*, 'Righteous People in the Holocaust', in Israel Charny (ed.), *Genocide: A Critical*

Bibliographical Review, vol. 2 (London: Mansell, 1991), 363–85. The Oliners studied 406 rescuers commemorated as 'Righteous Gentiles' by Yad Vashem for having saved Jewish lives in Occupied Europe.

21 Oliner and Oliner, *Altruistic Personality*, 186.

22 Ibid., 251.

23 Eva Fogelman, *Conscience and Courage: Rescuers of Jews during the Holocaust* (New York: Doubleday, 1994).

24 Ibid., p. xviii.

25 Ibid., 56.

26 Kristen R. Monroe et al. 'Altruism and the Theory of Rational Action: Rescuers of Jews in Nazi Europe', *Ethics*, 101 (1990), 103–22. Badhwar agrees that the rational choice model of self-interest and reward is wrong, but claims that altruistic actions are self-interested in the sense of being essential to rescuers' full moral worth and living up to their sense of self (Neera Kapur Badhwar, 'Altruism versus Self-Interest: Sometimes a False Dichotomy', in Ellen Frankel Paul et al. (eds), *Altruism* (Cambridge: Cambridge University Press, 1993), 90–117).

27 Oliner and Oliner, *Altruistic Personality*, 216.

28 Badhwar, 'Altruism versus Self-Interest', 98.

29 Ibid., 118.

30 Dorothy Rabinowicz, *New Lives: Survivors of the Holocaust Living in America* (New York: Knopf, 1977).

31 Erwin Staub, 'Transforming the Bystanders: Altruism, Caring and Social Responsibility', in Helen Fein (ed.), *Genocide Watch* (New Haven: Yale University Press, 1992), 162–81.

32 Petruska Clarkson, *The Bystander* (*An End to Innocence in Human Relationships?*) (London: Whurr Publications, 1996), 108.

33 E.g. *How to Make the World a Better Place; A Guide to Doing Good; The Campaigning Handbook, How Can I Help?* etc.

34 Angela Browne, 'The Victim's Experience: Pathways to Disclosure', *Psychotherapy*, 28/1 (Spring 1991), 150–6.

35 For a review, see Stephen J. Roth, 'Denial of the Holocaust as an Issue of Law', *Israel Yearbook of Human Rights*, 23 (1993), 215–35.

36 Cited (disapprovingly) by Priscilla Hayner, 'International Guidelines for the Creation and Operation of Truth Commissions', *Law and Contemporary Problems*, 59/4 (Autumn 1996), 173.

37 For a comprehensive summary of the issues, see Michael A. Menlowe and Alexander McCall Smith, *The Duty to Rescue* (Aldershot: Dartmouth, 1994).

38 The French version became most widely known in the aftermath of Princess Diana's fatal car accident. There was much talk about bringing photographers, journalists and other onlookers to trial, charged with failure or delay in rescuing.

39 Bok, *Secrets*, ch. 5.

40 Ibid., 68.

41 Carlo Felice, 'On the Obligation to Keep Informed about Distant Atrocities', *Human Rights Quarterly*, 12 (1990), 397–414.

42 Cat Cox, *Chocolate Unwrapped: The Politics of Pleasure* (London: Women's Environmental Network, 1993).
43 See Jane Turner et al., *Ethical Consumer Guide to Everyday Shopping* (Manchester: ECRA Publishing, 1996). This links innocuous brand names to their parent companies: Princess baked beans, we learn, is a sideline to Mitsubishi's plutonium supplies, Sarawak tropical timber and guided missiles. Everyone gets to do some denial work: the company gives out standard official denials; the unconvinced, lazy or burnt-out consumer says 'What do you expect me to do – consult the Guide about every can of baked beans?'
44 A 1993 NOP survey for Christian Aid found that 83 per cent of the public welcomes fairly traded products, and 73 per cent were prepared to pay more for them (cited in *Media Natura*, 'Café Direct Campaign', 1993).
45 On the third such banquet – in Santa Monica – see *Los Angeles Times*, 21 Nov. 1992.
46 Ronna Kabatznik, 'Hunger's Many Meanings', *Tikkun*, 7 (July 1992), 28.
47 Ibid., 65. If ever there was a case for hands-*off* altruism, this is it.
48 Hannah Arendt, *Eichmann in Jerusalem: A Report on the Banality of Evil* (New York: Penguin USA, 1994; orig. edn, 1965), 233; italics original.
49 Norman Geras, *The Contract of Mutual Indifference: Political Philosophy after the Holocaust* (London: Verso, 1998), 57–60.
50 Richard Flacks, *Making History: The Radical Tradition in American Life* (New York: Columbia University Press, 1988).
51 José Zalaquett, 'Discussion', in Alex Boraine et al. (eds), *Dealing with the Past: Truth and Reconciliation in South Africa* (Cape Town: IDASA, 1994), 105.

Chapter 11 Towards Cultures of Denial?

1 All quotes are from the Penguin edition (1969) of Sophocles, *King Oedipus*.
2 Michael Burleigh, *Death and Deliverance: 'Euthanasia' in Germany, 1940–1945* (Cambridge: Cambridge University Press, 1994), 7.
3 Ibid.
4 Hannah Arendt, 'Lying and Politics: Reflections on the Pentagon Papers', in *Crises of the Republic* (New York: Harcourt Brace, 1972), 3–47.
5 Ibid., 36.
6 Jean Baudrillard, 'La Guerre du Golfe n'a pas en lieue', *Liberation*, 29 Mar. 1991.
7 Jean Baudrillard, 'The Reality Gulf', *Guardian*, 11 Jan. 1991.
8 Christopher Norris, *Uncritical Theory: Postmodernism, Intellectuals and the Gulf War* (London: Lawrence and Wishart, 1992).
9 Ibid., 21.
10 See Pierre Vidal-Naquet, *Assassins of Memory* (New York: Columbia University Press, 1992).

11 Deborah Lipstadt, *Denying the Holocaust: The Growing Assault on Truth and Memory* (New York: Free Press, 1994).
12 Terence Des Pres, 'On Governing Narratives: The Turkish–Armenian Case', *Yale Review*, 75 (1986), 519.
13 Ibid., 521.
14 My reference is to Milton Rokeach's fine but neglected study, *The Three Christs of Ypsilanti* (New York: Columbia University Press, 1981; orig. pub. 1964).
15 Quoted in Erich Kulka, 'Denial of the Holocaust', in I. W. Charny (ed.), *Genocide: A Critical Bibliographical Review*, vol. 2 (London: Mansell, 1991), 55.
16 Mark Fritz, quoted by Susan D. Moeller, *Compassion Fatigue: How the Media Sell Disease, Famine, War and Death* (London: Routledge, 1999), 297.
17 Saul Friedlander, *Reflections of Nazism: An Essay of Kitsch and Death* (New York: Harper and Row, 1984), 89–92.
18 Ibid., 91.
19 Noam Chomsky, 'Writers and Intellectual Responsibility', in *Powers and Prospects: Reflections on Human Nature and the Social Order* (Boston: South End Press, 1996), 55–69. I have amalgamated two definitions (italics in original) from pp. 55 and 54.
20 Ibid., 62.
21 Ibid., 60–1.
22 Statistics taken from UNDP Human Development Report (New York: Oxford University Press, 1998).
23 Michael Ignatieff, *The Warrior's Honour: Ethnic War and the Modern Conscience* (London: Chatto & Windus, 1998).
24 Ibid., 90.
25 Frances Westley, 'Bob Geldof and Live Aid: The Affective Side of Global Social Innovation', *Human Relations*, 44 (1991), 1011–36.
26 Ignatieff's thesis on 'The Seductiveness of Moral Disgust' originally appeared in 1995 – rather soon for the optimistic narratives of moral engagement and the globalization of social suffering to have been so eroded by pessimism and chaos.
27 Zygmunt Bauman, *Postmodern Ethics* (Oxford: Blackwell, 1993), 18. On the need for 'an ethics of distance and distant consequences', see also Norman Geras, *The Contract of Mutual Indifference: Political Philosophy after the Holocaust* (London: Verso, 1998).
28 Michael Ignateiff, *The Needs of Strangers* (London: Vintage, 1994), 28.
29 Ibid., 29. We all have literal-minded friends who cannot tolerate expressions such as 'I'm dying of hunger', 'I'm famished', or 'I'm starving'. And 'these new boots are just *torture* to wear'.
30 Mary McCarthy, *Medina* (London: Wildwood House, 1973), 43.
31 David Morris, 'About Suffering: Voice, Genre and Moral Community', in Arthur Kleinman et al. (eds), *Social Suffering* (Berkeley: University of California Press, 1997), 25–47.
32 *Diane Arbus: An Aperture Monograph for The Museum of Modern Art* (New York: MOMA, 1972).

33 Susan Sontag, 'Freak Show', *New York Review of Books*, 15 Nov. 1973, 13 (the second of three essays later published as *On Photography*). All quotes below are from the original essay.
34 *Diane Arbus*, 2.
35 Ibid., 3.
36 Don McCullin, *Unreasonable Behaviour* (London: Vintage, 1992), 123–4.
37 John Berger, 'Photographs of Agony' (1972), reprinted in *About Looking* (New York: Pantheon, 1986), 38.
38 Ibid.
39 Ibid.

Index